Musa Lapidaria

A Selection of Latin Verse Inscriptions

AMERICAN PHILOLOGICAL ASSOCIATION
American Classical Studies

Series Editor

David L. Blank

Number 36

MUSA LAPIDARIA
*A SELECTION OF
LATIN VERSE INSCRIPTIONS*

by
E. Courtney

E. Courtney
Gildersleeve Professor of Classics
University of Virginia

Musa Lapidaria

A Selection of Latin Verse Inscriptions

Scholars Press
Atlanta, Georgia

MUSA LAPIDARIA
A SELECTION OF LATIN VERSE INSCRIPTIONS

by
E. Courtney

Library of Congress Cataloging in Publication Data
Courtney, E. (Edward), 1932–
Musa Lapidaria : a selection of Latin verse inscriptions / E. Courtney.
p. cm. — (American classical studies ; no. 36)
Includes bibliographical references (p.) and index.
ISBN 0-7885-0141-0 (cloth : alk. paper). — ISBN 0-7885-0142-9 (pbk. : alk. paper)
1. Inscriptions, Latin. 2. Latin poetry. I. Title. II. Series.
CN528.V4C68 1995
881'. 0180—dc20 95-30859
CIP

Printed in the United States of America
on acid-free paper

To
Robin Nisbet
and
Niall Rudd

CONTENTS

PREFACE

'Philologists have continued to demonstrate their appreciation of the linguistic usages which inscriptions incorporate, and while literary critics have inclined to acknowledge and neglect them as examples of Latin prose or verse, N. Horsfall has produced an interesting commentary on the funerary epigram commemorating Allia Potestas, a presage, one may hope, of a change of heart' (Reynolds - Beard - Roueché, *JRS* 76 (1986), 125).

This sentence may help to explain the idea behind this book. My selection envisages an audience primarily of graduate students and young professors, and I hope that they will find it a useful starting-point for research in various directions, not just in the areas of linguistics and literary criticism identified in the above quotation.

The study of inscriptions can help to bridge a widening, and deplorable, division in classical studies between historians (who nowadays often are to be found in history, not classics, departments) and philologists (this word used in its American and German sense, not, as in the opening quotation, to mean linguists). Philologists should not be just literary critics; historians should not be just historical theorists (these are of course simplified categories). All of us, whatever our specialism, should desire to understand texts in the fullest sense in order to reach a proper evaluation of evidence derived from them; my notes attempt to elucidate these poems from all angles, though this will inevitably mean that specialists will be able to find gaps in my knowledge of some areas. The fact that this is a selection of verse inscriptions will automatically make plain the literary and philological base from which I myself start; in selections of prose inscriptions inevitably the factual and historical predominates, but with most verse inscriptions the interesting element of artistic aspiration is added. Thus we find these two elements combined e.g. in the Scipio inscriptions (where linguistic and archaeological issues are also important) and those classed under my II A.

A selection necessarily raises the question of the principle of choice. One decision was to choose poems preserved complete, or at least complete enough for the situation behind them to be clear (this ruled out e.g. the intriguing *CLE* 1178). Another was that anything overtly Christian in content should be excluded, not because of any desire to erect intellectual boundaries but simply as a practical means of limiting the vast field and retaining a semblance of coherence and unity. Beyond that it was not my primary aim that my selection should be representative, since it then would have been necessary to include many trivial and repetitive items, particularly in the area of epitaphs. Rather I have chosen those poems from which there was most to be learned, or which seemed to me to stand out in some way. For convenience I have classified them under broad headings, so that at least the reader can see the most noteworthy specimens of any type in which he may be interested. Of course the poems often could be classed under either of two headings or headings other than those which I have chosen; some may miss a section on Women, but this would have been amorphous because of the large number of epitaphs devoted to them. When I wrote my *Fragmentary Latin Poets* I did not know that my next book would be this one; this has had the regrettable result that the boundaries between the two fluctuate a little.

I hope that the readers will find varied instruction in this selection and will enjoy picking out what is most useful or attractive to each of them singly; *lector intende, laetaberis*.

In conclusion it is a pleasant duty to thank the University of Virginia for a grant towards the cost of producing the maps, and those who have given their technological assistance in producing camera-ready copy, particularly Amanda McDaniel, John Miller and Tom Cichon.

E. C.

University of Virginia, April 1995

BIBLIOGRAPHY AND ABBREVIATIONS

Collections of Inscriptions

Bernand = *Les Inscriptions...du Colosse de Memnon*, ed. A. and E. Bernand (1960)

P. Burman, *Anthologia Veterum Latinorum Epigrammatum et Poematum* (1759-73)

CEG = *Carmina Epigraphica Graeca*, ed. P. A. Hansen (1983-9)

CIL = Corpus Inscriptionum Latinarum

1 (**All references to this in this book are to the second edition**) Inscriptiones Antiquissimae
2 Spain
3 Asia, Greek provinces of Europe, Illyricum
4 Pompeii, Herculaneum, Stabiae
5 Cisalpine Gaul
6 City of Rome
7 Britain
8 Africa
9 Calabria, Apulia, Samnium, Picenum, the Sabine territory
10 Bruttium, Lucania, Campania, Sicily, Sardinia
11 Aemilia, Etruria, Umbria
12 Gallia Narbonensis
13 Gallia Aquitanica, Lugdunensis, Belgica; Germany
14 Latium Vetus
Imagines, ILLRP ed. A. Degrassi (1965)

CLE = *Carmina Latina Epigraphica*, ed. F. Bücheler - E. Lommatzsch (1895-1926)

Epigr. anf. = *Epigrafia anfiteatrale dell' occidente romano* (1988-), ed. P. Sabbatini Tumolesi - G. L. Gregori - M. Buonocore

J. Geffcken, *Griechische Epigramme* (1916)

Gr. Pal. = *Graffiti del Palatino 2 Domus Tiberiana* (Acta Instituti Romani Finlandiae 4, 1970), ed. P. Castrén - H. Lilius
GVI = *Griechische Versinschriften I Grabepigramme*, ed. W. Peek (1955-7)
G. Herrlinger, *Totenklage um Tiere* (1930)
IG = *Inscriptiones Graecae*
IGM = *Inscriptiones Graecae Metricae*, ed. T. Preger (1891)
IGRR = *Inscriptiones Graecae ad Res Romanas Pertinentes*, ed. R. Cagnat and others (1906-27)
IGUR = *Inscriptiones Graecae Urbis Romae*, ed. L. Moretti (1968-90)
IIt = *Inscriptiones Italiae* (1931-)
ILA = *Inscriptions latines de l'Algérie* 1, ed. S. Gsell (1922); 2, ed. H.-G. Pflaum (1957-76)
ILCV = *Inscriptiones Latinae Christianae Veteres*, ed. E. Diehl (1925-31, repr. 1961 with suppl., ed. J. Moreau)
ILLRP = *Inscriptiones Latinae Liberae Rei Publicae*, ed. A. Degrassi 1 (ed. 2, 1965), 2 (1963)
ILS = *Inscriptiones Latinae Selectae*, ed. H. Dessau (1892-1916)
IRT = *Inscriptions of Roman Tripolitania*, ed. J. M. Reynolds - J. B. Ward Perkins (1952)
Musée Bardo = Zeïneb Benzina Ben Abdallah, *Catalogue des inscriptions latines païennes du Musée du Bardo* (CEFR 92, 1986)
P. Piernavieja, *Corpus de inscripciones deportivas de la España romana* (1977)
RIB = *Roman Inscriptions of Britain I*, ed. R. G. Collingwood - R. P. Wright (1965-83)
RIT = *Die röm. Inschriften von Tarraco*, ed. G. Alföldy (1975)
A. and J. Sasel, *Inscriptiones quae in Iugoslavia inter annos mcmii et mcmxl repertae et editae sunt* (1986), *...mcmxl et mcmlx...*(1963), *...mcmlx et mcmlxx...* (1978)
A. Varone, *Erotica Pompeiana* (1994)
G. Walser, *Römische Inschriftkunst* (ed. 2, 1993)
AE = *L'Année Épigraphique*
ZPE = *Zeitschrift für Papyrologie und Epigraphik*

Other Texts and Collections referred to

AL = *Anthologia Latina* (numeration of Riese).
FLP = E. Courtney, *The Fragmentary Latin Poets* (1993)
GLK = *Grammatici Latini*, ed. H. Keil (1857-80)
MGH, AA = *Monumenta Germaniae Historica, Auctores Antiquissimi*
MGH, PLAC = *...Poetae Latini Aeui Carolini*
MSG = *Musici Scriptores Graeci*, ed. C. Jan (1895)

J. U. Powell, *Collectanea Alexandrina* (1925)
SHA = Scriptor(es) Historiae Augustae
Suppl(ementum) Hell(enisticum, ed. P. H. J. Lloyd-Jones and P. J. Parsons (1983)

The *Annals* of Ennius are referred in the numeration of O. Skutsch (1985) and his tragedies in that of H. Jocelyn (1969), Lucilius in that of F. Marx (1904-5), Fronto according to the pagination of van den Hout (Teubner, 1988).

Other Works relating to Inscriptions and Palaeography

K. P. Almar, *Inscriptiones latinae* (1990)
S. Bassi, *La Scrittura greca in Italia* (1956)
B. Bischoff, *Latin Palaeography* (Eng. tr. 1990)
A. Brelich, *Aspetti della morte nelle iscrizioni sepolcrali* (1937)
I. Calabi Limentani, *Epigrafia latina* (ed. 3, 1974)
P. Colafrancesco - M. Massaro, *Concordanze dei CLE* (1986)
A. Colonna, *Epigrafia* (1974)
P. Cugusi, *Aspetti letterari dei CLE* (1985)
E. Diehl, *Inscriptiones latinae, tabulae* (1912)
M. Fele and others, *Concordantiae in CLE* (1988)
E. Galletier, *Étude sur la poésie funéraire romaine* (1922)
M. Gigante, *Civiltà delle forme letterarie nell' antica Pompei* (1979)
A. E. and J. S. Gordon, *Album of Dated Latin Inscriptions* (1958- 65)
A. E. Gordon, *Illustrated Introduction to Latin Epigraphy* (1983)
R. P. Hoogma, *Der Einfluss Vergils auf die CLE* (1959)
R. Ireland in M. Henig, *Handbook of Roman Art* (1983)
L. Keppie, *Understanding Roman Inscriptions* (1991)
R. Lattimore, *Themes in Greek and Latin Epitaphs* (1942)
B. Lier, *Topica carminum sepulcralium latinorum: Philol.* 62 (1903), 445 and 563; 63 (1904), 54
E. Lissberger, *Das Fortleben der röm. Elegiker in den Carmina Epigraphica* (1934)
M. R. Mastidoro, *Concordanza dei CLE compresi nella Silloge di J. W. Zarker* (1991)
Ernst Meyer, *Einführung in die lat. Epigraphie* (1973)
D. Pikhaus, *Répertoire des Inscriptions Latines Versifées de l'Afrique Romaine, I, Tripolitaine, Byzacène, Afrique Proconsulaire* (1994)
E. de Ruggiero, *Dizionario epigrafico* (1895-)
G. C. Susini, *The Roman Stonecutter* (Eng. tr. 1973), *Epigrafia romana* (1982)
H. Thylander, *Étude sur l'épigraphie latine* (1952)

B. Vine, *Studies in Archaic Latin Inscriptions* (1993)
R. Wachter, *Altlateinische Inschriften* (1987)

Language and Metre

W. S. Allen, *Vox Latina* (ed. 2, 1978)
ALL = *Archiv für lat. Lexicographie*
F. Biville, *Les Emprunts du Latin au Grec* (1990)
F. Hallbauer, *De numeralibus latinis epigraphicis* (1936)
HS = J. B. Hofmann - A. Szantyr, *Lateinische Syntax und Stylistik* (1965)
KS = R. Kühner - C. Stegmann - A. Thierfelder, *Grammatik der lateinischen Sprache* (ed. 3, 1955)
W. Konjetzny, *De idiotismis syntacticis in titulis urbanis, ALL* 15 (1908), 297
B. Kübler, *Die lat. Sprache auf afrikanischen Inschriften, ALL* 8 (1893), 161
M. Leumann, *Lateinische Laut- und Formenlehre* (ed. 2, 1977)
W. M. Lindsay, *Early Latin Verse* (1922)
E. Löfstedt, *Syntactica* 1 (ed. 2, 1956), 2 (1933); *V(ermischte) S(tudien)* (1936)
LSJ = *Greek - English Lexicon*, Liddell - Scott - Jones (ed. 9, 1925-40; suppl. 1968)
P. Mastandrea, *De Fine Versus* (1993)
L. Mueller, *De Re Metrica* (ed. 2, 1894)
NW = F. Neue - C. Wagener, *Formenlehre der lateinischen Sprache* (ed. 3, 1902)
OLD = *Oxford Latin Dictionary*, ed. P. G. W. Glare (1968-82)
E. Pieske, *De titulorum Africae latinorum sermone* (1913)
M. L. Porzio Gernia, *Contributi metodologici allo studio del latino arcaico: la sorte di M e D finali* (*MAL* 17, 1973)
F. Sommer, *Handbuch der lat. Laut- und Formenlehre* (ed. 2-3, 1948)
SP = F. Sommer - R. Pfister, *Handbuch...I Einleitung und Lautlehre* (ed. 4, 1977)
TLL = *Thesaurus Linguae Latinae* (1900-)
V. Väänänen, *Le Latin vulgaire des inscriptions pompéiennes* (references to ed. 2, Abhl. Berlin Akad. 1958, 3; ed. 3, 1966).
A. Walde - J. B. Hofmann, *Lateinisches etymologisches Wörterbuch* (ed. 3, 1930-54)
E. O. Wingo, *Latin Punctuation* (1972)
E. Wölfflin, *Über die alliterierenden Verbindungen der lat. Sprache*, in *Ausgewählte Schriften* (1933), 225.

Other

A(cta) Ant(iqua Academiae Scientiarum) Hung(aricae)
A(tti del) C(entro) S(tudi e) D(ocumentazione)

W. Altmann, *Die röm. Grabaltäre* (1905)
ANRW = *Aufstieg und Niedergang der röm. Welt*, ed. H. Temporini - W. Haase (1972-)
G. Appel, *De Romanorum Precationibus* (1909)
A(nalecta) R(omana) I(nstituti) D(anici)
A(rchiv für) R(eligions)W(issenschaft)
J. P. V. D. Balsdon, *Life and Leisure in Ancient Rome* (1969)
H. Blümner, *Die röm. Privataltertümer* (1911)
G. Boulvert, *Esclaves et affranchis impériaux* (1970)
V. Brouquier - Reddé, *Temples et Cultes de Tripolitaine* (1992)
Bull(ettino della) Comm(issione archeologica comunale di Roma)
CEFR = Collection de l'École Francaise de Rome
CL = Collection Latomus
F. Cumont, *L(ux) P(erpetua)* (1949), *Recherches sur le symbolisme funéraire* (1942)
DAC = *Dictionnaire d'Archéologie Chrétienne*, ed. F. Cabrol - H. Leclercq - H. Marrou (1907-)
DS = C. Daremberg and E. Saglio, *Dictionnaire des Antiquités Grecques et Romaines* (1877-1919)
S. Demougin, *L' Ordre équestre sous les julio-claudiens* (CEFR 108, 1988)
EPRO = *Études préliminaires aux religions orientales dans l'empire romain*
E. C. Evans, *The Cults of the Sabine Territory* (Papers and Monographs, American Academy in Rome 11, 1939)
G. Fabre, *Libertus* (CEFR 50, 1981)
E. Fraenkel, *Elementi Plautini in Plauto* (1960)
T. Frank and others, *Economic Survey of Ancient Rome* (1933-40)
L. Friedlaender, *Darstellung aus der Sittengeschichte Roms* (ed. 9-10, 1921-2, by G. Wissowa, followed by reference to the English translation by L. Magnus and others, 1907-13)
P. Ginestet, *Les Organisations de la Jeunesse* (CL 213, 1991)
H(arvard) Th(eological) R(eview)
W. Heraeus, *Kleine Schriften* (1937)
A. E. Housman, *Classical Papers* (1972)
O. Kajanto, *The Latin Cognomina* (SSF, CHL 36.2, 1965), *Supernomina* (SSF, CHL 40.1, 1967)
(Der) kl(eine) Pauly (1964-75)
D. E. Kleiner, *Roman Imperial Funerary Altars with Portraits* (1987)
K. Latte, *Röm. Religionsgeschichte* (1960)
Lex(icon) Icon(ographicum Mythologiae Classicae) (1981-)
M(emorie della classe di scienze morale e storiche dell') A(ccademia dei) L(incei); ser. 5 begins in 1893, ser. 8 in1948
J. Marquardt, *Das Privatleben der Römer* (ed. 2 by A. Mau, 1886)

W. O. Moeller, *The Wool Trade in Ancient Pompeii* (1976)
T. Mommsen, *Röm. Staatsrecht* (ed. 3, 1887-8)
MRR = T. R. S. Broughton, *Magistrates of the Roman Republic* (1951-86)
E. Nash, *Pictorial Dictionary of Ancient Rome* (1961-2)
A. D. Nock, *Essays on Religion* (1972)
E. Norden, *Agnostos Theos* (1913)
NS = *Notizie degli scavi di antichità* (ser. 7 vol. 1 is 1940, ser. 8 vol. 1 is 1947)
A. Otto, *Die Sprichwörter...der Römer* (1890), with *Nachträge zu A. Otto, Sprichwörter...* (ed. R. Häussler, 1968)
PIR = *Prosopographia Imperi Romani*, E. Klebs - P. von Rohden - H. Dessau (1897-8), ed. 2 by E. Groag - E. Stein (1933-)
PLRE = *Prosopography of the Later Roman Empire*, A. H. M. Jones - J. R. Martindale - J. Morris (1971-)
R(eallexicon für) A(ntike und) C(hristentum) (1950-)
R(endiconti della classe di scienze morale, storiche e fililogiche dell') A(ccademia dei) L(incei); ser. 8 begins in 1946
RE = *Realencyclopädie der klassischen Altertumswissenschaft*, ed. A. Pauly - G. Wissowa and others (1893-1974)
L. Richardson, *New Topographical Dictionary of Ancient Rome* (1992)
W. H. Roscher (and K. Ziegler, eds.), *Ausführliches Lexicon der griechischen und römischen Mythologie* (1884-1937)
O. Salomies, *Die röm. Vornamen* (SSF, CHL 82, 1987)
W. Schulze, *Zur Geschichte lateinischer Eigennamen* (1904)
H. Solin, *Die griechische Personnamen in Rom* (1982)
V. Spinazzola, *Pompeii alla luce degli scavi nuovi* (1953)
SSF, CHL = Societas Scientiarum Fennica, Commentationes Humanarum Litterarum
J. M. C. Toynbee, *Death and Burial in the Roman World* (1971)
S. M. Treggiari, *Roman Marriage* (1991)
H. Walther, *Proverbia Sententiaeque Latinitatis Medii Aevi* (1963-9), *Initia Carminum ac Versuum Medii Aevi Posterioris* (1959)
J. P. Waltzing, *Étude historique sur les corporations professionelles chez les Romains* (1895-1900)
O. Weinreich, *Kleine Schriften* 1-3 (1969-79)
G. Wille, *Musica romana* (1967)
G. Wissowa, *Religion und Kultus der Römer* (ed. 2, 1912)
H. Wrede, *Consecratio in formam deorum* (1981)

Other abbreviations are as in *L'Année Philologique* or more explicit. The bibliographies to individual poems are selective. I regret that M. Massaro, *Epigrafia Metrica Latina di Età Repubblicana* (1992) came into my hands too late to be used.

INTRODUCTION

The first collection of inscriptional verse not mixed up among other heterogeneous poetry was the *Carmina Latina Epigraphica* of F. Bücheler (1895-7), a supplement to which was published by E. Lommatzsch in 1926; in this work the poems are arranged by metre. No doubt Bücheler took for his model G. Kaibel's *Epigrammata Graeca* (1878), which was published in association with *IG* as Bücheler's work was in association with *CIL*. Almost simultaneously with Bücheler (1897; ed. 2, 1904) appeared a collection of epitaphs by J. Cholodniak; this is of comparatively little importance. Bücheler's work shows to the full the 'patient ingenuity' and 'unforgettable brevity' that have been ascribed to him, together with a profound understanding of the Latin of the common man; it is a minor flaw that occasionally these qualities led him into explaining and defending the inexplicable and indefensible, and his supplements are sometimes rash. The highly compressed but invaluable notes are concerned with individual details of text and interpretation and do not pretend to present anything like a complete commentary or overall assessment of the poems. Such an overall commentary on a selection of 67 epitaphs was produced in 1905 by F. Plessis (Épitaphes, textes choisis et commentés), a work which met with appreciation and which is the sole forerunner of my own; one difference is that the progress of philology offers to a student in our days information and methodologies with which he can dig deeper, particularly in linguistic and historical areas, than Plessis, who was most interested in literary evaluation, sought to do. In particular the appearance of the concordances by Fele and Colafrancesco - Massaro, with the supplement by Mastidoro, has greatly facilitated research. The best introduction to epigraphical verse generally, though his title specifies epitaphs, is the book of E. Galletier (see the bibliography);

his three chapters deal with their religious and philosophical, historical and literary evaluation. R. Lattimore's book, though its focus is specifically what may be gathered from epitaphs about attitudes to death, is also valuable. This collection is not intended to work inductively as they do in tracing topics by a survey of the whole body of inscriptions within a particular field; this procedure inevitably makes it impossible to appreciate the individual poems as unitary creations. Rather I seek to apply deductively the conclusions reached by them and others where they help to illuminate these individual poems. Moreover it should be noted that, unlike them, I seek to cover a wide range of subject-matter, not just epitaphs, and it would have been impractible to provide separate introductions to each area (e.g. an essay on love of animals among the Romans in relation to 200-204). I therefore draw attention to points of more general applicability in the notes on the individual poems, which are directed to assist those interested to discern what they need to look for in order to assess properly an epigraphic poem.

One feature of Latin epigraphic verse is that, unlike our generally upper-class and highly cultured literary texts, it comes from all social classes and every variety of occupation (and class and occupation are much more often indicated in inscriptions from the status-conscious Roman society than they are in Greek inscriptions). Another quality which all inscriptions share is that they come unmediated, whereas the writings of a Catullus or a Vergil are to us loaded with associations. This of course is not to say that the facts presented by an inscription may not have been manipulated; in this respect the Res Gestae of Augustus stands on exactly the same plane as the Commentarii of Julius Caesar, and such manipulation is suggested in the notes on my no.10. But with very rare exceptions inscriptions have not been filtered through a refined artistic sensibility seeking to build up a complex literary structure; the highly individual poet of 199A may in a sense count as one of those exceptions. The vast majority of inscriptions is in prose form, and the majority of these consists of a record of facts which it is desired to perpetuate. On occasion however these facts can be presented in an emotional tone, as in the so-called 'Laudatio Turiae'. Naturally this is eminently the case in most verse inscriptions, particularly epitaphs. To go to the trouble and expense of commissioning or composing such implies that prose has been felt inadequate to convey the desired impression of solemnity or the depth of feeling. Appeasement of the grief of the bereaved is often the dominating impulse; who can deny the profundity of affection and the sense of loss in the picture of the red-headed tomboy with the crew-cut and pigtail (179)? This is not to say that perpetuation (see e.g. 74, 123.15 and note) is not also important in a society whose civic religion lacked any firm assurance of a satisfying afterlife or any clear picture of such beyond mythological fancies, and which often had to settle for survival of memory in default of personal survival.

Verse form also has a specific function in religious contexts, and has a natural connection with other forms of artistic production (see some of the instances grouped under II B); these two motives for versification unite in dedications. For those who are attracted by such things, the lineation of verse gives scope for acrostichs and the like. In the case of graffiti verse form can concentrate the wit by its concision, and it is also the natural medium for the expression of erotic feelings. Humour too fits verse much better than sober-sided prose. The paradoxical point (which seems to have been a tradition going back to Greek verse dedications; see the note) that ends 6 would have appeared out of place in prose; the same applies to the joking allusion to Hercules (the same god as addressed in 6; he is a deity who can enjoy rough humour) as a money-lender like the dedicator in 7. Humour also comes through e.g. in 124, 185 and, naturally, in poems addressed to Priapus (which may include 148).

Direct addresses to the reader, such as are common, or to the deceased are also much less appropriate to prose, though not by any means totally excluded from it (as in the 'Laudatio Turiae'). The same applies to representing the deceased as speaking from the tomb, with the similar reservation that literary prose can on occasion introduce this effect by the figure of prosopoeia; a special variety of this is the apparition of the deceased, as in the highly literary 183, which in its situational framework has something in common with verse descriptions of the deified Romulus (see on 183.31) and the like. In general a literary background (as in some of the poems collected under II C) makes verse form suitable in some cases; so with Greek literary epigram in 17, 169, 181.5, or humorous Plautine allusion in 2.

Some of these poems are indeed highly literary and elegantly written; I instance 151, 155 (if genuine), 180, 202, 204. At the opposite end of the range we find literary adornment grafted on to basically sub-literary material, which is an interesting testimony to an aspiration, sometimes almost painful, towards culture. This is particularly apparent with the ubiquitous tags picked up from Vergil (a topic discussed by Hoogma), but echoes of less popular writers (one may instance 28.1, 34.1 and 5, 91-2) and literary flourishes (e.g. in 184, 187, 189, 190) can also be found in incongrous surroundings. Even poets who are proud enough of their work to include their own name, like Laberius (188; he calls himself a *uates*) and Lupus (199), can be convicted of metrical or stylistic lapses.

The final point which needs to be made in these brief introductory remarks is that the whole idea of writing an inscription in verse is derived from Greece, and the Greeks had developed this practice into the composition of purely literary pieces in inscriptional form by the time the Romans took up the idea of verse inscriptions; I have already mentioned how 6 culminates in a point derived from Greek inscriptional verse (and 135 is also based on a Greek precedent), and some other poems draw on Greek literary epigram. The Hellenizing influence on the Scipio epigrams right at the beginning of the Roman development is remarked on p. 219 (see also on 11.6). Channels of Greek influence through the theatre and the large element of Greek origin among the population of Rome are noted on 16, 20, 21 (see also the Grecisms in 177). Lier in particular has attempted to trace back topics of Latin epitaphs to Greek, though he often fails to carry conviction. Yet one can observe certain widespread characteristics of Roman epitaphs which are rare in Greek; in particular commonly much more detail is given not only about status and occupation, as remarked above, but also about age (see on 70.3; even when one is unsure of it, as in 133) and offices held (this even in verse, though naturally it is particularly at home in prose).

TEXTUAL CRITICISM AND PRESENTATION OF INSCRIPTIONS

North-west of Callistoga, California, there is a small geological museum which was opened, as a plaque records, by the then Vice-President, George Herman Walker Bush. Mr Bush's second name is of course Herbert. Such an error raises interesting questions. How did it arise? How did it come to escape detection until too late (if it was detected at all)? What is the reaction of readers who observe the error?

In a literary text the steps by which the text reaches us are in most cases clearly marked: first an author's text (autograph or produced by dictation to a secretary), then duplication by scribes and a continuous succession of copying until the invention of printing. A literary author may commit slips of the pen, but normally his Latinity will observe the canons of cultivated usage of his time (with due allowance made for creative linguistic innovation), and usually deviations from this will be scribal errors. With an inscription on stone (graffiti on plaster or pottery etc. are a different matter) the potential stages are much more complex:

1) The commissioner of an inscription.

2) Its composer.

3) A functionary now known as the ordinator who marks out on the stone in paint or charcoal or with a sharp point the letters to be carved. This name is derived from *CIL* 10.7296 = *ILS* 7680 = *IG* 14.29 στῆλαι ἐνθάδε τυποῦνται καὶ χαράσσονται ... *tituli heic ordinantur et sculpuntur* (*aidibus sacreis qum operum publicorum*; the spelling indicates republican date); the Greek and Latin of this inscription (illustrated by Ireland 221, Calabi Limentani, tav. I between pp. 16-

17, J. Mallon, *De l'Écriture* (1986) 262) are not meant to be synonymous (Pliny, *NH* 35.128 *typos scalpsit* means 'he engraved reliefs', and something like this may be meant by τυποῦνται), but the word *ordinare* must imply that part of the function was to plan the lay-out of the inscription. On other inscriptions we have *scripsit et sculpsit* or *scalpsit* (Susini, *Stonecutter* 11, Keppie 13, Meyer 22; add *CIL* 6.2105), but it does not seem that these refer to different stages of operation. An idea of the work of the ordinator can be formed from unfinished inscriptions (Susini 30). It cannot be assumed that an ordinator was invariably employed, or that his operations necessarily went beyond the laying out of guidelines; Di Stefano Manzella, *Epigraphica* 42 (1980), 25 lists cases in which the right-hand margins are so uncomfortably crowded that there can have been no preparatory tracing. Susini, *Epigrafia* pl. l-li (cf. p.85) shows the rehearsal and the proper cutting of the same inscription; Buonopane, *Epigraphica* 50 (1988), 226 adduces a stone on which the *ordinatio* is visible beneath the cut letters.

4) The carver.

It should be kept in mind that these personages may overlap; e.g. the commissioner of an inscription may also be its composer, particularly when one's own tomb is prepared in advance of death. In this collection 63 and 188, perhaps 130, involve similar situations.

This sequence cuts out the layers of errors which accumulate as literary texts are successively copied during their transmission, but leaves other occasions for error. If we may ignore the commissioner, who in many cases probably had nothing more than a vague general idea of what he wanted, the composer will have written out his text on papyrus, wax or parchment, using the ordinary handwriting of the day, not formal book or inscriptional capitals; so at least argues J. Mallon in his *Paléographie Romaine* (1952), 57 § 103 sqq. and many other publications, mostly collected in his abovementioned *De l'Écriture*, and before him Le Blant, *Rev. Arch.* 1896, 2.183, Cagnat in DS s.v. *Inscriptiones* 3.535. This creates the potentiality for misreadings by the ordinator (such as *tnumpe* for *triumpe* in the second occurrence in the refrain of the *Carmen Aruale* and other misreadings in that inscription), and these misreadings will have no palaeographical relationship to the capital script into which the text is transferred. The ordinator will have needed some degree of literacy to lay out the text, but the degree and the consequent potentiality for error will have varied from person to person. Moreover the same mental process as in manuscript transmission may at this stage cause the introduction of phonetic errors. These are often, but quite illogically, taken to be evidence for the production of texts by dictation. In fact the procedure is that a scribe memorizes a block of text from his exemplar, and then looks from that to his blank page and transfers to it what he has memorized. As he does this, he mentally pronounces the words to himself as he writes them, and he will be doing this in his own pronunciation, which is liable to introduce phonetic errors. Just so the ordinator transfers the composer's text to the stone.

This therefore is the stage at which errors of misreading (as e.g. 135.3) and pronunciation are likely to cluster. The carver will normally follow mechanically the ductus traced out for him, and errors at this stage, if a full *ordinatio* has taken place, will be few, though not non-existent, and mostly visual. For instance, the ordinator might trace such a short horizontal stroke on a T that it could be carved as an I; Susini, *Stonecutter* 27 quotes an instance of an intended C carved as an O because the ordinator's compass had traced out a full circle and the carver had failed to eliminate an arc on the right-hand side. Sidonius Apollinaris, *Ep.* 3.12.5 speaks of errors committed by the mason (*peto ut (carmen) tabulae...celeriter indatur; sed uide ut uitium non faciat in marmore lapidicida, quod factum siue ab industria seu per incuriam mihi magis quam quadratario liuidus lector adscribet*), but he may be ignoring technicalities.

But the composer himself may well not speak the cultivated Latin of a literary text, since the producers of inscriptions and the public for which they are produced embrace a much wider social range than with literary works. Therefore when we encounter what is, by the standards of cultivated Latin, an error of phonology or morphology, in each case the attribution of this error to composer or executant respectively will depend on an act of judgment based on our assessment of the general level of the inscription, and such an act of judgment is bound to lack objectivity. It is therefore safest generally not to correct such errors (though in 111.2 I have ventured to do so; see also on 128.3), since we may be correcting the composer, whose text it is that we seek to present. Errors of syntax will nearly always be due to the composer.

Distinct from errors such as those just considered are the cases (as in my 38) in which wholly irrational errors, such as sequences of unintelligible letters, appear, no doubt in most cases because of lapses by the ordinator. We have as much right to emend these as we have to emend similar manuscript readings, bearing in mind that palaeographically we should not on Mallon's view think wholly in terms of capital script. Here we may also recall that some inscriptions are recorded only via a medieval manuscript tradition (see below).

Many objections have been raised to Mallon's view, but most of them are based on cases in which the process outlined by him has been over-rigidly applied; as indicated above, not everything must be supposed always to have been executed according to formula. The most vulnerable point is the claim that the script supplied to the ordinator will have been in cursive writing; e.g. one may well imagine the proprietor of the atelier drafting out the inscription as eventually carved in capitals so that the commissioner can have a clear idea how it will look on the stone. Keppie 13 fig. 1 (cf. p. 12 and Ireland 220-2) illustrates from a papyrus what may be the model, in large capitals, for an inscription. Yet Mallon's view certainly provides a satisfying explanation for many phenomena; we only have to avoid presenting it as a panacea, and recognize that the circumstances of production must have varied considerably from inscription to inscription. One will note an inscription drafted out in cursive on the back of a formal carving of the same inscription with a different lineation (Priuli, *Epigraphica* 46 (1984), 49).

One other complication. Naturally enough, for epitaphs in particular a number of set formulae were developed, and we sometimes find even whole inscriptions appearing identically in different parts of the empire. For example, *CLE* 519 (= J. G. Fernández, *Corpus de Inscr. Lat. de Andalucia I Huelva* (1987?) no. 75 and fig. 65)

> Terrenum corpus, caelestis spiritus in me,
> quo repetente suam sedem nunc uiuimus illic,
> et fruitur superis aeterna in luce Fabatus

appears identically in Italy (with a prose prescript to C. Clodius Fabatus) and in Spain (Bücheler 2 p. 586); Canto, *Archivo Español de Arqueologia* 55 (1982), 115-6 (with photo p. 118) shows that the nomenclature links with Italy, not Spain, points out that the Italian stone is much larger, and supposes that Fabatus died and was buried in Spain and had a cenotaph in Italy. Similarly *CLE* 1498 from a sarcophagus on the Via Appia reappears with the same name and two added corruptions on a tile, which must have marked a niche in a columbarium, in Dacia (Tudor, *Latomus* 39 (1980), 639-46; 40 (1981), 109-11). On this see further S. Mariner Bigorra in *Atti del III Congresso internazionale di Epigrafia, 1957* (1959), 207. Other cases show adaptation of a prototype (Cagnat, *Rev. Phil.* 13 (1889), 61). For instance, *CLE* 1055 begins *quicumque Albana tendis prope[rare per arua]* (so I suggest should be restored), and 1056 adapts this to *quiqumque Nol[a]na t[en]di[s]s per [rura] uiator*, becoming even more unmetrical in the process; the two continue with minor variations. Two explanations have been put forward for this phenomenon. Cagnat l.c. 51 suggested that the proprietors of masonic firms kept manuals or pattern-books from which clients could choose or adapt wording to suit their needs, without the necessity to call at first hand on the services of a composer. Others have thought that clients in need of an inscription might remember one read elsewhere (and no doubt travellers did sometimes actually heed the admonitions on tombs by the roadside and read the epitaphs), so that such inscriptions could travel over the empire; an explanation of this type, only with the substitution of word of mouth for memory, is certainly correct for the spread of graffiti, illustrated in my 103 and passim in II E.

Instances of such recurring phrases and verses will be found in my 18-19, 168.1 and the notes on 70.13, 119.20, 178.4; other cases not involving geographical proximity are *CLE* 76 and 1876,965-6, 991-2, 1091-4, 1179-82, 1537-42, and there are more in Cagnat l.c. and Leclercq in *DAC* 8.1338. Outside the area of epitaphs see my note on 135b; 61 spans both graffiti (in the case of which pattern-books cannot be involved) and epitaphs. I do not see that any of these can establish the use of manuals (I should perhaps make it clear that I consider the 'epitaph' of Pacuvius quoted on 19 not to be a genuine epitaph). Nevertheless I am convinced that such manuals existed, on the basis of such evidence as *AE* 1931. 112 = A211 Pikhaus *hic corpus iacet pueri nominandi*, where clearly a phrase from one with the name left undetermined has been mechanically reproduced (three hexameters follow). In other cases (21.1, 68.4, 189.10) inscriptions show features best explained by deviation from a model, which might of course have been another inscription. If such pattern-books really did exist, we must take into account a possible accumulation of errors in them also.

The question arises whether those who commissioned inscriptions found errors in them acceptable. In formal documents, which must have been carefully executed and supervised, such errors are rare. Some of the commissioners of private inscriptions no doubt were not observant or literate enough to notice errors, others will have been deterred by the expense of correction or replacement (the costs involved in commemoration by inscriptions have been discussed by R. Duncan -Jones, *The Economy of the Roman Empire*, ed. 2, 1982; see also Friedlaender, *SG* 4.304 = Eng. tr. 4.279), for others the impression of the monument as a whole will have been more important than the detailed accuracy of the inscription. As for the portentous error in *AE* 1931.112, we do not know that this stone was actually used.

Apart from certain particular features of archaic script (see p. 21), republican inscriptions in general use rather squat capitals, not executed with a sharp chisel and therefore with no effect of shading. Early imperial inscriptions use serifs and shaded capitals, i.e. with broad and narrow strokes as in writing with a pen or brush; the painting of the letters in red would accentuate the effect. There was also employed *scriptura actuaria*, which is more upright and narrow, less square and spacious, with at least some letter-forms less angular and more flowing and cursive, in the manner of rustic capital book-script. In the third century this turned into a debased style with ugly, shallow, crowded lettering (see the photos of 1). Some broad datings can be established from this general progression, but the early imperial style of lettering is so standardised that a purely palaeographical dating in most cases depends largely on subjective impression; it would also be fruitless without the provision of a photo for every inscription. In addition there is the complication that in the fourth century an archaising trend sought to reproduce classical lettering. For these reasons, and because the exact dating of an imperial inscription rarely affects the reason for which I include it, I say virtually nothing about this aspect, and seldom rely on it for dating.

The original publication of an inscription demands the fullness of detailed reporting and the utmost precision. No inscription is published in this book for the first time, and I do not write specifically for specialists in epigraphy; I therefore feel entitled to ask the reader to refer to the other publications which I list for precise details which do not seem to affect central points. Accordingly, especially since I provide a skeleton apparatus as if for literary texts and a commentary in which I can note what needs explanation, I do not need the full battery of critical signs which technical epigraphical publications require and on the use of which not all are agreed. The signs which I employ are as follows.

[ ] Letters lost or illegible, but restored by conjecture. Where the restoration is uncertain it is desirable that the approximate number of letters missing be indicated if that can be done, but, since I cannot do it with consistency where no photo is available, I content myself with giving no more than a general notion. Likewise, where publications do not give precise information about the size of gaps, some supplements which I suggest are to be understood as *exempli gratia* (e.g. 108.13).

() Expansion of abbreviations; e.g. *lib(ertus), (uiginti)* = *xx* on the stone. This sign is also employed as a brief and convenient means of indicating phonetic errors, so that the reader encountering e.g. *uende(n)s* knows that it is a participle and not a second person finite verb. My use of it in this sense is sparing but, I think, justified, since, unlike the next item, it is not misleading.

<> Omitted letters which the composer intended to be present. Some epigraphical publications unfortunately also employ this sign to enclose correct letters which have been restored by conjecture in place of erroneous; this ambiguous use ought to be eliminated.

(*sc.*) An unexpressed abbreviated form of expression, e.g. Metella Crassi (*sc.* uxor).

A sublinear dot marks a letter not clearly legible.

.... A stretch of text in which only a few letters giving no continuous sense can be read. It would be desirable if each dot could represent one letter, but that is not always practicable, and in this book no significance should be attached to the number of dots.

********* A line of verse now missing from the stone.

<< >> Erased text.

* following my number marks an inscription known only or mainly from medieval manuscript transmission.

** following my number marks an inscription known from humanistic and scholarly reports, but not seen by the compilers of *CIL* or their informants nor since.

| Line-end on the stone; I record this only where there is a particular reason for doing so (e.g. to account for a preceding abbreviation).

DATING INSCRIPTIONS

The following is a list of criteria which occur in the republican inscriptions of this selection and which help to establish dating, with a brief postscript on imperial developments. It should be realised that this is merely a simplified sketch of a highly complex and sometimes controversial subject.

Graphical

For general palaeographical development see p. 18.

The letters L and P in particular have characteristic archaic shapes, for which see the introduction to the Scipio epitaphs and to 16.

The omission of *-s* after a short is common until about 200 B.C.; for omission of *-m* see on 1.4-6, 19.4. For associated metrical phenomena see Metre I b, h.

Around 110 B.C. (Oliver *AJP* 87, 1966, 159) the habit is introduced of indicating *ī* with *I* (Leumann 13 is wrong in seeing a reference to this in Plautus). This is really *i* super-imposed on *i*.

From about 100 B.C. (Oliver 150) the apex (e.g. *á*) is introduced to indicate long vowels; but its application is seldom consistently executed. It is intended as a help to reading the inscription aloud correctly.

In my text the apex and long I are reproduced when they affect the dating of the inscription, not otherwise.

Orthographical

Double consonants are indicated by single until early in the second century B.C., and the spelling with single consonants finally disappears around 100 B.C.

During the period c. 135 - 75 B.C. and sporadically thereafter (Oliver 155; see on 85.1) vowels may be doubled to indicate long quantity (*i* only very rarely in this form, since the sequence *ii* is too common in Latin morphology for it to represent *i*, and also two upright strokes represent *e* in some scripts; see however *uiitam* 2 B).

The aspirate with *c t p* comes in about 150 B.C. (see on 3).

Phonological

ai begins to be replaced by *ae* early in the second century B.C., and generally dies out about 120 B.C., though it lingers in some proper names and official words (e.g. *Caicilius, praifectus*).

ei and *ī* originally indicated different sounds; in common inflections the genitive singular of the second declension was properly -*ī*, the nominative plural -*ei*, the dative and ablative plural -*eis*, the dative singular of the third declension -*ei*. However these sounds began to get confused about 160 B.C., and eventually *ī* takes over, though *ei* spellings (sometimes improperly applied) persist into the empire (e.g. 136.3; see Lommatzsch, *ALL* 15 (1908), 129). *ei* is sometimes simplified to *e* in early inscriptions (see on 9.1).

oi (as in 9.1) changes to *ū* (first in 11.4), but lingers until about 50 B.C.

ou changes to *ū*, beginning around 200 B.C., but the process is not fully accomplished until early in the first century.

du- (as in 9.2) in certain words changes to *b*- around 250 B.C., though the older forms sometimes remain as archaisms (e.g. *duellum*).

-ol(-) (cf. 6.5, 9.4) generally changes to *-ul(-)* about 150 B.C.

In the nominative and accusative singular and the original genitive plural of the second declension *-os* and *-om* pass into *-us* and *-um* shortly before 200 B.C., except that they survive after *u* (e.g. *diuom*).

In superlatives and similar words *-imus* begins to replace *-umus* late in the second century B.C.

Morphological

The ablative *-d* begins to disappear early in the third century B.C. and dies out totally around 125 B.C., except that the monosyllabic pronouns are a little more tenacious (*sed CIL* 1.582 of 125 B.C., though Terence no longer uses such forms). This same ending also is found in adverbs and then disappears; but *hau* (16.2), which is on a different level (see Leumann 229, HS 59*), never drove out *haud*.

In early verse it has to be remembered that some terminations which classical Latin shortened retain their original length; so *censōr* 9.4, *posidēt* 12.2, *cluēt* 14.3.

In imperial times the chief phonological developments are the interchange of *ae* and *e*, for which see Metre Ia, and that of *b* and *u*, which begins in early first century A.D. (see Leumann 159, SP 129, 152, Väänänen 50).

METRE

Like the stylistic level, the nature of the versification in Roman inscriptions varies widely, from the highly polished to such helplessness as we see in e.g. 34 and 117. Occasionally we even encounter the sheer inability to count six feet in a hexameter, as e.g. in 132 (a similarly extended septenarius in 85.3); where I suggest means of reducing or expanding to a hexameter, I think that in each case it will be apparent whether my intention is to indicate faulty reproduction of a model or simply to show that there was no technical obstacle to a correct verse. Other factors which dictate this range are as follows:

(1) in prosody, vulgar pronunciation; e.g reduction of *ae* to ĕ, non-pronunciation of *-m* even before a following consonant.

(2) late Latin metrical developments; e.g. recognition of *h* as a consonant (this is not due to pronunciation, in which, quite the contrary, *h* tended to disappear, as may be seen in Romance languages) and of *qu* as a double consonant, lengthening of a short final open vowel before initial mute and liquid. The second of these probably has a phonological basis, the first and third seem to be due to artificial scholastic theorizing, which had to replace natural instinct for Latin language and versification as that weakened.

(3) even in poems with correct prosody, such things as the formation of line-ends may not be executed with classical refinement; features which in themselves are not non-classical, such as lengthening by the metrical beat and hiatus, may be extended beyond classical boundaries, particularly to short final open vowels at caesura and diaeresis.

One feature which applies overall to epigraphic verse is that the metre may simply be suspended to incorporate such potentially intractable items as proper names; see 8.1, 9.3, 19.3, 27.2, 68.4?, 69.1, 179.19 (some scholars misguidedly try to fit the first two instances into schemes of the Saturnian metre). Other expressions in this category are official titles (29.9, 162.7; at 76.4 the line is a hexameter with the last word scanned as written in abbreviated form, but becomes a heptameter if it is read in full) and arithmetical sums (69.5, 133.2; Galletier 295). In 69.1 and 5 the metre would run correctly with the removal of a few words, and so also 133.2 *natŭm arbitror* (see Ic below) would pass with the numeral *xxxv* discounted.

It must also be observed that the spelling often does not match the prosody; see on 7.1 (and 4?), 12.3 (?), 13.3, 15.1, 20.4, 39.5, 40.1, 41.7, 69.4 (?), 78.2 (?), 117.1-2, 118.5, 135a.1, 187.7, 188.10, 190.3, 199A.A26, 202.11. Note also the lineation in 185.3-4.

The following illustrate the most notable divergences from classical usage.

I *Prosody*

a) The reduction of *ae* to ē had started even in archaic Latin. In imperial times it is further reduced to ĕ, the earliest example known to me being *ustulatae* (83.2) at Pompeii; see also 30 A 7 *primaeue*, where spelling indicates the difference of prosody, 179.5 *femine*, and shortenings in prosody with the diphthong retained in spelling at 39.2 (twice) and 10, 161.2, 190.7 and other more doubtful instances. See Leumann 56, SP 64 (but they are wrong about *Priapea* 3.9), L. Mueller 445. The reverse confusion (Leumann 68, SP 63-4, Väänänen 24) is shown graphically at 95.2 *aedeo* = *edo*, 117 *maea, praecor, diae(m)* (but also *fam(a)e* 5), 159.2 *quae* = *que*; this is hypercorrection.

b) *-m* may be ignored in scansion before a consonant, particularly in the fifth foot of the hexameter (70.1, 119.4, 130.3, 159.3, 176.4, 179.11); outside that location see 140.3, 199.8. Cf. Leumann 224, SP 220-1, Väänänen 71. The writer of 40 ignores *-m* so often that in compunction he introduces the hyper-correct *quandium* (8).

On the oldest inscriptions *-m* is very often unwritten (e.g. 1.4-6), but during the second century B.C., coinciding with the obsolescence of the saturnian metre, it becomes usual to write it (cf. on 19.4). Then again on later vulgar inscriptions it is frequently omitted. See Leumann 224, SP 220, Porzio Gernia 135.

c) Conversely a final syllable ending in *m* may count as a short before a following vowel instead of suffering elision; see 27.1, 109.15, 138. 9-10, 161.1, 172.10, 179.12.

d) With notable frequency *i* is treated as a consonant (which I indicate by using *j*) before a following vowel (cf. Leumann 130, SP 108); see 39.11, 40.8?, 70.1, 112.1, 115.9, 129.7, 130.5, 157, 164.2, 179.3 and 11, 185.3, 189.5? and L. Mueller 299, 325. Since the combination consonant + consonantal *i* should lengthen a preceding short (SP 209-10), and does so at 102b.2 *rātjonem*, it is hard to see how to justify *religione* ⏑ ⏑ - - ⏑ at 161.1 (see the note there). A special case is names ending in *-ianus* (L. Mueller 446); 26.6 (but see the note there) and 126.3 *Hadrianus*; 74.4 and 164.9 (unless the metre is simply suspended for the proper names there; see above); see on this Salomies, *Arctos* 17 (1983), 74.

e) Initial *h* may count as a consonant to lengthen a preceding monosyllable ending in a consonant (instances in L. Mueller 370, 391), as 40.2 *īn hac*, 192.3 *ēt Hermas* (perhaps 189.10 *ēs Heroe*, though there the metrical beat of the line may be in play), or to prevent elision, as 59.2 *mortuă heic*, 175.4 *leuĕ hiberni*.

f) A short may be lengthened before *qu*, usually in *que*; so 108.2 *annonāque* (nominative), 109.4 *nēque*. See *Class. et Med.* 40 (1989), 201, A. M. Devine and L. D. Stephens, *Two Studies in Latin Phonology* (1977), 51.

g) A short final open vowel may be lengthened before initial mute and liquid, as 108. 8 *inuidiā* (nom.) *creuit*, 115.7 *hydraulā grata*. In literary texts this comes in during the fourth century, unless Q. Serenus, *De Medicina* 28 *inductā prosunt* is earlier (the conventional dating of this work depends on a false identification of its author; see *FLP* 406). See also on 159.3.

h) Whereas the discounting of *-s* in scansion before an initial consonant disappeared from literary usage during the 50s B.C., it persisted in epigraphic verse, with a high proportion of the instances in the fifth foot of the hexameter (C. Proskauer, *Das auslautende -s* (1910), 198), as 28.1 (where however a reminiscence of Ennius is probably at work), 59.2; for other locations see 30 A 3, 39.3?, 155.51?, 188.3? Of these instances 59.2 is a rare case which does not involve *-us* or *-ŏs*. In 78.1 *s* is not written but its presence is probably intended to be felt. See Väänänen 77 sqq.

i) The accent may create a long, as 78.2 and 5, 188.1? See too 151.18 and (for what it is worth) 138.1 and 3 *Iouīgena*. Cf. also on 177.5. See L. Mueller 442-3, Väänänen 19, Hodgman, *HSCP* 9 (1898), 143.

j) Unaccented syllables may be shortened, particularly final syllables; one may note especially the following categories:

(i) Ablatives of the first and second declension, as (of the first) 29.7, 115.9 and 119.4 (both of *pia*, cf. *CLE* 750.7, 769.11), 150 passim, 189.1, 119.8 (L. Mueller 421 quotes fifth-century literary instances of this) and (of the second) 39.6, 119.3 and 9, 192.4 (Mueller ibid. quotes *CLE* 543.4, which like Bücheler he attributes to the second century). In the second case the shortening of *-o* in verbs (as *portŏ*), third declension nouns (as *leŏ*) and adverbs etc. (as *uerŏ*) spread to dative and ablative gerunds in silver literary verse (as 200.3 *cursanŏ*), but not beyond. One may also note *trigintă* (see on 28.2), *substă* 117.1, and (assisted by false etymology) *posteă* 109.14, 130.5, *anteă* 139.6 (L. Mueller 421).

(ii) Syllables in *-s*, as (verbs) 163.15 and (particularly harsh) 4 *intonăs nubigenam*; (nouns and adjectives) 49.8, 115.5, 117.7 *gladiantes in*, 199.6 and (again harsh) 53.4 *dolŏs iurgia*. For the latter one may compare a verse quoted by the *Historia Augusta* 11.12.6.3 *gentĕs amant*.

(iii) The perfect ending *-i*, with a particular concentration in the fifth foot of the hexameter, as 70.5, 109.5 and 119.3 (both *uixĭ*), 130.1 and 5; elsewhere 70.7, 130.3? Here one may also count *uintĭ* 179.3, *cunctĭ* ibid. 15, both in the fifth foot.

k) Double consonants may be reduced phonetically to single, as *Cŏmmodus* 28.4, *ĭmminet* 164.1; see also 118.6 and L. Mueller 447.

l) Forms of the possessive adjectives *meus, tuus, suus* are scanned as monosyllables at 7.3 (twice), 13.1, 16.2. These are from republican inscriptions; at 39.8 *suae* may be a pyrrhic, and the versification of 179 (10 *meo*, cf. 11 the pronoun *mei*) is too inaccurate to permit close analysis. See O. Skutsch, *Annals of Ennius* 382 n.8.

II *Metrical Forms*

A *Dactylic Metres*

a) Hiatus at the caesura of the hexameter (29.4, 115.7, 187.5) or diaeresis of the pentameter (66.2) or before a pause (177.2 and 8) or in other places of the line (7.2, 29.5, 112.2, 145.1, 174.3). Most of these are not essentially unclassical.

b) Lengthening of closed syllable at the caesura of the hexameter is quite common, as in classical verse; for similar lengthening in the fourth foot see 49.1, 62b.1, 115.6, 151.7, 175.2, 199.1; elsewhere 176.1 and in the pentameter 71.2 *uendēs* (present) *acuam*.

c) Lengthening of closed syllable at the diaeresis of the pentameter 50.6, 109.19.

d) Lengthening of short open vowel at the caesura of the hexameter 29.7, 39.2 and 62a.1 (both *lapidĕ*), 115.2, 190.1, 199.8 (instances in 109.17 and 26, the latter in any case before mute and liquid, 189.7 are hardly significant in view of the general usage of these authors); in the fourth foot 39.11, 179.8.

e) Similar lengthening at the diaeresis of the pentameter 109.6, ibid. 14 (if that is not an error), ibid. 26 (mute and liquid follow); cf. Galletier 305.

f) Hiatus and lengthening combined at the caesura of the hexameter 59.3, 199.7, 66.1 and 70.15 (in these two cases *h* follows); note also 39.5 *quondām Alexand[*, 59.2 *sūm et*. Similarly at the diaeresis of the pentameter 115.9, 145.4; note too 71.2 *acuām et*, 181.4 *castarūm h[*.

(g) Pentameters may be irregularly placed (as by Trimalchio, Petron. 34.10, 55.3); so in 29, 70, 89, 109.17-24, 112, 115, 150, 171, 177, 189, 192-4. 101 is an isolated pentameter.

h) In the sequence ⏑ ⏑ ⏑ the first may be artifically lengthened, as cultured verse does with *religio, reliquiae, relicuus, Italia,* to fit the words into dactylic metre; so *mēmoriam* 39.8, *īnanimem* 76.2.

i) Spondaic hexameters are rare in inscriptions (33.15 with a proper name, 46.1), but spondees may be admitted into the second half of the pentameter, as 94b, 145 (see P. Kessel, *De Pentametro Inscriptionum Lat.* (1908), 71, Galletier 305).

j) Elision of a long in the second half of the pentameter is rare (193.6 and, unless *subitŏ* is implicit, 185.2); even elision in *-m* is not common (168b.4, 187.12, 188.14). See Galletier 305.

B *Iambic and Trochaic Metres*

a) Iambic shortening is found in 85.2 *manŭ*; prima facie there is also an instance in primitive hexameters at 16.1, and another at 89.3 (q.v.). *uidĕ* in 193.2 is more acceptable (L. Mueller 418).

b) Lengthening before mute and liquid within a word, not found in the old scenic verse but occurring as early as Lucil. 923 *fēbris* and quite common in Phaedrus, appears in 107 *pātre*, 124.4 *Agrippae* ; cf. Hodgman, *HSCP* 9 (1898), 145.

c) Hiatus at a pause is found in 124.6, at the caesura of the senarius 124.8 and 10, 63.10 (Plautus at least seems to have permitted this); 164.7 is both at a pause and at the caesura.

d) The senarius lacks a caesura in 24.1 and 7, 68.6, 198.3.

e) A proceleusmatic is apparently split at 69.4 in a way which transgresses the rule that the first two syllables of an anapaest or proceleusmatic may not constitute the end of a longer word (see ad loc.); cf. also on 40.8. 78.1 is probably not a case of an incorrectly split tribrach. For the Bentley-Luchs Law, which states that with certain exceptions a final word of iambic shape may not be preceded by another iambus, see on 32.39 (p. 254), 164.3, 63.8.

C *The Saturnian Metre*

Even if it were possible to give a comprehensive account of this metre, that would occupy a full-length treatise and would involve consideration of the literary as well as the inscriptional examples; that cannot be contemplated here. What follows is strictly an empirical account of the main forms which will be encountered in this selection, and a doxography about the metre is deliberately avoided. It will be apparent that I take my stand with those who think that this a quantitative metre.

A Saturnian line consists of two cola of very variable form, with the second almost always shorter than the first, or at most of equal length (as in 9.1-2, 10.2 and in four out of six lines in 12). The exceptions to this are 2.1 and 5; these come in the inscription of the Faliscan cooks, whose Saturnians, aptly christened 'kitchen Saturnians', are abnormal in several respects. A paradigmatic line is that of Naevius *nouem Iouis concordes filiae sorores* (English readers might like to use as a paradigm the nursery-rhyme line 'The queen was in the parlour, eating bread and honey', which Coventry Patmore in his *Essay on English Metrical Law* identified as a Saturnian!); this form is found 2.6, 6.3, 8.2-3, 9.4, 10.4, 12.4-5 and the verses quoted under 5, perhaps also 4.5, and these particular cola predominate. 9.5 and 12.5 show hiatus at the diaeresis (perhaps also 4.5). It is a natural result of the shape of the line that five-element and six-element cola are found predominantly in the second half of the line, seven-element predominantly in the first.

Most occurrences of two consecutive shorts appear to be resolved longs (at least the lines in which they occur usually fit into well-established patterns on this assumption); for this reason I prefer to speak of 'elements' rather than 'syllables'. There are however cases in which word-boundary seems to indicate that consecutive shorts are to be regarded as separate elements (2.2b, 9.2b and the identical phrase in the elogium of Calatinus; 9.6b and 11.2b must also belong here, perhaps also 12.6a); see F. Leo, *Der Saturnische Vers* (Abhl. Göttingen Gesellsch. 8 (1905), 5), 58.

In my analyses x means an element which may be represented by - or ⏑, y one which may be represented by - or ⏑ ⏑, z one which may be represented by ⏑, - or ⏑ ⏑.

Five-element cola show no clear pattern; 2.5 and 9.2 are the only occurrences in the first half of the line.

Six-element cola. A very cohesive group can be analysed as y ⏑ - | z y x; this is found only in the second half of the line, and almost invariably has the word-boundary indicated (8.2 is an exception, and in 11.3 the break comes after *atque*). Other six-element cola show no clear pattern, and occur in either half of the line.

Seven-element cola. Here there enters the factor of the so-called caesura Korschiana, thus defined by Cole, *YCS* 21 (1969), 19: 'In any half-line that contains seven or more syllables, the last three or (more rarely) the last four must be preceded by word-end. This rule is violated only when absolutely necessary - to allow for the inclusion within a half-line of a word of five or more syllables' (2.5b and 9.6a are instances). Note

(a) that a seven- or eight-syllable colon may be in my terminology a six-element colon, and that the Korsch caesura applies to the particular form analysed above with the modification that, whereas in the seven-element colon a word of five syllables is needed to excuse violation, a four-syllable word *restitistei* justifies it in a six-element colon in 8.2;

(b) that if we speak of word-break three elements rather than three or four syllables from the end, we shall have very few exceptions (2.3a and 4a, in the abnormal Faliscan inscription; 9.3a, with proper names which often defy the metre (see above)).

A cohesive group can be analysed as z - z - | z y x. This colon appears as the second half of a line only in the primitive 1.7-9, the eccentric 2.1, and perhaps 4.5. In 1.4b - 6b and probably 4.1a we have a phenomenon like what we know in the hexameter as the quasi-caesura. 2.1b quite exceptionally involves elision at the caesura; on the contrary in 11.3, 12.6, perhaps 10.3, 11.1, possibly but not probably at 12.3 the element preceding the caesura is after a long treated as syllaba anceps(not in 9.4, 10.4, where we probably have the archaic *censōr*).

The other seven-element cola, all in the first half of the line, show no clear pattern.

The eight-element cola (only in 1 and 2) do not seem to conform to a pattern, except that 1.4a - 6a and 2.2a show a caesura Korschiana three elements from the end, and the violation in 2.5b is excused by a long word.

D *Index of Metres* (other than hexameters, elegiacs and senarii)

choriambic tetrameter and trimeter catalectic 151. 8-14
cretic 151. 15-20
glyconic and pherecratic 131. 5 and 22, 140
hendecasyllables 105, 116, 143.5-7, 155, 186, 204
iambic dimeter 30 A, 131, 137, 138, 141. 10-13, 200; catalectic 129.1 and 4
iambic trimeter (to be distinguished from senarii) 27, 32, 75, 98, 143.1-2, 149, 153
ionic dimeter 129, 136
sapphic 155. 6, 10, 23
trochaic septenarius 84, 85, 166, 169
trochaic tetrameter 75, 134, 141. 14-19, 188. 1-3?; uersus quadratus 100

141 and 151 are polymetric; the metre changes in mid-line in 59.1, 78.3.

E *Metrical Features*

ădicit 127.15
Correption 184.18
Elision of *quae* 155.9
Greek accent becomes Latin long vowel 177.5
Lengthening due to beat in hendecasyllables 155.15; of *quis* 87.1, *quit* = *quid* 80.4, *quod* 169
Proceleusmatic replacing dactyl 7.4?
Pronouns, dative: *cŭī* 159.3 (q.v.), *hŭic* 187.2, *hūic* 187.12
'Prosodic hiatus' 124.11
Syncope; of *Hercules* 135a.1?; of *sacculi* 102.2; of *facilia* 7.4?
Synizesis of *quoius* (10.3?), 18.2, of *eius* 68.10, of *ei* 115.3; of *quandium* 40.8?; of *quies* 99.1
Verse intermingled with prose 125 (q.v.); accidental 147

u consonantal scanned as vocalic 155.24 and 49; vocalic scanned as consonantal 40.15; *acua* = *aqua* 71.2

x scanned as *s* 39.5

TEXT AND TRANSLATION

I A: SATURNIAN INSCRIPTIONS

1

ibi sacerdotes clusi succincti libellis acceptis carmen descindentes tripodauerunt in uerba haec

e nos Lases iuuate
e] nos Lases iuuate
e nos Lases iuuate
neue lue(m) rue(m) Marma<r> sins incurrere in pleores
neue lue(m) rue(m) Marmar [si]ns incurrere in pleoris
neue lue(m) rue(m) Marmar serp incurrere in pleoris
satur fu, fere Mars, limen [sa]li, sta berber
satur fu, fere Mars, limen sali, sta berber
satur fu, fere Mars, limen sali, sta berber
Sem]unis alternei aduocapit conctos
Semunis alternei aduocapit conctos
Simunis alternei aduocapit [conct]os
e nos Marmor iuuato
e nos Marmor iuuato
e nos Ma<r>mor iuuato
triumpe triumpe triumpe trium[pe tri]umpe.

post tripodationem deinde signo dato publici introierunt et libellos receperunt.

2

Iouei, Iunonei, Mineruai
Falesce quei in Sardinia sunt
donum dederunt. magistreis
L. Latrius K. f., C. Salu[e]na Voltai f.
coiraueront.

gonlegium quod est aciptum aetatei age(n)d[ai]
opiparum a[d] uiitam quolundam festosqu[e] dies
quei soueis aastutieis opidque Volgani
gondecorant sai[pi]sume comuiuia loidosque
qu<o>quei huc dederu[nt i]nperatoribus summeis
utei sesed lubent[is be]ne iouent optantis.

A1 D]iouei *Wachter*
B2 uiitam *Wachter,* ueitam *priores*

1

The priests, shut in there and with their robes tucked up, receiving the prayer-books and reciting (?) the formula, performed the three-step dance to these words.

Help us, Lares,

and, Mars, do not allow disease and disaster to attack the multitude.

Be sated, fierce Mars; leap (on to? over?) the threshold.

In turn you [*plural*] shall summon all the Semones.

Help us, Mars.

triumpe!

Then after the dance the sign was given, and the public slaves entered and took back the books.

2

The Falerians who are in Sardinia presented a gift to Jupiter, Juno, Minerva; supervised by their officials, Lucius Latrius son of Kaeso and Gaius Salvenus son of Volta.

Cooks, a guild welcome for passing a pleasant time, well endowed for cheering life and festal days, who full often give luxury to banquets and games with their own ruses and by the help of Vulcan, presented this to the Supreme Rulers, desiring that of their grace they should generously help them.

3

L. Mummi(us) L. f. cos. duct(u)
auspicio imperioque
eius Achaia capt(a), Corinto
deleto Romam redieit
triumphans. ob hasce
res bene gestas, quod
in bello uouerat,
hanc aedem et signu(m)
Herculis Victoris
imperator dedicat.

4

]re et Tauriscos c[
]us coactos m[
]r quineis qua[ ]auit
]signeis consi[lieis]os Tudita | nus
Roma]e egit triumpu[m]dedit Tim | auo
]ria ei restitu[it]reis tradi | t

*5**

Caesius Bassus, *GLK* 6.265 apud nostros autem in tabulis antiquis quas triumphaturi duces in Capitolio figebant uictoriaeque suae titulum saturniis uersibus prosequebantur talia repperi exempla: ex Regilli tabula

duello magno dirimendo regibus subigendis

...in Acilii Glabrionis tabula

fundit fugat prosternit maximas legiones.

Atilius Fortunatianus, *GLK* 6.293 (on the saturnian): maxime tamen triumphaturi in Capitolio tabulas huiusmodi uersibus incidebant

summas opes qui regum regias refregit.

3

When Achaea had been taken and Corinth wiped out under his leadership, his auspices and his command, Lucius Mummius, son of Lucius, consul, returned to Rome in triumph. For these successes he, the commander, dedicates this shrine and statue of the Victorious Hercules, as he had vowed during the war.

4

...and the Taurisci...coerced...whom in fifteen days he four times defeated (?)...standards and counsels...he celebrated a triumph at Rome...gave to Timavus...restored ? to it...handed over to...

5

Among the Romans I have found the following examples among the ancient tablets which generals about to triumph used to affix in the Capitol, equipping the inscription of their victory with Saturnian verses: from the tablet of Regillus:

> By settling a great war and subduing kings.

...In the tablet of Acilius Glabrio :

> He routs, puts to flight, lays low great battalions.

Particularly those about to celebrate a triumph inscribed tablets on the Capitol with verses of this type:

> Who broke the great regal power of kings.

Epitoma Disciplinarum 14.14 (Censorinus ed. Sallmann (1983), p. 83.10) numerus saturnius

magnum numerum, triumphat   hostibus deuictis.

6

M. P. Vertuleieis C. f. |
quod re sua d[if]eidens   asper | afleicta
parens timens | heic uouit   uoto hoc soluto
[de]cuma facta | poloucta   leibereis lube(n) | tes
donu(m) danunt | Hercolei   maxsume mereto,
semol te | orant se uoti   crebro condemnes.

7

sancte
de] decuma, Victor, tibei Lucius Munius donum
mor]ibus antiqueis pro usu[r]a hoc dare sese
uis]um animo suo perfecit, tua pace rogans te
co]gendei dissoluendei tu ut facilia faxseis.
per]ficias decumam ut faciat uerae ration[is
pro]que hoc atque alieis donIs des digna mere[nti.

8

hoc est factum monumentum | Maarco Caicilio. |
hospes, gratum est quom apud | meas   restitistei seedes. |
bene rem geras et ualeas, | dormias sine qura.

The Saturnian metre:

A great number, after the defeat of the enemy he celebrates a triumph.

6

Marcus and Publius Vertuleius, sons of Gaius.

In payment of the vow which their father, despairing and embittered at the ruin of his fortunes, vowed here, his sons Marcus and Publius Vertuleius gladly present a gift to Hercules, the great benefactor, having set aside a tithe and given to the god his share of the sacrifice. At the same time they beseech you often to exact payment of a vow.

7

Holy One! Lucius Munius has achieved what he had decided in his mind, that he should give this gift to you, Conqueror, according to ancient custom, as interest from a tithe, asking you of your indulgence to make easy work of collecting money and paying it out. See to it that he totals up a tithe of true reckoning, and in return for this and other gifts give worthy return to him, as he deserves.

8

This memorial was made for Marcus Caecilius. Thank you, stranger, for stopping at my resting place. Good luck, good health, and worry-free sleep to you.

I B: THE SCIPIO EPITAPHS

9

L.] Cornelio(s) L. f. Scipio | aidiles, cosol, cesor.

honc oino(m) ploirume(i) cosentiont R[omai
duonoro(m) optumo(m) fuise uiro(m),
Luciom Scipione(m) filio(m) Barbati.
consol, censor, aidilis hic fuet a[pud uos,
hec cepit Corsica(m) Aleria(m)que urbe(m),
dedet Tempestatebus aide(m) mereto[d.

3 filio(m) *L. Havet, De Saturnio Latinorum Versu (1880), 221*: filios *lapis*

10

L. Corneli]o(s) Cn. f. Scipio

<<********************************** | ****************>>
Cornelius Lucius Scipio Barbatus,
Gnaiuod patre | prognatus, fortis uir sapiensque,
quoius forma uirtutei parisuma | fuit,
consol, censor, aidilis quei fuit apud uos,
Taurasia(m) Cisauna(m) | Samnio cepit,
subigit omne(m) Loucanam opsidesque abdoucit.

11

quei apice(m) insigne Dial[is fl]aminis gesistei, |
mors perfec[it] tua ut essent omnia | breuia,
honos fama uirtusque, | gloria atque ingenium,
quibus sei | in longa licuiset tibe utier uita, |
facile facteis superases gloriam | maiorum.

9

Lucius Cornelius Scipio, son of Lucius, aedile, consul, censor.

Most people agree that this man, Lucius Scipio, son of Barbatus, was uniquely best among the good men at Rome. He was consul, censor, aedile among you, he captured Corsica and the city of Aleria, he gave to the Storm-deities a temple, as they deserved.

10

Lucius Cornelius Scipio, son of Gnaeus.

Lucius Cornelius Scipio Barbatus, begotten of his father Gnaeus, a brave and sapient man, whose handsome form was fully a match for his courage, who was consul, censor, aedile among you, captured Taurasia, Cisauna, Samnium, reduced all of Lucania and took hostages from there.

11

You who wore the cap, the mark of the flamen Dialis, death caused everything that belonged to you, your honour, reputation, courage, glory and talents, to be short-lived. If you had been allowed to enjoy these in a long life, you would easily have outshone the glory of

qua re lubens te in gremiu(m), | Scipio, recipit
terra, Publi, | prognatum Publio, Corneli.

3 in.genium *lapis*

12

L. Cornelius Cn. f. Cn. n. Scipio

magna(m) sapientia(m) | multasque uirtutes
aetate quom parua | posidet hoc saxsum.
quoiei uita defecit, non | honos, honore(m),
is hic situs, quei numquam | uictus est uirtutei,
annos gnatus (uiginti) <h>is | l[oc]eis m[a]ndatus,
ne quairatis honore(m) | quei minus sit mandatus.

13

Cn. Cornelius Cn. f. Scipio Hispanus pr(aitor) aid(ilis) cur(ulis) q(uaistor) tr(ibunus) mil(itum) II Xuir sl(itibus) iudik(andis) Xuir sacr(is) fac(iundis)

uirtutes generis mieis moribus accumulaui,
progeniem genui, facta patris petiei,
maiorum optenui laudem ut sibei me esse creatum
laetentur; stirpem nobilitauit honor.

your ancestors. Therefore, Publius Cornelius Scipio, scion of Publius, the earth gladly receives you into her bosom.

12

Lucius Cornelius Scipio, son of Gnaeus, grandson of Gnaeus.

This stone holds great prudence and many fine qualities coupled to a brief span of life. Here lies that man whose life, not (lack of) respect, denied him office, who was never outdone in merit. So that you may not enquire why office was not entrusted to him, he was entrusted to this place at the age of twenty.

13

Gnaeus Cornelius Scipio Hispanus, son of Gnaeus, praetor, curule aedile, quaestor, twice tribunus militum, member of the Board of Ten for settling lawsuits, Member of the Board of Ten for supervising ritual.

By my noble character I built still higher the glorious deeds of my family ; I begat offspring and emulated the deeds of my father. I upheld the praise of my ancestors, so that they rejoice that I was born to them. My public career ennobled my family.

I C: OTHER REPUBLICAN INSCRIPTIONS

14*

Fragmenta Poetarum Latinorum ed. W. Morel p. 32

Plin. *NH* 35.115 decet non sileri et Ardeatis templi pictorem, praesertim ciuitate donatum ibi et carmine, quod est in ipsa pictura his uersibus

dignis digna. +loco+ picturis condecorauit
Reginae Iunonis supremi coniugis templum
Plautius Marcus: cluet Asia lata esse oriundus,
quem nunc et post semper ob artem hanc Ardea laudat

eaque sunt scripta antiquis litteris Latinis.

15

quod neque conatus quisquanst neque[ ]au[
noscite rem ut famaa facta feramus uirei.
auspicio [Antoni Marc]i pro consule classis
Isthmum traductast missaque per pelagus.
ipse iter eire profectus Sidam, classem Hirrus Atheneis
pro praetore anni e tempore constituit.
lucibus haec pauc[ei]s paruo perfecta tumultu
magna[a qu]om ratione atque salut[e
q[u]ei probus est lauda[t], quei contra est in[
inuid[ea]nt dum q[u d]ecet id u[

16

Protogenes Cloul(i) | suauei(s) heicei situst | mimus,
plouruma que | fecit populo soueis | gaudia nuges.

Fort. Cloul[i] *et* que[i] *lapis*

14

One should also mention the painter of the temple at Ardea, especially since he was presented there with citizenship and a verse inscription, which is on the actual painting:

Worthy rewards to the worthy. Marcus Plautius adorned with paintings the temple of Queen Juno, wife of Highest Jupiter; he is spoken of as sprung from broad Asia. Because of this artistic achievement Ardea now praises him and (will praise him) subsequently for ever.

This is written in ancient Latin lettering.

15

Learn of a deed which no-one has either ever attempted..., so that we may exalt with fame the exploits of a hero. Under the auspices of Marcus Antonius a fleet was transported over the Isthmus and sent across the sea. He himself set out on his journey to Sida, the propraetor Hirrus based the fleet at Athens in view of the season of the year. All this was achieved within a few days with great prudence and no danger; there was hardly any turmoil. Upright men are full of praise, those who are of the opposite disposition, of envy; let them envy...

16

Protogenes, the genial mime-actor, slave of Cloelius, lies here; he gave the people great pleasure with his clowning.

17**

hospes, quod deico paullum est, asta ac pellege.
heic est sepulcrum hau pulcrum pulcrai feminae.
nomen parentes nominarunt Claudiam.
suom mareitum corde deilexit souo.
gnatos duos creauit; horunc alterum
in terra linquit, alium sub terra locat.
sermone lepido, tum autem incessu commodo.
domum seruauit, lanam fecit. dixi. abei.

18

rogat ut resistas, hospes, t[e] hic tacitus lapis,
dum ostendit quod mandau[i]t quoius umbram te[git].
pudentis hominis, frugi, c[u]m magna fide,
praeconis Oll Grani sunt [o]ssa heic sita.
tantum est. hoc uoluit nescius ne esses. uale.
A. Granius M. l. Stabilio, praeco.

19

adulescens, tametsi properas, | hic te saxsolus
rogat ut se | aspicias, deinde ut quod scriptust | legas.
hic sunt ossa Maeci Luci sita | Pilotimi uasculari. |
hoc ego uoleba(m) | nescius ni esses. uale.
posteris ius. |
L. Maeci L. l. Salui, Manchae Manchae f(iliae). | Rutilia Rutiliae l. Hethaera, | Maecia L. f.

20

Eucharis Licini[ae l.], docta, erodita omnes artes uirgo, u[ixit an(n.) xiiii]

heus oculo errante quei aspicis léti domu[s,
morare gressum et titulum nostrum perlege,

17

Stranger, what I have to say is brief, halt and read it. This is the unlovely tomb of a lovely woman. Her parents gave her the name Claudia. She loved her husband with all her heart. She gave birth to two sons; one of them she leaves on earth, the other she places (placed?) beneath it. She was charming in conversation and modest in gait. She kept to the house and made wool. That is all I have to say; be on your way.

18

This stone, silent as it is, requests you to halt, stranger, while it discloses the instructions of the man whose shade it covers. Here lie the bones of a modest, thrifty, trustworthy man, the auctioneer Aulus Granius. That is all. He did not want you to be unaware of this. Farewell.

Aulus Granius Stabilio, freedman of Marcus Granius, auctioneer.

19

Young man, even if you are in a hurry, this little stone asks that you contemplate it and then read what is inscribed. Here lie the bones of Lucius Maecius Philotimus the vessel-maker. I wanted you not to be unaware of this. Farewell.

[Later additions].

20

Eucharis, freedwoman of Licinia, a virgin learned and cultivated in all accomplishments; she lived for fourteen years.
Ho there, you who with random eye survey the homes of death, stay your step and read my epitaph, which the love of my father

amor parenteis quem dedit natae suae,
ubei se reliquiae conlocarent corporis.
heic uiridis aetas cum floreret artibus
crescente et aeuo gloriam conscenderet,
properauit hóra tristis fatalis mea
et denegauit ultra ueitae spiritum.
docta, erodita paene Musarum manu,
quae modo nobilium ludos decoraui choro
et Graeca in scaena prima populo apparui,
en hoc in tumulo cinerem nostri corporis
infistae Parcae deposierunt carmine.
studium patronae, cura, amor, laudes, decus
silent ambusto corpore et leto tacent.
reliqui fletum nata genitori meo
et antecessi, genita post, leti diem.
bis hic septeni mecum natales dies
tenebris tenentur Ditis aeterna dom[u.
rogo ut discedens terram mihi di[cas leuem.

21

PrImae PompeIae ossua heic.
Fortuna spondet multa multIs, praestat nemini.
uIue in dies et horas, nam proprium est nihil.
Saluius et Heros dant.

22

Stallius Gaius has sedes Hauranus tuetur,
ex Epicureio gaudiuigente choro.

23

Publi(us) progenies Appi cognomine Pulchri
occubuit letum.

gave to his daughter so that the remains of my body might bestow themselves there. When my blossoming youth was flowering here on earth with accomplishments and, as my age grew, was mounting glory's chariot, the gloomy hour of my destiny hurried and denied the breath of life any longer. I was taught and educated, one might say, at the hands of the Muses, I who lately adorned the games of the nobility with my dancing and was the first woman to appear before the people on the Greek stage. Behold, the Fates, turning their chant to hostility, laid the ashes of my body in this tomb. Now that my body is burnt the favour of my patroness [Licinia], her concern and love, my glories and distinction are silent and quiet in death. I left tears to my father and, though born later, preceded the day of his death. Fourteen birthdays are held with me here in the eternal house of Dis. I request that, as you depart, you wish the earth to rest light on me.

21

Here lie the bones of Prima (slave of?) Pompeia. Fortune pledges many things to many people, but pays up to none. Live for the day and the hour, for nothing is held in perpetuity.

The gift of Salvius and Heros.

22

Gaius Stallius Hauranus is in possession of this abode, a member of the revelling Epicurean band.

23

Publius, scion of Appius, surnamed Pulcher, has succumbed to death.

II A: EMPERORS, NOTABLES, MATTERS OF STATE, PUBLIC BUILDINGS

24

templum hoc sacratum her[edibus, quei] quod ger[unt
Augusti nomen felix [ ] remaneat,
stirpis suae laetetur u[t] parens.
nam quom te, Caesar, tem[pus] exposcet deum
caeloque repetes sed[em qua] mundum reges,
sint hei tua quei sorte ter[rae] huic imperent
regantque nos felicibu[s] uoteis sueis.
L. Aurelius L. f. Pal. Rufu[s] primopilaris l[eg] xvi militans st[ ]
imp. Caesaris [

25

M. Aurelius Cottae Maximi l. Zosimus accensus patroni.
libertinus eram, fateor, sed facta legetur
patrono Cotta nobilis umbra mea,
qui mihi saepe libens census donauit equestris,
qui iussit natos tollere quos aleret,
quique suas commisit opes mihi semper et idem
dotauit natas ut pater ipse meas,
Cottanumque meum produxit honore tribuni
quem fortis castris Caesaris emeruit.
quid non Cotta dedit? qui nunc et carmina tristis
haec dedit in tumulo conspicienda meo.
Aurelia Saturnina Zosimi.

26

Inuicti ueneranda ducis per saecula uellent
Victrices Musae, Pallas, crinitus Apollo
Laeta serenifico defundere carmina caelo,

24

This shrine is dedicated to his heirs; may Augustus' name which they bear remain lucky for them, so that their father may rejoice in the (government) of his offspring. For when the due time demands you, Caesar, as a god, and you return to a place in heaven from which you can rule the world, may these be the men who in succession to you govern this land and rule us with all their vows coming to fruition.

Lucius Aurelius Rufus, son of Lucius, of the Palatine tribe, head centurion of the sixteenth legion, serving...

25

Marcus Aurelius Zosimus, freedman of Cotta Maximus, adjutant to his patron.

I was a freedman, I admit, but men will read that my shade was ennobled by the patronage of Cotta, who often willingly gave to me the sums of the equestrian census and bade me to beget children whom he would rear, who always entrusted his wealth to me and also dowered my daughters as if he himself were their father, and promoted my Cottanus with the post of tribune, which he bravely served out in Caesar's camp. What did Cotta not give? Now in sorrow he has also given this epitaph for public view on my tomb.

Aurelia Saturnina, wife of Zosimus.

26

The victorious Muses, Pallas and Apollo would have wished to pour down happy verses from a clear sky during the august era of the invincible emperor, but the undefiled deities fled from the

Intemerata malas hominum set numina fr[u]d[es
Iurgiaque arcanis et perfida pectora curis
Fugere. Hadriani tamen ad pia saecula verti
Ausa peroccultas remeant rimata latebras,
Vt spirent cautes ac tempora prisca salute[nt;
Sacra Mamertino sonuerunt praeside sig[na.
Tum superum manifesta fides stetit: inclutu[s - x
Inachias sospes diti pede pressit harena[s.
Namque inter celsi densata sedilia tem[pli,
Incola quo plebes tectis effunditur at[
Munera caeli[colum **********************
****

27

Pro salute imp. Caesaris Traiani Hadriani Aug. domini n(ostri).

Voto Serenus aram inst[r]u[x]it Ioui,
biduo secutus Agriophagos nequissimos,
quorum fere pars maior in pugna perit,
neque uulnera. . . . .
praedamque totam cum camelis apstulit.

ὕπερ σωτηρίας αὐτοκράτορος Καίσαρος Τραιανοῦ Ἀδριανοῦ Σεβαστοῦ τοῦ κυρίου Σουλπίκιος ὑιὸς Γναίου Σερηνὸς Ἀγριοφάγους δει[νοτ]ά[τους

28

M oribus hic simplex situs est Titus Aelius Faustus,
A nnis in lucem duo de triginta moratus,
C ui dederant pinguem populis praebere liquorem
A ntoninus, item Commodus, simul induperantes.
R ara uiro uita et species, rarissima fama,
I] nuida sed rapuit semper Fortuna probatos.
V t signum imuenias quod erat dum uita maneret
S elige litterulas primas e uersibus octo.

wicked deceits of men and their quarrels and their hearts perfidious with secret preoccupations. Yet they dared to turn back at the conscientious era of Hadrian, and they return searching out hidden recesses so that stones may breathe and greet the [revived] olden days; the sacred statue gave voice while Mamertinus was prefect. The manifest proof of the reliability of the gods was established; the noble < >, arrived safely, pressed with enriching foot the sands protected by Isis. For amid the thronged benches of the lofty temple, into which the neighbouring mob poured from its (crowded?) dwellings, the gifts of the gods...

27

For the welfare of our lord, the emperor Caesar Trajan Hadrian Augustus.

According to his vow Serenus set up an altar to Jupiter, having chased the wicked Agriophagi for two days; pretty well the majority of them perished in battle, and no wounds <were suffered by us>. He also took from them all their booty together with the camels.

For the welfare of our lord, the emperor Caesar Trajan Hadrian Augustus; Sulpicius Serenus, son of Gaius, (defeated) the savage Agriophagi.

28

Here lies the modest Titus Aelius Faustus, who sojourned in life for twenty-eight years. Marcus Aurelius and Commodus too during their joint reign had granted to him the function of providing rich oil to the people. His life and handsomeness were rivalled by few, his reputation by still fewer, but envious Fortune always snatches away those who win approval. So that you may find the surname which was his during life, take the first letters from these eight verses.

29

Cerne age, principio uenerandum numen adorans,
quos similes fecit, nos, manus artificis.
sub laeua posui Marcum me nomine Carpum,
qui procuraui auro sanctaeque Monetae,
sed iam cesso mihi senio hortante libenter
et merui laudis bonae sub principe famam.
altera de parte situs est mihi karus Achilles,
prudens et doctus nostro qui Caesare dignus;
hunc merito iuuenem cernimus a memo[ria.
signum etiam posui nostri maioris Ach[illis
in medio fulgens ut caelo stella Boo[tes,
qui solus longe tutatus nobiliter [nos.

30

*********** | [ ] . . stallus alumnus | Postumi praef(ecti) class(is)
aput fluent[u]m I[b]e[r]ic(um)
Romanus infans editus
alumnus castris mar.[
Hibera postquam uider[at]
et Maura longe moenia
acta quiescit Moesica
primaeue pubis indigus
ut uerna florum germin[a]
uento feruntur Thracio.

Achelous alumnus | Postumi praef(ecti) class(is)
extima Cappadocum, Ponti qua iungitur orae,
me genuit tellus; moenia sunt Tyan[ae],
Hermogenes genitor, nom[en] Acheloo,
artibus [ ]s editus ingen[uis
f]orma homine[s
iam gemitu

[K]rystallus *uel* [C]rystallus *Dorutiu-Boila et Vassileiou, et certe*]ry *lapis ut uid.*
A1 *fort.* apud *lapis*
A3 mari[timis *uel* Mart[iis *Solin*
B6 iam gemitu *legit Solin*

29

Come, initially venerating the majestic divine power, look on us, whom the artist's hand has portrayed realistically. On the left I have placed myself, Marcus Carpus by name, who supervised the gold of the sacred mint. But at the prompting of old age I now relax in retirement, and I earned the report of a good reputation under my emperor. On the other side is placed my dear Achilles, who for his prudence and training was worthy of our Caesar; we see this young man in the imperial secretariat, deservedly so. I have also set up the representation of our ancestor Achilles, like the star Bootes shining in the middle of the sky; he alone from a distance nobly protected us.

30

A. Krystallus, foster-son of the admiral Postum(i)us.

Born as a Roman infant and a nurseling in the (martial?) camp by the river Ebro, after seeing the towns of Spain and, from a distance, of Morocco, he rests on the Moesian shore, robbed of his tender youth, as the spring buds of flowers are carried off by the Thracian wind.

B. Achelous, foster-son of the admiral Postum(i)us.

The outer Cappadocian land, where it borders on Pontus, produced me; the city was that of Tyana, my father was Hermogenes, the name Achelous (was bestowed on me), given birth...with humane accomplishments...

31**

Patris opus munusque [ ] tibi, Roma, dicauit
Augustus [Constan]tius orbe recepto,
et quod nulla tulit tellus nec uiderat aetas
condidit ut claris exa[equ]et dona triumfis.
hoc decus ornatum genitor cognominis urbis
esse uolens caesa Thebis de rupe reuellit,
sed grauior diuum tangebat cura uehendi
quod nullo ingenio nisuque manuque moueri
Caucaseam molem discurrens fama monebat.
at dominus mundi Constantius omnia fretus
cedere uirtuti terris incedere iussit
haut partem exiguam montis pontoque tumenti
credidit et placido [flu]ctu
litus ad Hesperium [ ] mirante carinam.
interea Romam ta[et]ro uastante tyranno
Augusti iacuit donum studiumque locandi
non fastu spreti, sed quod non crederet ullus
tantae molis opus superas consurgere in auras.
nunc ueluti rursus ruf[is] auulsa metallis
emicuit pulsatque polos. haec gloria dudum
auctori seruata suo c[um c]aede tyranni
redditur, atque aditu Ro[mae ui]rtute reperto
uictor ouans urbiq[ue]e tropaeum
principis et munus condi[t]que triumfis.

9 *v.l.* moneret
23 q[ue fauens ex host]e *Bücheler, cf. Verg. Georg.* 3.32

32

(in fronte)
D. M. Vettius Agorius Praetextatus augur, p[o]ntifex Vestae, pontifex Sol[is], quindecimuir, curialis Herc[u]lis, sacratus Libero et Eleusi[ni]is, hierophanta, neocorus, tauroboliatus, pater patrum, in [r]epublica uero quaestor candidatus, pretor urbanus, corrector Tusciae et Vmbriae, consularis Lusitaniae, pro consule Achaiae,

31

When Constantius Augustus had recovered the world, he dedicated the < > work and gift of his father to Rome and established what no land brought forth and no epoch had seen, so that he makes (might make?) his gift match his triumph(s). His father, wishing this monument to adorn the city named after him, hewed it from the rock at Thebes, but a greater worry troubled the sanctified emperor, in that far-spread rumour warned that the mass of Caucasian proportions could not be moved by any ingenuity or physical effort. But Constantius, lord of the world, confident that everything yields to excellence, gave orders that the sizeable slice of mountain should roll over the land and entrusted it to the swelling sea, and (had it carried) to the shores of Italy while the calm waves wondered at the (huge?) boat. In the meantime while the foul usurper was devastating Rome the gift of Augustus and zeal to put it in situ were abandoned, not because it was rejected in contempt, but because nobody believed that such a massive work could be raised into the air. But now, as if again hewn from the red quarry, it has leaped up and knocks at heaven's door. This glory, long kept in store for its author, is now duly awarded to him along with the death of the usurper, and the celebrating victor, having found the path to Rome through his courage and (favouring) the city, has established his trophy and an emperor's gift and (consecrates it) by his triumph.

32

To the spirit of Marcus Vettius Agorius Praetextatus, augur, priest of Vesta, priest of the Sun, member of the Board of Fifteen, curial priest of Hercules, consecrated to Bacchus and the Eleusinian goddesses, hierophant (of Hecate), sacristan (of Serapis), initiated in the taurobolium, father of fathers (in the Mithraic hierarchy); in politics Caesar's candidate as quaestor, praetor urbanus, corrector of Etruria and Umbria, consular governor of Lusitania, proconsul praefectus urbi, legatus a senatu missus V, praefectus praetorio II Italiae et Illyrici, consul ordinarius designatus, et Aconia Fabia Paulina c(larissima) f(emina) sacrata Cereri et Eleusiniis, sacrata apud Eginam Hecatae, tauroboliata, hierophantria: hi coniuncti simul uixerunt ann. XL.

(in tergo)

Sple]ndor parentum nil mihi maius dedit
quam] quod marito digna iam tum uisa sum.
se]d lumen omne uel decus nomen uiri
Agori, superbo qui creatus germine
patriam, senatum coniugemq(ue) inluminas
probitate mentis, moribus, studiis simul,
uirtutis apicem quis supremum nanctus es.
tu namque quidquid lingua utraq(ue) est proditum
cura soforum, porta quis caeli patet,
uel quae periti condidere carmina
uel quae solutis uocibus sunt edita,
meliora reddis quam legendo sumpseras.
sed ista parua: tu pius mystes sacris
teletis reperta mentis arcano premis
diuumque numen multiplex doctus colis
sociam benigne coniugem nectens sacris
hominum deumque consciam ac fidam tibi.
quid nunc honores aut potestates loquar
hominumque uotis adpetita gaudia,
quae tu caduca ac parua semper autumans
diuum sacerdos infulis celsus clues?
tu me, marite, disciplinarum bono
puram ac pudicam sorte mortis eximens
in templa ducis ac famulam diuis dicas.
te teste cunctis imbuor mysteriis,
tu Dindymenes Atteosque antistitem
teletis honoras taureis consors pius,
Hecates ministram trina secreta edoces
Cererisque Graiae tu sacris dignam paras.
te propter omnis me beatam, me piam
celebrant, quod ipse me bonam disseminas;
totum per orbem ignota noscor omnibus.
nam te marito cur placere non queam?
exemplum de me Romulae matres petunt
subolemque pulchram, si tuae similis, putant.
optant probantque nunc uiri nunc feminae

of Achaea, urban prefect, sent on five embassies by the senate, twice praetorian prefect, of Italy and Illyricum, designated consul ordinarius. Also Aconia Fabia Paulina, a lady of senatorial rank, consecrated to Ceres and the Eleusinian goddesses, consecrated to Hecate at Aegina, initiated in the taurobolium, hierophant (of Hecate). They lived together united for forty years.

The distinction of my parents gave me no greater gift than that even then I appeared worthy of my husband. But all my glory and honour consisted in your name, my husband Agorius, who, born from proud stock, give lustre to your country, the senate, and your wife with your integrity of mind, your character and also your studies, through which you have attained the summit of merit. Whatever has been set forth in both languages by the devotion of the wise, to whom the gate of heaven stands open, either the poetry which skilled writers have produced or what has been put forth in prose - all this you leave in a better state than when you took it up for your reading. But these are trivialities: you, a pious initiate, keep silent in the recesses of your mind the things discovered in secret mysteries, and in scholarly wise worship the manifold divinity of the gods, of your kindness linking your wife, the faithful companion who shares the thoughts of your heart, to the sacred things of men and gods. Why should I now speak of offices and positions of authority and the joys sought by the prayers of men? For you always declared them to be transient and trivial, and have your fame as the priest of the gods, marked out by the sacred headband. You, my husband, rescuing me from the lot of death, bring me, made pure and chaste by the blessing of your teachings, into the temples and consecrate me as a servant to the gods. In your presence I am initiated into all mysteries; you, my dedicated husband, honour me as priestess of Cybele and Attis with the ceremony of the bull's blood; while I function as servant of Hecate you teach me her threefold secrets; you make me worthy of the rites of the Greek Ceres. Because of you, all celebrate me as blessed and holy, because you yourself spread abroad fair report of me; though unknown, I am known to all throughout the world. For why should I not win favour when you are my husband? The Roman mothers seek a pattern from me and think their offspring handsome if it is like yours. Both men and women approve and long for the marks

quae tu magister indidisti insignia.
his nunc ademptis maesta coniunx maceror,
felix, maritum si superstitem mihi
diui dedissent, sed tamen felix, tua
quia sum fuique postque mortem mox ero.

(in latere sinistro)

Vettius Agorius Praetextatus Paulinae coniugi
Paulina nostri pectoris consortio,
fomes pudoris, castitatis uinculum
amorque purus et fides caelo sata,
arcana mentis cui reclusa credidi,
munus deorum qui maritalem torum
nectunt amicis et pudicis nexibus,
pietate matris, coniugali gratia,
nexu sororis, filiae modestia
et quanta amicis iungimur fiducia,
aetatis usu, consecrandi foedere,
iugi fideli simplici concordia
iuuans maritum diligens ornans colens.

(in latere dextro)

Vettius Agorius Praetextatus Paulinae coniugi
Paulina ueri et castitatis conscia,
dicata templis atq(ue) amica numinum,
sibi maritum praeferens, Romam uiro,
pudens fidelis pura mente et corpore,
benigna cunctis, utilis penatibus,
. . . .

13 mystes *Haupt*: mouestes *lapis*
26 atteos qui *lapis*
33 cui *Schrader ap. Burman 2 p. lxix*
34 exempla *edd.*
post 58 *sequitur uersus unus in quo pauca tantum legi possunt*

33

Ius ad iustitiam reuocare aequmque tueri
Dalmatio lex est, quam dedit alma Fides.
bis sex scripta tenet praetorisque omne uolumen
doctus et a sanctis condita principibus.
hic idem interpres legum legumque minister

of distinction which by your teaching you bestowed on me. Now that these have been taken away I, your wife, pine in sorrow. I would have been happy if the gods had granted that my husband should survive me, yet I am still happy because I am and was and presently after death shall be yours.

Vettius Agorius Praetextatus to his wife Paulina.

Paulina, partner in my heart, the kindler of modesty, the bond of chastity, pure love and fidelity born in heaven, to whom I disclosed and entrusted the secrets of my mind, gift of the gods who bind the marriage-bed with affectionate and modest links; you helped, loved, adorned, respected your husband with maternal affection, wifely attraction, sisterly closeness, a daughter's submission, with all the loyalty which unites us to our friends, with the experience of maturity, with partnership in ritual, with ever-flowing, faithful, frank concord.

Vettius Agorius Praetextatus to his wife Paulina.

Paulina, ever aware of truth and chastity, consecrated to the temples and god-loving, setting her husband above herself and Rome above her husband, modest, faithful, pure in mind and body, kindly to all, stay of her household...

33

Dalmatius has for his law, a law given by fostering integrity, to match jurisdiction with justice and to protect equity. He has a learned grasp of the Twelve Tables and every praetorian edict and what the worshipful emperors have laid down. Moreover, as interpreter and administer of the laws, his expert skill is matched by

quam prudens callet tam bonus exequitur.
multis pro meritis, Valeri, iustissime rector,
multis pro meritis haec stat imago tibi,
quam positi longe testantes publica uota
usque procul patriae mittimus in gremium.
hinc praefecturae summos uen<e>ramur honores,
hoc te gaudentes omine prosequimur.
quisquis scire uolet quorum celebreris amore,
ille hoc indicium sumserit ex titulo:
Dalmatio posuit prouincia Lugdunensis
tertia, patrono grata clienta suo.

34

frag]ilem [po]stquam rate[m
ue]nerat ad portum uitata pericula cred[ens
a]missam classem saepe in statione defl[ebat,
i]ncusansque deos talia est fortasse [locutus:
'q]uid pelagi trucis profuit euasis[se
s]i mihi in portu pelagus naufragia [?'
ha]nc cladem inspiciens factis nomen [superauit.
cond]oluit miseris obiectaque scrup[ea tollens
rettu]lit in melius hanc Eusebi cura r[uinam,
portui no]men amissum et reddidit usu[i portum.
pos]teritas ne haec obliuisc[
stat lapis hic] mansurus i[

3 *uel* defl[euit
5 [se furorem *uel sim.*
6 [patrat *Courtney; cetera pleraque suppl. Stroux*

35

Constanti uirtus studium uictoria nomen
dum recipit Gallos, constituit Ligures,
moenibus ipse locum dixit duxitque recenti
fundamenta solo iuraque parta dedit.
ciues, tecta, forum, portus, commercia, portas

the uprightness with which he puts things into effect. Valerius, our just ruler, this portrait is set up for you in return for your many services - yes, many. Though situated far away we despatch it from all that distance to the bosom of your native land, bearing witness to the prayers of the populace. This is the cause for which we humbly pray for the high office of a prefecture, this is the omen with which we happily escort you. Whoever wants to know who it is whose affection celebrates you, let him take his information from this inscription: The province Lugdunensis Tertia set this up to Dalmatius, a grateful dependent to its patron.

34

After...the fragile craft...(many a one) had come to harbour thinking that dangers had been avoided, he often lamented his ship lost at anchor, and accusing the gods spoke words perhaps like this: 'What good was it to escape the (fury) of the stormy sea if that sea (inflicts) shipwreck in harbour on me?' Contemplating this disaster he surpassed his name with deeds. The diligent Eusebius sympathised with the afflicted and, removing the rocky barrier, turned this collapse to good effect. He restored its lost repute to the harbour and the harbour to use. Lest posterity forget this, (this stone is erected) to remain (for ever).

35

While the courageous, diligent, victorious, aptly-named Constantius was recovering Gaul and putting Liguria in order, he himself appointed a site for the walls and traced the foundations in the freshly-cut sod and gave an established constitution. Constructing buildings he set up a citizen body, habitations, a forum, harbours,

conditor extructis aedibus instituit,
dumque refert orbem, me primam protulit urbem
nec renuit titulos limina nostra loqui,
et rabidos contra fluctus gentesque nefandas
Constanti murum nominis opposuit.

36

Haec loca Theudosius decorat post fata tyranni.
aurea saecla gerit qui portam construit auro.

37

Munera parua quidem pretio sed honoribus alma
patribus ista meis offero cons(ul) ego.

commerce and gates, and, while he was recovering the world, he promoted me to be a leading city. He did not refuse that my gate should speak in an inscription, and to the furious waves of wicked tribes he opposed the wall of the name Constantius.

36

Theodosius adorns this place after the death of the usurper. He who builds a gate of gold brings with him a Golden Age.

37

I, the consul, offer to my senators this gift, small indeed in value but affectionate with marks of respect.

II B: BATHS AND SPRINGS, PRIVATE BUILDINGS, WORKS OF ART, FURNITURE

38

Debilis Albuleo steterat qui gurgite Samis
articulum medicis ut tenuaret aquis,
dente quod Aetrusco turgebat saucius apro
et Russellano forte solutus erat,
hinc graciles ubi ian nerui tenuisque cicatrix
et celer accepto currere coepit ecus,
dat tibi pro meritis semet de marmore donum
qua media(m) gaudes, Lymfa, subire uiam,
Tiburis aduersae dominus qua despicit aedem
frontibus et pictis Aelia uilla nitet.

3 turgebat *Guarini*: tergebat *lapis*
5 graciles *Haupt*: giacius *uel* ciacius *lapis*
7 semet *Lachmann*: seat *lapis ut uid.*
10 nitet *Guarini*: uidet *lapis*

39

Alma lauacrorum de sax[is deci]do lympha
Et sunt ex lapide perfecta[e balnea]e pulchrae
Laetis inque locis natus la[cus.] tamen ipsis,
Tunc cum sospes erat, coniux s[i]t in usum
Emeritis quondam Alexand[r] nomine dignae.
Raucisoni lapidoso cadunt [de fon]te liquores.
Tam laudati operis dominus [ ] et auctor
In suae memoriam uoluit con[stare] maritae.
Vt tamen et lector nomen [cognosce]re possis,
Singulae declarant exordia [li]t[ter]ae primae.
Aelia cum Tertia subole de coniuge [ ]ta.

2 balnea]e *Marcovich*:]pi[scina]e *priores, quod neque legi potest neque spatio conuenit*
4 s[ecreui]t *Courtney, alii* s[acraui]t *uel* s[eruaui]t
7 ue[teranus] *aliqui, eidem culpae cui in 2 obnoxii*
8 con[stare] *Courtney*

38

Samis (?) had stood injured in the Aquae Albulae so that with the medicinal waters he might reduce his joint, since it was swollen and dislocated because of a wound from the tusk of a boar from Etruscan Russellae. But when the sinews had gone down and the scar was slight and his horse began to run swiftly with him on its back, for this reason in return for your services he gives you, Spring-Goddess, himself in marble as a gift, where you take pleasure in running under the road midway, where the lord of Tibur [= Hercules] looks down on your shrine as you face him and the painted facade of Hadrian's villa gleams.

39

I, the refreshing water of the baths, fall from rocks, and a handsome bath-house has been constructed from stone, and a pool has come into being in a delightful situation. However a married woman, while she was still alive, set me aside (?) for the use of old-timer veterans alone of Alexander's legion, worthy of its name. Plashing waters fall from a rocky spring. The owner and developer of the construction that has won such praise desired it to be established as a memorial to his wife. However, so that you also, reader, may be able to ascertain her name, the individual initial letters reveal it. With Aelia Tertia, his daughter by his (chaste?) wife (Fausta?).

40

Quaesii multum quot memoriae tradere(m),
Agens prae cunctos in hac castra milites,
Votum communem, proque reditu exercitus
Inter priores et futuros reddere(m).
Dum quaero mecum digna diuom nomina,
Inueni tandem nomen et numen deae
Votis perennem quem dicare(m) in hoc loco.
Salutis igitur quandium cultores sient,
Qua potui sanxi nomen, et cunctis dedi
Veras salutis lymphas, tantis ignibus
In istis semper harenacis collibus
Nutantis Austri solis flammas feruidas
Tranquille ut nando delenirent corpora.
Ita tu qui sentis magnam facti gratiam
Aestuantis animae fucilari spiritum,
Noli pigere laudem uoce reddere
Veram, qui uoluit esse te sanum tib[i],
Set protestare uel salutis gratia.

41

Post fla]mmas cinere[sque] suos noua surgere foenix
scit; nu]nc ut pulcra r[e]nouetur fabrica mole
]ne, facis, cui la[u]dem nobile corpus
]es peperere suae quibus omnia polles,
]Romuleo genitum quem stem[m]ate p[atru]m
]m Mauris claro [p]ermisit honore.
]turis thermis [h]onos iste resurget
que]m gaudet sibimet [n]utrisse Satafis.
(*sc.* anno) pr(ouinciae) CCCXX[ ]II.

3 *fort.*]nte *lapis*
6 rectore]m *uel* custode]m *Courtney*

40

I, in charge of all soldiers in the camp, pondered much what vow in the common interest I should put on record and discharge, among previous and future vows, for the return of the army. While I was pondering worthy names of gods, I at last found a name and divinity of a goddess to consecrate in this place in perpetuity with my vows. Therefore, as far as I could, I have consecrated the name of Health for as long as worshippers exist, and I have given to all the waters which truly belong to Health (health), so that in these ever sandy dunes of the south their bodies, swimming at leisure, may palliate the burning flames of the sun. So you who feel great gratitude for the fact that the breath of your panting respiration is refreshed, do not feel shy about rendering vocal and accurate praise to the man who desired you to be healthy; on the contrary bear witness because of health (Health) at least.

41

The phoenix knows how to rise renewed after the flames of its own pyre; now you, [ ]us, see to it that the construction is renewed in a handsome pile, you for whom your fine body and the appropriate [ ], with which you can achieve anything, have evoked praise. You were born from a family tree of Roman ancestors, and (the emperor) placed you over the Moors in a position of high honour. That honour will rise again from the baths, which themselves will rise again through your agency (?); Satafis rejoices that it nurtured you for itself.

In the year 3.. C.E.

42*

Fausta nouum domini condens Fortuna lauacruM
Inuitat fessos huc properare uiaE.
Laude operis fundi capiet sua gaudia praesuL
Ospes dulciflua dum recreatur aquA.
Condentis monstrant uersus primordia nomeN
Auctoremque facit littera prima legI.
Lustrent pontiuagi Cumani litoris antrA:
Indigenae placeant plus mihi deliciaE.

4 Ospes *L. Mueller*: hospis *cod.*
6 summa *Courtney, Hermathena 129 (1980), 41*

43

Cerne salutiferas s[plendent]i marmore Baias
qui calidos aest[us fran]gere quaeris aquis.
hic ubi Vulcano Ne[ptunus] certat amore,
nec necat unda f[ocum n]ec nocet ignis aquas.
gaude operi, Gebam[unde, tu]o, regalis origo;
deliciis sospes ute[re cum] populo.

2 fran]gere *Dessau, alii alia spatio breuiora*
3 Ne[ptunus] *Engelmann ap. Gauckler, CRAI 1907.792*

44

F]elix Urania, mecum partire laborem
Et Nymfis aude recidiuos pandere fontis.
Latex ubi sentibus horrens merserat ante
Incassum funditus superante ruina,
Currit iter liquidum prisco de more fluore,
Ecce gradatim nosces quo curante si qu(a)eras.

5 de more prisco *lapis*

42

Prosperous Fortune, establishing the proprietor's new baths, invites those weary of travelling to hasten here. The landlord of the estate will derive pleasure from the praise of his creation, while guests are refreshed by the sweetly flowing water. The beginnings of the line indicate the name of the developer, and the first (?) letter makes the initiator to be read. Let sea-roamers frequent the grottoes of the Campanian shore, but may luxury at home be my delight.

43

See this health-giving 'les-Bains' with its shining marble, you who seek to overcome the seething heat with waters. Here where Neptune rivals Vulcan in affection, the water does not quench the fire and the fire does not hurt the water. Rejoice in your creation, Gebamund, royal scion; enjoy luxury with the people in good health.

44

Propitious Urania, share the task with me and venture to expound the springs ever-renewed by the Nymphs, where the water, overgrown with briars, had previously submerged (its streams), with the collapsed building totally overcoming their vain (efforts). It runs on its watery path in a stream after its former fashion; behold, if you look you will step by step recognize under whose supervision.

45

Nectareos sucos, Baccheia munera cernis,
quae bitis genuit aprico sole refecta.

46

Si nitidus uiuas, eccum domus exornata est;
si sordes, patior, sed pudet, hospitium.

47

(a) abluat unda pedes, puer et detergeat udos;
mappa torum uelet, lintea nostra caue.
(b) lasciuos uoltus et blandos aufer ocellos
coniuge ab alterius; sit tibi in ore pudor.
(c) insanas] litis odiosaque iurgia differ,
si potes, aut gressus ad tua tecta refer.

48

P raesidium aeternae firmat prudentia paci S,
R em quoque Romanam fida tutat undique dextr A,
A mni praepositum firmans munimine monte M,
E cuius nomen uocitauit nomine Petra M.
D enique finitimae gentes deponere bell A
I n tua concurrunt cupientes foedera, Samma C,
V t uirtus comitata fidem concordet in omn I
M unere Romuleis semper sociata triumfi S.

45

You see nectar-sweet juices, the gift of Bacchus to which the vine, refreshed by the radiant sun, has given birth.

46

If you live a cleanly life, behold a house furnished; if you are dirty, I submit to entertaining you, though I don't like it.

47

(a) Let water wash your feet and a slave towel them while they are wet; let a coverlet drape the couch, take good care of my linen.

(b) Take your lascivious expressions and coaxing eyes off another man's wife; let modesty dwell on your face.

(c) If you can, postpone (mad) disputes and hateful quarrels; otherwise turn your steps back to your own house.

48

The circumspection of eternal peace strengthens the fortress (*or* circumspection governs the castle which protects eternal peace), and also protects Roman interests on all sides with its loyal right hand, strengthening with fortification the mount set over the river, the mount from whose name it gave the name Petra (to the fortress). Moreover the neighbouring tribes, desiring to lay aside war, eagerly embrace treaties with you, Sammac, so that courage and loyalty combined may unite in every task, for ever associated with Roman triumphs.

49

Mantua si posset diuinum redder[e] uate[m],
inmensum miratus opus hic ceder[et] antro
adq(ue) dolos Ithaci, fl<a>mmas et lumen ademtu[m
semiferi somno pariter uinoque grauati,
speluncas uiuosq(ue) lacu[s, Cy]clopea saxa,
saeuitiam Scyllae fract[amq(ue) in g]u[rgi]te pupp[im
ipse fateretur nullo sic ca[rmine - x
uiuas ut artificis express[
quam sola exsuperat natur[a
Faustinus felix dominis ho[c

50

uatum digna m[odis] monumenta uirorum,
uites [l]ucos, uiolaria, tecta.
Graiorum uultus et Musis dedita templa
lilia, poma, rosae, uites, arbusta coronant.
Socratis os [ ] et uiuida corda Catonis
produnt signa satis ut genus [

1 m[odis ueterum] *Ussani ap. Paribeni*
2 [antra uides *Courtney*

51

Fecerat Eufranor Bacchum, quem Gallus honorat
fastorum consul carmine, ture, sacris.

52

Fl]amm[i]fugas fratre[s], pietatis maxima dona,
quos tulit hostilit[as], reddidit hos Merulus
[u.c.] et spectabilis consul[aris p]rouinciae Siciliae.

49

If Mantua could bring the divine poet back to life, he, admiring the wondrous structure, would yield to the grotto and would himself admit that no poem could (represent) the subterfuges of Odysseus, the fire and the blinding of the eye of the monster oppressed simultaneously by sleep and wine, the caves and natural pools, the Cyclopean rocks, the savagery of Scylla and the ship wrecked in the water, as well as the (hand) of the sculptor (moulded) the living shapes; only nature excels that hand. Faustinus [ ] this (grotto) which is fortunate in its owners.

50

(You see) the monuments of great men which are worthy of the strains of poets, (you see) vines, groves, beds of violets, canopies. Lilies, fruits, roses, vines, shrubs crown the countenances of men of Greece and shrines dedicated to the Muses. The busts show the face of Socrates and stout-hearted Cato well enough for the type (to become apparent).

51

Euphranor had sculpted a Bacchus, whom Gallus, the consul of the annual record, honours with verse, incense and ritual.

52

The brothers who escaped the flames, a great reward for their filial devotion, were carried off by the enemy, but recovered by Merulus, *uir clarissimus et spectabilis,* consular governor of the province of Sicily.

53

Ales, homo, numen, uirtus et gloria palmae,
Romuleis praepes uirgo fecunda tropeis
sic stetit ut Romam uictus cognosceret orbis.
omine quo residens metum dolos iurgia uincas
et comitatus agas prouectus, gaudia, palmas.

54

escipe qu(a)e ferimus felicia munera libe/ utere felix.

55*

quisquis amat d[ictis absentum rodere uitam,
hanc mensam in[dignam nouerit esse sibi.

56

quae paruis mater natis alimenta parabat
fortuna in patrios uertit iniqua cibos.
aeuo dignum opus est: tenui ceruice seniles,
as[pice, ia]m uenae lacte . . [
]q(ue) simul uultu fri<c>at ipsa Miconem
Pero; tristis inest cum pietate pudor.

4 aspice qua]m *Engelmann (Jahresb. Phil. Vereins 30 (1904), 281),* iam *Mau (uel* as[picite] ut); as[pice iam] ut *Wick.*
re[plente *Bücheler* (re *non omnino certum), tum in fine* tument *(Mau) uel* micant *(Wick) uel* micent.

53

A winged but human creature, a deity, the glory of courageous victory, the flying virgin pregnant with Roman triumphs, took up such a position that the conquered world acknowledged Rome. Reposing on this omen may you overcome fear, trickery and quarrels, and accompanied (by her) may you celebrate promotions, joys and victories.

54

Receive the joy-bringing gifts which we (gladly?) bring; use them with good luck.

55

Whoever likes to carp at the way of life of the absent with witticisms, let him know that this table is unworthy of him.

56

The nourishment which a mother was readying for her small children was turned into sustenance for her father by cruel fortune. This creation merits eternity; see, the old man's veins in his wizened neck now (swell) with milk, and at the same time with [ ] countenance Pero herself massages Micon; sad modesty together with daughterly love is incorporated (in the picture).

II C: POEMS WITH LITERARY, EDUCATIONAL AND PHILOSOPHICAL CONNECTIONS

57

zetema
mulier ferebat filium similem sui. |
nec meus est nec mi similat, sed | uellem esset meus. |
ego
et uoleba(m) ut meus esset.

58

Pulueris aurati pluuia sit sparsa papyrus,
rescribet Danae sollicitata 'ueni'.

59

Cara meis uixi, uirgo uitam reddidi.
mortua heic ego sum et sum cinis, is cinis terrast;
sein est terra dea, ego sum dea, mortua non sum.
rogo te, hospes, noli ossa mea uiolare.
Mus uixit annos xiii.

1 mieis *(cf. ad 13.1) corr. in* meis *lapis*

60

Fullones ululamque cano, non arma uirumq(ue).

57

A riddle.

A woman was giving birth to an infant resembling herself. He is not mine nor is he like me, but I could have wished that he were mine.

I too wished that he were mine.

58

Let the papyrus be spattered with a shower of golden dust; then Danae, if you tempt her, will write 'come' in return.

59

I lived beloved by my circle, I died a virgin. Here I am in death and am ashes, those ashes are earth; but if earth is a goddess, then I am a goddess, not a dead woman. I beseech you, stranger, not to disturb my bones.

Mus lived thirteen years.

60

I sing of cleaners and the owl, not arms and the man.

61

discite 'dum uiuo, mors inimica uenit'.

62a

D. [M.]
Forte s[ub hoc la]pide iac[eo Ma]trona s[epulta]
nocte di[e

62b

D. M. S. Seuerus Aug. lib. uixit annis lxxu.
Monte sub hoc lapidum tegitur his ipse sepultus;
nocte uia tutus carpe uiator iter.
Seuerianus Aug. lib. patri et matri carissimis posuit.

63

D. M. M. Pomponio M. fil(io) M. n(epoti) M. pron(epoti) M. abn(epoti)
Cor(nelia) Bassulo IIuir(o) q(uin)q(uennali)
Ne more pecoris otio transfungere[r
Menandri paucas uorti scitas fabulas
et ipsus etiam sedulo finxi nouas.
id qualequalest chartis ma[n]datum diu.
uerum uexatus animi cu[r]is [a]nxiis,
nonnullis etiam corpo[ris dol]oribus,
utrumque ut esset taedi[io mi ultr]a modum,
optatam mortem sum pot[itus] mihi
suo de more cuncta [dat leu]amina.
uos in sepulchro [h]oc elo[gium inc]idite
quod sit documento post...........ibus
inmodice ne quis uitae sco[pulos hor]reat
cum sit paratus portus.........ibus
qui nos excipiat ad quiet[em perpet]em.
set iam ualete donec ui[ ]it.
Cant(ria) Long(ina) marit(o) opt(imo) b(ene) m(erenti) f(ecit).

61

Learn the lesson 'while I am living (an enjoyable life), hostile death comes'.

62a

I, Matrona, lie buried beneath this stone. By night and day...

62b

Severus, freedman of the emperor, lived seventy-five years.

He himself, buried beneath this mount of stones, is covered by them. By night (and day), traveller, journey in safety.

Severianus, freedman of the emperor, erected this to his dear father and mother.

63

To Marcus Pomponius Bassulus, son of Marcus, grandson of Marcus, great-grandson of Marcus, great-great-grandson of Marcus, of the Cornelian tribe, *duovir quinquennalis*.

So that I should not pass my life in idleness like the dumb beasts, I translated a few witty plays of Menander, and also I myself industriously created new ones. Whatever its quality, that was long ago given written form. However, distressed by severe nervous anxieties and also by some physical pain, so that each was intolerably irksome, I laid hold of the death for which I longed, and, in its fashion, it gives me every alleviation. Do you carve this epitaph on my tomb to be a lesson to subsequent...that no-one should excessively fear the rocks of life, seeing that a harbour is available to..., which can receive us into everlasting rest. But now farewell until (?as long as)...

Set up by Cantria Longina to her excellent and meritorious husband.

64

quinq(u)agenta ub<i> erant exinde oc<c>idi[t Achilles

64A

littera prima dolet, iubet altera, tertia mittit,
quarta dolet, facti quinta habet inuidiam.

65a

Roma tibi subito

65b

Roma tibi

66

Primigeniae Nucer[in]ae
uellem essem gemma hora non amplius una
ut tibi signanti oscula pressa darem.

1 gemma uelim fieri hora non *CLE* 359 = *CIL* 4.1698

67

R(ufius) Festus u(ir) c(larissimus) de se ad deam Nortiam.
Festus Musoni suboles prolesque Auieni,
unde tui latices traxerunt, Caesia, nomen,
Nortia, te ueneror lare cretus Vulsiniensi,
Romam habitans, gemino proconsulis auctus honor[e,
carmina multa serens, uitam insons, integer aeum,
coniugio laetus Placidae numeroq(ue) frequenti
natorum exsultans. uiuax sit spiritus ollis;
cetera composita fatorum lege trahentur.

64

Where there were (a hundred) Achilles killed fifty of them **OR** where there were fifty, Achilles killed (a hundred) of them.

64A

The first letter indicates sorrow, the second pleasure, the third an order to go, the fourth sorrow; the fifth conveys disdain at an act.

65

Rome, your love, (will) suddenly (come to you through movement).

66

To Primigenia of Nuceria.

I could have wished to be a gem-stone for one hour, no longer, so that I might implant kisses on you while you were stamping your seal.

67

Rufius Festus, *uir clarissimus*, to the goddess Nortia about himself.

Festus, the descendant of Musonius and offspring of Avien(i)us, from whom the Caesian waters derived their name, I, a native of Vulsinii domiciled at Rome, worship you. I was twice honoured with appointment as proconsul, I wove many poems, lived an innocent life, was in my prime, blessed in my marriage to Placida and rejoicing in my numerous children. May they have a long life; all else will be drawn along by the established law of destiny.

Sancto patri filius Placidus.
Ibis in optatas sedes, nam Iuppiter aethram
pandit, Feste, tibi candidus, ut uenias;
iamq(ue) uenis: tendit dextras chorus inde deorum
B4 et toto tibi iam plauditur ecce polo.

A3 lari *et fort*. B1 ibus *lapis*

68

qui, dum, cum haberet clausam in castello ani[mu]lam
mortalem, ad superos licitum est, [f]initam ad diem
p[a]rce pudensque uixit omni tempore,
Auruncus era[t], Fu[r]ius erat nomine
magister ludi litterari Philocalus,
summa quom castitate in discipulos suos,
idemque testamenta scripsit cum fide,
nec quoiquam ius negauit, laesit neminem.
ita [de]cucurrit uitam fidus sine metu.
eius ossa nunc hic sita sunt posita a cen[t]uris.

1 dum cum *repudiauit Bücheler*: cum dum *lapis*
4 Furius *Zangemeister*, Fu.ius *Mommsen*, Fusius *Nissen (Hermes 1 (1867), 148).*
8 ius *dubitanter Mommsen*, suum *Shackleton Bailey (Phoenix 31(1978), 322), alii alia; lapis lectu difficilis*

69

Terentius Sabinianus fons et camena litteris,
sapiendo opimus et dicendo splendidus.
hoc praeter ceteros etiam Hippo dicti[tat
diarrytos, ubi magister praestans floruit,
uixitque numerum in se de analogia Pythagorae primarium.
p(ius) u(ixit) a(nnos) xxxvi, h(ic) s(itus) e(st).

5 anologia *lapis*

His son Placidus to his worshipful father.

You will go to the home for which you long, for propitious Jupiter opens heaven to you, Festus, so that you may come. And now you do come; thence the company of the gods extend their right hands to you and, behold, over all the heavens applause for you echoes.

68

He who, while he was permitted on earth, when he had his mortal soul enclosed in its sentry-box, lived ever thrifty and modest until the end of his days - he was an Auruncan, Furius (?) Philocalus by name, a schoolmaster who never molested a pupil. He was also a trustworthy writer of wills, and never denied to anyone what he was entitled to, never harmed anyone. So he loyally ran life's race with no qualms. His bones now lie here, laid to rest by his fellow-clubmen.

69

Terentius Sabinianus, the fount and muse of literary culture, a treasure-house of discrimination and a brilliant speaker. As well as all the others Hippo Diarrhytos, where he flourished as an outstanding teacher, declares this; and he lived the square of the base number from the ratio of Pythagoras.

He lived honourably for thirty-six years, and lies here.

70

D. M. Petronii Antigenidis

Tu pede qui stricto uadis per semita(m), uiator,
siste, rogo, titulumque meum ne spreueris, oro.
bis quinos annos mensesque duos, duo soles
at superos feci tenere nutritus, amatus.
dogmata Pythagorae sensusque meaui sophorum
et lyricos legi, legi pia carmina Homeri,
sciui quid Euclides abaco praescripta tulisset.
delicias habui pariter lususque procaces.
haec Hilarus mihi contulerat pater, ipse patronus
si non infelix contraria fata habuissem.
nunc modo ad infernas sedes, Acheruntis ad undas
  taetraque Tartarei sidera possideo.
effugi tumidam uitam. spes et fortuna, ualete:
nil mihi uobiscum est, alios deludite, quaeso.
haec domus aeterna, hic sum situs, hic ero semper.

15 aeterna est *testis unus*

70A

ut bene cacaret, uentrem palpauit Solon.
durum cacantes monuit ut nitant Thales.
uissire tacite Chilon docuit subdolus.

70

To the soul of Petronius Antigenes.

You, traveller, who make your way along the path with your foot laced up, halt, I ask you, and, I beseech you, do not spurn my epitaph. Delicately nurtured and loved I lived on earth for ten years, two months, two days. I traversed the doctrines of Pythagoras and the views of the philosophers, I read the lyric poets and the holy epics of Homer, I knew what Euclid had laid down on his abacus. At the same time I enjoyed diversions and impudent amusements. All this my father Hilarus had bestowed on me, and he himself (would have been) my patron had not I, with my unhappy lot, encountered the hostility of destiny. Now in the underworld by the waters of infernal Acheron I dwell under murky stars. I have escaped tempestuous life. Farewell, hope and fortune; I have nothing to do with you, cheat others, please. This is my eternal home, here I lie, here shall I be for ever.

70A

To have a good shit, Solon rubbed his stomach.
Thales instructed the constipated to strain.
Crafty Chilon taught how to fart silently.

II D: INNS, TRAVEL AND TOURISM

71

Talia te fallant utinam me(n)dacia, copo;
tu ue(n)des acuam et bibes ipse merum.

72

Edone dicit
assibus hic bibitur, dupundium si dederis, meliora bibes,
quattus si dederis, uina Falerna bib(es).

2 quadtus *in* quantus *corr. paries ut uid.*

73

Miximus in lecto; fateor, peccauimus, hospes.
si dices 'quare?', nulla matella fuit.

*74**

Vidi pyramidas sine te, dulcissime frater,
et tibi, quod potui, lacrimas hic moesta profudi
et nostri memorem luctus hanc sculpo querelam.
sic nomen Decimi Gentiani pyramide alta
pontificis comitisque tuis, Traiane, triumphis
lustra<que> sex intra censoris consulis exstet.

4 sic *uel* sit *auctor, idem* Cētianni
6 exstet *Bücheler,* esse *auctor*

71

May cheating like this trip you up, barman. You sell water and yourself drink undiluted wine.

72

(H)edone says: a drink here costs one *as*; if you pay two *asses*, you will drink better quality; if you give four, you will drink Falernian wine.

73

I have wet the bed; I admit that I have done wrong, innkeeper. If you say 'why?', (the answer is that) there was no chamber-pot.

74

I have seen the pyramids without you, my dear brother, and in sorrow I have here shed tears, all I could do, and inscribe this lament in record of my grief. So may the name of Decimus Gentianus, pontifex and participant in the triumph(s) of Trajan, census-supervisor and consul before his thirtieth birthday, survive on the lofty pyramid.

75

Memnonem uates canorum Maximus Statilius
audit et donat camenas, musa nam cordi deis.

meas quoque auris Memnonis uox accidit:
nomen cieto quisque 'uatem Maximum'.

2 camenas *Bernand*, -a *priores*

76

Memnonis [uocem] clarumque sonor[em
exanimi inanimem mi[ssum] de tegmine bruto
auribus ipse meis cepi sumsique canorum
praefectus Gallorum al[ae], praefectus item Ber(onices),
Caesellius Quinti f. [| Abararo....

75

Statilius Maximus the poet hears harmonious Memnon and presents verses to him, for the gods love poetry.

The voice of Memnon comes to my ears too; let everyone invoke the name 'greatest of poets (OR Maximus the poet)'.

76

I myself absorbed and took in with my own ears the voice of Memnon and the distinct harmonious sound, animate though emitted from an insensible, inanimate surface - I, Caesellius (Abararo?), son of Quintus, prefect of the troop of Gauls and prefect of Beronice.

II E: EROTIC

77

Admiror, paries, te non cecidisse ruina,
qui tot scriptorum taedia sustineas.

1 ruina *2461*, ruinis *1904 ut uid., om. 2487*

78

Amoris ignes si sentires, mulio,
magi(s) properares, ut uideres Venerem.
diligo iuuenem uenustum. rogo, punge, iamus.
bibisti, iamus. prende lora et excute.
Pompeios defer, ubi dulcis est amor.
meus es

3 iuuenem *scriptum super erasum* puerum.

79

amat qui scribet, pedicatur qui leget,
qui opscultat prurit, paticus est qui praeterit.
ursi me comedant; et ego uerpa qui lego.

2 opscultat *2360 (cf. CIL 4 p. 219)*, obscultat *4008; post* 2 scribit pedicator Septumius *ut uid. 4008 omisso* 3

80

qui uerpam uissit, quid cenasse illum putes?

77

I am surprised, wall, that you have not collapsed and fallen, seeing that you support the tedious effusions of so many writers.

78

Muleteer, if you felt the fire of love you would make more haste to see your charmer. I love a charming youth (boy). Please goad the mules, let's be on our way; you have had your drink, let's be on our way. Grasp the reins and shake them. Bring me to Pompeii, where sweet love is. You are mine...

79

He who writes is in love, he who reads is buggered, he who listens lusts, he who passes by is a fairy. May bears eat me, I too who read am a prick.

80

When a man shits a prick, what do you think he dined on?

81

accensum qui pedicat, urit mentulam.

82

seni supino colei culum tegunt.

83

Chie, opto tibi ut<i> refricent se ficus tuae
ut peius ustulentur quam ustulatae sunt.

84

Futuitur cunnus pilossus multo melius quam glaber:
eadem continet uaporem et eadem u[ell]it mentulam.

85

                    fueere quondam Vibii opulentissimi,
non ideo tenuerunt in manu sceptrum pro mutunio
itidem, quod tu factitas cottidie in manu penem tene(n)s.

86

quoi scripsi semel et legit, mea iure puella est:
        quae pretium dixit, non mea sed populi est.

81

He who buggers an adjutant (a man on fire) scorches his cock.

82

When an old man lies on his back, his scrotum covers his arse.

83

Chius, I wish for you that your piles irritate themselves anew so that they may be inflamed worse than they were inflamed.

84

A hairy cunt is fucked much better than a depilated one; it simultaneously holds in the heat and plucks the prick.

85

The Vibii were once very wealthy, but they did not for that reason hold a sceptre in their hands instead of a prick, as you do every day, holding your penis in your hand.

86

She to whom I have written once and who has read (my letter) is rightly reckoned to be my girl; she who has set a price belongs not to me but to the populace.

87

alliget hic auras, si quis obiurgat amantes,
et uetet assiduas currere fontis aquas.

88

quis]quis amat ualeat, pereat qui nescit amare,
bis tanto pereat quisquis amare uetat.

89

quisquis amat, ueniat. Veneri uolo frangere costas
fustibus et lumbos debilitare deae.
si potest illa mihi tenerum pertundere pectus,
quit ego non possim caput i[ll]ae frangere fuste?

90

quisquis amat, calidis non debet fontibus uti,
nam nemo flammas ustus amare potest.

91

si potes et non uis, cur gaudia differs
spemque foues et cras usque redire iubes?
er]go coge mori quem sine te uiuere cogis:
munus erit certe non cruciasse boni.
quod spes eripuit, spes certe redd[i]t amanti.

87

He who chides lovers might as well bind the winds and forbid the spring's waters to flow continuously.

88

Good luck to whoever loves, damn whoever doesn't know how to love, double damnation to whoever forbids love.

89

Whover loves, let him come. I want to break Venus' ribs with cudgel-blows and belabour the goddess' rump. If she can smite my susceptible breast, why should I be unable to break her skull with a cudgel?

90

Whoever is in love should not use hot water, for nobody who has been scorched can like flame.

91

If you can but are unwilling, why do you postpone pleasure and foster hope and continually tell me to come back tomorrow? So force me, whom you force to live without you, to die. At any rate to have refrained from torturing will be the gift of a good man. Assuredly hope restores to a lover what (lack of) hope has taken away.

92

o utinam liceat collo complexa tenere
braciola et teneris | oscula ferre label(l)is.
i nunc, uentis tua gaudia, pupula, crede. |
crede mihi, leuis est natura uirorum.
saepe ego cu(m) media | uigilare(m) perdita nocte
haec mecum medita(n)s: 'multos | Fortuna quos supstulit alte,
hos modo proiectos subito | praecipitesque premit;
sic Venus ut subito coiunxit | corpora amantum,
diuidit lux, et se |
paries quid ama

93a

si quis forte meam cupiet uio[lare] puellam,
illum in desertis montibus urat amor.

93b

Cresce(n)s: quisque meam futuet riualis amicam,
illum secretis montibus ursus edat.

94a

Hic ego nu[nc f]utue formosa(m) fo[r]ma puella(m)
laudata(m) a multis, set lutus intus erat.

94b

hic [ego] nu(n)c futue formosam fo[rt]e puellam,
morbus qu[oi ta]lis form[o]sam facie[m

94c

Hic eg[o] me memin[i qu]ondam futuisse puellam
in cuiiu[s] cunno frig[o]re paene peri.

92

Would that I might hold my (your) arms embraced around your (my) neck and give kisses with my tender lips. Go now, poppet, and entrust your joys to the winds. Believe me, men's nature is fickle. When in my desperation I was lying awake in the middle of the night, often, thinking over things with myself, (I said) 'Many whom Fortune has raised aloft, these she subsequently oppresses, suddenly hurled down headlong. Similarly after Venus has suddenly united the bodies of lovers, daylight separates them...'

93a

If anyone should want to violate my girl-friend, may love set him on fire in lonely mountains.

93b

Crescens (says): whatever rival fucks my girl-friend, may a bear eat him in remote mountains.

94a

Here I have now (happened to) fuck a beautiful girl; though praised by many, inside she was slime.

94b

Here I have now happened to fuck a beautiful girl, whose beautiful face (was affected by) such a disease...

94c

I remember that here I once fucked a girl in whose cunt I almost perished of cold.

94d

Hic ego me memini quendam futuisse puellam.
in cuius] cunno - non dico, curiose.

94e

Hic] ego memini quenda[m] crissasse puella[m]
cuius cineres aurea terra tegat

95

Quisquis amat nigra(m), nigris carbonibus ardet;
nigra(m) cum uideo mora libenter aedeo.

96

Candida me docuit nigras odisse puellas.
odero si potero, si non, inuitus amabo.

2 se...sed *1520*

97

Hic ego cum domina resoluto clune [p]er[eg]i -
cetera se]d uersu scribere [turp]e fuit.

(c) elsewhere

98

mentulacessas uerpalumbos abstulit

94d

I remember that here I fucked a certain girl (in whose) cunt - I won't say any more, prurient reader.

94e

Here I remember that a certain girl wiggled; may golden earth cover her ashes.

95

Whoever loves a black girl burns with black coals. Whenever I see a black girl, I gladly eat blackberries.

96

A blond taught me to spurn brunettes; I shall spurn them if I can, if not, I shall love them against my will.

97

Here with my mistress, my haunches heaving, I performed - but to write out (the rest?) in verse would have been shameful.

98

Are you to harass me? Spring has robbed us of the doves **OR** Prick, are you idle? Cock has won the prize of rump.

99

] nulla est animi, non somnus claudit ocellos,
noctes at[que] dies aestuat omnis amor.

1 quies] *uel* ques] *Walter, WS 45 (1926-7), 110*
2 omnes *paries (cf. Väänänen 21)*

100

Li[nge] Lel[i, l]inge L[eli], linge Leli Fa[lc]ula[m].
Lici(nius) fec(it).

100A

Cunne, licet plores uel tota nocte mineris,
eripuit culus quod tua praeda fuit.

101

S]tatio loc(i) felix. [T]utela Her[c]ules Fides Fortuna hic.
inuide qui spectas hec tibi poena manet.

102a

Quisquis ammat pueros sene finem puellas
rationem saccli no(n) refert.

102b

Quisquis amat pueros, etiam sin[e] fine puellas
rationem saccli non h[a]bet ille sui.

99

There is no mental (repose), sleep does not shut the eyes; all love seethes night and day.

100

Laelius, suck, suck, suck Falcula.

Composed by Licinius.

100A

Cunt, though you lament or threaten throughout the night, arse has stolen from you what was your booty.

101

The assembly-place is of good omen; here are Protection, Hercules, Trustworthiness, Good Luck.

This punishment awaits you who watch with the evil eye.

102

Whoever incessantly loves boys and girls too has no regard for his purse.

II F: MUNICIPAL POLITICS AND INSTITUTIONS

103a

ita candidatus quod petit, fiat, tuus,
et ita perennes, scriptor, opus hoc praeteri.
hoc si impetro a te, felix uiuas, bene uale.

103b

ita candidatus fiat honoratus tuus
et ita gratum edat munus tuus munerarius
et tu s[is] felix, scriptor, si hic non scripseris.

103c

quisquis honorem agitas, ita te tua gloria seruet,
    praecipias puero ne linat hunc lapidem.

103d

****
    haec est quam coniux condidit atque [pater.

parce opus hoc, scriptor, tituli quod luctibus urgen[t:
    sic tua praetores saepe manus referat.

104

communem nummum diuidendum censio est,
nam noster nummus magna(m) habet pecuniam.

103a

May what your candidate seeks come about and may you, bill-poster, have long life, on condition that you pass by this work. If you grant my request, may you live happy. Fare well.

103b

May your candidate gain office, and may your games-giver put on a show to please you, and may you, bill-poster, have good luck if you don't write here.

103c

Whoever you are who have office as your ambition, may your glory stick by you on condition that you tell your slave not to daub this stone.

103d

This is she whom her husband and father laid to rest.

Bill-poster, spare this work which epitaphs weigh down with grief; so may your arms often carry home (newly-elected) praetors.

104

There is a vote that our communal funds should be shared out, for our funds have plenty of cash.

105

Mulsum crustula, municeps, petenti
in sextam tibi di[u]identur hora[m.
de] te tardior au[t] piger quereri[s.

106

M. Epidium Sabinum d(uumuirum) i(ure) dic(undo)...faciatis.

Sabinus dissignator cum plausu facit.

107

Non est ex albo iu[dex] patre Aegyptio.

108

E]dideram munus m[m]ense [N]ou[embri
a]nnonaq(ue) meo su[mptu est lax]ata ter an[te.
solliciti insonte[s] proponi magna put[antes
sperantesq(ue) mihi se munera ferre fere[bant
funera. set sanctus deus hic felicius i[lla
transtulit in melius; sic denique fata tuler[unt.
a]uratam faciunt generatis undique nummi[s.
inuidia creuit de nomine magna, patronu[m
si]c tamquam domini ciues expellere temp[tant
] praecisus pudor e[s]t. ut forte lucus[tae
]an[t]es timidae neque[u]nt defendere ses[e,
agmi]nibus iuncti[s q]uae pabula saepe secat[a
a]uidae campis hominum pecudumque [
sic pop]ulus fuerat constans, disiunctu[s
] quisque sibi timidus, ut protin[us

1 m[irandum, m[irabile; *sed breuius spatium nuntiatur (item 2)*
2 ter an[te *Bücheler; alii aliter legunt et supplent*
13 dant a]uidae *et* [ruinae *uel* aluo a]uidae *et* [recondunt *Courtney*
14 [s at errat; *Courtney*
15 fit male] *Courtney*

105

Mead and pastries will be shared out to you, fellow-townsman, when you seek them at mid-day. If you are too late or lazy you will only have yourself to blame.

106

Vote for Marcus Epidius Sabinus as duumvir for legal verdicts.

Sabinus the theatre-usher votes for him with applause.

107

A juror with an Egyptian father is not on the panel **OR** a juror does not issue from a white Egyptian father.

108

I had put on a (wonderful) gladiatorial show in the month of November, and thrice before that the price of grain was lowered at my expense. Solicitous men, quite innocently, thinking that great tributes were being offered and hoping that they were bringing a gift to me, were actually bringing a rift. But this holy god turned these events to a happier issue; that was the destined outcome. Collecting funds from all sources they made a gilt statue. Great envy grew up because of the title (of patron); the citizens, like proprietors, tried to drive me out; shame was abandoned. As timid locusts cannot defend themselves, locusts who in united ranks often in the fields cut down and (consume) the food of men and beasts, just so the people, previously reliable, when disunited (became fickle). In apprehension it was each man for himself...

109

. . . .
pau[p]ere progenitus lare sum paruoq(ue) parente,
cuius nec census neque domus fuerat.
ex quo sum genitus, ruri mea uixi colendo:
nec ruri pausa nec mihi semper erat,
et cum maturas segetes produxerat annus,
demessor calami tu(n)c ego primus eram.
falcifera cum turma uirum processerat aruis,
seu Cirtae Nomados seu Iouis arua petens,
demessor cunctos ante ibam primus in aruis,
pos tergus linquens densa meum gremia.
bis senos messes rabido sub sole totondi
ductor et ex opere postea factus eram.
undecim et turmas messorum duximus annis
et Numidae campos nostra manus secuit.
hic labor et uita paruo co<nte>nta ualere
et dominum fecere domus, et uilla paratast
et nullis opibus indiget ipsa domus.
et nostra uita fructus percepit honorum,
inter conscriptos scribtus et ipse fui.
ordinis in templo delectus ab ordine sedi
et de rusticulo censor et ipse fui.
et genui et uidi iuuenes carosq(ue) nepotes.
uitae pro meritis claros transegimus annos,
quos nullo lingua crimine laesit atrox.
discite mortales sine crimine degere uitam:
sic meruit, uixit qui sine fraude, mori.

18, 20 *dextrorsus ut pentametros*, 19 *sinistrorsus ut hexametrum trahit lapicida*
26 laedit *legunt aliqui*

109

I was born in a poor home from an insignificant father, who had neither property nor house. Ever since I was born, I have lived by cultivating my land in the country; neither country nor I ever had any rest, and when the season produced ripe crops, then I was the first harvester of the stalks. When the sickle-bearing team of men came out into the fields, making its way either to the estates of Numidian Jupiter or of Cirta, I as harvester would outpace all others in the fields, leaving heaped sheaves behind my back. For twelve harvest-times I cut under the torrid sun, and afterwards was promoted from workman (?) to foreman. I led teams of harvesters for eleven years, and our hands cut the fields of the Numidians. This labour and life content with little made me flourish and turned me into the proprietor of a house; I also acquired a country estate, and my actual house lacked no resources. My life received the reward of offices, and I, even I, was enrolled among the enrolled (council). Chosen by the decurions I sat in the council-chamber of the decurions, and from a peasant I, even I, became a censor. I begat sons and saw dear grandchildren. I passed years of distinction corresponding to the merits of my life, years which hostile tongues attack with no reproach. Men, learn to live your life free from reproach; this is how the man who has lived with no cheating deserves to die.

110

C. Luxsilius C. f. Pom. Macer
Arma haec quae cernis princeps lu[dendo] fui;
id ita fuisse campus urbis te[stis est].
u(ixit) a(nn.) xuiiii

1 *suppl. M. Della Corte (Archivio Storico della Provincia di Salerno, 5.3 (1926), 3)*
2 *suppl. Holland (Ph. W. 1927, 1504)*

110

Gaius Luxilius Macer, son of Gaius, of the Pomptine tribe.

I was champion in sporting with these weapons which you see. The exercise-field of the city (bears witness) that this was so.

II G: GAMES, PUBLIC PERFORMANCES AND PERFORMERS

111**

Litoribus uestris quoniam certamina laetum
ex<h>ibuisse iuuat, Castor uenerandeque Pollux,
munere pro tanto faciem certaminis ipsam,
magna Iouis proles, uestra pro sede locaui
urbanis Catius gaudens me fascibus auctum
Neptunoque patri ludos fecisse Sabinus.

112

(d. m.?)

Factionis Venetae Fusco sacrauimus aram
de nostro, certi studiosi et bene amantes,
ut scirent cuncti monimentum et pignus amoris.
integra fama tibi, laudem cursus meruisti,
certasti multis, nullum pauper timuisti,
inuidiam passus semper fortis tacuisti,
pulchre uixisti, fato mortalis obisti.
quisquis homo es, quaeres talem; subsiste, uiator,
perlege, si memor es, si nosti quis fuerit uir.
Fortunam metuant omnes, dices tamen unum:
    'Fuscus habet titulos mortis, habet tumulum.
contegit ossa lapis. bene habet. Fortuna, ualebis.
fudimus insonti lacrimas, nunc uina. precamur
    ut iaceas placide. nemo tui similis'.
    τοὺς σοὺς ἀγῶνας αἰὼν λαλήσεται.

113**

Florus ego hic ịaceo bigarius infans,
qui, cito dum cupio currus, cito decidi ad umbr[as].
Ianuarius alumno dulcissimo.

111

Since it gives me great pleasure to present contests on your shores, august Castor and Pollux, great offspring of Jupiter, in return for such a great privilege I, Catius Sabinus, have placed the very image of the contest in front of your shrine, rejoicing that I have been honoured with the city fasces and have celebrated the games of father Neptune.

112

We, steadfast and devoted supporters, have from our own resources set up an altar-tomb for Fuscus of the Blue team, so that all might know the record and token of devotion. Your reputation is unsullied, you won fame for speed, you contended with many, though not rich you feared nobody, though you experienced envy you always bravely maintained silence, you lived a fine life, being mortal you died, but a natural death. Whatever sort of man you be, you will miss such a one as Fuscus; halt, traveller, read, if you remember and know who the man was. Let all men fear Fortune, yet you will make one remark: 'Fuscus has the epitaph and tomb that belong to death. The stone covers his bones. All is well with him. Away with you, Fortune. We poured out tears for this good man, now (we pour out) wine. We pray that you rest in peace. No-one is like you'.

The ages will talk of your contests.

113

I, Florus, the child with the two-horse chariot, lie here. In my premature desire for a chariot, I prematurely fell to my death.

Ianuarius to his sweet foster-son.

114

D(is) Man(ibus) | Sex[t]o Vetuleno Lauica[n]o. |
Delicium populi, circi quoque nuntiu(s) | ampli,
septima quem regio sextaqu(e) | amauit idem,
hunc mihi coniuuenes | titulum posuere sepulto
et | scalpsere sua nomina nostra fide. |
di, tales seruate diu, seruate, sodales
qui | nostri memores quique fuere sui. |
u(ixit) a(nn.) xliiii.

115

Clausa iacet lapidi coniunx pia cara Sabina.
artibus edocta superabat sola maritum.
uox ei grata fuit, pulsabat pollice cordas,
set cito rapta silet. ter denos duxerat annos,
heu male quinque minus, set plus tres me(n)ses habebat
bis septemque dies uixit. hec ipsa superstes
spectata in populo hydraula grata regebat.
sis felix quicumque leges, te numina seruent
et pia uoce cane 'Aelia Sabina uale'.
T. Aelius Iustus hydraularius salariarius leg(ionis) II ad(iutricis)
coniugi faciendum curauit.

4 silet *Thewrewk*: silpi *lapis (qui etiam alia peccat)*

116

****

fluxa aut syrmata Bacchici coturni,
hic Phoebus fuit, hic superbus Euhan.
plaude istis, populare uolgus, umbris,
si sum dignus adhuc fauor[e] uestro,
si, post praemia rixulasq(ue) uestras,
ut tiro ac rudis in quiete u[iua]m.

114

To the soul of Sextus Vetulenus from Labicum.

The darling of the populace, messenger also of the spacious Circus, whom both the sixth and the seventh regions loved - my fellow club-members placed this epitaph over me where I lie buried and with their characteristic loyalty engraved my name. You gods, preserve for long such comrades, who have been mindful both of me and of themselves.

He lived for 44 years.

115

My loyal, dear wife Sabina lies enclosed in stone. Cultivated with accomplishments she was the only one to excel her husband. Her voice was attractive, she plucked the strings with her thumb, but she has been quickly plucked away and is now silent. She had lived for thirty years less (alas) five, but she had three extra months and lived fourteen days (more). While alive she herself, watched in public, was a popular organ-player. Whoever you are who read this, good luck to you, may the gods preserve you, and recite this due tribute, 'Farewell, Aelia Sabina'.

Commissioned by Titus Aelius Justus, fee-earning organ-player of *legio II adiutrix*.

116

...or the flowing robes of the Bacchic buskin. He was Apollo, he was proud Dionysus. Applaud this corpse, my public, if I still deserve your enthusisam, if, after your rewards and brawls, I shall live in peace like an inexperienced beginner.

117

d.m.s.
substa, praecor, paulum festina(n)s ire uiator
et maea post hobitum rogantis concipe uerba,
tale(m) co(m) speres et ipse uenire diae(m).
Iustus ego non patrio set materno nomine dictus,
paupere patre quidem set fam(a)e diuite uixi.
tibicinis cantu modulans alterna uocando
Martios ancentu stimulans gladiantes in arma uocaui.
qui uixi annis XXI m. XI d. XXVIIII
Iustus ego morte acerba peri.
parentes filio incomparabili.

118

caedere] qui tauros ualidisq(ue) [feri]re lacertis
] Sabinus erat, cui [com]minus ictum
taurus sp]umatus mutilata [uoln]ere cauda
ingem]inans Stygias mi[se]rum dimisit ad umbras.
infeli]x iuuenis, munere deco[r]ate suppremo,
Ti]gimma te genuit, tenet Tihgibba sepultum.

119

(A)
Paulo siste gradum, iuuenis pie, quaeso, uiator,
ut mea per titulum noris sic inuida fata.
uno minus quam bis denos ego uixi per annos
integer, innocuus, semper pia mente probatus,
qui docili lusu iuuenum bene doctus harenis
pulcher et ille fui uariis circumdatus armis.
saepe feras lusi, medicus tamen is quoque uixi,
et comes ursaris, comes his qui uictima sacris
caedere saepe solent et qui nouo tempore ueris
floribus intextis refouent simulacra deorum.
nomen si quaeris, titulus tibi uera fatetur:
Sex. Iul. Felicissimus.
Sex. Iulius Felix alumno incompara[bili et] Felicitas f[ratri?

117

As you hasten on your way halt briefly, traveller, I beseech you, and absorb the words of my posthumous request, seeing that you too expect a day like this to arrive. I am Justus, so called after my mother, not my father; I lived (born) of a father who was poor but rich in repute. Ringing the changes by calling upon the oboe-player's melody I roused up and stirred martial gladiators to combat by my playing. I Justus lived twenty-one years, eleven months, twenty-nine days and died a premature death.

His parents to their incomparable son.

118

(This was) Sabinus, who (was accustomed to slaughter) bulls and smite them with his strong arms; a bull covered with foam, its tail mutilated by a wound, inflicting repeated blows at close quarters on him sent the poor fellow down to the infernal shades. Unhappy man, honoured by the final tribute, Tigimma gave birth to you, Tihgibba holds you in the grave.

119

Halt your steps briefly, humane young man on your journey, so that in this way you may learn my spiteful death from my epitaph. I lived one less than twenty years, upright, innocent, always approved for my sense of duty. I was well instructed in the skilful sport of young men in the arena, and was that 'Good-looker' girt with a variety of weapons. I often made sport of wild animals, but I also lived as their veterinarian and a pal of the bear-baiters, of those who regularly kill victims for sacrifices and who in the fresh spring-time revive the images of the gods with twined flowers. If you ask my name, the inscription tells you accurately: Sextus Julius Felicissimus.

Sextus Julius Felix to his unmatched foster-son and Felicitas to her brother (?).

(B)

Tu quicumque leges titulum ferale(m) sepulti,
qui fuerim, quae uota mihi, quae gloria, disce.
bis denos uixi depletis mensibus annos
et uirtute potens et pulcher flore iuuentae
e]t qui praeferrer populi laudantis amore.
q]uit mea damna doles? fati non uincitur ordo.
spe]s hominum sic sunt ut [citr]ea poma:
aut matur]a cadunt aut [immatura l]eguntur.

20 spe]s *Courtney*, re]s *plerique breuius spatio*

120

Se]rpentis lusus si qui sibi forte notauit,
Sepumius iuuenis quos fac<i>t ingenio,
spectator scaenae siue es studiosus equorum,
sic habeas lances semper ubique pares.

121**

lau]datus populo, solitus mandata referre,
adl]ectus scaenae, parasitus Apollinis idem,
quar]tarum in mimis saltantibus utilis actor

122

Gaius Theoros lux uictor pantomim(orum).
Si deus ipse tua captus nunc a[rte] Theorost,
a[n] dubitant h[omines] uelle imi[tare] deum?

You, whoever you be, who read the funereal epitaph of the man here buried, learn who I was, what my ambitions were, what my glory. I lived for twenty years with some months subtracted, strong in my courage, handsome in the flower of my youth, winning the preference of the populace which affectionately praised me. Why do you grieve over what I have lost? The orderly progression of destiny is invincible. The hopes of men are like citron fruits; they either fall when ripe or are picked when unripe.

120

If anyone happens to have remarked the serpent-diversion which Sepumius (?) ingeniously devises, whether you are a theatre-spectator or a fan of chariot-racing, then may you always and everywhere find scales evenly balanced.

121

Praised by the populace, playing the regular role of performing commissions, an associate of the stage and member of Apollo's guild, a good performer in pantomimes of the fourth actor's role.

122

Gaius Theoros, the illustrious, the victor of pantomimes.
If a god himself has now been captivated by your artistry, Theoros, can men hesitate to wish to imitate a god?

123

d.m.

Ti. Claudius Esquilina Aug. Tiberinus his situs est: fecit Tampia Hygia mater filio pientissiimo.

Tu, quicumque mei ueheris prope limina busti,
supprime festinum, quaeso, uiator, iter.
perlege, sic numquam doleas pro funere aceruo;
inuenies titulo nomina fixa meo.
Roma mihi patria est, media de plebe parentes,
uita fuit nullis tunc uiolata malis.
gratus eram populo quondam notusque fauore,
nunc sum defleti parua fauilla rogi.
quis bona non hilari uidit conuiuia uoltu
adque meos mecum peruigilare iocos?
quondam ego Pierio uatum monimenta canore
doctus cycneis enumerare modis,
doctus Maeonio spirantia carmina uersu
dicere, Caesareo carmina noto foro:
nunc amor et nomen superest de corpore toto,
quod spargit lacrimis maestus uterque parens.
serta mihi floresque nouos, mea gaudia, ponunt;
fusus in Elysia sic ego ualle moror.
quod meat in stellis Delphin, quod Pegasus ales,
tot mea natales fata dedere mihi.

10 locos *lapis, ut contra* nuliis 6.

124

Vrsus togatus uitrea qui primus pila
lusi decenter cum meis lusoribus
laudante populo maximis clamoribus
thermisTraiiani, thermis Agrippae et Titi,
multum et Neronis, si tamen mihi creditis,
ego sum. ouantes conuenite pilicrepi
statuamque amici floribus, uiolis rosis,
folioque multo adque unguento marcido
onerate amantes et meum profundite
nigrum Falernum aut Setinum aut Caecubum

123

Tiberius Claudius Tiberinus, Augustalis of the Esquiline tribe, lies here; his mother Tampia Hygia made (this monument) for her affectionate son.

Whoever you are who ride by the threshold of my tomb, I beseech you, traveller, halt your hurried journey. Read, and if you do so may a premature death never cause sorrow to you. You will find my name attached to my epitaph. Rome is my native city, my parents were middle-class, my life then was afflicted by no troubles. I was once in favour with the populace and their enthusiasm made me well-known; now I am a handful of dust from a lamented pyre. Who did not see with a cheerful face good dinner-parties and my merriment persisting with me until dawn? I was once skilled in reciting the legacy of poets in strains as sweet as Muses and swans, skilled in delivering poetry pulsating with Homeric verse, verse well-known in Caesar's forum. Now all that remains of my whole body, which both parents in sorrow bedew with tears, is affection and reputation. They lay down for me garlands and fresh flowers, in which I take pleasure. That is how I am laid out and linger in the vale of Elysium. My destiny gave me as many birthdays as the stars in which the Dolphin and winged Pegasus revolve.

124

I am Ursus, the first toga-wearing Roman, if you will believe me, to play gracefully with glass balls together with my fellow-players to the loud applause of the people in the Baths of Trajan, Agrippa and Titus, and also often in those of Nero. Ball-players, assemble rejoicing and affectionately load the statue of your friend with flowers, violets and roses, and with much foliage and matured perfumes, and with my permission pour out my dark Falernian or Setian and Caecuban wine from my proprietorial cellar to me while

uiuo ac uolenti de apotheca dominica
Vrsumque canite uoce concordi senem
hilarem iocosum pilicrepum scholasticum,
qui uicit omnes antecessores suos
sensu, decore adque arte suptilissima.
nunc uera uersu uerba dicamus senes:
sum uictus ipse, fateor, a ter consule
Vero patrono, nec semel sed saepius,
cuius libenter dicor exodiarius.

I am alive, and with united voice celebrate Ursus, the merry, witty, ball-playing old fellow who frequents the schools of rhetoric, who has excelled all his predecessors in tact, grace and refined expertise. Now let us old men speak true words in this poem; I myself was defeated, I admit it, by my patron Verus, thrice consul, and that not once but repeatedly; I am glad to be called his appendage.

II H: TRADES AND PROFESSIONS

125

M. Rupilius Serapio hic ab Ara Marmor(ea)
oculos reposuit statuis, quaad uixit, bene.

*126**

Ille ego Pannoniis quondam notissimus oris,
inter mille uiros primus fortisque Batauos
Hadriano potui qui iudice uasta profundi
aequora Danuuii cunctis transnare sub armis,
emissumque arcu dum pendet in aere telum
ac redit, ex alia fixi fregique sagitta;
quem neque Romanus potuit nec barbarus umquam
non iaculo miles, non arcu uincere Parthus,
hic situs hoc memori saxo mea facta sacraui.
uiderit anne aliquis post me mea gesta sequatur!
exemplo mihi sum, primus qui talia gessi.

127

Tu quae Tarpeio coleris uicina Tonanti,
uotorum uindex semper Fortuna meorum,
accipe quae pietas ponit tibi dona merenti,
effigiem nostri conseruatura parentis,
cuius ne taceat memorandum littera nomen,
Caesius hic idemq(ue) Titus Primusq(ue) uocatur,
qui largae Cereris messes fructusq(ue) renatos
digerit in pretium, cui constat fama fidesq(ue)
et, qui diuitias uincit, pudor, ire per illos
consuetus portus cura studioq(ue) laboris
litor<a> qui praestant fessis tutissima nautis,
notus in urbe sacra, notus quoq(ue) finibus illis

125

Rupilius Serapio here, in the quarter of the Marble Altar, expertly replaced eyes in statues while he was alive.

126

I (was) that man once famous in the lands of Pannonia who, first among a thousand brave Batavians, according to Hadrian's judgement could have swum over the wide stream of the deep Danube with all my armament; who, while an arrow shot from my bow was hanging in the air and coming back to earth, split and broke it with another arrow; whom no Roman soldier could ever surpass with his javelin nor barbarian Parthian with his bow. Here I lie, canonizing my deeds with this recording stone. It is up to others to see whether someone after me matches my achievements; I, who first achieved such things, am my own model.

127

You, Fortune, who are worshipped next door to Capitoline Jupiter, and who have always championed my vows, receive the gift which filial duty sets up to you, the benefactress, purposing to preserve the statue of my father. So that the written record may not pass over his distinguished name, he is called Titus Caesius Primus. He parlays the harvests of generous Ceres and the reborn crops into profit; his reputation and trustworthiness and (a quality which surpasses riches) restraint are unchallenged. He is accustomed with careful devotion to his work to visit those harbours which

quos Umber sulcare solet, quos Tuscus arator.
omnibus hic annis uotorum more suorum
centenas adicit numero crescente coronas,
Fortunae simulacra colens et Apollinis aras
Arcanumq(ue) Iouem, quorum consentit in illo
maiestas longae promittens tempora uitae.
accipe, posteritas, quod per tua saecula narres.
Taurinus kari iussus pietate parentis
hoc posuit donum, quod nec sententia Mortis
uincere nec poterit Fatorum summa potestas,
sed populi saluo semper rumore manebit.

128**

D. M. is cuius per capita uersuum nomen declaratur fecit se uibus sibi et suis omnibus libertis libertabusque posterisque eorum.

Liber nunc curis fuerim qui, respice, lector.
Notus in urbe sacra uendenda pelle caprina
Exhibui merces popularibus usibus aptas,
Rara fides cuius laudata est semper ubique.
Vita ueata fuit, struxi mihi marmora, feci
Secure, solui semper fiscalia manceps,
In cunctis simplex contractibus, omnibus aequus
Vt potui, nec non subueni saepe petenti,
Semper honorificus, semper communis amicis.
Maior ad<huc> hic laudis honor, potior quoque cunctis,
Ipse meis quod constitui tutamina membris
Talia, qu(a)e feci non tam mihi prouidus uni:
Heredum quoque cura fuit. tenet omnia secum
Re propria quicumque iacet. me fama loquetur;
Exemplum laudis uixi dum uita manebat,
Sollicitus multis requiem feci quoque multis.
L. Nerusius Mithres.

provide safe shores to weary sailors; he is known in the Holy City, known too in those lands which the Umbrian and Tuscan ploughmen turn over. Every year with habitual vows he adds cumulatively one hundred coronets, worshipping the statue of Fortune and the altars of Apollo and Secret Jupiter; the majesty of all these gods is focussed on him, promising a long life-span. Listen, posterity, for a message for you to repeat through your generations. Taurinus, under the instructions of his dear father's sense of obligation, set up this gift, which can be overthrown neither by the verdict of Death nor the supreme power of Destiny, but will always remain with its popular applause unimpaired.

128

He whose name is revealed by the initial letters of the lines set up (this monument) during his lifetime for himself and all his freedmen and freedwomen and their descendants.

Reader, regard who I, now free from worries, was. Well known in the Holy City for selling goat-skins I set out wares suitable for the uses of the people. My trustworthiness was matched by few and was always praised everywhere; my life was prosperous, I built a tomb for myself, I lived without worry, as a contractor I paid my taxes, I was open in all my dealings, fair to every one so far as it lay in my power, often I aided those who requested this, and was always respectful and obliging to my friends. This tribute of honour is still greater, in fact preferable to all, namely that I personally set up a shelter like this for my body, and constructed it not so much looking after myself; I was also thinking of my heirs. He who lies at rest in his own property has everything with him. Fame will speak of me; while life remained I lived a pattern of good repute, and, solicitously looking after many, I also provided a resting-place for many.

L. Nerusius Mithres.

129

Marcellus hic quiescit
medica nobilis arte,
annis qui fere uixit
triginta et duobus.
sed cum cuncta parasset
edendo placiturus,
tertium muneris ante
ualida febre crematus
diem defunctus obiit.

130

Dum sum Vitalis et uiuo, ego feci sepulcrhum
adque meos uersus, dum transseo, perlego et ipse.
diploma circaui totam regione(m) pedestrem
et canibus prendi lepores et denique uulpis.
postea potionis calices perduxi libenter,
multa iuuentutis feci, quia sum moriturus.
quisque sapis iuuenis, uiuo tibi pone sepulcrhum.

131

Hoc hoc sepulcrum respice
qui carmen et Musas amas
et nostra communi lege
lacrimanda titulo nomina.
nam nobis pueris simul
ars uaria, par aetas erat.
ego consonanti fistula
Sidonius acris perstrepens ***
Hoc carmen, haec ara, hic cinis
pueri sepulcrum est Xantiae,
qui morte acerba raptus est,
iam doctus in compendia
tot literarum et nominum
notare currenti stilo

129

That distinguished physician Marcellus lies here. He lived about thirty-three years, but when he had got everything ready to win praise by putting on games, on the third day before the games, burnt up by powerful fever, he ended his days and died.

130

While I am Lively and alive, I have built a tomb, and I myself read my own verses as I pass by. With the official pass I have traversed the whole mainland area, and with dogs I have caught hares and foxes. Afterwards I have taken pleasure in draining bumpers of liquor and have engaged in many youthful diversions, because I am destined to die. Young man, if you have any sense, build a tomb for yourself while you are still alive.

131

You who love song and the Muses, regard this tomb, and read our bemoaned names in a shared epitaph. For we, boys together, had the same age but different accomplishments. I, Sidonius, blowing on shrill (pipes) with a harmonious reed...This epitaph, altar, ashes constitute the tomb of the slave-boy Xanthias, who was snatched away by a premature death, though he was already skilled with a fluent pen in taking down what the fluent tongue said into abbreviations of so many letters and words. Already no-one would

quod lingua currens diceret.
iam nemo superaret legens,
iam uoce erili coeperat
ad omne dictatum uolans
aurem uocari at proximam.
heu morte propera concidit
arcana qui solus sui
sciturus domini fuit.

132

D. M. Q. Candi[di] Benigni fab(ri) tign(arii) corp(oris) Ar(elatensis)
Ars cui summa fuit fabricae, studium doctrina pudorque,
quem magni artifices semper dixsere magistrum.
doctior hoc nemo fuit, potuit quem uincere nemo,
organa qui nosset facere aquarum aut ducere cursum.
hic conuiua fuit dulcis, nosset qui pascere amicos,
ingenio studio docilis animoq(ue) benignus.
Candidia Quintina patri dulcissimo et Val. Maxsimina coniugi kar(issimo).

133

[P. M]urrius PP. (= Publiorum) l(ibertus) Zetus [Pla]centinus, mercator [pur]purarius, hic situs est.
[hospes] consiste et casus hominum cogita.
[anno]rum natu(m) xxxu arbitror fuisse m[e].
[modo] plurumi fui et florebam maxume.
[ce]cidi longe ab domo et meis amantibus.
[P. M]urrius PP. l. Eros [con]libertus et socius uiuus [hoc] monumentum fecit ossaque [tran]stulit Placentiam ind[

3 [modo] *Courtney*

surpass him in reading, already, flying to every dictate (uttered) by his master's voice, he had begun to be summoned to be closest confidant (?). Alas, he who alone was marked out to know the secrets of his master has fallen in early death.

132

To the soul of Q. Candidius Benignus, carpenter of the union of Arles.

Nobody was more skilled than this man, who possessed highest expertise in workmanship, diligence, skill and modesty; whom great craftsmen always acknowledged as their master; whom no-one could surpass; who know how to construct hydraulic equipment or trace a channel. He was a delightful boon-companion, who knew how to feed his friends, expert because of native talent and diligence, and generous in spirit.

Candidia Quintina to her darling father and Valeria Maximina to her dear husband.

133

Here lies P. Murrius Zet(h)us, freedman of Publius and Publius, from Placentia, trader in purple dye.

(Stranger,) halt and reflect on the lot of man. I think that I was thirty-five years old. (Just lately) I was of great importance and flourished mightily; I have fallen far from home and my loving circle.

P. Murrius Eros, freedman of Publius and Publius, fellow-freedman and partner in life, constructed this monument and transferred the bones to Placentia.

II J: RELIGION

134

Hercules inuicte, Catius hoc tuo donu[m libens
numini sancto dicauit praetor urbis [
cum pia sollemne mente rite fecisset [sacrum
tradidisti quod Potitis Euandreo [saeculo
administrandum quodannis hic ad A[ram Maximam.

135a

Hercules [i]nuicte, san[c]te Siluani nepos,
hic aduenisti; nequid hic fiat mal[i].
g(enio) p(opuli) R(omani) f(eliciter)

135b

Felicitas] hic habitat; nihil intret mali.

136

Alfeno Fortunato
uisus dicere somno
Leiber Pater bimater
Iouis e fulmine natus
basis hanc nouationem
genio domus sacrandam.
uotum deo dicaui
praef(ectus) ipse castris.
ades ergo cum Panisco
memor hoc munere nostro
natis sospite matre.

134

Catius as urban praetor gladly consecrated this gift to your divinity, invincible Hercules, when with pious intent and in due fashion he had performed the ceremony which you entrusted to the Potitii in Evander's day, to be carried out annually here at the Ara Maxima.

135a

Invincible Hercules, holy grandson of Silvanus, you have arrived here; let nothing harmful take place here.

To the guardian spirit of the Roman people, with good omens.

135b

Luck dwells here; let nothing harmful enter.

136

Alfen(i)us Fortunatus dreamed that Father Liber, the god with two mothers, born of the thunderbolt of Jupiter, ordained this pedestal renovation, to be consecrated to the guardian spirit of the house. I myself, commander of the camp, have consecrated the vow to the god. So, with Pan, protect my sons, keeping their mother safe too, prompted by this gift of mine. Ensure that Rome sees me (? I see

memor hoc munere nostro
natis sospite matre.
facias uidere Romam
dominis munere honore
mactum coronatumque.

1 *fort.* Alfenio *lapis (cf. Schulze 120)*
3 bimater *Henzen*: bimatus *lapis*

137

Liber Pa[t]er [sa]nctissime
arcem [qui p]ossides,
[e]t ad s[acellu(m) uoue]ram
u[r]bis [uicemq(ue) coni]ugis
et hi[c tibi] uotum dico
dentes duos Lucae bouis.

3 *suppl. Guey,* 4 *Courtney*

138

Iouigena Liber Pater,
uotum, quod destinaueram
Lari Seueri patrio
Iouigenae solis mei,
Pudens pater pro filio
ob tribunatus candidam
et ob praeturam proximam
tantamque in nos princip(um)
conlatam indulgentiam
compos uotorum omnium
dentes duos Lucae bouis
Indorum tuorum dico.

8 principp (*i.e.* principum) *potius quam* principi[s *lapis*

Rome) elevated and begarlanded with an honorific presentation by our imperial lords.

137

Holy Father Liber, who possess the [ ] acropolis, I had on behalf of (?) the city and my husband vowed at your sanctuary two elephant-tusks, and here I consecrate this vow to you.

138

Father Liber, born from Jupiter, I Pudens, having obtained all my vows, dedicate two elephant-tusks of your Indians, (constituting) the vow which I, as father, had promised to the native Lar, born from Jupiter, of my sun Severus, for my son, on account of his imperially-supported candidature for the tribunate and his impending praetorship and the great indulgence of the emperors bestowed on us.

139

Incola Tifatae, uenatibus incluta uirgo,
haec, Latona, tuis statuit miracula templis
cunctis notus homo, siluarum cultor et ipse,
laudibus immensis uitae qui seruat honorem,
Delmatius signo, prisco de nomine Laetus.
credo quidem donum nullis hoc antea natum
collibus aut siluis; tantum caput explicat umbris
****

140

um]brarum ac nemorum incolam,
ferarum domitricem,
Dianam deam uirginem
Auxentius u. c. ubique piu[s] suo numini sedique restituit.

141

(*in fronte*)
Dianae sacrum Q. Tullius Maximus leg(atus) Aug. leg(ionis) uii gem(inae) felicis
(*in tergo*)
aequora conclusit campi diuisque dicauit
et templum statuit tibi, Delia uirgo triformis,
Tullius e Libya rector legionis Hiberae
ut quiret uolucris capreas, ut figere ceruos,
saetigeros ut apros, ut equorum siluicolentum
progeniem, ut cursu certare, ut disice ferri,
et pedes arma gerens et equo iaculator Hibero.
(*in dextro latere*)
dentes aprorum quos cecidit Maximus
dicat Dianae, pulchrum uirtutis decus.

139

Dweller in Tifata, virgin famed for hunting, a man known to all, like you a frequenter of the forest, who perpetuates respect for his life with unbounded encomiums, surnamed Delmatius but originally called Laetus, has set up this wondrous object in your temple. I believe that such a gift never came to light previously in any hills or woods; so great is the head which it unfolds in the shadow (of the antlers) (?).

140

Auxentius, *uir clarissimus*, universally pious, restored to her proper sanctity and position

the maiden goddess Diana, the dweller in shady groves, the subduer of wild beasts.

141

Sacred to Diana. Quintus Tullius Maximus, commander of the seventh legion Gemina Felix.

The Libyan Tullius, commander of a Spanish legion, enclosed the level plains and consecrated them to the gods, and set up a shrine to you, Delian maiden of three figures, so that he might be able to spear swift roes and deer and bristling boars and the offspring of forest-dwelling horses, to compete in swiftness and with a lethal implement of iron (?), carrying weapons on foot and hurling spears from a Spanish horse.

Maximus dedicates to Diana the tusks of the boars which he slew, a fine trophy to his courage.

(*in sinistro latere*)
ceruom altifrontum cornua
dicat Dianae Tullius
quos uicit in parami aequore
uectus feroci sonipede.
(*in tabella marmorea*)
donat hac pelli, D[iana,
Tullius te Maxim[us,
rector Aeneadum [
legio quis est se[ptima,
ipse quam detrax[it apro
laude opima p[raeditus.

142**

munere te hoc dono, Latonia sancta uirago:
cornigeram cepi uirtute et laude potitus
exuuieisque eius templum tuum decoraui.

143

'Ερμῆς
Lucri repertor atque sermonis dator
infa(n)s palaestram protulit Cyllenius.

(*five mutilated Greek verses*)

(*in latere sinistro*)
interpres diuum, caeli terraeq(ue) meator,
sermonem docui mortales atq(ue) palaestram.
]usque terrae
sermonis dator atq(ue) somniorum,
Iouis nuntius et precum minister.

Tullius dedicates to Diana the antlers of the lofty-headed deer which he overcame on the plain of the plateau (? of El Páramo), riding on his high-spirited charger.

Tullius Maximus, commander of the sons of Aeneas belonging to the seventh legion, presents you, Diana, with this hide, which he himself, endowed with ample honour, skinned from (a boar).

142

I present you, holy warrior lady born of Leto, with this gift. I caught an antlered deer, gaining praise for my courage, and I have ornamented your shrine with a trophy stripped from it.

143

Discoverer of gain and giver of speech, the god of Cyllene invented wrestling as a child.

Go-between of the gods, traveller over heaven and earth, I taught men speech and wrestling.

...giver of speech and dreams, messenger of Jupiter and helper of prayers.

144

Cutius has auris Gallus tibi uouerat olim,
Phoebigena, et posuit sanus ab auriculis.

145

En dea, en praesens semper comitata tribunal
adsistit Pallas numine sacrato,
effigiem cuius simulacro adoremus in isto,
orantes iura et mage dicentes.

146

(*in fronte*)
V(irgini) V(estali) Cossiniae L. f(iliae) L. Cossinius Electus
(*in tergo*)
undecies senis quod Vestae paruit annis
hic sita uirgo manu populi delata quiescit.
l(ocus) d(atus) s(enatus) c(onsulto).

147

Coeliae Claudianae u(irgini) V(estali) max(imae) sanctissim(ae) ac super omnes retro maximas religiosissimae, cuius sanctimonia a cunctis praedicatur.
nunc certe pertinet esse
te talem, cuius laudem numen quoque Vestae
honorauit. Fl. Eucharistus Septim(ius) Epictetus i(uuenis) p(erfectissimus) Aur. Optatus sacerdotes sacrae u[rb]is de x prim(is).

144

Long ago Cutius Gallus had vowed these ears to you, son of Apollo, and, with his ears healed, he affixed them.

145

Behold, Pallas, the goddess who has always accompanied the judge's bench in person, stands by us with her sanctified divinity. Let us adore her likeness in this effigy as we plead the laws and, even more so, lay them down.

146

Lucius Cossinius Electus to the Vestal Virgin Cossinia, daughter of Lucius.

Given a public funeral because she served Vesta for sixty-six years, here lies in rest a Virgin.

Space granted by decree of the senate.

147

To Coelia Claudiana, chief Vestal Virgin, most holy and scrupulous above all preceding chief Vestals, whose sanctity is praised by all.

Now at any rate it is to the point that you are such, you whose praises even the divinity of Vesta adorned.

Flavius Eucharistus Septimius Epictetus, *iuuenis perfectissimus*, and Aurelius Optatus, priests of the Holy City, senior members of the college.

148

]eo pede claudus utroque
]ii diu[ ]t procul hinc reg[e p]laustra, bubulc[e.
quod si fort[e t]uus non me uitauerit axis,
excutiere rotis [e]t tractus ut He[c]tor Home[ri
debilior nobis i[n]ter tua plaustra iacebis.

1 sed]eo *uel* man]eo
2 *uel*]ti diu

149

Siluane sacra semicluse fraxino
et huius alti summe custos hortuli,
tibi hasce grates dedicamus musicas
quod nos per arua perq(ue) montis Alpicos
tuique luci suaue olentis hospites,
dum ius guberno remque fungor Caesarum,
tuo fauore prosperanti sospitas.
tu me meosque reduces Romam sistito
daque Itala rura te colamus praeside:
ego iam dicabo mile magnas arbores.
T. Pomponi Victoris proc(uratoris) Augustor(um).

150

S[iluano sac]rum Athe[nio? An]nii Laterani lib(ertus) proc(urator) et Eutyches disp(ensator)
Magne deum, Siluane potens, sanctissime pastor,
qui nemus Idaeum Romanaque castra gubernas,
mellea quod docilis iunctast tibi fistula cera
(namque procul certe uicinus iungitur amnis,
labitur unda leui per roscida prata Tirinus
gurgite non alto, nitidis argenteus undis),

148

I stay, lame in both feet...steer your wagons far from here, oxherd. If your axle does not avoid me, you shall be thrown from your cart, and, dragged along like Hector in Homer, we shall find you lying maimed among your wagons.

149

Silvanus, half-enclosed by a sacred ash-tree, supreme guardian of this lofty garden, I dedicate to you this poem of thanksgiving, because you protect me with your propitious favour through the fields and mountains of the Alps and the inhabitants of your fragrant grove while I keep law and order and transact the business of the emperors. Bring me and mine back in safety to Rome and grant that we dwell in the countryside of Italy under your protection; then I shall consecrate a thousand large trees.

Belonging to Titus Pomponius Victor, imperial superintendent.

150

Gift dedicated to Silvanus by Athenio (?) freedman of Annius Lateranus, superintendent, and Eutyches, steward.

Great among the gods, mighty Silvanus, holy herdsman, who supervise the Idaean grove and the Roman camp, because your well-trained flute is fastened with beeswax (for assuredly at a distance the neighbouring river has its confluence; the Tirinus in its shallow bed glides with placid waters through the dewy meadows,

et teneram ab radice ferens, Siluane, cupressum:
adsis huc mihi, sancte, fauens numenq(ue) reportes
quod tibi pro meritis simulacrum aramq(ue) dicaui
haec ego quae feci dominorum causa salutis
et mea proque meis orans uitamq(ue) benignam
officiumque gerens. fautor tu dexter adesto
dum tibi quae refero quaeq(ue) aris, inclute, reddo
ex uoto meritoque libens mea dicta resoluo
ille ego qui inserui nomen in ara meum.
nunc uos o laeti bene gestis corpora rebus
procurate uiri et semper sperate futurum.
d(onum) d(ederunt).

4 iugiter *Lachmann*

151

Omnisata omnigena e terra [quae gramina surgunt
quaeque effeta tulit tellus cata sol[e calente,
cuncta iubant, animant, uiridant nem[us; undique frondes
sollicitae de flore nouo, de uere mari[to.
quare cette deo patrium dedam[us honorem
Siluano, de fonte bouant cui frond[ea tecta,
gignitur e saxo lucus inque arb[ore gemmae.

hunc tibi de more damus difficil[em ⏑ - x
hunc tibi de uoce patris falciten[entis haedum,
hunc tibi de more tuo pinifera es[t corona.

sic mihi senior memorat sa[cerdos:
ludite Fauni, Dryades puell[ae
ludite, canite iam meo sacel[lo
Naides e nemore meo colon[ae.

cantet adsueta de fistul[a
adsit et ludo de more pa.[
cantet et rosea de tibia [

silvered by its bright ripples), and you, Silvanus, carrying an uprooted young cypress-tree: visit me here with your favour, holy one, and confer your divinity, because in return for your benefactions I have dedicated to you this statue and altar which I have constructed for the safety of my masters and my own, requesting a pleasant life for those of my circle and executing my duty. Support me with well-omened favour, famed deity, while I, who have added my name to the altar, willingly as is due according to my vow pay off my promises, of which I here make return and delivery to the altar. Now, gentlemen, that all has been auspiciously performed, gladly give yourselves to enjoyment, and always hope for the future.

151

Vegetation of all kinds which rises from the multi-planted earth, and the plants (?) which the ground, exhausted by the hot sun, has produced, all gladden, animate, give greenery to the grove; on all sides is foliage, anxious about the new flowers and about spring, its spouse. So, come along, let us give to the god Silvanus his ancestral honour; he has leafy bowers rustling from the spring, a grove growing from rock, and buds on the trees.

According to custom we give you this intractable [ ], according to your sickle-bearing father's utterance we give you this (goat); according to custom you have this garland of pine.

The aged priest says this to me: 'Disport yourselves, Fauns, and, Dryad maidens, disport yourselves; Naiad dwellers, sing now from my temple out of my grove'.

Let [ ] make music from his usual pipe, and according to custom let Pan (?) attend the sport, and let [ ], rosy from playing

et] premat biíuges deus A[pollo
desi]nat bello deus ho[rrido
tuque] uenias pater [
****

2 sata *Courtney*
7 gemmae *Pighi, alii* rami
16 *fort.* Pan
19-20 *suppl. Pighi*
Cetera suppleuerunt Héron de Villefosse (CRAI 1909. 467), Chatelain, Diehl (DLZ 1913. 2147)

152

Stercorari ad murum progredere.
si pre(n)sus fueris, poena(m) patiare neces(s)e est.
caue.

pueris *paries*

153

Custos sepulcri pene destricto deus
Priapus ego sum. mortis et uitae locus.

154*

Vilicus aerari quondam, nunc cultor agelli,
    haec tibi perspectus templa, Priape, dico.
pro quibus officiis, si fas est, sancte, paciscor
    adsiduus custos ruris ut esse uelis,
improbus ut si quis nostrum uiolabit agellum
    hunc tu, sed tento - scis, puto, quod sequitur.

1 *vv. ll.* rusticus aerari quondam nunc uilicus horti, aerari quondam custos nunc cultor agelli
5 *v. l.* uiolarit
6 *v. l.* taceo *(Brit. Mus. Burn. 268 al.)*; teneo *ed. Plant. Tibulli 1569 in mg.*

the pipe, make music, and let divine Apollo halt his chariot. Let the god (Mars) cease from wild war, and you, father, come...

152

Go to the wall to relieve yourself (?).

If you are caught, you must undergo the punishment.

Beware.

153

I am the god Priapus, guarding the tomb with my penis unsheathed. The place of life and death.

154

I, tried and trusty, once the steward of the public monies, now the cultivator of a little plot, dedicate this shrine to you, Priapus. If I may, holy one, in return for these services I bargain that you consent to be the perpetual protector of my garden, so that if any wicked fellow harms my estate, him you may, and that too with your erect phallus - I think you know the rest.

155**

(*in fronte*)
Genio numinis Pria[pi] | potentis polle[nti]s [inui]cti | Iul. Agathemerus Aug. lib. a | cura amicorum | somno monitus.
(*in tergo*)

Salue, sancte pater Priape rerum,
salue. da mihi floridam iuuentam,
da mihi ut pueris et ut puellis
fascino placeam bonis procaci
lusibusque frequentibus iocisque
dissipem curas animo nocentes
nec grauem timeam nimis senectam,
angar haud [miser]ae pauore mortis
quae ad domu[s] trahet inuida[s Auer]n[i,
fabulas manes ubi rex coercet,
unde fata negant redire quemquam.
salue, sancte pater Priape, sal[ue.

(*in latere*)

conuenite simul quot est[is om]nes,
quae sacrum colitis [ne]mus [pu]ellae,
quae sacras colitis a[q]uas puellae,
conuenite quot estis atque [be]llo
uoce dicite blandula Priapo
'salue, sancte pater Priape rerum'.
in]guini oscula figite inde mille,
fasci]num bene olentibus [cor]onis
cing]ite illi iterumque dicite omnes
'salue, san]cte pater Priape rerum'.
nam malos arcens homines [cr]uentos
ire per siluas dat ille uo[b]is
perque opaca silentia incruenta;
ille fontibus arcet et scelestos,
inprobo pede qui sacros liquores
transeunt faciuntque turbulentos,
qui laua[n]tque manus nec ante multa
inuocant prece uos, deae pu[ellae.
'o Priape, faue, alme' dicite [omnes,
'salue, sancte pater Priape, [salue'.

155

To the *genius* of the mighty, powerful, invincible god Priapus, (set up) by Julius Agathemerus, freedman of Augustus in charge of access to the emperor, on the admonition of a dream.

Hail, Priapus, holy father of the world, hail. Grant to me flourishing youth, grant that with my rampant phallus I may find favour with boys and girls, and that with constant sport and revelry I may dispel the worries that gnaw at the mind and may not be over-fearful of oppressive old age, may not be tormented by terror of wretched death, which will drag me to the grudging abodes of Avernus, where the spirits of which legend tells are constrained by their king, whence destiny forbids return to anyone. Hail, holy father Priapus, hail.

Assemble together, each and every one of you, you lasses who dwell in the sacred grove and the sacred waters, assemble all and in winning tones say to handsome Priapus 'Hail, Priapus, holy father of the world'. Next fasten a thousand kisses on his crotch, gird his phallus with fragrant garlands and again all say 'Hail, Priapus, holy father of the world'. For he, warding off wicked blood-stained men, enables you to go through the woods and the shady silences undefiled by blood, and he excludes from the springs criminals who pass through the sacred waters with wicked feet and make them muddy, who wash their hands without previously calling on you, youthful goddesses, with many a prayer. All of you say 'Kindly Priapus, show favour; hail, holy father Priapus, hail'.

(*in latere altero*)

o Priape potens ami[ce, salue,
seu cupis genitor uo[cari] et auctor
orbis aut physis ipsa Panque, salue.
namque concipitur tuo uigore
quod solum [repl]et, aethera atque pontum.
ergo salue, Priape, salue, sancte.
saeua [Iuppiter] ipse te uolente
ultro fulmina ponit atque [se]des
lucidas cupidus suas relin[quit.
te Venus bona, feruidus Cupido,
Gratia et ge[minae] colunt [sor]ores
atque laeti[tiae da]tor Lyaeus.
namque te si[ne n]ec Venus proba[tur,
Gratiae illepidae, Cupi[do, Ba]cchus.
o Priape potens amice, salue.
te uocant prece uirgi[nes pudi]cae
zonulam ut soluas diu ligatam,
teque nupta uocat, sit ut mar[ito
neruus saepe rigens potensque sem[per.
salue, sancte pater Priape, s[alue.

9 *v.l.* domos

156

DServ. Aen. 8.564 (de Feronia): in huius templo Tarracinae sedile lapideum fuit, in quo hic uersus incisus erat

bene meriti serui sedeant, surgunt liberi;

quam Varro (*Ant. rer. hum.* 222 *Cardauns*) Libertatem dicit.

157

otiosis locus hic non est, discede morator.

Priapus, potent friend, hail, whether you desire to be called parent and origin of the world or nature itself and Pan, hail. For it is through your potency that everything is conceived that fills sky, sea and land. Therefore hail, Priapus, hail, holy one. At your will Jupiter himself spontaneously lays down his fierce thunderbolts and in lust abandons his bright abode; fair Venus, hot-blooded Cupid, the three Graces, Lyaeus who grants joy honour you, for without you Venus does not win favour, the Graces, Cupid, Bacchus lose their charm. Priapus, potent friend, hail. Chaste maidens call on you in prayer that you untie their girdle long knotted, and married women call on you that their husbands have pricks often erect and always potent. Hail, holy father Priapus, hail.

156

In the temple of Feronia at Terracina there was a stone seat, in which this verse was carved:

Let meritorious slaves seat themselves, and they rise free men.

Varro calls her Freedom.

157

This is not the place for the idle; depart, loiterer.

158

Antinoo et Beleno par aetas formaque si par,
cur non Antinous sit quoque qui Belenus?

159

[Hic iacet Bacc]hi dei nota [sacer]dos
pastophorus]quae deae Nilo[tidis p]udica
Ale[xandria, cui flos [ ]um iuuentae
P]arcarum nota sustu[lit] inuida Diti.
ἐνθά]δε 'Αλεξάνδρια κόρη πρόπολος Διονύσου
παστοφόρος τε θεᾶς Νειλώτιδος Εἴσιδος ἁγνῆς
εἴκοσι δὶς πληρώσασα χρόνω [κεῖται λυκαβάντων
****

160

Σώματος ἐν καμάτοις μογεροῖς ψυχῆς τε πόνοισιν
[ἄ]χρι τανηλέγεος θανάτου Τυχιός ποτε κάμνων
εὐξάμενος Ληνῶ προφυγεῖν χαλέπ' ἄλγεα νούσων
Ἄρηι κρατερῶ δῶρον τόδε θῆκε σαωθείς.

C]orporis adque animi diros sufferre labores
dum nequeo, mortis prope limina saepe uagando,
seruatus Tychicus diuino Martis amore
hoc munus paruom pro magna dedico cura.

161

I(oui) O(ptimo) [M(aximo)] L. Sept[imius] u(ir) p(erfectissimus) pr(aeses) B[r(itanniae)] resti[tuit] ciuis R[

[si]gnum et [e]rectam [p]risca re[li]gione co[l]umnam
Septimius renouat primae prouinciae rector.

158

If Antinous and Belenus match each other in age and handsomeness, why shouldn't Antinous be actually identified with Belenus?

159

Here lies the well-known priestess of the god Bacchus and shrine-bearer of the goddess of the Nile, chaste Alexandria, who had not yet lost (?) the bloom of youth; the grudging mark of the Fates took her away to Dis.

160

I Tychicus was unable to tolerate sore afflictions of body and mind, and often strayed near the gates of death, but I was preserved by the divine love of Mars, and dedicate this small gift in return for his great concern.

161

Restored by L. Septimius, citizen of..., governor of Britain, in honour of Jupiter Greatest and Best.

Septimius, governor of the first province, renews the statue and the column erected by ancient piety.

162

Pan]thea cornigeri sacris adiuncta Tonantis,
q]uae Libycis Maurisque simul uenerabilis oris
his] etiam colitur te[rr]is, quam Iuppiter Hammon
inter] utrumque lat[us] m[e]diam cum Dite seuero
dext]er sede tegit - hanc puluinaribus altis
]que dicat solio diuosque frequentis
]ianus a militiis de suplice uoto,
] facie renouans dominamque biformem.
ded(icatum anno) pr(ouinciae) ccuii.

8 signa deum] *Bücheler, fort.* et reliquos]
renouam *lapis*

163

****
a]c sceptrum regi cessit, quod solus habe[ret.
tu nimbos uentosq(ue) cies. tibi, Iuno, sono[ros
perfacilest agitare metus, nam fratre q[uieto
intonas nubigenam terris largita mado[rem.
forsitan et superis ammossent saecula [mortem
ni tu per teneras discrimen poneres au[ras.
quin etiam caeli moles uix firma man[eret
haec eadem regina deum ni cuncta p[rofundo
aere consurgens fulcires sidera, Iuno.
incomprensa oculis presens non cern[eris ullis
alternos curans anima redeunte mea[tus,
et sentire iubes quod cernere posse negasti.
nesciris tam nota tuis. sic peruia Phoeb[o,
sic pluuiis, caelum prohibes concurrere t[errae
cum lucis non claudas iter, nec noscere fas est
cur eadem uirtus pariter contraria s[
s[alue, ue]ra deum rectrix, Saturnia pro[les.

16 s[umas *uel* s[erues

162

Panthea, sharing in the rites of horned Jupiter, who, worshipped equally in the lands of Libya and Mauretania, is adored in this area too, whom Jupiter Hammon, seated on the right, with stern Dis respectfully places in the middle between the sides of each of them - this deity [ ]ianus, serving the military career, according to his suppliant vow consecrates with a lofty couch and a throne, renovating the company of the gods and the goddess of double figure with a [refurbished?] look.

Dedicated 246 C.E.

163

...and the sceptre was handed over to the king for his sole possession. You, Juno, summon up clouds and winds, it is easy for you to stir up echoing terrors, for when your brother is quiet you thunder, bestowing on the earth moisture born of the clouds. Perhaps the centuries would have brought death to the gods too, did you not place a separation through the fine air. Why, even the massy frame of heaven would hardly remain firm did not you, Juno, this same queen of the gods, rising through the recesses of the air prop up all the stars. You cannot be grasped, and are not seen personally by any eyes, but you supervise the alternate movements as the breath goes back and forth, and you bid us feel what you denied us the ability to see. Though you are so well known, you are unknown to your devotees. Thus, permitting passage to the sun's rays and rain, you prevent the sky from mingling with the earth since you do not shut off light's path, and we may not know why you with one divine power simultaneously discharge opposite functions. Hail, true governess of the gods, offspring of Saturn.

164

Imminet Leoni Virgo caelesti situ
spicifera, iusti inuentrix, urbium conditrix,
ex quis muneribus nosse contigit deos.
ergo eadem mater diuum, Pax, Virtus, Ceres,
dea Syria, lance uitam et iura pensitans.
in caelo uisum Syria sidus edidit
Libyae colendum; inde cuncti didicimus.
ita intellexit numine inductus tuo
Marcus Caecilius Donatianus militans
tribunus in praefecto dono principis.

165

Iucundus Liuiae Drusi Caesaris (*sc.* libertus), f(ilius) Gryphi et Vitalis

In quartum surgens comprensus deprimor annum
    cum possem matri dulcis et esse patri.
eripuit me saga manus crudelis ubique
    cum manet in terris et nocit arte sua.
uos uestros natos concustodite, parentes,
    ni dolor in toto pectore fixsus eat.

164

In her heavenly location Virgo, carrying the ear of grain, she who established justice and founded cities (from these gifts flowed knowledge of the gods), hovers over Leo. So she is also mother of the gods, Peace, Goodness, Ceres, the Syrian Goddess, weighing out life and justice on her scales. Syria produced a star seen in the heavens to be worshippped by Libya; thence we have all learned. Marcus Caecilius Donatianus, prefect (of a cohort) but serving as tribune (of soldiers) through the bounty of the emperor, led on by your divinity came to this understanding.

165

Iucundus, freedman of Livia wife of Drusus Caesar, son of Gryphus and Vitalis.

Rising towards my fourth year, when I could have given pleasure to my mother and father, I was caught and suppressed. I was snatched away by a coven of witches (**OR** a witch's hand), universally cruel while it remains on earth and causes harm by its lore. Parents, guard your children, lest pain pierce and spread through your whole breast.

II K: EPITAPHS

166

Hoc sepulcr[um con]frequentent, a me qui sint liberi,
c[ir]cumuersos quos relinquam uel manumitti uolam;
at postrema pateat ipsis quique ex is prou[e]nerint.
Volusia Q. f. Pia Annia A....ena sic mandaui, sic [fia]t dis Manibus sacrum.

1 *fort.* sepulcr *sic breuiatum lapis*

167

Hei age, q[u]isque uoles, moriturus inemptor, amice,
ac[c]ipe, perpe[t]ua set m[odo lege], locum.
d[e]sulcanda prius mihi danti cerea prata,
ne post pa[e]niteat non tetulisse [tuu]m.
In fr(onte) p(edes) lxx, in agr(um) p(edes) xlu.

168a

Hospes, ad hunc tumulum ne meias ossa precantur
tecta hominis, set si gratus homo es, misce bibe da mi.

168b

Hospes, adhuc tumuli ni meias ossa prec[antur,
nam, si uis (h)uic gratior esse, caca.
Urticae monumenta uides; discede, cacator.
non est hic tutum culu(m) aperire tibi.

166

Let my freedmen, those whom I shall leave ritually whirled around or desire to be manumitted, throng this tomb; let it be available to them and those born of them for the final rites.

These are the instructions of Volusia Pia Annia A[ ]a, daughter of Quintus; so may it become sacred to the souls of the dead.

167

Attention, friend, whoever you be, who, aware of impending death, wish to buy in, receive a plot, but only on condition of perpetuity. I who give the plot must first furrow the waxy field, so that you may not later complain that you have not received your due.

70 feet wide, 45 deep.

168a

Stranger, the buried bones of a man request you not to piss at this tomb, but, if you are an agreeable man, mix a drink, drink it, and give me some.

168b

Stranger, the bones ask you not to piss at this tomb, for, if you want to be more agreeable to this man, shit.

You see Nettle's tomb; away from here, shitter; it is not safe for you to open your bowels here.

169

D. M. T. Flauius Martialis hic situs est.
Quod edi bibi, mecum habeo, quod reliqui, perdidi.
u(ixit) a(nn.) lxxx.

170a**

u(ixit) an(n.) lii
D. M. Ti. Claudi Secundi: hic secum habet omnia.
Balnea uina Venus corrumpunt corpora nostra,
set uitam faciunt b(alnea) u(ina) V(enus).
Karo contubernal(i) fec(it) Merope Caes(aris l.) et sibi et suis p(osterisque) e(orum).

170b

Balnea uina Venus faciunt properantia fata.
θύων τήρι τὴν κήλην σου.

171

D. M. C. Domiti Primi
Hoc ego su(m) in tumulo Primus notissimus ille.
uixi Lucrinis, potabi saepe Falernum,
balnia uina Venus mecum senuere per annos.
hec ego si potui, sit mihi terra lebis.
set tamen ad Manes foenix me seruat in ara,
qui mecum properat se reparare sibi.
L(ocus) d(atus) fun[e]ri C. Domiti Primi a tribus Messis, Hermerote Pia et Pio.

169

Titus Flavius Martialis lies here.

I have with me what I have eaten and drunk, I have lost what I left behind.

He lived for eighty years.

170a

He lived for fifty-two years; to the soul of Tiberius Claudius Secundus; he has everything with him.

Baths, wine, love break down our bodies, but life is made by baths, wine, love.

Erected by Merope, freedwoman of Caesar, for her dear partner and herself and their family and descendants.

170b

Baths, wine, love make our destiny speed up.

Watch your groin while sacrificing.

171

To the soul of Gaius Domitius Primus.

I, that widely-known Primus, am in this tomb. I lived on Lucrine oysters, I often drank Falernian wine; baths, wine, love aged with me through the years. If I was able to manage this, may the earth be light on me. Yet in the afterlife I am preserved by the phoenix on the altar, which hastens to renew itself along with me.

Site granted for the burial of Gaius Domitius Primus by the three Messii, Hermeros, Pia and Pius.

*172***

L. Licinius Priscus et Fabia Euplia L. Licinio Seuero filio pientissimo parentes.

De genitore mihi domus Vmbria, de genetrice
Ostia; Tybris ibi uitreus, Nar hic fluit albus.
ille ego qui uixi bis deno circine solis,
flore genas tenero uernans et robore pollens,
miles eram. sum deinde cinis de milite factus.
nec solum hoc, quia me rapuit, Fatum male fecit:
quod pater et mater plangunt, hoc plus male fecit.
actust, excessi, Spes et Fortuna ualete;
nil iam plus in me uobis per secla licebit.
quod fuerat uestrum, amisi; quod erat meum, hic est.

*173***

L. Cominio L. f. L. n. Pal. Firmo pr(aetori) q(uaestori) aer(arii) et alim(entorum), Oppiae Sex(ti) et (Gaiae) l(ibertae) Eunoeae.

Exemplum periit castae, lugete, puellae.
Oppia iam non est, erepta est Oppia Firmo.
accipite hanc animam numeroque augete sacr[atam
Arria Romano et tu Graio Laodamia.
hunc titulum meritis seruat tibi fama superstes.

sibi suis posterisq(ue) eorum.

*174***

Iam datus est finis uitae, iam paussa malorum
Vobis, quas habet hoc gnatam matremq(ue) sepulcrum
Litore Phocaico pelagi ui exanimatas
Illic, unde Tagus et nobile flumen Hiberus
Vorsum ortus, uorsum occasus fluit alter et alter,
Stagna sub Oceani Tagus et Tyrrhenica Hiberus;
Sic etenim duxere ollim primordia Parcae

172

Lucius Licinius Priscus and Fabia Euplia, parents, to their loving son Lucius Licinius Severus.

My home is Umbria on my father's side, Ostia on the mother's; in the latter flows glassy Tiber, in the former white Nar. I who lived for twenty circuits of the sun, covering my cheeks with the soft bloom of my spring and strong in my vigour, was a soldier, and then turned from a soldier into ash. And it was not destiny's only reproach that it snatched me away; it was an even worse reproach that my father and mother bewail me. All is over, I have departed; farewell, Hope and Fortune; you have no more power over me during the ages. I have lost what had been yours; what was mine is here.

173

To Lucius Cominius Firmus, son of Lucius, grandson of Lucius, of the Palatine tribe, praetor, quaestor of the treasury and the child-allowance, and to Oppia Eunoea, freedwoman of Sextus and Gaia.

Mourn, the pattern of a chaste young woman has perished; Oppia is no longer, Oppia has been snatched away from Firmus. Welcome this soul and honour it, you, Arria, with the Roman group, and you, Laodamia, with the Greek. Surviving repute preserves this epitaph for you because of your merits.

To themselves, their family and their descendants.

174

Now the end of life and relief from troubles has been granted to you, mother and daughter held in this tomb. You were deprived of life off the coast around Marseilles by the violence of the sea, in the area from which the Tagus and the famous river Ebro flow respectively west and east, the Tagus to the waters of the Atlantic and the Ebro to those of the Mediterranean. For that is how the Fates long ago laid out their web and spun the threads of life over you, so that your

Et neuere super uobis uitalia fila
Cum primum Lucina daret lucemq(ue) animamque,
Vt uitae diuersa dies foret unaque leti.
Nobis porro alia est trino de nemine fati
Dicta dies leti, quam propagare suopte
Visum ollis tacito arbitrio cum lege perenni,
Sisti quae cunctos iubet ad uadimonia mortis.

175

D. M. Marcanae C. f. Verae T. Caesius Lysimachus coniugi sanctissimae et sibi uiuos posuit.

Ver tibi contribuat sua munera florea grata
Et tibi grata comis nutet aestiua uoluptas
Reddat et autumnus Bacchi tibi munera semper
Ac leue hiberni tempus tellure dicetur.

176

Innocuus Aper ecce iaces non uirginis ira
nec Meleager atrox perfodit uiscera ferro:
mors tacita obrepsit subito fecitq(ue) ruinam
quae tibi crescenti rapuit iuuenile(m) figuram.

*177***

Aeternam tibi sedem Hermes aramq(ue) dicaui,
Nice, optassemque utinam tua fata, superstes
ut mihi tu faceres, sed iniqua sorte maligna
rapta iaces annis iam uiduata tuis.
ia tibi Cybeles sint et rosa grata Diones
et flores grati Nymphis et lilia serta,
sitq(ue) precor meritis qui nostra parent tibi dona

birthdays should be different but the day of your death identical. For me yet a different day of death has been appointed from the triple spinning of destiny. They resolved to postpone this according to their unuttered decision linked with the everlasting law which orders all to appear to answer the bail which they have given to death.

175

Titus Caesius Lysimachus erected this in his lifetime for Marcana Vera, daughter of Gaius, his beloved wife, and for himself.

May spring allot to you its delightful gifts of flowers, and may the delightful charm of summer nod with its foliage for you, and may autumn ever deliver to you the gifts of Bacchus, and may the season of winter be consecrated to you with the earth not weighing down on you.

176

Behold, you, Hogg, lie in your innocence not because of the wrath of the maiden goddess, nor did fierce Meleager pierce your flesh with his spear; death silently and suddenly crept up on you and caused the havoc which robbed you as you were still growing of your youthful form.

177

I, Hermes, have consecrated to you, Nice, an eternal abode and an altar, and would that I had prayed for your lot, so that you might have survived and done the same for me; however, because of unfair malign destiny you lie at rest, robbed of your years. May you have the violets of Cybele and the rose of Venus and the flowers that please the Nymphs and entwined lilies, and, I pray, may there be those who will produce for you my annual tribute because of your

annua, et manes placida tibi nocte quiescant,
et super in nido Marathonis cantet aedon.

3 *fort.* maligne

*178***

Hic iacet Optatus pietatis nobilis infa(n)s,
cui precor ut cineres sint ia sintque rosae,
terraq(ue), quae mater nunc est, sibi sit leuis oro,
namque grauis nullis uita fuit pueri.
ergo, quod miseri possunt praestare parentes,
hunc titulum nato constituere suo.

179

Geminiae Agathe Matri dulcissimae.
Mater nomen eram mater non lege futura,
quinque etenim solos annos uixisse fatebor
et menses septem diebus cum uinti duobus.
dum uixi lusi, sum cunctis semper amata.
nam pueri uoltum, non femine, crede, gerebam,
quam soli norant Agathen qui me genuerunt,
ingenio docili, forma pulchra ac ueneranda,
rufa coma, tonso capite posttrema remisso.
conuiuae cuncti nunc mi bona pocula ferte
diciteque ut semper meo corpori terra leuis sit.
nec paruae doleat requiem mei perqua(m) Fauentius,
nutritor plus quam genitor, qui solam amauit.
est mihi nam mater, pater et praecesserat olim
nec doluit casum, soror est et matris amoenae
tristis et ipsa meae mortis. quos cuncti parentes
solando uitae dulci retinete precantes
ne dolor augescat seu maeror tristis abundet.
qui legitis, totum nomen si nosse uelitis,
noscetis Geminiam Agathen, quam mortis acerbus
eripuit letus teneramque ad Tartara duxit.
hoc est, sic est, aliut fieri non potest; hoc ad nos.

14 *uel* Amoenae

merits, and may your soul rest in undisturbed night, and above you may the nightingale of Marathon sing in its nest.

178

Here lies Optatus, an infant known to all for his affection; I pray that his ashes be violets and roses, and that the earth, which is now his mother, be light on him, for the boy's life was oppressive to none. Therefore his wretched parents have set up this epitaph to their son, all that they can do.

179

To the sweet Geminia Agathe Mater.

My name was Mother, though I was not destined to be a regular mother; for I shall disclose that I lived for only five years, seven months and twenty-two days. While I lived I played games, and everyone always loved me, for, believe me, I looked like a boy, not a girl, and only my parents knew me as Agathe. I had a docile temperament, a pretty appearance which evoked respect, red hair let down at the back with my head cropped. Bring now auspicious beakers to me, all you guests, and pray that the earth for ever rest light on me. May Faventius, rearer rather than father, who loved me alone, not grieve overmuch at the repose of my little body. For I have a mother, and my father had long ago gone before me, not sorrowing at my fate; there is also my dear mother's (OR mother Amoena's) sister, she too grieving at my death. Consoling them hold them back, all my relatives, for pleasant life, praying that their pain not grow and their bitter grief overflow. If you who read would like to know my full name, you will recognize Geminia Agathe, whom premature death snatched away and led her tender form to the underworld.

That is it, that is how it is, it cannot happen otherwise; this much for us.

180

(*in fronte*)
Atimetus Pamphili Ti. Caesaris Aug. l(iberti) l(ibertus) Anterotianus sibi et Claudiae Homonoeae conlibertae et contubernali.

ἡ πολὺ Σειρήνων λιγυρωτέρη, ἡ παρὰ Βάκχῳ
  καὶ θοίναις αὐτῆς χρυσοτέρη Κύπριδος,
ἡ λαλιὴ φαιδρή τε χελειδονὶς ἔνθ' Ὁμόνοια
  κεῖμαι Ἀτιμήτῳ λειπομένη δάκρυα,
τῷ πέλον ἀσπασίη βαιῆς ἄπο, τὴν δὲ τοσαύτην
  δαίμων ἀπροϊδὴς ἐσκέδασεν φιλίην.

permissu patroni, in fronte longum p(edes) V, latum p(edes) IV.

(*in sinistro latere*)

Tu qui secura procedis mente, parumper
  siste gradum, quaeso, uerbaque pauca lege.
illa ego quae claris fueram praelata puellis
  hoc Homonoea breui condita sum tumulo,
cui formam Paphie, Charites tribuere decorem,
  quam Pallas cunctis artibus erudiit.
nondum bis denos aetas mea uiderat annos,
  iniecere manus inuida fata mihi.
nec pro me queror hoc: morte est mihi tristior ipsa
  maeror Atimeti coniugis ille mei.
'sit tibi terra leuis, mulier dignissima uita
  quaeque tuis olim perfruerere bonis'.

(*in dextro latere*)

Si pensare animas sinerent crudelia fata
  et posset redimi morte aliena salus,
quantulacumque meae debentur tempora uitae
  pensassem pro te, cara Homonoea, libens.
at nunc, quod possum, fugiam lucemque deosque
  ut te matura per Styga morte sequar.
'parce tuam, coniunx, fletu quassare iuuentam
  fataque maerendo sollicitare mea.
nil prosunt lacrimae nec possunt fata moueri.
  uiximus, hic omnis exitus unus habet.
parce: ita non unquam similem experiare dolorem
  et faueant uotis numina cuncta tuis,
quodque mihi eripuit mors immatura iuuentae,
  id tibi uicturo proroget ulterius'.

180

Atimetus Anterotianus, freedman of Pamphilus the freedman of Tiberius Claudius Augustus, for himself and Claudia Homonoea, his fellow freedwoman and partner.

She who was far sweeter-voiced than the Sirens, who was more golden than Aphrodite herself at drinking-parties and banquets, I, the talkative and glossy swallow Homonoea, lie here, leaving tears to Atimetus, to whom I was dear since I was a little girl; but a divine power indifferent to the future disrupted this great affection.

By the permission of their patron, 5 feet wide, 4 deep.

You who make your way with nothing on your mind, halt briefly, please, and read a few words. I, that Homonoea who had been given the palm over famous women, am laid to rest in this small tomb. To me Venus gave beauty, the Graces comeliness; Athena trained me in every accomplishment. My youth had not yet seen twenty years when grudging destiny laid hold of me. I do not make this complaint for myself; that grief of my husband Atimetus is more bitter to me than death itself. 'May the earth lie light on you, woman who deserved life and enjoyment of your blessings long ago'.

If cruel destiny permitted exchange of life and survival could be purchased by another's death, I should gladly have exchanged for you, dear Homonoea, whatever time is due to my life. But as matters stand in reality, I shall shun the light of day and the gods, which is all I can do, so that I can follow you over the Styx in speedy death. 'Husband, do not convulse your manly form with weeping or distress my soul with mourning. Tears achieve nothing, and destiny cannot be influenced. My life is over, this same end dominates everyone. Cease; so may you never experience pain like this, and may all the divine powers favour your vows, and may my premature death prolong for you as you live into the future that part of the prime of life which it has taken from me'.

181

L. Carisius L. l. Gemellus Iuniae Q. l. [M]ela[?niae
Terra leui tumulo leuior, ne degrauet ossa,
pau[pe]ris inpositum sustinet arte super.
Iunia formosas inter memoranda puella[s,
Iunia castarum h.....s in orbe decus,
in cineres uerssa ess tumuloque inclusa cicadae:
diceris coniunxs una fuisse uiri.

182

Scita hic sit[a est.
Papilio uolita(n)s texto religatu[s] aranist.
illi praeda rep<e>ns, huic data mors subitast.

183

Memoriae M. Luccei M. f. Nepotis Sex. Onussanius Sex. f. Com...
Quum praematura raptum mihi morte Nepotem
flerem Parcarum putria fila querens
et gemerem tristi damnatam sorte iuuentam
uersaretque nouus uiscera tota dolor,
me desolatum, me desertum ac spoliatum
clamarem largis saxa mouens lacrimis,
exacta prope nocte suos quum Lucifer ignes
spargeret et uolucri roscidus iret equo,
uidi sidereo radiantem lumine formam
aethere delabi. non fuit illa quies,
sed uerus iuueni color et sonus, at status ipse
maior erat nota corporis effigie.
ardentis oculorum orbes umerosq(ue) nitentis
ostendens roseo reddidit ore sonos:

181

Carisius Gemellus, freedman of Lucius, for Julia Melania (?), freedwoman of Quintus.

The earth, lighter than the mound which itself is light so that it may not weigh down on the bones, holds above itself that mound laid on it by such skill as a poor man can afford. Junia, memorable among beautiful women, Junia, glory of chaste women while you sojourned (?) on earth, you have been turned into ashes and shut into a cicada's tomb. You will be remembered as the only wife of your husband.

182

Here lies Scita.

A fluttering butterfly has been caught in a spider's web; one of them gains a quick prey, the other a swift death.

183

Sextus Onussianus Com..., son of Sextus, to the memory of Marcus Lucceius Nepos, son of Marcus.

When I was lamenting my loss of Nepos through premature death, complaining of the easily-snapped threads of the Fates, and was bemoaning his manhood condemned by a cruel destiny, and pain not previously experienced was torturing my whole heart; when I was bewailing my bereft, abandoned, deprived state, moving the rocks with my floods of tears; almost at the end of night, when the dewy Dawn-Star was spreading his rays and riding his swift horse, I saw a shape, glowing with stellar light, glide down from the sky. That was no dream, but the man had his actual complexion and voice, though his stature was greater than the familiar shape of his body. Showing the blazing orbs of his eyes and shining shoulders

'adfinis memorande, quid o me ad sidera caeli
ablatum quereris? desine flere deum,
ne pietas ignara superna sede receptum
lugeat et laedat numina tristitia.
non ego Tartareas penetrabo tristis ad undas,
non Acheronteis transuehar umbra uadis,
non ego caeruleam remo pulsabo carinam
nec te terribilem fronte timebo, Charon,
nec Minos mihi iura dabit grandaeuus et atris
non errabo locis nec cohibebor aquis.
surge, refer matri ne me noctesque diesque
defleat ut maerens Attica mater Ityn.
nam me sancta Venus sedes non nosse silentum
iussit et in caeli lucida templa tulit'.
erigor et gelidos horror perfuderat artus;
spirabat suaui tinctus odore locus.
die Nepos, seu tu turba stipatus Amorum
laetus Adoneis lusibus insereris,
seu grege Pieridum gaudes seu Palladis [arte,
omnis caelicolum te chor[u]s exc[ipiet.
si libeat thyrsum grauidis aptare co[rymbis
et uelare comam palmite, Liber [eris;
pascere si crinem et lauro redimire [⏑ - que
arcum cum pharetra sumere, Ph[oebus eris.
indueris teretis manicas Phrygium[que ⏑ - x,
non unus Cybeles pectore uiuet a[mor.
si spumantis equi libeat quatere ora [lupatis,
Cyllare, formosi membra uehes e[quitis.
sed quicumque deus, quicumque uocaber[is heros,
sit soror et mater, sit puer incolu[mis.
haec dona unguentis et sunt potiora c[orollis
quae non tempus edax, non rapi[t - ⏑ ⏑ x.

39 [que galerum *uel* tiaran

he spoke from his rosy lips. 'My noble kinsman, why do you complain that I have been snatched away to the stars of the sky? Cease to bewail a god, lest your affection, unaware that I have been welcomed in the celestial abode, may mourn and by its sorrow distress a supernatural being. I shall not gloomily make my way to the underworld streams and shall not as a ghost be ferried across the waters of Acheron; I shall not with my oar drive forward the dark boat nor shall I fear Charon with his terrifying countenance, nor will ancient Minos pass judgment on me; I shall not wander in those dark places nor be pinned in by the rivers. Rise, tell my mother not to lament me night and day, as the mourning Attic mother does Itys. For holy Venus has forbidden me to know the abodes of the silent and has carried me to the bright halls of heaven'. I jumped up, and trembling had pervaded my cold limbs; the place was fragrant, redolent with a sweet smell. Sanctified Nepos, the whole heavenly chorus will welcome you, whether, escorted by a crowd of amorini, you happily mingle with the amusements of Adonis, or you rejoice in the crowd of the Muses or in the artistic skill of Athena. If you should want to fasten heavy clusters of ivy-berries to the thyrsus and veil your hair with vine-shoots, you will be Bacchus; if you should want to grow your hair and garland it with bay and take up bow and quiver, you will be Apollo. Put on fine sleeves and a Phrygian (cap), more than one love will quicken in Cybele's breast. Should you desire to shake the mouth of a foaming horse with the bridle, then Cyllarus will carry the body of a handsome rider. But whatever god, whatever demigod you shall be called, may your sister, mother and young son be safe and sound. These gifts, which gnawing time and ... do not take away, are better than perfume and garlands.

184

Si dolor infractum potuit conuellere pectus
Herculium, cur me flere tamen pigeat?
nam uelut Aeacide laudauit corpus A[ch]illi
clarus Homerus, item non tua laus similis.
te sortita Paphon pulchro minus ore notabat
diua, set in toto corde plicata inerat.
sobria quippe tuo pollebat pectore uirtus
non aetate minor n[e]c minor inde loco.
hec mihi per ualidos rapto te morte dolores
quamuis aequanimo dat, puer, ut lacrimem.
cr]uciamur uolnere uicti
et reparatus item uiuis in Elysiis.
sic placitum est diuis aeterna uiuere form[a
qui bene de supero numine sit meritus:
quae tibi castifico promisit munera cursu
olim iussa deo simplicitas facilis.
nunc seu te Bromio signatae mystides †aise†
florigero in prato congregi in Satyrum
siue canistriferae poscunt sibi Naides aequ[e
qui ducibus taedis agmina festa trahas,
sis quodcumque, puer, quo te tua protulit aetas,
dummodo [

17 mystidis, 19 naidis *lapis*
21 quoicumque *lapis* (= quotcumque ?)

185

Quod superest homini, requiescunt dulciter ossa
nec sum sollicitus ne subito esuriam
et podagram careo nec sum pensionibus arra
et gratis aeterno perfruor hospitio.

184

If pain could break down and tear the heart (OR could tear the unbreakable heart) of Hercules, why should I despite all be reluctant to weep? For your praise is not the same as that which glorious Homer bestowed on the physique of Achilles, descendant of Aeacus. The goddess who has taken over Paphos did not mark you out with a handsome face, but was entwined throughout your whole disposition. For temperate goodness reigned in your breast, greater than your age and than your station too. Now that you have been taken from me by an agonizing death she allows me, calm though I am, to weep ... beaten down by the wound I am tortured, and you, resurrected, are alive in Elysium. This is the decree of the gods, that he who has served the divine will should live with everlasting beauty; these are the gifts, long ago ordained by the gods, which your obliging frankness promised to you because of your innocent way of life. Whether in the flowery meadow, among the assembly of the Satyrs, the initiates marked by Bacchus with ? demand you for themselves, or the basket-bearing Naiads equally demand you to lead their festal ranks with torches preceding, be now anything to which your age has brought you, provided that...

185

My bones rest pleasantly (all that remains in the end for a man), and I have no worries that I may suddenly experience hunger, and I am free from gout and am not a deposit for my rent, and without payment I enjoy an eternal lodging.

186

****
et, quae rara fides tori[s ⏑ - x ,
multos cum caperet superba forma,
blando iuncta uiro pudica mansit.
qui nunc pro meritis bene atque caste
corpus, quod potuit negare flammae,
unguento et foleo rosisque plenum
ut numen colit anxius merentis.
parcas, oro, uiro, puella, parcas,
ut possit tibi plurimos per annos
cum sertis dare iusta quae dicauit,
et semper uigilet lucerna nardo.

187

Heu crudele nimis fatum. dua funera maerens
plango uir et genitor flebile mersa deo.
sat fuerat, Porthmeu, cumba uexsisse maritam
abreptamque mihi sede iacere tua.
adiecit Chloto iteratum rumpere filum,
ut natum raperet tristis, ut ante, mihi.
me decuit morti prius occubuisse suppremae
tuque mihi tales, nate, dare exsequias.
ad tu ne propera, simili qui sorte teneris,
dunc annos titulo, nomina ut ipse legas.
illa bis undenos uixit, natus quoque senos;
nomen huic Probus est, huic quidem Athenaidis.
quas ego, quas genitor pro te dabo, nate, querellas,
raptum que(m) Stygio detinet unda lacu!
quam bene bis senos florebas, parue, per annos,
credebantque deis uota placere mea!
stamina ruperunt subito tua candida Parcae
apstuleruntque simul uota precesque mihi.
cum te, nate, fleo, planctus dabet Attica aedo
et comes ad lachrimas ueniet pro coniuge Siren,
semper et Alcyone flebit te uoce suprema
et tristis mecum resonabet carmen et Echo
Oebaliusque dabit mecum tibi murmura cycnus.

186

···and, though superlative in her beauty she captivated many, united to her loving husband she remained chaste, a loyalty rare among married couples. Her husband now in return for her benefactions devotedly honours the body of the benefactress as a divinity, that body which he was able to deny to the flames and fill with unguents and perfume and rose-petals. Spare, I beseech you, spare your husband, so that for many years he may be able to give you the garlands and offerings which he has vowed, and so that the lamp may ever be kept alight by nard.

187

Alas my over-cruel fate! In grief I, husband and father, bemoan two corpses lamentably drowned by destiny. It would have been sufficient, ferryman, to have carried my wife in your boat, and for her, snatched from me, to rest in your abode. Clotho proceeded to attack and snap a second thread so that, harsh as previously, she might rob my son from me. I should have succumbed to death's finality before you, my son, and you should have given me obsequies like this. But do not hurry to read the names yourself, you who are in the grip of the same destiny, until you read the years in the epitaph. She lived twenty-two years, my son twelve; his name is Probus, hers Athenais. What lamentation can I, your father, produce for you, my son, whom the water of the Stygian stream holds kidnapped from me? How well you flourished for twelve years, boy! People believed that my vows were acceptable to the gods. Suddenly the Fates broke your white threads, and simultaneously robbed me of my vows and prayers. When I lament you, my son, the Attic nightingale will beat her breast, and the Siren will come to accompany my tears for my wife, and Alcyone will also bewail you with her last cries, and Echo too in grief will with me re-echo the dirge, and the Spartan swan with me will bestow lamentation on you.

188

Bassa, uatis quae Laberi coniuga, hoc alto sinu
frugeae matris quiescit, moribus priscis nurus.
animus sanctus cum maritost, anima caelo reddita est.

Parato hospitium; cara iungant corpora
haec rursum nostrae, sed perpetuae, nuptiae.

In spica et casia es, benedora stacta et amomo.
inde oro gramenue nouum uel flos oriatur,
unde coronem amens aram carmenque meum et me.
purpureo uarum uitis depicta racemo
quattuor amplesast ulmos de palmite dulci.
scaenales frondes detexant hinc geminam umbram
arboream procaeram et mollis uincla maritae.

Hic corpus uatis Laberi, nam spiritus iuit
illuc unde ortus. quaerite fontem animae.

Quod fueram non sum, sed rursum ero quod modo non sum.
ortus et occasus uitaque morsque itidest.

189

Omnes uicisti specie doctrina, puella
Iulia cara mihi, fatis abducta paternis.
auro nil aliud pretiosius atque cylindro,
nil Tyrio suco formosius adque Lacone,
marmore nil Pario splendentius adq(ue) Caris<t>io;
nil forma melius s[eu] pulchrius esse lic[ebat,
lanifica nulla potuit con<ten>dere Arachne,
cantu Sirenas Pa[nd]i[o]nidasque sorores
et specie superasti quae sunt super omnia dicta
tu quae Graiugeno sata es Heroe parente.
nata bis octonos, letali funere rapta,
hoc sita nunc iaceo Iulia Paula rogo.

188

Bassa, wife of the poet Laberius, rests in the deep bosom of the fruitful (earth-)mother, a married woman of old-fashioned morality. Her chaste thoughts are with her husband, her soul has been restored to heaven.

Prepare a lodging; let this marriage of ours once again, but this time for ever, unite our loving bodies.

You are in spikenard and cinnamon, fragrant myrrh and balsam; I pray that from these may rise a new herb or flower with which, out of my mind, I can garland the altar and my dirge and myself. The vine painted with the purple bunches of grapes has embraced four elm-trees with its darling shoots. Let the foliage which forms a back-drop weave twofold shadow out of this, the tall shadow of the trees and the bonds of their pliant spouse.

Here is the body of the poet Laberius, for his spirit has departed to the place from which it arose. Look for the fountain-head of the soul.

I am not what I was, but I shall be again what I am not now. Rising and setting, birth and death are the same.

189

Youthful Julia, dear to me but taken away because of your father's destiny, you excelled all in beauty and culture. Nothing is more precious than gold and gems, nothing more beautiful than Tyrian and Spartan purple, nothing more resplendent than the marble of Paros and Carystos; nothing could be (?) better or fairer than (your) beauty. No wool-spinning Arachne could rival you, you excelled in song the Sirens and the daughters of Pandion, and in beauty you surpassed all the above-mentioned, you who were born of a Greek father, Heros, grown to the age of sixteen and then snatched away by death. I, Julia Paula, now lie buried in this tomb.

190

D. M. memoriae.
Iulia Sidonia, Felix de nomine tantum,
cui, nefas, ante diem ruperunt stemina Parcae
quam procus, heu, nuptiis hymeneos contigit ignes
(ingemuere omnes, Dryades doluere puellae,
et Lucina facis demerso lumine fleuit,
uirgo quod et solum pignus fueratque parentum) -
Memphidos haec fuerat diuae sistratae sacerdos;
hic tumulata silet aeterno munere somni.
u(ixit) a. xuiiii m. iiii d. xiiii: h(ic) s(ita) e(st).

191

filio
infelicis]sim<a> mater
[aetatis pri]mo qui mihi flore perit
percussus cornu, bubus dum pascua ponit;
ad quem dum curro, dum miser ante perit.
infelixs genetrix Diti tria funera duxsi;
lugebam natas cum mihi natus obit.
quod superest matri saltem concedite, Manes,
ut sint qui uoltus post mea fata premant.
M. Octaui Pulli f. Rufi.

192**

Hic sit[us est] | | prima iuuenta fuit |
dum uarias cupit spec[ies] | museo figere in alto |
decidit et Hermas hoc nunc | est pondere clausus |
aeternasq(ue) lacrimas reli | quit Carpo parenti
qui uixit ann(is) xxi m(ensibus) uiiii dieb(us) xx. Carpus coloniae (*sc.* seruus) pater infelicissimus fec(it).

190

Julia Sidonia, Joy in name only, whose threads (what an abomination!) were snapped by the Fates on the day before her bridegroom lit the hymeneal torch at her wedding; all groaned, the Dryad maidens grieved and Lucina wept at her torches with their fire put out, because she had been a virgin and her parents' only child. She had been a priestess of the rattle-shaking goddess of Memphis; she is buried here silent because of the eternal gift of sleep.

She lived nineteen years, four months, fourteen days; here she lies.

191

...most unhappy mother...to her son...whom I lost in the first bloom of his youth. He was gored while laying out fodder for the oxen; while I was running to him, he expired beforehand. I, an unlucky mother, have led three funeral corteges; I was still mourning my daughters when I had my son die. Gods of the underworld, grant a mother at least what remains, that there be those who can close my eyes after my death.

Belonging to Marcus Octavius Rufus, son of Pullus.

192

Here lies...it was his earliest youth. Hermas fell down while he trying to fix shapes of varied colours in the roof of an academy, and he is now enclosed in this massy monument and has left everlasting tears to his father Carpus.

He lived twenty-one years, nine months, twenty days. Erected by his unhappy father Carpus, municipal slave.

193

Iucundus M. Terenti l(ibertus) pecuarius.
Praeteriens quicumque legis, consiste, uiator,
et uide quam indigne raptus inane querar.
uiuere non potui plures (triginta) per annos,
nam erupuit seruos mihi uitam et ipse
praecipitem sesse deiecit in amnem.
apstulit huic Moenus quod domino eripuit.
patronus de suo posuit.

194

Quicumque legis titulum iuuenis, quoi sua carast,
auro parce nimis uincire lacertos.
illa licet collo laqueatos inliget artus
et roget ut meritis praemia digna ferat,
uestitu indulge, splendentem supprime cultum:
sic praedo hinc aberit, neq(ue) adulter erit.
nam draco consumpsit domina speciosus ab artus
infixumq(ue) uiro uolnus perpetuumq(ue) dedit.

195

dis Manibus Q. Volusi Sp. f. Lem(uria) Anthi
Paruolus in gremio comunis forte parentis
dum ludit, fati conruit inuidia.
nam trucibus iunctis bubus tunc forte noueli<s>
ignarum rector propulit orbe rota<e>.
maestus uterque parens postquam miserabile funus
fecit <et> inferi<i>s munera suma dedit,
hunc Antho tumulum male deflorentibus annis
pro pietate pari composuere suo.
Q. Volusius Q. l. Anthus pater fecit sibi et Siliae (Gaiae) l. Feliculae coniugi sanctissumae, Volusiae Q. f. Nice, Q. Volusio Q. f. Antho, Siliae (Gaiae) l. Nice, C. Silio Antho.
in fr(onte) p(edes) ui, in ag(ro) p(edes) iii s(emis).

3 noueli<s>, 4 rota<e> *F. Osann, Sylloge Inscriptionum Antiquarum* (1834), p. 458

193

Iucundus the herdsman, freedman of Marcus Terentius.

Traveller, whoever you are who read this as you pass by, halt, and see how undeservedly I, who make these useless complaints, was snatched away. I was not able to live for more than thirty years, for a slave deprived me of life and hurled himself headlong into the river. The Main took from him what he took from his owner.

Set up by his patron at his own expense.

194

Whatever young man who loves his girl reads this epitaph, do not overload her arms with gold. Even though she loop and entwine her arms around your neck, and ask you to give her gifts matching her deserts, indulge her with clothes, but avoid resplendent adornment; so will robbers stay away and there will be no adulterer. For a showy serpent devoured the limbs from my mistress, and gave to her lover a wound implanted for ever.

195

To the soul of Q. Volusius Anthus, son of Spurius, of the tribe Lemuria.

While the little boy was playing in the bosom of the mother of all, he was cut down by the envy of destiny. For just at that moment a carter had yoked skittish young oxen and with the orb of his wheel struck the unwary child. After the two mourning parents performed the piteous funeral and gave the final gifts as grave-offering, now they have set up this tomb with equally matched affection to their Anthus as his years unhappily wither.

Constructed by the father, Quintus Volusius Anthus, freedman of Quintus, for himself and Silia Felicula, freedwoman of Gaia, his chaste wife [etc.]

6 feet wide, 3 1/2 deep.

196

Vmmidiae manes tumulus tegit iste simulque
Primigeni uernae, quos tulit una dies.
nam Capitolinae compressi examine turbae
supremum fati competiere diem.
Vmmidia<e> Ge et P. Vmmidio Primigenio, uix. ann. xiii. P. Vmmidius Anoptes lib. fecit.

197**

Murrae et Verecundo Murrani filis.
Qui legis, has pueri moribundas perlege uoces
et lacrimam fatis da gemitumque meis.
Murra patris primam referens e nomine partem
amborum effigiem matre fauente tuli.
bis mihi septenos aetas ostenderat annos
certaque iam nostri fama pudoris erat,
cum subito mortis, pro fallax, causa fuisti
lusus et aequalis non inimica manus.
nam temere emissus non ad mea funera clauus
haesit et in tenero uertice delituit.
uos non hoc] primum perculsi uulnere manes
parcite iam luctu sollicitare meos.
uix luctum alterius] posuistis funere nati:
trimus et in decimo mense sepulte iaces.
] uocarunt
immunes: nostris ossibus urna sat est.

7 *v.l.* subitae
11, 13 *sic fere suppl. Courtney*

198

Attia M. l. Ampliata annor(um) xxiii h(ic) s(ita) e(st).
Florente aetate depressere ueneficae

196

This tomb covers the spirit of Ummidia and also of the home-born slave Primigenius, who were snatched away on the same day. For together they attained the last day of destiny, crushed in the throng of the Capitoline crowd.

Publius Ummidius Anoptes, freedman, raised this to Ummidia Ge and Publius Ummidius Primigenius, who lived thirteen years.

197

To Murra and Verecundus, sons of Murranus.

You who read, read to the end these dying words of a young boy and bestow tears and groans on my death. I Murra, reproducing the first part of my father's name, to my mother's joy resembled both parents. My age had shown fourteen years to me, and the repute of my chastity was now well-established, when suddenly sport (treacherous, alas) and the arm of a playmate intending no harm caused my death. For a training javelin carelessly thrown, not intended to kill me, hit and penetrated my tender head. Refrain from vexing my spirit with your grief, my parents, smitten by another blow before this (?); you have hardly laid aside grief at the death of another son (?); you (,my brother,) lie buried in the tenth month of your fourth year....; an urn is sufficient for my bones.

198

Attia Ampliata, freedwoman of Marcus, lies here at the age of twenty-three.

As her youth was flourishing, witches cut her down, snatched away

mensesq(ue) quinq(ue) et annum cum aegrotauerit
abreptam aetate in inferi Ditis specus.
hunc titulum posuit Faustus libertae suae.

199

Memoriae Q. [Ael. Apoll]oni mil(iti) coh(ortis) (milliariae) nou(a)e Suror(um) stip(endiorum) iii uix(it) ann. xx Aelia Marcia mater filio dulcissimo et Aelia Apollonia soror eius faciendum curauerunt.

Lubrica quassa leuis fragilis bona uel mala fallax
Vita data est homini, non certo limite cretae,
Per uarios casus tenuato stamine pende(n)s.
Viuito, mortalis, dum dant tibi tempora Parc(a)e,
Seu te rura tenent, urbes seu castra uel (a)equor.
Flores ama Veneris, Cereris bona munera carpe
Et Nysii larga et pinguia dona Mineruae;
Candida(m) uita(m) cole iustissima mente serenus.
Iam puer et iuenis, iam uir et fessus ab annis,
Talis eris tumulo superumque oblitus honores.

7 Nysti, Nysyi *lapides*

199A

A

Sint licet exiguae fugientia tempora uitae
paruaq(ue) raptorum cito transeat hora dierum
mergat et Elysiis mortalia corpora terris
adsidue rupto Lachesis male conscia penso,
iam tamen inuenta est blandae rationis imago
per quam prolatos homines in tempora plura
longior excipiat memoratio multaq(ue) seruet
secum per titulos mansuris fortius annis.

from her youth into the caverns of infernal Dis when she had been ill for a year and five months.

Faustus set up this epitaph for his freedwoman.

199

Aelia Marcia, his mother to her dead son, and Aelia Apollonia his sister supervised the erection of this monument to the memory of Quintus Aelius Apollonius, soldier of new miliary cohort of Syrians; served for three years, lived for twenty.

To a man is given life that is slippery, shaky, fleeting, fragile, good or bad, treacherous, hanging on a slender thread through a variety of chances with no clearly-marked finishing-post. Live to the full, mortal, while the Fates grant you time, whether the country embraces you or cities or a military camp or the sea. Love the flowers of Venus, pluck the benign gifts of Ceres and the generous gifts of Bacchus and the viscous gifts of Athena; cultivate a serene life, calm because of your clear conscience. Speedily a boy and a youth, speedily a man and then worn out by old age, you will be like this in the tomb, with no memory of the honours of men alive on earth.

199A

Even though the period of short life is fleeting, the brief hour of our days passes quickly and they are snatched from us (*or* of the days at which we snatch), guilty Lachesis breaks her thread and continually submerges mortal bodies in the territory of Elysium; yet there has been discovered a seductively-devised substitute, so that by means of it a longer-lasting report can embrace men, their life prolonged for a greater time, and preserve many details, since the years will endure with it more firmly because of inscribed records.

ecce recens pietas omni placitura fauore
ingentem famae numerum cum laude meretur
exemplo iam plena nouo, quam Flauius alto
more Secundus agens patrio signauit honore.

quis non iam pronis animi uirtutibus adsit,
quis non hoc miretur opus fusasq(ue) uidendo
diuitias stupeat tantos se cernere census,
per quos aetherias surgunt monimenta per auras?

haec est fortunae melius laudanda facultas,
sic sibi perpetuas faciunt impendia sedes,
sic immortales scit habere pecunia mores,
aeterno quotiens stabilis bene figitur usu.

uiderit ille furor, nimio qui ducitur auro,
quem trahit argenti uenalis sanguine candor,
uiderit et fusae uanis in amoribus errans
gloriae luxuriae, peregrinas quaerere magno
quae didicit uestes gemmasq(ue) nitore placentes
aut ab Aeruthraeo uenientia munera fluctu,
quam laedunt gentes uario certamine rerum,
Graecia cum pueris, Hispania Pallados usu,
uenatu Libyae tellus, orientis amomo,
Aegyptos Phariis leuitatibus, artibus actis
Gallia semper ouans, diues Campania uino.

haec cito deficiunt et habent breue munus amoris
momentis damnata suis, set si quis ad omnes
respiciat uitae casus hominemque laboret
metiri breuitate sua, tunc credere discet
nil aliut melius fieri nisi uiribus aeui
quot possit durare diu sub honore deorum.
    nunc ego non dubitem tacitis Acherontos in umbris,
si post fata manent sensus, gaudere parentem
saepe, Secunde, tuum, reliquas et spernere turmas,
quod sciat hic tantam faciem superesse sepulchri
perpetua nouitate sui, sic stare nitentes
consensus lapidum, sic de radice leuatos
in melius creuisse gradus, ut et angulus omnis
sic quasi mollitae ductus sit stamine cerae.

(9) See, a recent filial gesture, which will meet with total approval, deserves a great mass of fame and praise, a gesture pregnant with a novel precedent; Flavius Secundus, acting in his father's style, has marked that gesture with a lofty mark of honour. Who would decline to approve this with the support of the noble instincts of the mind, who would not admire this work, who, as he sees riches poured out, would not be amazed at beholding such wealth, by means of which the monument rises through the breezes of the ether? This is the use of wealth which deserves higher praise, this is how spending creates an ever-lasting abode, this is how money finds a way to have eternal merit, when in stability it is grounded in a use that lasts for ever. (21) Let that madness see to itself which is swayed by over-much gold, which the brightness of silver bought with blood drags captive; let the vagrant vanity of extravagance poured out on meaningless amours see to itself, that extravagance which has learned to seek at great cost foreign attire and gems which seduce with their brightness, or gifts coming from the Indian Ocean, that extravagance which is corrupted by the peoples of the world with their rival commodities, Greece with young slaves, Spain with the fruits of Pallas, the land of Libya with wild beasts hunted down and that of the Near East with its amomum, Egypt with cheeky Alexandrian slaves, Gaul with works of art which it produces with continual pride, rich Campania with wine. (32) These things swiftly fade and carry but a brief meed of attractiveness, condemned by their own quick passing; but if one considers all the hazards of life and strives to measure man by his brief span, then he will learn to believe that nothing better is achieved than what is able to last long in vigorous aging, with respect for (*or* the respect of) the gods.

(38) Now, if sensation survives after death, I would not doubt that your father, Secundus, in the silent shades of Acheron often rejoices and spurns the other groups of ghosts because he realises that here on earth there remains this impressive tomb in its eternal novelty, that the shining well-fitted slabs stand as they do, that the levels of steps raised from the foundation have grown finer, so that every corner has been traced as if with the stuff of malleable wax.

mobilibus signis hilaris scalptura n[ou]a[t]ur
et licet atsidue probet hos uaga turba d[e]cores,
lucentes stupeat pariter pendere columnas.
quit cum militiae titulos ipsumq(ue) parentem
numinibus dederis haec gaudia saepe uidentem
quae quondam dedit ipse loco, dum munera Bacchi
multa creat primasq(ue) cupit componere uites
et nemus exornat reuocatis saepius undis?
permittant mihi fata loqui noctisq(ue) timendae
regnator Stygius: sic immortalis haberi
iam debet pater ecce tuus Ditisque relicti
tristem deseruisse domum, dum tempore toto
mauolt haec monumenta sequi scriptisq(ue) per aeuom
uiuere nominibus, solitis insistere lucis,
adsi]due patrias hinc cernere dulciter arces
quosq(ue) dedit natis prope semper habere penates.

forsitan haec multi uano sermone ferentes
uenturae citius dicant praesagia mortis,
si quis dum uiuit ponat monimenta futuris
temporibus. mihi non tales sunt pectore sensus,
set puto securos fieri quicumque parare
aeternam uoluere domum certoque rigore
numquam lapsuros uitae defigere muros.
fatis certa uia est neq(ue) se per stamina mutat
Atropos: ut primo coepit decurrere filo,
crede, Secunde, mihi, pensatos ibis in annos.
set securus eris, set toto pectore diues,
dum nulli grauis esse potes nec plena labore
testamenta facis, tuus hoc dum non timet heres,
ut sic aedificet. iam nunc quodcumq(ue) relinques
totum perueniet tua quo uolet ire uoluntas.

sed reuocat me cura operis celsiq(ue) decores.
stat sublimis honor uicinaq(ue) nubila pulsat
et solis metitur iter. si iungere montes
forte uelint oculi, uincuntur in ordine colles;
si uideas campos, infra iacet abdita tellus.

non sic Romuleas exire colossos in arces
dicitur aut circi medias obeliscus in auras,

Sprightly sculpture constitutes an innovation in a mobile effigy, and the crowd passing by can continually applaud these adornments and be amazed at the matching columns which gleam overhead. (49) What about when you gave to the sainted dead the inscription recording your father's military career and your father himself? He often sees the delights which he himself bestowed on the place in producing an abundance of the gifts of Bacchus and desiring to lay out the first vines and making the grove flourish by many diversions of the stream. May destiny and the infernal ruler of dread darkness permit me to say that in this way your father now deserves to be considered immortal and to have departed from and abandoned the gloomy halls of Dis, namely that through all time he prefers to accompany this monument and to live for eternity in the inscribed record, to dwell in the grove to which he was accustomed, from here to see with continuous pleasure the buildings of his native city, and to have by him for ever the home which he gave to his children.

(62) Perhaps many people, commenting in empty words, say that it is a presage of death destined to arrive sooner if a man during his lifetime establishes a monument for time yet to come. Such opinions are not in my heart, but I believe that freedom from care comes to those who have resolved to prepare an eternal abode and with unswerving rectitude of life to establish walls that will never fall. Destiny has its fixed path and Atropos does not alter herself in her spinning; as she has begun to draw out the first thread, so (believe me, Secundus) will you proceed to years measured out. But you will be free from care and rich in all your being when you can no longer be oppressive to anyone and do not make wills filled with obligations, when your heir does not fear that he may have to build (a monument) in this style. Whatever you leave now will in its totality end up where your wishes desire it to go.

(77) But I am called back by consideration of the work and its lofty beauties. Its impressiveness reaches into the sky, impinges on the neighbouring clouds and measures the course of the sun. If the eyes should happen to desire to survey the hills one after another, each summit in turn is dominated; if you should view the plains, the ground lies thrust far below. No match for this is the colossus said to be level with the hills of Rome or the obelisk of the circus said to reach into the air, or the lighthouse which points out the channels

nec sic sistrigeri demonstrat peruia Nili
dum sua perspicuis aperit Pharos aequora flamis.

quid non docta facit pietas? lapis ecce foratus
luminibus multis hortatur currere blandas
intus apes et cerineos componere nidos,
ut semper domus haec thymbraeo nectare dulcis
sudet florisapos, dum dant noua mella, liquores.

B

Huc iterum, Pietas; uenerandas erige mentes
  et mea quo nosti carmina more foue.
ecce Secundus adest iterum, qui pectore sancto
  non monimenta patri, sed noua templa dedit.
quo nunc, Calliope, gemino me limite cogis,
  quas iam transegi rusus adire uias?
nempe fuit nobis operis descriptio magni,
  diximus et iunctis saxa polita locis,
circuitus nemorum, currentes dulciter undas
  atque reportantes mella frequenter apes.

hoc tamen, hoc solum nostrae, puto, defuit arti,
  dum cadis ad multos, ebria Musa, iocos:
in summo tremulas galli non diximus alas,
  altior extrema qui, puto, nube uolat;
cuius si membris uocem natura dedisset,
  cogeret hic omnes surgere mane deos.
et iam nominibus signantur limina certis
  cernitur et titulis credula uita suis.
opto, Secunde, geras multos feliciter annos
  et quae fecisti tu monimenta legas.

of the sistrum-rattling Nile while disclosing the waters around itself with its far-visible flames. What does this filial loyalty linked with expertise not achieve? See, the stone perforated with many apertures encourages docile bees to fly inside and set up their waxy hives, so that this abode, sweetened with thyme nectar, may exude flower-scented juices while they produce fresh honey.

B

'Filial affection, once again arouse your awe-inspiring mind to this purpose and nurture my song in the way familiar to you. See, here again is Secundus, who with pure heart has given to his father not a monument but a new type of shrine. For what purpose, Calliope, do you constrain me on a double path to approach again the roads which I have already traversed? For I have executed the description of the great work and described the polished stones well set together, the surrounding groves, the waters running charmingly and the bees which regularly bring back their honey. (11) Yet this thing, this alone, I think, was lacking in my accomplishment in which, intoxicated Muse, you stoop to many frivolities, namely that I did not tell of the fluttering wings of the cock which flies, I dare say, higher than the final cloud. If nature had given a voice to its body, it would constrain all the gods to rise in the morning. Now that the facade is marked with the words decided on and one can see a biography that places its trust in its record of achievement, I pray that you, Secundus, may enjoy many happy years and read the monument which you have set up.'

II L: EPITAPHS OF ANIMALS

200

D. M.
Gaetula harena prosata,
Gaetulo equino consita,
cursando flabris compara,
aetate abacta uirgini
Speudusa Lethen incolis.

201

Coporusque tuli[sse(n?)t
nec T]usci saltus pascua nec Sicula,
qui u]olucris ante ire uaga[s], qui flamina Chori
uincere suetus eras, hoc stabulas tumulo.

202

Gallia me genuit, nomen mihi diuitis undae
concha dedit, formae nominis aptus honos.
docta per incertas audax discurrere siluas
collibus hirsutas atque agitare feras,
non grauibus uinclis unquam consueta teneri
uerbera nec niueo corpore saeua pati.
molli namque sinu domini dominaeque iacebam
et noram in strato lassa cubare toro,
et plus quam licuit muto canis ore loquebar;
nulli latratus pertimuere meos.
sed iam fata subii partu iactata sinistro,
quam nunc sub paruo marmore terra tegit.

200

Born from sandy Gaetulia, conceived in a Gaetulian stud, matching the winds in speed, you, Quickfoot, reft from your virgin youth dwell in Lethe.

201

(Such a horse neither...) and Coporus would have produced, nor the Tuscan valleys nor the Silician pastures. You who were accustomed to outrunning the roaming birds and defeating the blasts of the North-Easterlies now have your stable in this tomb.

202

Gaul gave me birth, the oyster of the rich sea gave me my name, my precious name matched my prettiness. I was expert in racing boldly through trackless forests and in chasing shaggy wild beasts on the hills, I was never accustomed to being restrained by an oppressive lead nor to enduring cruel blows on my snow-white body. For I used to lie in the loving laps of my owners, husband and wife, and I had worked out how to lie on the made-up bed when I was tired, and with my dumb canine mouth I used to say more than nature permitted; nobody ever feared my barking. But now, distressed by complications in giving birth, I have undergone my destiny; the earth covers me beneath a miniature marble tomb.

*203***

Portaui lacrimis madidus te, nostra catella,
quod feci lustris laetior ante tribus.
ergo mihi, Patrice, iam non dabis oscula mille
nec poteris collo grata cubare meo.
tristis marmorea posui te sede merentem
et iunxi semper manib(us) ipse meis,
morib(us) argutis hominem similare paratam;
perdidimus quales, hei mihi, delicias!
tu, dulcis Patrice, nostras attingere mensas
consueras, gremio poscere blanda cibos,
lambere tu calicem lingua rapiente solebas
quem tibi saepe meae sustinuere manus,
accipere et lassum cauda gaudente frequenter
****

204

Quam dulcis fuit ista, quam benigna,
quae cum uiueret, in sinu iacebat
somni conscia semper et cubilis.
o factum male, Myia, quod peristi!
latrares modo siquis adcubaret
riualis dominae licentiosa.
o factum male, Myia, quod peristi.
altum iam tenet insciam sepulcrum
nec seuire potes nec insilire
nec blandis mihi morsibus renides.

203

Bedewed with tears I have carried you, our little dog, as in happier circumstances I did fifteen years ago. So now, Patrice, you will no longer give me a thousand kisses, nor will you be able to lie affectionately round my neck. You were a good dog, and in sorrow I have placed you in a marble tomb, and I have united you forever to myself when I die. You readily matched a human with your clever ways; alas, what a pet we have lost! You, sweet Patrice, were in the habit of joining us at table and fawningly asking for food in our lap, you were accustomed to lick with your greedy tongue the cup which my hands often held for you and regularly to welcome your tired master with wagging tail.

204

How sweet and friendly she was! While she was alive she used to lie in the lap, always sharing sleep and bed. What a shame, Midge, that you have died! You would only bark if some rival took the liberty of lying up against your mistress. What a shame, Midge, that you have died! The depths of the grave now hold you and you know nothing about it. You cannot go wild nor jump on me, and you do not bare your teeth at me with bites that do no hurt.

COMMENTARY

I : REPUBLICAN INSCRIPTIONS

A: SATURNIAN INSCRIPTIONS

1

CLE 1 = *CIL* 1.2 = 6.2104 = *ILS* 5039 = *ILLRP* 4 = A(E). Pasoli, *Acta Fratrum Arualium* (1950), 167 = Gordon, *Album* 3.41 no. 276.
Photo: Gordon, *Album* pl. 130, *Introduction* pl. 49; A. Rostagni, *La Letteratura di Roma repubblicano ed Augustea* (1940), tav. iv facing p. 64.
Discussions: E. Norden, *Aus altrömischen Priesterbüchern* (1939), 109; *CIL* 1.2.4 p.855; I. Paladino, *Fratres Aruales* (1988), 195; J. Scheid, *Romulus et ses Frères* (1990), 618, 644. Though the song offers a standing invitation, often eagerly accepted, to manic conjecture, Norden's interpretation has proved generally convincing, and the notes derive most of their matter from it; one caveat is that Norden sometimes bases his elucidations on literary floscules. There is a recent, but very unconvincing, discussion by Considine in *Historical Philology, Greek, Latin and Romance*, ed. B. Brogyanyi and R. Lipp (1992), 211.

This inscription records the proceedings of the Arval Brethren for 218 A.D. In the prose introduction *ibi* means 'inside the shrine of the Dea Dia', and *descindentes*, which is replaced by *dicentes* in the Acts for 219, is probably merely a mistake motivated by *desciderunt* = *descenderunt* just above. The priests are *succincti* so that they can perform their dance; they recite their song from ritual books which they receive from *serui publici* and hand back to them. On the stone the song is written out in prose with only a few dots dividing words, some of them evidently misplaced; in the above version a few minor lapses of no significance are eliminated. It is disconcerting that Gordon (*Album*) in 7-9 nowhere sees *sali*, but *[sa]le, sall, sni* (others here see *saii*); he complains of the difficulty of reading this inscription. A translation into classical Latin might be: nos, Lares, iuuate, neue luem ruinam, Mars, sine incurrere in plures. satur esto, fere Mars, (in? super?) limen sali, sta ?. Semones alterni aduocabitis cunctos. nos, Mars, iuuato.

Language

In transcription of the libelli some modernisms have crept in. *Lases* (cf. *TLL* vii.2.964.45) is a form which pre-dates rhotacism, but *pleores* post-dates it. *incurrere* would be *incurere* before the second century B.C. In archaic Latin *iuuate, iuuato* should be *iouate* (see 2.6, Leumann 596, Walde - Hofman s.v.), *iouatod* (Leumann 228-9, Sommer 518-9, Porzio Gernia 171).

1-3 *e Lases* go together; they are pushed apart because *nos* thrusts itself into second position as enclitics and related words tend to do, a tendency identified by Wackernagel (cf. Fraenkel on Aesch. *Ag.* 1215); cf. 11.2 and in particular *ob uos sacro* (Festus 190). Compare *ecastor* and *eiuno, edi medi = ediusfidius, mediusfidius* (like *mecastor;* Charisius 258 B); *equirine, iusiurandum per Quirinum* (Paul. Fest. 81). The difficulty is that this *e*, like ἦ μήν, is elsewhere used in adjuration, not in entreaty, but none of the many other explanations is nearly so convincing.

4-6 *lue = luem, rue = ruem = ruinam*; the latter is a word known only from the evidence of glossaries, collected *CGL* 7.216. *Marmar* (of which *Marmor* 13-15 is probably just a corruption) is hard to explain philologically, but must be a variant form of *Mars*; the dative *Mamartei* has cropped up on an inscription of about 500 B.C. from Satricum (*AE* 1979, 136 = *CIL* 1.2832a). See *Kl. Pauly* s.v. *Mars* 1046, Giacalone Ramat, *Archivio Glottologico Ital.* 50 (1968), 8, Leumann 434, C. Simone in C. M. Stibbe and others, *Lapis Satricanus* (1980), 85, Wachter 378, *CIL* l.c.

sins is presumably an imperative formed with -*s* like some Greek forms (E. Schwyzer, *Gr. Gramm.* 1.800), though these themselves are philologically obscure; the third occurence looks more like *serp* than (as is often reported) *sers*, but must be just an error. *pleoris* is a formation not satisfactorily explained, but it must surely mean *plures*; cf. Leumann 496, Sommer 455. The third occurrence could be read as *pleoius*.

7-9 *fu* is part of the same conjugation system as the subjunctive *fuam*, perfect *fui*, participle *futurus*. *berber* has not been satisfactorily explained; Norden's explanation is plainly unacceptable (Latte, *Philol.* 97 (1948), 152 n.1).

10-12 *aduocapit* = *aduocabite*, with *-e* subject to apocope as generally in early Latin (Leumann 92-3, SP 120, 214). The ending *-tis* in the second person plural is an innovation of Latin; the inherited ending is *-te* (Leumann 512, 515; Sommer 489), which Latin specialises to the imperative. For such apocope cf. e.g. *it'* Plaut. *Poen.* 1237. The *p* in *aduocapit* and the *u* in *Semunis* (for *Semonis*) seem to be forms due to other Italic dialects, unless *[Se]munibus* is to be read on *CIL* 1.2436 = *ILLRP* 290 (from the *ager Capenas*).

For *conctos* see Leumann 48-9.

Metre

The song is mainly written in cola which later crystallised into the Saturnian metre; 1-3, 4b-6b, 7b-9b, 13-15 are the standard seven-element colon, 10b-12b the standard six-element. 4a-6a, with *neue* scanned as *neu*, are eight-element cola.

For 7a-9a Norden compares a phrase quoted by Varro, *LL* 7.49 from the *carmen Saliare* (fr. 15 Morel and Büchner), *Mamuri Veturi*, which scans - x - ⏑ ⏑ - (but a parallel involving a proper name is not very satisfactory, cf. p. 23; it would be better to compare 6.4b, 11.5b below). Fraenkel, *Eranos* 49 (1951), 170 points to the fact that the hymn of the Curetes (see below on liturgy) begins with two of these units ἰὼ μέγιστε Κοῦρε, / χαῖρέ μοι Κρόνειε, but the rest of the hymn makes no use of them, and one must remark that the first of them does not observe the *caesura Korschiana*.

Liturgy

This song is to be placed in relation to the prayer recorded in Cato, *De Agr.* 141.2-3, which I have laid out in order to illustrate its structure:

Mars pater, te precor quaesoque
    uti sies uolens propitius
    mihi domo familiaeque nostrae;
quoius rei ergo
    agrum terram fundumque meum
    suouitaurilia circumagi iussi;
uti tu morbos uisos inuisosque
    uiduertatem uastitudinemque calamitates intemperiasque
    prohibessis defendas auerruncesque;
utique tu fruges frumenta uineta uirgultaque
    grandire beneque euenire siris,

pastores pecuaque salua seruassis
duisque bonam salutem ualetudinemque
mihi domo familiaeque nostrae.
harunce rerum ergo
fundi terrae agrique mei
lustrandi lustrique faciendi ergo,
sicuti dixi,
macte hisce suouitaurilibus lactentibus immolandis esto.
Mars pater, eiusdem rei ergo
macte hisce suouitaurilibus lactentibus esto.

The Lares were not in origin house-gods, but protected the whole estate (Latte 90 sqq.). Mars appears in Cato as an agricultural god, but that is apparently a later development (see G. De Sanctis, *Storia dei Romani* 4.2.149); here he is *ferus*, the god of the wild land outside the cultivated bounds of the estate (cf. Cato 83 *Marti Siluano in silua*). He is traditionally insatiable (Nisbet - Hubbard on Hor. *Odes* 1.2.37), but is now asked to curb this quality and not to send pestilence to the crops from his domain. Hence in Cato he has developed into a protective deity, on the principle that one tries to turn the god who has power to inflict harm into a protector against that harm, as the Erinyes are turned into the Eumenides (promises made by them in Aesch. *Eum.* 938-47 resemble what we have here). The statement by Tertullian, *De Spect.* 5.8 that games were celebrated to Mars and Robigo has also been adduced (and the Robigalia were held at the edge of ancient Roman territory), but this statement is of little help because (a) it is entirely unsupported elsewhere: (b) it is not even clear that Tertullian is speaking of one festival (E. Castorina in his edition (1961) thinks that he is not, M. Turcan in his (1986) hesitates).

It is not clear why Mars is asked to leap on (?over) the threshold (the word cannot mean 'border', one of the literary turns imported by Norden; Latte 65 n.2); perhaps the threshold in question is that of the storage barn, not the house. At any rate, leaping dance is associated with this god; he may be referred to as *Salisubsal(i)us* on the bridge (another boundary) at Catull. 17.6, and the Palatine college of Salii at Rome was associated with him. One may compare θόρε addressed to Zeus in the hymn of the Curetes (Powell, *CA* 161) 47; he is to leap to the herds and fields to protect them. The Curetes of course are also dancing priests. The Semones are a group (hence *conctos*) of obviously agricultural deities (from *sero, semen*; Leumann 371 compares *semen - semo* with *termen - termo*); we find mention of a *Salus Semonia* (i.e. the protecting power of the *Semones*) and of a *Semo Sancus*.

The question has been raised whether 10-12 is meant to be part of the text of the song or was a rubric in the *libelli* intended to give an instruction for performance but wrongly incorporated as part of the text. The latter alternative may be supported by Verg. *Buc.* 3.58-9

incipe Damoeta, tu deinde sequere, Menalca;
alternis dicetis; amant alterna Camenae.

One may compare the performance instruction at the end of the psalm (ch.3) of Habakkuk, 3.19 in the Authorised Version 'To the chief singer on my stringed instruments' (cut out of some versions). On the former hypothesis, the chorus-leader gives instructions to his colleagues to call antiphonally on the names of the Semones, not recorded as part of the text.

The assonance *lue rue* is of a type common in religious and magical formulae; a close parallel is λιμὸς καὶ λοιμός (Hes. *Op.* 243, where see West, and two oracles in Parke - Wormell, *The Delphic Oracle, Responses* 261.1, 487.13 etc.; see also Plut. *De Fort. Rom.* 322 A). For assonant pairs of supernatural entities in general see West on Hes. *Theog.* 135. Cf. Verg. *Aen.* 3.138-9 *miserandaque uenit / arboribusque satisque lues*, Livy 4.21.3 *pestilentia populum inuasit...ruere in agris nuntiabantur tecta*, Lucan 2.199-200 *subitaeque ruinae / aut terrae caelique lues*. The combination may be compared to *uiduertatem uastitudinemque* in Cato.

For threefold repetitions in religious contexts cf. Norden 242, HS 810-11, Weinreich 2.250; see instances in J. W. Poultney, *The Bronze Tables of Iguvium* (1959), pp. 164, 198, 276. Horace, *Odes* 4.2.50 states that the shout *io triump(h)e* will go up *non semel*, and some emend 49 to specify this to *ter*. The verb *tripodare* describes a ritual dance in which each movement is thrice repeated.

The word *triumpe* is usually related to θρίαμβος (so first Varro, *LL* 6.68, but tentatively), and the first element of this is often linked with τρίς, 'thrice' (the five-fold repetition of the ritual cry here is unexplained). The exact nature of the relationship is disputed (the question is best surveyed by H. S. Versnel, *Triumphus* (1970), 11-55):
(1) The Greek word may have been mediated through Etruscan; so e.g. Bonfante Warren in *Studies in Honor of J. A. Kerns* (Janua Linguarum 44, 1970), 108 = *Out of Etruria* (1981) 93, and in *JRS* 60 (1970), 52.
(2) The word came from Etruscan, but was independently derived by that and Greek from a pre-Greek Aegean language.
(3) It came from the Greeks of south Italy. In form *triumpe* may be

an Etruscan nominative or a vocative, but in any case it is quite likely that it came to Rome first as an inarticulate shout and only later, taken as a vocative, re-created a declined noun *triumpus*. Similarly the cry ἰὼ Βάκχε produced a noun Iobacchos, and the same doubtless happened with e.g. ὑμέναιε and Ἴακχε ; Versnel 32 suggests the same for θρίαμβε itself.

That leads on to the question of the date of this song. A priori one would think that it belongs to the very earliest days of Rome, a conclusion perhaps encouraged by the apparent dialectal forms, but theories (1) and (2) of *triumpe* (which still seem more probable to me than (3)), would seem to put it after the Etruscan takeover symbolised by the elder Tarquin. This hardly appears to be a great problem; cultural influence does not have to imply political domination.

2

CLE 2 = *CIL* 1.364 = 11.3078, 7483 = *ILS* 3083 = *ILLRP* 192 = *Corpus Inscr. Etruscarum* 8341 = G. Giacomelli, *La Lingua Falisca* (1963), p. 264 = E. Pulgram, *Italic, Latin, Italian* (1978), pp. 205-7.

Photo: *CIL* 1.364, 11. 7483; *Imagines* 93; *CIE*; Diehl, *Tabulae* 3 a-b; Peruzzi (see below).

Discussions: *CIL* 1.2.4 p. 877; Linderski, *PP* 13 (1958), 47; Peruzzi, *Atti e Memorie dell' Accademia Toscana, La Columbaria* 31 = n.s. 17 (1966), 113; Wachter 441.

Translation into classical Latin: collegium quod est acceptum aetati agendae, opiparum ad uitam colendam festosque dies, qui suis astutiis opeque Volcani condecorant saepissime conuiuia ludosque, coci hoc dederunt imperatoribus summis, ut sese lubentes bene iuuent optantes.

This is a bronze tablet with the first (as I present it) prose inscription on one side and the second verse one on the other, found at Falerii novi, which was established on the plain after the destruction of the original Falerii on its hill site in 241 B.C. as punishment for a revolt. The two inscriptions seem to be of the same date and even probably by the same engraver, but it is puzzling that, since the tablet was attached by four nails to the dedicated object, it would have been possible to read only one side. Therefore it is suggested that the verse inscription, which, apart from its errors, is uncomfortably crowded, was discarded and the other side of the tablet was re-used for the prose inscription. This conclusion is confirmed by the fact that the nails were driven in from the prose side (*coiraueront* is inset because the positioning of this was foreseen), and it removes the problem of having to assume the presence of a whole collegium of Faliscan cooks in Sardinia, made a province in 238. If the collegium was at Falerii itself, we may compare the collegium of *coques atriensis Fortunae Primigeniae* at Praeneste (*CIL* 1.1447 = 14.2875 = *ILS* 3683a = *ILLRP* 104), i.e. cooks who assembled in the atrium of the temple of Fortuna, or were perhaps attached to the temple for the sacrifices (Jerome, *Adv. Iovinianum* 2.29 *sunt et culinae in templis*). The *inperatores summi* are the gods to whom the dedication is made (cf. *TLL* vii.1.554.21), probably the triad listed on the reverse; this triad must have belonged to a Capitol at Falerii. A temple found at Falerii veteres used to be thought to have a triple cella (Stefani, *NS* 1947, 73), but see now A. Comella, *I materiali votivi di Falerii* (1986), 180. This tablet was found with half of another dedicatory tablet to Minerva (*CIL* 1.365 = 11.3081 = *CIE* 8340 = *ILS* 3124 = *ILLRP* 238 = Giacomelli p. 68 = Pulgram p.207). In later times the Faliscan cult of Juno outshone the others.

A note of warning should be added about the above deductions, in that some bronze tablets, both Greek and Latin, read continuously from front to back and yet have nail-holes, which cannot always be plausibly attributed to fastening in a frame (πλαίσιον). The problem which this presents seems to be still unresolved.

In the second century B.C. (see 'Language' for this date), as in classical Athens, cooks were not domestic servants but independent professionals who were hired for special occasions, as still happens in Juv. 7.185; cf. Pliny, *NH* 18.108 *cocos uero habebant in seruitiis, eosque ex macello conducebant* (talking about c. 175 B.C.), Livy 39.6.9 *tum coquos, uilissimum antiquis mancipium et aestimatione et usu, in pretio esse, et quod ministerium fuerat, ars haberi coepta* (187 B.C.). Bücheler points out that Faliscan cooks must have invented the recipe for *Falisci* or the *Faliscus uenter*, a kind of sausage (Varro, *LL* 5.111, Mart. 4.46.8, Stat. *Silv.* 4.9.35).

These cooks know their Plautus, and play up to their traditional comic type-casting as pretentious boasters. For the grand *opid Volgani* cf. Plaut. *Aul.* 359 *Volcano studes* (said to the cook Congrio), *Men.* 330 *ego haec appono ad Volcani uiolentiam* (said by the cook

Cylindrus), Alexis 149.14 Kock; Bücheler also quotes Vespa, *Iudicium Coci et Pistoris* (*AL* 199) 8 *hic est Vulcanus iudex, qui nouit utrosque.* Note too e.g. Plaut. *Most.* 728 *musice hercle agitis aetatem...uino et uictu...uitam colitis*. The word *opiparus* is not found between Plautus and Apuleius, though the adverb struck somewhat deeper roots in colloquial Latin. At the same time this boasting also conveys an advertisement.

Language

The double consonant in *summeis* and the spelling *aetas* for *aitas* give a terminus post quem of the early second century B.C. The marking of the long vowel with *aa* in *aastutieis* (this reading can now be taken as assured) and *uiitam* bring us down into the second half of the second century. These spellings jostle with *aciptum, saipisume* and *comuiuia*, though there seems to be a balance between *ui̯itam festosque dies* and *comui̯uia loidosque*. Other forms give a patina of antiquity; *opid* and *sesed, soueis* = Homeric ἑ(ϝ)οῖς = *sewois (cf. 16.2, 17.4). For *loidos* cf. *coiraueront* in the prose inscription; for *huc* = *hoc, TLL* vi.3.2697.6; for the nominative plural *optantis* 32.30, Leumann 440, Sommer 382, NW ii.60, Nyman, *Glotta* 68 (1990), 216; for the ablative *opi(d)* in a consonant-stem 12.4, 43.5, 115.1, Leumann 436, Sommer 375, Wachter 297 § 122d and n.78 (sometimes perhaps to differentiate between e.g. *ope* and *ope(m)*); for *qu<o>quei, quol Undam* (this contrasts with *agE(n)dai*, for which see on 71) Leumann 137, SP 126. *gonlegium* (contrasted with *comuiuia*), *Volgani, gondecorant* (which has both *g* and *c*; we should have expected a point to be made with *condecorant conuiuia*) appear not to be due to any dialectal substratum underlying the Latin imposed on Falerii noui but to represent the engraver's own pronunciation. For *comuiuia* (*CLE* 1186.8) cf. *comuouise* in the *SC de Bacanalibus*, but both are probably etymological rather than phonetic spellings; *aciptum* is also probably etymological (as in *accipio*), cf. the converse *uootum...cuncaptum* on the dedicatory tablet to Minerva mentioned above.

Metre

This dedication is clearly intended to be in Saturnians, but shows many irregularities commented on in the metrical introduction. In 5, which seems to be a five-element followed by an eight-element colon, it is probably without significance that the tablet actually has *inperato.ribus*. Peruzzi 145-6 points out that the 'regular' Saturnian 6 is also a formulaic line which could have been taken over from other dedications (for *bene iouent* cf. Plaut. *Pers.* 755, Livy 29.27.2). Note how alternate lines are inset, as if elegiacs were being engraved.

3

CLE 3 = *CIL* 1.626 = 6.331 = *ILS* 20 = *ILLRP* 122

Photo: Strong, *JRS* 29 (1939), 143; *Imagines* 61; Gordon, *Introduction* pl. 7; Calabi Limentani 271 pl. 61; A. M. Colini, *Storia e Topografia del Celio* (Mem. Pontif. Accad., ser. 3, 7 (1944)) 41; Colonna tav. 10; Bassi tav. xxxv.97; Almar 23.

Discussion: *CIL* 1.2.4 p.921.

Mummius razed Corinth in 146 and triumphed in 145 (*MRR* 1.465, 470; 3.146). This stone was found on the Caelian hill (though it had been reused and was not on its original site), where the shrine was probably built. The stone (.55 metres horizontal, .60 vertical) and its writing are small (only *Herculis Victoris* is in larger letters), and, as Jordan, *Hermes* 14 (1879), 573-5 points out, it could never have been the inscription on the front of a proper temple. He concludes that the shrine was just an *aedicula* (cf. 38.9), and that the inscription comes from a statue-base, comparing *CIL* 1.1503 = 10.5961 = *ILS* 5440 = *ILLRP* 135. The shrine was apparently dedicated in 142 B.C., when Mummius was censor (*MRR* 1.474; Livy 53 *periocha*; Plut. *Praec. rei p. gerendae* 20.816c, though he has garbled the story, as A. E. Astin, *Scipio Aemilianus* (1967), 121 indicates). Ziolkowski, *Phoenix* 42 (1988), 309, agreeing that the stone could not have been the inscription on a temple, thinks that it comes from one of the lesser monuments of Mummius but that it refers to a round temple (about 15 metres in diameter) by the Tiber in the Forum Boarium area; this seems improbable. We have specimens of votive inscriptions in Saturnians set up by conquering generals in temples (see 4-5 below, and also in prose Livy 41.28.8-9), and it is natural that there are coincidences in phraseology; cf. Livy 40.52.5 *auspicio imperio felicitate ductuque eius*, 41.28.8-9 *Ti. Semproni Gracchi consulis imperio auspicioque legio exercitusque populi R. Sardiniam subegit...re p. felicissime gesta...triumphans in urbem Romam rediit* (Plautus mimics the vocabulary at *Amph.* 196 *ductu imperio auspicio suo*). This inscription also shows the habit of conveying the achievements in ablatives absolute (Fraenkel 228 with addenda; cf. 5d below).

Unless the ordinator has made a mistake, *Corinthus* is masculine, as it is sometimes in Greek (LSJ s.v.); on another inscription of Mummius we have *<Co>rintho capta* (*CIL* 1.630 = *ILLRP* 331), but in his addenda Degrassi states that the lettering is not contemporary, and moreover the inscription is restored otherwise by Canto, *Epigraphica* 47 (1985), 9. A neuter form *Corinthum* is a variant at Livy 33.31.11 (not mentioned in the OCT), but is very unlikely to be right. Prop. 3.5.6. is not a reliable instance of the masculine. Note *Corinto* but *Achaia* and *triumphans* (contrast *triumpum* 4.5); the aspirate was just coming in in such cases, and in fact the only earlier occurrence is on *CIL* 1.2940 = *ILLRP* 1283 (vol. 1 p. 308).

Formal grammar might prefer *suo* to *eius*; for the spelling *redieit* see on 9 Metre and Leumann 600, 607.

The recovery of the stone of *CLE* 248 has proved that that has nothing to do with Mummius; see no. 7 below.

'Metre'

This is usually supposed to be in Saturnians, but the stone does not in any way indicate verse, if it is Saturnians they show various abnormalities, and there is an odd number (9) of cola, which never happens in Saturnians. I think that this is prose, but nevertheless have felt it necessary to include it.

4

CLE 1859 = *CIL* 1.652 = 5.39*, 8270 = *ILS* 8885 = *ILLRP* 335 = *IIt* 10.4.317, 13.3.no. 90 with photo p. 74 = J. (=G.) B. Brusin, *Inscriptiones Aquileiae* (1991) 28 with photo

Photo: *Imagines* 147; *CIL* 1.652; Calabi Limentani 240 no. 44; Reisch (see below) 278-9; A. Rostagni, *La Letteratura di Roma repubblicano ed Augustea* (1940), tav. vi facing p. 96, and *Storia della Letteratura Latina* 1 (1954), 247; Brusin (see below) fig. 1.

Discussion: *CIL* 1.2.4 p.926 ; Bücheler, *Rh. Mus.* 63 (1908), 321; Reisch, *JÖAI* 11 (1908), 276; Birt, *Rh. Mus.* 73 (1920), 306; Brusin, *Aquileia Nostra* 33 (1968), 15; Morgan, *Philol.* 117 (1973), 40; G. Bandelli, *Ricerche sulla Colonizzazione romana della Gallia cisalpina* (1988), 78 and *Antichità Altoadriatiche* 35 (*Aquileia repubblicana e imperiale*, 1989), 111.

This inscription was found near Aquileia in two pieces, each damaged on the left; our ignorance of the size of the lost portions and the elasticity of the Saturnian metre in which this was clearly written deprive us of sure foundations for restoration, which has often been applied with great rashness. However Bücheler's reconstruction of the beginning of 5 has much plausibility (it contrasts the site of the celebration with that of this titulus); he suggested that *Romae* was preceded by something like *ita*. For 3 he suggested *diebus te]r*, which goes well with the insistence which we find elsewhere on the brevity of campaigns (Morgan 41 n.64, Bandelli (1989) 121 n. 51); for the numerical periphrasis at this early date cf. Plaut. *Pseud.* 345, Lucil. 107. An improvement rhythmically would be to insert e.g. *quos* after *diebus*; then the rest of the line might be e.g. *qua[ter ibei fug]auit*. Bücheler's supplement in 4, printed above, also seems very appropriate; he compared Hor. *Odes* 4.4.23 *cateruae consiliis iuuenis reuictae*. In 6 he proposed *sacra pat]ria ei restitu[it et magist]reis tradit* (Birt suggested *aes* in place of *et*), and nothing better has been put forward though a precise explanation of *sacra patria* is not given (the obvious *dona]ria* seems much too short); it is no doubt presumed that plunderers took dedicated objects. At the ends of 3-6 the letters indicated have been folded round on to the side of the stone; see Vine 303.

C. Sempronius Tuditanus was consul in 129 B.C. and on 1 October of that year celebrated a triumph *de Iapudibus* (*MRR* 1.504, 3.190). This stone might be part of the base of the statue mentioned by Pliny, *NH* 3.129 *Tuditanus, qui domuit Histros, in statua sua ibi inscripsit ab Aquileia ad Titium flumen stadia M<?M>*, but Pliny's report is more likely to be part of an inscription of Tuditanus found near the mouth of the Timavus (*CIL* 1.2503 = *ILLRP* 334 = *IIt* 10.4.317); see on this Cuscito in *Antichità Altoadriatiche* 10 (1976), 53. In the same place as that was found *CIL* 1.2647 = *ILLRP* 261 = *IIt* 10.4.318 *Temauo uoto [suscep]to*; for the cult of the Timavus, which had some sort of shrine there, cf. Strabo 5.1.8.214, *CIL* 1.2195 (= *ILLRP* 262), 3416, *AE* 1990.391. Aquileia would have been an obvious base for an advance into Illyria; hence the presence of the inscription of Tuditanus there. Ennius, *Ann.* 305 scans *Tudītanus*, and (despite Skutsch there), it is unnecessary to postulate *Tudĭtanus* here; the line was probably like e.g. 9.1b, 12.1b.

For the historic present in 6 after the perfect cf. 10.6.

As regards metre, it is unusual to have a seven-element colon in the second half of the line, as apparently in 5 unless a monosyllable such as *hoc*] is to be supplied (for the consequent hiatus at the diaeresis cf. 12.5).

5*

Here I collect literary references to other Saturnian so-called tabulae triumphales.

a Aemilius Regillus celebrated a triumph in 189 B.C. for the victory of Myonessus won in 190 (*MRR* 1.356, 362); the whole inscription is paraphrased by Livy 40.52.5 (the lost Mainz manuscript, our only source for this part of the text, has garbled whatever Livy wrote for this line).

Acilius Glabrio celebrated a triumph in 190 for the victory of Thermopylae won in 191 (*MRR* 1.352, 3.2), cf. Livy 40.34.5-6. *fundit fugat* is one of the alliterative pairs in which Latin is rich (Wölfflin 261). For the general style cf. Naevius 39 Morel *insulam integram / urit, uastat, populatur, rem hostium concinnat* (text uncertain in detail), Cic. *Phil.* 14.27 *hostesque...prostrauit fudit occidit*. For *legiones* applied to non-Roman forces cf. Cato ap. Gell. 15.9.5 etc.

In Caesius Bassus *apud nostros* is contrasted with Greek 'saturnians'. He is wrong with *triumphaturi*, since Livy explicitly states that the temples to which these inscriptions were attached were dedicated respectively 10 and 9 years after the triumphs. He is also wrong with *in Capitolio*; for Livy's phrase (40.52.7) *eodem exemplo tabula in aede Iouis in Capitolio supra ualuas fixa est*, which does not mean an exact copy but 'after the same pattern', see H. Roth, *Untersuchungen über die lat. Weihgedichte* (1935), 29 n.14. These are all votive inscriptions, not triumphal (Roth 28).

b This verse, quoted also by Diomedes, *GLK* 1.512, shows a striking alliteration of *r*. Cf. Prop. 3.3.44 *Teutonicas Roma refringat opes*.

All of these verses are standard Saturnians, with *duello* scanned as a spondee.

The Scholia Bobiensia to Cic. *Pro Archia* 27 (p. 179 Stangl) mention saturnians composed by Accius to commemorate the triumph won by D. Iunius Brutus (Callaicus) for his campaigns in 138-6 B.C. (cf. Cic. l.c., Val. Max. 8.14.2).

6

CLE 4 = *CIL* 1.1531 = 10.5708 = *ILS* 3411 = *ILLRP* 136.
Photo: Panciera, *Epigraphica* 29 (1967), 57 fig. 11.
Discussion: *CIL* 1.2.4 p. 1003.

This came from the neighbourhood of Sora. Gaius Vertuleius (for the name on other inscriptions from Sora cf. *CIL* 10. 5731, 5757) had met with disaster in his business, and vowed a tithe to Hercules if it should recover. When it did so, after his death his sons Marcus and Publius discharge the vow. The offering of a tithe to Hercules, a protector of commerce (see on 101), was a traditional measure, imported from Greece (*RE, Hercules* 567, Wissowa 277, Latte 215, Ruggiero, *Hercules* 694, J. Bayet, *Les Origines de l'Hercule Romain* (1926), 326, Evans 74-6, Bodei Giglioni, *Riv. Stor. Ital.* 89 (1977), 51-4, Pease on Cic. *De N. D.* 3.88, G. Dumezil, *Archaic Roman Religion* (Eng. tr. 1970), 437). *Pollucere* means to give part of a sacrifice to a god, while the rest is given to the participants in the sacrifice; this latter is called *profanare*, and *pollucere decumam* is the other side of *profanare decumam*. Here *decuma facta poloucta* (the participles in asyndeton, as often in formal expressions) means that the tithe had duly been given to Hercules in the form of money, and the money had been used for the sacrifice and the ceremonial meal. Other inscriptions like this are *ILLRP* 134 (= *ILS* 3412), 142?, 155, *ILS* 3413, *CLE* 5 = *CIL* 1.1805 = 9.3569 (Bücheler there also quotes *CIL* 9.4071a) and the next poem here. For other parallels see Naevius, *com.* 27 CRF (p. 210 Marmorale) *qui decimas partes? quantum <mi> alieni fuit / polluxi{t} tibi iam publicando epulo Herculis / decimas*; Plaut. *Stich.* 233 *ut decumam partem Herculi polluceam*; Masurius Sabinus ap. Macrob. *Sat.* 3.6.11 *M. Octauius Hersennus, prima adulescentia tibicen, postquam arti suae diffisus est, instituit mercaturam et bene re gesta decimam Herculi profanauit* (cf. DServ. *Aen.* 8.363); Festus 253 *pollucere...merces liceat...Herculi autem omnia esculenta, posculenta.*

The alliterations in the second halves of the lines are striking; so too is the assonance *parens timens*.

For the form of the nominative plural in *Vertuleieis* and *leibereis* cf. *magistreis* in the prose of 2 and Leumann 427, Sommer 346; Vine 218 points out that here, as often, it refers to two individuals. For *Hercolei* see Leumann 86; for *mereto* 9.6, Leumann 84, SP 84. *Semol* = *simul* (a form due to the analogy of *similis*), cf. the form *co(n)sol* in 9-10; the mss. of Plautus sometimes offer *semul*. The diphthongs in *afleicta* and *poloucta* seem to indicate vowel length before *ct*. Altogether the

orthography suggests a date around 150 B.C.
1 C. Vertuleius was embittered (*asper*) by his misfortunes. Bücheler compared Verg. *Aen.* 8.364 *te quoque dignum / finge deo rebusque ueni non asper egenis,* said by Evander exhorting Aeneas not to spurn the humble hospitality which had been acceptable to Hercules. This notably close parallel might have drawn the attention of editors of Vergil and deterred epigraphists from wishing to see an error or abbreviation in *asper.*
2 *heic* = at this very altar.
5 For *uoti condemnare* cf. *TLL* iv.124.72, to which *CIL* 2.1044 should be added; *damnare* is commoner. The line is a paradox; normally one does not ask to be frequently condemned, but if one is condemned to pay a vow, then the god has granted one's request. Fraenkel 437 compares *CEG* 227 = Geffcken 12 = *IG* 1 (ed. 3) 728 and literary parallels.

Metre

The Saturnians are not written as verse, but the lines of verse are separated by intervals on the stone, as in 11 and 19. 3 is a standard Saturnian line; in all the other lines the second colon is of five elements.

7

CLE 248 = *CIL* 1.632 = 9.4672 (cf. p. 684) = *ILS* 3410 = *ILLRP* 149 = A. M. Reggioni, *Rieti, Museo Civico* (1981), 50 no. 87 = A. M. R., *Museo Civico di Rieti* (1990) 68 no. 115
Photo: *Imagines* 71; Evans (pl. III 1) and Giglioli (see below); Reggioni (1981) tav. xxvi, (1990) tav. xxxiv; C. Pietrangeli and others, *Rieti e il suo territorio* (1976), 118.
Discussion: *CIL* 1.2.4 p. 922; Evans 69 (confused); Giglioli, *Athen.* 28 (1950), 267; Riposati, *Epigraphica* 12 (1950), 137; Bass, *MEFRA* 97 (1985), 295 with fig. 2 p. 298.

This hexameter poem is placed here because of its connection in subject with the preceding. The stone was discovered at Reate in the fifteenth century, lost in the seventeenth, and rediscovered in the twentieth. While it was lost most scholars (with Dessau and Wissowa notable exceptions) overrode the evidence, read *Mummius* in the first line (and took *uictor* as nominative), and related it to 3; this can now be rejected. For the name *Munius* cf. Schulze 195, 362,

424; Giglioli 270 n.2.; Bass 307. He was evidently a banker, who jokingly alludes to his profession by presenting this dedication 'as interest' (*pro usura* Cic. 2 *Verr*. 3.168); in return he asks the god to make easy work of bringing in the money and paying it out (Bass 308 draws attention to the title of an Atellan by Novius, *Hercules coactor*), and also to supervise the correctness of Munius' calculation of what is due as a tithe, so that the god is not cheated of his due. The *do ut des* character of Roman religion is well illustrated by the antithesis *perfecit...ut faxseis*)(*perficias ut faciat*.

For the title Hercules Victor cf. 3.4 etc. For *sancte* as a title of this god cf. *CIL* 1.2.4 p.922, Roscher, *Sanctus* 311, Evans 72 n.1, H. Delehaye, *Sanctus* (1927), 15-16 (often wrongly altered at Prop. 4.9.71-2). *Tibei* keeps its original spelling, though iambic shortening has now reduced it to a pyrrhic, cf. 13.3, 20.4, Leumann 462, Sommer 410. A famous line of Ennius (*Ann.* 156) begins *moribus antiquis*; this is probably not a deliberate allusion, but simply means that Munius regards the custom of giving a tithe as long-established. 1-3 must mean 'L. Munius has achieved what he had decided in his mind, namely that he should give this gift to you, Victor, according to ancient custom as interest from a tithe'. For *tua pace* cf. *CLE* 5 = *CIL* 1.1805 = 9.3569 (another tithe inscription) *quei tou(am?...) pacem petit...adiouta*; 'of your indulgence'. The syntax of 4 is mysterious (the genitives seem to lie in the general area covered by HS 75), but it must mean what is indicated by the vernacular paraphrase given above. The metre is also problematical; he either intended the substitution of a proceleusmatic for a dactyl in *facilia* (perhaps following Ennius' *capitibus*) or the syncope *faclia* (with which one may compare *ful(i)ca* restored in Furius Antias fr. 4 and other examples in my note on Juv. 3.361; according to Wachter § 94 i *uiglias* on *CIL* 1.1466 = *ILLRP* 653 is probably an error). 2 is also defective, since there must be a hiatus either before or after *usura*; in 3 *suo* and *tua* are monosyllables (see Metre I 1). The metrical and syntactical problems of 2 combine to give colour to suggestions that in the cutting somehow a finite verb in this line has been eliminated, e.g. *usura* <*auet*> Stowasser, *WS* 25 (1903), 261 (with a full stop at the end). There is stylisation in the etymological figure *facilia faxseis* (cf. 11.5) and the alliteration of *d* in 6. The long I in *donIs* dates this inscription not much earlier, if at all, than the first century B.C. (cf. 18.4). On the other hand the scansion *Luciu' Muniu'* in urbane poetry at any rate is not found later than the middle of that century.

The brackets indicate trimming of the rediscovered stone; before its loss it could be read complete. Originally there were relief sculptures on either side of the inscription, which even in the fifteenth century were badly damaged; they were cut away in the seventeenth. The descriptions of these by the humanists are rather vague (reported in *CIL* 9), but they state that one was of Hercules with eight Muses (he is shown on an Athenian relief with eight women; *Lex. Icon.* s.v. Herakles no. 1480, illustrated p. 815, Cumont, *Recherches* pl. 25.1 facing p. 296); he carried his club and the typical lion-skin on his head, but was dressed in a transparent robe which they described as of feminine type (Ligorio's drawing is reproduced by Bass, fig. 3 p. 303). This is interpreted by van Berchem, *Syria* 44 (1967), 317-9 as the dress of the priests of the Phoenician Melqart, who was equated with Heracles, transferred to the god himself (hence the story of the transvestism of Heracles in the service of Omphale); van Berchem also adduces a relief from Tibur (Bass, fig. 5 p.318). However, whatever may be the case concerning Phoenician (i.e. Carthaginian) influence in archaic Rome, it can hardly be postulated in Rieti c. 100 B.C. It is hard to know what to make of the statement by John Laurentius the Lydian, *De Mensibus* 4.46 (67), p. 120 Wuensch, that men dressed as women at the April festival of Hercules Victor.

The stone is slightly convex, and in the fifteenth century formed part of a whole hollow circle, so the gift of Munius was a *puteal*, a surround for a well.

8

CLE 11 = *CIL* 1.1202 = 6.13696, cf. 34072 = *ILS* 8121 = *ILLRP* 970.
Photo: J. Ripostelli - H. Marucchi, *La Via Appia* (ed. 2, 1908), 250; Almar 15.

Found at Rome on the Appian way, where it still stands. *Maarco* is not on the same level as *seedes*, but represents an Oscan spelling taken into Greek too (Leumann 13, Lazzeroni, *ASNSP* 25 (1956), 132). The spelling *seedes* indicates a date in the range 135-75 B.C. For *qura* see Leumann 10, SP 31, *TLL* iv.1451.76, 1496.47, *CLE* 2092.1. *meas seedes* = my grave, cf. 22.1; so this sense is not first found in Vergil, as Norden on *Aen.* 6.152 says.

This inscription imports the Greek habit of addressing the passer-by as ξεῖνος (cf. 17.1, 18.1 etc.; Lattimore 230); *hospes resiste* is a common beginning of epitaphs. For the final good wishes cf.

ualebis hospes, *CLE* 62.4, 63.7, *ualeas uiator*, *CLE* 112.10, *sine omni cura dormias* Plaut. *Trin.* 621. Cf. also *CEG* 110 = *GVI* 62 τὺ δ' εὖ πρᾶσ', [ὀ̑] παροδο̑τα.

Metre

Each line of verse is split into two lines of writing with the second in each case inset; in 1 and 3, but not in 2, the break comes at the end of a metrical colon.

2-3 are standard Saturnians, 1 would be except that the need to include the name upsets the pattern, as often in inscriptions (see p. 23). No attempt should be made to analyse *Maarco Caicilio* as any type of colon. I assume that *meas* 2a is monosyllabic.

I B: THE SCIPIO EPITAPHS

Unlike most aristocratic families at Rome, the Cornelii until Sulla maintained the tradition of being inhumed, not cremated (Cic. *De. Leg.* 2.56, Pliny, *NH* 7.187). An early tomb (of the late fourth - early third century) belonging to them has been discovered (Blank, *Röm. Mitt.* 73-4 (1966-7), 72; Solin, *Arctos* 6 (1970), 110), but the epitaphs with which we are concerned come from a hypogeum on the Appian way (begun 312) outside the Porta Capena (Cic. *Tusc.* 1.13) but inside the subsequent Aurelian wall. This was discovered in the seventeenth century, rediscovered and excavated in the eighteenth (the names of Piranesi and Visconti are associated with the later occasion). Restoration was carried out in 1926; earlier descriptions are in some respects misleading. The most comprehensive account is by F. Coarelli, *Dial. di Arch.* 6 (1972), 36 (also published separately as *Il Sepolcro degli Scipioni*); see also Nash 2.352-6, and, for a fresco on the tomb, Cambridge Ancient History, plates 4 pp. 82-3 b, J. D. Evans, *The Art of Persuasion* (1992), 10.

The family tree, as far as concerns those members with whom we shall be dealing, is this, with the probable subjects of epitaphs (not all in verse) in italics:

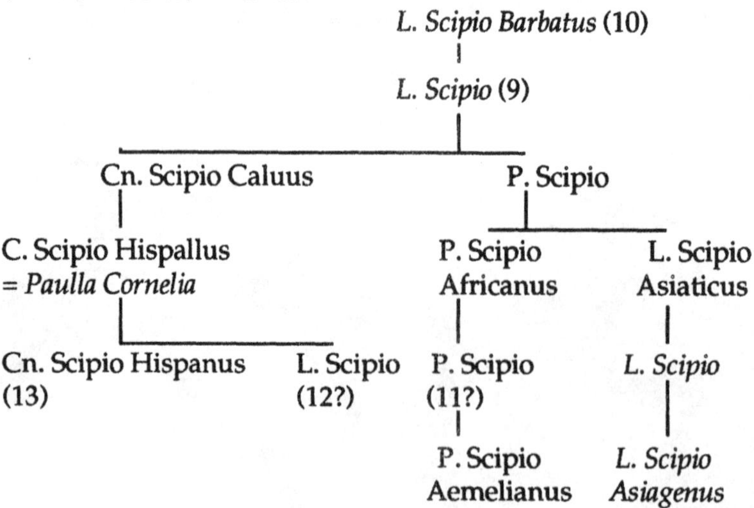

The burials therefore extend c. 240 B.C. - c. 130 B. C. The latest are probably those of Scipio Hispanus and his mother; her sarcophagus was squeezed behind that of Barbatus, with the back wall of the latter acting as the front of hers. By this time there were over thirty burials in the main tomb, so a lateral gallery at an angle to the main chamber was added in which there were six or seven subsequent burials. This is the time of the revival of the Scipio glory with Aemilianus, and it seems to have been then that a monumental facade was added, facing north towards the city not on the side of the Appian Way but of a minor road connecting the Appia with the Latina. At the lowest level of this facade there were three arches, of which the central was the entrance to the main chamber, the right that to the side-gallery, and the left that to a round chamber with an exhedra, not used for burial. Above this level probably stood the three marble statues supposed to be of Africanus (who was buried not at Rome but at Liternum), Asiaticus and Ennius (Livy 38.55-6, whose expressions seem to indicate that these identifications were merely guess-work). Coarelli fig. D-E shows this facade in its actual state and as reconstructed by him, but a warning is needed that the above account, based on him, is not without its difficulties (in particular the three arches are not placed symmetrically), and Lauter-Bufe, *Röm. Mitteil.* 89 (1982), 35 prefers to date the facade to early in the second century; in that case the lack of symmetry may be due to the fact that the entry to the lateral gallery was a subsequent addition.

This hypogeum was intended not just as a burial-site but also as a monument to the family glory. As one entered the central door to the main square chamber, directly in front at the far end was the sarcophagus of Barbatus, the only one with any decoration; it is in the form of an altar, with volutes, triglyphs and rosettes. Consistently with this, the later inscription, like that on the sarcophagus of his son, speaks to the Romans (*apud uos*). The tomb was no doubt constructed by Barbatus himself in anticipation of his death or by his son. In the first century A.D. the tomb was reused by the Cornelii Lentuli for urn-burials.

To understand this monument one must start from the firmly-established basis that the poetical inscription of Barbatus is younger than that of his son. This is established by the forms of some words (see below), but more particularly by the shapes of the letters L and P; in the son's inscription the bottom stroke of the former is turned sharply upwards and the second stroke of the latter is rectangular, not rounded, both in the antique style. On the front side of the top face each has a simple painted identification presenting the nominative *Cornelio*, which in the case of Barbatus at least (note the forms in line 1) is more antique than the morphology in the verse. On the front face each has a poem, but on the sarcophagus of Barbatus this begins in the middle of a line and is preceded by a line and a half which has been erased. In this erasure Hülsen read <*c*>*eso*<*r*>; the inference has been drawn that a cursus honorum stood there. From this the following sequence has been constructed:

1) Sarcophagi with a painted inscription of the name and, in the case of the son, a cursus honorum.
2) Addition of an incised cursus to the sarcophagus of Barbatus
3) Addition of a poem to the sarcophagus of his son
4) Replacement of the cursus on the sarcophagus of Barbatus by a similar poem.

Underlying this was the assumption that stage 1 represented the original Roman simplicity, and that we should see neat stages of progressive elaboration. That notion has been weakened by the discovery of the earlier tomb of the Cornelii with two simple but incised inscriptions, including mention of the office of pontifex maximus (cf. *ILLRP* 1274a, *CIL* 1.4.2835 p. 861 and tav. 3.6; illustrated also *Roma medio repubblicana* (1977), tav. li.372, cf. p. 240). Moreover, nobody has ever been able to verify Hülsen's decipherment, and Wachter 320 correctly points out that before the first word *Cornelius* of the verse on the Barbatus inscription there stood in the erasure a dash like those which separate the Saturnian lines in the rest of the inscription. He argues (convincingly) that two Saturnian lines stood under the erasure and (unconvincingly) that these two lines were much like 9.1-2 and the Calatinus-inscription (see below); it does not seem to me that two such lines would fit on at all well to the beginning of this epitaph, or that they would sit well with 2-3. Wachter's argument about parallelism with 9 depends on keeping the improbable *filios* there and on the false assumption that 10.1-2 are in anacoluthon. Moreover he can give no reasonable explanation for the erasure (his attempts on 322 and 339 n.804). It seems simplest to me to assume that the mason made a mess of the first two lines and had to start again. The son must have died about 240 B.C., and we have no reason to date his sarcophagus any later, but the sculpture on that of Barbatus seems, at least to many, to forbid such an early date (some indeed find it difficult to put it before c. 150 B.C., which will import further complications), so we need to split the first stage above into two:

1a Sarcophagus of the son
1b Sarcophagus of Barbatus replacing original receptacle.

Stage 1b must represent a deliberate attempt to impress, and, if art history will permit this, one will be tempted to link it with the glory of the Scipiones at the end of the third century. The great Africanus himself was evidently buried in an altar-tomb (Sen. *Ep.* 86.1) but at Liternum, not at Rome, because of his withdrawal from the city (Livy 38.55.2 records confusion about this point, and such confusion can be seen in the rhetoric of Pliny, *NH* 7.114). One can hardly say that the attempt to impress is a complete success. The sarcophagus itself, doubtless executed by a Greek sculptor, is elegant, but the later inscription is awkward, with no consideration of horizontal alignment or symmetrical arrangement; the poem goes out to the right margin while leaving a considerable space on the left. The Romans were still unpractised in writing long inscriptions on tombs and grave-stones, and the Scipiones were among the first to have this done (see on 9.1-2 for Calatinus). It is characteristic of this family (see e.g. E. S. Gruen, *Culture and National Identity* (1992), 242-3 on Africanus) that we catch an atmosphere of Hellenising in a detail (see on 10.3), in the sculpture of the Barbatus sarcophagus, and in the aesthetic judgment that a bare recital of name and, in the case of the son, cursus seemed too dry and that poetic ornament was called for.

The upshot is that a very tentative absolute chronology might be something like this:

Construction of the tomb and of the sarcophagus of the son with painted inscription: by c. 240 B.C.

Sarcophagus of Barbatus with painted inscription, shortly before 200 B.C.

Addition of poem to sarcophagus of son (after 205 B.C., see on 9. 1-2) at the same time or soon after.

Addition of poem to sarcophagus of Barbatus, perhaps 186-5 B.C., when L. Scipio attempted to revive the sagging popularity of the family by giving magnificent games. The reason for not adding this poem simultaneously with that on the son's sarcophagus will have been the consciousness, discussed below, that Barbatus had not really much to his credit, whereas in 186-5 the family will have been ready to clutch at straws.

Construction of (? facade and) lateral gallery: c. 130 B.C.

The above presents what has been the usual view; this has been challenged by Wachter, who argues that the sarcophagus of Barbatus and the inscription on it are to be placed soon after his death and before those of his son. He challenges the epigraphic arguments based on the letters L and P, stating for instance that the latter in 10.5 is more angular than in 9.1, which on the photographs hardly seems to me to be the case. Altogether his arguments here (323-4) are weak, and in the end for 9 he has to resort to that disreputable device of desperate epigraphists, the elderly and old-fashioned mason (matched in this case with an old-fashioned poem). On the linguistic side he makes two fair points, the need to allow for archaism particularly in verse, and the paucity of securely dated evidence for the state of the language at any precise point. One can indeed argue e.g. that, in the light of *cepit*, *fuet* and *dedet* in 9 are archaisms, but the problem is that time and time again Wachter has to argue that things are the reverse of what they seem, too often to carry conviction. One must also remark that his account does not in any way help with the explanation of the problems of these epitaphs.

Discussion: Coarelli (see above); *CIL* 1.2.4 pp. 859-60; Wölfflin, *Rev. Phil.* 14 (1890), 119, *Sitzb. bay. Akad. München* 1892, 188; Zevi, *Stud. Misc.* 15 (1968-9), 69; Fraenkel, *Studi Urbinati* 31 (1957), 11-13; Till, *Festschrift K. Vretska* (1970), 276; Wachter 303; Van Sickle, *BICS* suppl. 51 (1988), 143.

9

CLE 6 = *CIL* 1.8-9 = 6.1286-7 = *ILS* 2-3 = *ILLRP* 310.
Photo: *Imagines* 133; Coarelli fig. 10-11 (drawing fig. F-G); Nash pl. 1130; Colonna tav. 9; Bassi tav. xxxiv.95.

L. Cornelius (*RE* no. 323) Scipio was consul in 259, censor in 258; it is unknown when he was aedile. While the offices are chronologically arranged in the prose, in the verse they are ordered according to the convention which, as often, puts the consulship first and the other two offices in reverse order; cf. 10.4, Mommsen 1.562 n.4, Cic. *De Fin.* 5.82 *Q. Metellus...cum ipse consul* (143 B.C.), *censor* (131), *augur* (before 140) *fuisset et triumphasset*. It is odd that Scipio's triumph in 258 for his victory in Corsica is not mentioned. Cf. *MRR* 1.206.

1 Cf. the beginning of the elogium of Atilius Calatinus, consul in 258 and 254, preserved by Cicero (*De Fin.* 2.116, *Cato* 61)

hunc unum plurimae   consentiunt gentes
populi primarium   fuisse uirum

(the first two words corrupt in Cicero's citations, and the spelling of course modernised); here with *gentes* (which can hardly mean 'races') we catch a hint of the family pride and emulation which the Scipio tomb suggests. The tomb of Calatinus was also outside the

Porta Capena, near that of the Scipiones (*De Fin.* l.c.,*Tusc.* 1.13). That was probably earlier than the present inscription, since this seems to recall the judgment passed on Scipio Nasica, the son of Scipio Calvus and grandson of our L. Scipio, in 205 B.C. when he was nominated to receive the Magna Mater into Rome; Livy 29.14.8 *P. Scipionem Cn. f....iudicauerunt in tota ciuitate uirum bon<or>um optimum esse.* It should be added that some scholars think that the relationship between this epitaph and the commendation of Nasica could be the opposite of that indicated by me, but it seems natural to suppose that the Calatinus formulation was adjusted into a reminder of a striking glory of the Scipiones. The supplement *R[omai* (rather than *R[omane(i)*) is commended by Livy's *in tota ciuitate* and ibid. 29.11.6 *qui uir optimus Romae esset.* For the antithesis *oino - ploirume* see Fraenkel on Aesch. *Ag.* 1455.
3 The nominative *filios* would have to go with what follows, but that would break up the verse, and it naturally goes with what precedes. Corroboration is supplied by the structure of the epitaph of Barbatus, which on the usual view imitates this (that is what justifies the supplement in 4); each has three lines for name and family, three for offices and achievements. Doubtless the executant was supplied with a script which had just *filio*, wrongly expanded by him. This would suggest that this was inscribed when the form *-os*, not *-us*, was still in currency; but of course this argument depends on a conjecture. J. Svennung, *Anredeformen* (1958), 257 retains the nominative but still links it with the preceding, comparing e.g. *CIL* 2.2054 for slippage back into the nominative, but none of his parallels is as stylized as this.
6 The dedication of this temple is mentioned by Ovid also, *Fasti* 6.193 *te quoque, Tempestas, MERITAM delubra fatemur*, and the Fasti Antiates (*ILLRP* 9 = *IIt* 13.2 p. 25, cf. p. 463); it was quite near the tomb of the Scipiones. Oddly enough the former puts the dedication on June 1, the latter on Dec. 23; the former date is probably that of a later restoration (see A. Ziolkowski, *The Temples of Mid-republican Rome* (1992), 162).

Language
aidiles, cosol, cesor contrast with *consol, censor, aidilis* in the verse, but one can hardly say that the forms of the prose are earlier than those of the verse (which has *cosentiont, Tempestatebus*). For *aidilEs* cf. Leumann 51, SP 57, Sommer 369 (similarly *TempestatEbus, merEtod*); for the omission of *n* Leumann 145-6, SP 103; for *co(n)sOl* on 6.5. *honc* = **homce*; *honce* is on *CIL* 1.366 = *ILS* 4911 = *ILLRP* 505.

oino, ploirume: In each of these *oi* was subsequently replaced by *ū*. Cic. *De Leg.* 3.9 seems to have *oenus* (*ones* codd.), which (according to the traditional explanation) is implicit in *noenum* = *ne-oenum* = *non*. The superlative of *plus* offers added complications (cf. 1.4a-6a, 16.2), for which see Leumann 496, Sommer 458; Cicero, *De Leg.* 3.6 evidently had no warrant for his pseudo-archaic *ploera*. For *-e* representing *-ei* cf. the prose of the Faliscan inscription (2 above), 11.4, 16.2, and perhaps *fuet* below; see Allen 53.
duonoro = *bonorum*, cf. *duello* 5.1 (Leumann 131, SP 169). For the termination cf. *ol[or]om*, *CIL* 1.25 = 6.1300 = *ILS* 65 = *ILLRP* 319 (i.e. *illorum*); the first declension **-āsom* caused the corresponding form to replace *-om* in the second.
uiro The Calatinus elogium makes it likely that this and *uirum* in Livy are accusative singular, not genitive plural.
Luciom Both in its first vowel and in the writing of *m* (cf. on 10.6) this is more modern than the rest of the inscription.
fuet, dedet but *cepit*; for *-et* (which is older; see below on metre) cf. *adouxet*, *CIL* 1.2443 (which also has *dedit*), Leumann 514, 606-7, Sommer 576-7.
hec is a form not found elsewhere, and contrasts with *hic* 4; it represents *hĭc* (as with *Tempestatebus* and *meretod*), not *he(i)c*, since *hīc* is not found until Lucilius. One notices an attempt at anaphora.
Tempestatebus cf. *nauebos* (perhaps a false archaism; Wachter 361) *CIL* 1.25 (cf. on 2) and *meretod* (cf. 6.4).

Metre
4 is a standard Saturnian if we scan *censōr* (above p. 21, 29) and *fŭēt*. Archaic Latin shows two terminations of the third person singular perfect indicative, *-ĕd* (which derives from an aorist) and *-eit* (*-īt*); though the latter survives sometimes even in classical Latin in the combination *-iīt* (cf. *redieit* in 3 above), both end up as *-ĭt*, the former via *-id* (cf. *fecid*, *CIL* 1.561) or *-et*. *-ēt* here might represent *-eit*, cf. *fuueit* or *fueit*, *CIL* 1.1297 = *ILS* 7998 = *ILLRP* 918. Another possibility might be that there is a lengthening due to metrical reasons, either analogous to the locus Jacobsohnianus in iambics and trochaics or like lengthenings due to the metrical beat in hexameters.

3a is irregular because the proper name has to be fitted in (cf. p. 23 and see Leo (above p. 28) 50). In 5 we are uncertain of the prosody of Aleria except that the second syllable is represented by epsilon. Attempts to stretch out 2 by adding a word are refuted by the Calatinus elogium and the considerable space after *uiro*.

10

CLE 7 = *CIL* 1.6-7 = 6.1284-5, 31587-8 = *ILS* 1 = *ILLRP* 309.

Photo: *Imagines* 132; Nash pl. 1131; Coarelli fig. 8-9 (drawing fig. H-I), fig. 5 (Piranesi's drawing); Gordon, *Introduction* pl. 5; Scamuzzi, *RSC* 5 (1957), 256; Diehl, *Tabulae* 4; Ireland 223 (photos often show this as it now stands in the Vatican Museum, with *Cornelius* wrongly restored in the painted prose inscription and an extraneous bust standing on top).

Discussion: E. Innocenti Prosdocimi, *Annali dell' Istituto di Storia, Università di Firenze* 2 (1980-1), 1; Radke, *Rh. Mus.* 134 (1991), 69 (both refer to other discussions).

It has been explained above why, in defiance of genealogical sequence, the epitaph of Barbatus has been placed after that of his son. Barbatus (*RE* no. 343) was consul in 298 (*MRR* 1.174), censor maybe 280 (ibid. 1.191, *IIt* 13.1 p.113), aedile at an unknown date.

Livy's narrative (10.11.10 sqq.) of the events of his consulship runs thus. After his election with Cn. Fulvius an embassy arrives from the Lucanians asking for protection against a Samnite invasion, and expressing willingness to provide hostages. The alliance is forged, and Scipio sets out to the Etruscan front while Fulvius proceeds to Samnium; each consul wins a narrow victory, Fulvius a triumph over the Samnites (the Fasti Triumphales say over the Etruscans and Samnites). Frontinus too (*Strat.* 1.6.1, 11.2) brings Fulvius to Samnium; the former passage begins *Fuluius Nobilior cum ex Samnio in Lucanos exercitum duceret*, which reads as if it agrees with this inscription against Livy in implying the hostility of the Lucanians. Modern historians tend to support the statements of the inscription, dismissing Livy's account as a Fabian distortion (so e.g. Meyer, *ANRW* i.2.970; the Fulvii and Fabii had a close association), but it must be remembered that this inscription on the usual view is a century or more later than these events. The contradictions are such that we can hardly hope to recover the historical truth, but it rather looks as if Scipio had not much to boast of, and that fairly minor achievements had to be magnified; that while (against Livy) he did operate in Samnium, the real achievements belonged to his colleague. If we follow Livy, the Lucanian hostages were submitted voluntarily, not exacted, and again *omne(m) Loucanam* looks like exaggeration. Cisauna is unknown elsewhere, Taurasia is known only from Livy 40.38.3 and an entry in Stephanus of Byzantium;

these insignificant hamlets cannot be put on a level with Aleria, an important city of Corsica, in the inscription of Barbatus' son. The parallel of *Corsica(m) Aleria(m)que* favours understanding *Samnio(m)* here, which might magnify Barbatus' exploits more, though the forms in 1 suggest that *Samniu(m)* might have been preferred (not that one can confidently expect consistency). Porzio Gernia 172 n.5 quotes inscriptions from statue-bases etc. in which an ablative after *capere* denotes the locality from which the booty was brought, and takes *Samnio* here as ablative; *Gnaiuod* might make us look for *Samniod*, but the ablative *-d* had begun to disappear on inscriptions before the end of the third century (Porzio Gernia 172 sqq.). This however is refuted by Wachter 288-9 and 309, and is not validated by *CIL* 11.1827 *Appius Claudius...complura oppida de Samnitibus cepit*. Another possibility is dative of disadvantage, but again Wachter 309 refutes this. Still less likely is it that *Samnio(m)* is a genitive plural = *Samnitium* (said to have been suggested by E. Fraenkel). If the conclusion that *Samnio* is accusative is correct, this strengthens the impression that this line imitates the corresponding line in 9.

In the prose inscription the initial]*o* is no longer legible and has been replaced by *Cornelius*, but was read by the first discoverers.

1 For the order *Cornelius Lucius* see 14.3, 15.3, 19.3 and the epitaph of Pacuvius there quoted, 22.1, Skutsch on Enn. *Ann.* 329. This form of the termination, as opposed to the older *Cornelio(s)*, is first found on a securely dated inscription in 211 B.C. (*CIL* 1.608, quoted just above), though there are a few examples likely to be earlier (Wachter 309-10 §131, and 376-7 §173 on *CIL* 1.47 = 14.3563 =*ILS* 3143 = *ILLRP* 222, which has *-os* on one side and *-us* on the other). As in 9, *Lucius* contrasts with an older form, here *Loucanam* (cf. also *abdoucit*).

2 *Gneuus* is on *CIL* 6.16322. Even by this date *prognatus* seems to convey archaic grandeur, cf. 11.7, Livy 1.40.3, E. Fraenkel, *Horace* (1957), 82 n.4. *Fortis uir sapiensque* too varies from straightforward prose order; for the combination see Cic. *Pro Mil.* 96, *Tusc.* 5.36 (translating ἀνδρεῖος and φρόνιμος Plato, *Menex.* 248a), Hor. *Epist.* 2.1.50 (see Brink's commentary p. 94), *TLL* vi.1.1149.67. Plut. *Gracch.* 8.4 comments that *sapiens* covers both σοφός and φρόνιμος (Cic. *De Off.* 1.153 disagrees). The latter is no doubt what is envisaged here, practical prudence, as in 12.1; cf. Pliny, *NH* 7.139 *Q. Metellus in ea oratione quam habuit supremis laudibus patris sui L. Metelli...scriptum*

reliquit decem maximas res optimasque...consummasse eum: uoluisse enim primarium bellatorem esse...fortissimum imperatorem...summa sapientia esse, and see also my note on Cic. *Consulatus Suus* fr. 10 (= 11 Morel) 69 (*FLP* 170). Wheeler, *Historia* 37 (1988), 166 wishes to see in the word a particular implication of wily military stratagems, and (184-5) points out stratagems associated with Barbatus in other campaigns; but this is too limiting, and cannot be intended in 12.1, which Wheeler has to explain by a change in Roman values. See in general U. Klima, *Unters. zu den Begriff Sapientia* (1971), 61; Pesando, *Boll. di Arch.* 1-2 (1990), 23; Homeyer, *AC* 25 (1956), 301.
3 *Forma* on the other hand seems a hellenising, un-Roman thing to mention, though I would not want to link 2-3 as closely as some to καλοκἀγαθία. One may note that the earliest known Claudius Pulcher (*Ciceronis Orationum Scholiastae* p. 90 Stangl) was the consul of 249 B.C. *Parisuma* is elsewhere found only Plaut. *Curc.* 506 and (a certain emendation) Gell. 2.1.34. For similar phrases in later eulogies of women see Alton - Wormell - Courtney, Ovid *Fasti* pp. xx-xxi. As in 9.4-5, we see an attempt at anaphora in 3-4, but here the parataxis of 9 becomes hypotaxis, cf. *quod...quei* 2.1-3.
6 For the historic presents after perfects cf. 4.6. The name Lucania is not found until Horace; before that it was usual to refer to Lucani (see my note on Juv. 8.180). What we have here is singular, *Loucana(m)* sc. *terram*; one may compare *Taurica*, *CIL* 8.619 and *Celtica* (see *TLL onom.* s.v. 311.24). It is a question whether the final *m* in this word was written (see Scamuzzi 256-9), but Gordon p. 81 is fairly sure that it was; if so, it contrasts with the forms in 5, perhaps because the next word begins with a vowel. For *abdoucit* cf. *adouxet* quoted on 9.4. etc.

Where 9 has *Lucio(m), fuet*, 10 has *Lucius, fuit* (and in 10 *-it* is invariable), both younger forms.

Metre

A dash separates the lines of verse, though it is missing between 1 and 2; Professor Vine suggests to me that, though the first line is clearly part of the six-line Saturnian structure, it may have been felt in a way to be 'extra metrum', being entirely composed of proper names (cf. p. 23). 4 is a standard Saturnian; see on 9.4. *Taurāsiam* in 5 would give a regular colon.

11

CLE 8 = *CIL* 1.10 = 6.1288 = *ILS* 4 = *ILLRP* 311.
Photo: *Imagines* 134; Coarelli fig. 12 (drawing fig. L).
Discussion: Bandelli, *Epigraphica* 37 (1975), 84; Moir, *CQ* 36 (1986), 264 and 38 (1988), 258; Tatum, *CQ* 38 (1988), 255.

This is usually supposed to be the son (*RE, Cornelius* 331) of Africanus, who suffered from poor health and died prematurely; we do not know that he was flamen Dialis, and, though there is nothing very much against the identification, there is nothing very much for it either. Another possibility is a son (otherwise unknown) of that man (*MRR* 3.70; G. V. Sumner, *The Orators in Cicero's Brutus* (Phoenix suppl. 11, 1973), 36); his early death will have motivated the adoption of Aemilianus, which had taken place by 168 B.C. Moir 1986 argues against Sumner. Bandelli suggests an otherwise unknown grandson of P. Scipio Asina cos. 221, who was son of Cn. Scipio Asina, who was a second son of Barbatus.

Bücheler points out that the other Saturnian Scipio epitaphs are of six lines, that the first line here is written in smaller letters, that it starts to the left of the others, and that it stands on a separate line whereas the rest is written continuously, though with small intervals between the verses; he concludes that the first line with the mention of the flaminate is a subsequent addition. Coarelli 95 suggests that it was added when the tomb was remodelled c. 130 B.C., and Moir 1988 points out that Aemilianus would have been interested in doing this for his adoptive father.

In this epitaph the deceased is directly addressed, which emphasises, though in restrained fashion, the pathos of his early death.

The consonants are doubled in *essent* and *terra*, but left single in *gesistei, superases, licuiset*. *utier* is the earliest occurrence of this spelling, replacing *oitier*.

1 *insigne(m)* might be intended, but the neuter noun is appropriate (*TLL* s.v. 1899.73); for the metre see above p. 29. For the *apex* cf. Latte 157, 203, 404.

2 *tua omnia* go together, with *ut* in the Wackernagel position (see on 1.1-3). *breuia* is contrasted with *longa* 4.

4 For *tibe(i)* cf. on 9.1 and *sibe* attested by Quintil. 1.7.24.

5 Cf. 13.4. *facile facteis* is a striking homoearchon following the alliteration in 4; it is also an etymological pun (cf. 7.4).

6-7 Cf. Cic. *De Leg.* 2.63 *ut sinus et gremium quasi matris mortuo tribueretur*; this is a Greek literary floscule, γαῖα κόλποις ἐδέξατο (cf. *CEG* 2.551, 606.9, 611 and Lier (1903) 586, Geffcken p. 53 on his 143.8, Brelich 38), in connection with which one will recall that the Cornelii persisted in inhumation. Cf. also 178.3, 188.1-2, 195.1, *CLE* 809 *mater genuit materq(ue) recepit*, Pliny, *NH* 2.154. It is also an artificial literary technique to hold back the name of the deceased until the end (cf. 68.4-5 and Geffcken p. 48 on his 130.5), and the splitting and arrangement of the name *Publi Scipio Corneli* are even more artificial; cf. 19.3, 68.4-5, 111.5-6 and HS 397, who quote Coelius Antipater (correct their reference from 'Cael. or.') fr. 1 Peter *has res ad te scriptas, Luci, misimus, Aeli* (criticised by Cicero, *Or.* 230). For *prognatum* cf. on 10.2.

The earth 'gladly' absorbs one of such merit.

Metre
For 1 see above; in 4 scan *quibu'*. For the lay-out see on no. 6.

12

CLE 9 = *CIL* 1.11 = 6.1289 = *ILS* 7 = *ILLRP* 312.
Photo: *Imagines* 135; Coarelli fig. 13 (drawing fig. M).

This is assumed to be a son (RE Cornelius 326) of Hispallus and Paulla Cornelia and a brother of Hispanus, but again with no certainty. The inscription is distinguished by alliterations and a taste for verbal point in the form of antithesis and adnominatio; like 9-10 it addresses the Roman public (*ne quairatis*). It has a single consonant in *posidet* but a double in *annos*; note also *aetate* but *quairatis*.

1 For *sapientia* see on 10.2.

2 *quom* in the preposition is a pseudo-archaic spelling; 15.8, 68.6, *TLL* iv.1339.82, Leumann 137, SP 126.

3 *honore* has been taken as ablative, dative or accusative, but the last is surely established by Grattius 291 *ille tuos olim non defecturus honores* 'the pup who will not fall short in the positions of authority entrusted by you', on which Barth comments *'scite honores ut in re p. dicit, cum gradus sint officiorum inter canes'*. We therefore have an elaborate pun, 'whose life-span, not (lack of) respect, denied him office'; *honos* is an instance of the idiom *res pro rei defectu* (Madvig on Cic. *De Fin.* 2.73, C. F. W. Müller in Friedlaender's note on Juv.

2.39, Kühner - Gerth, *Gr. Gramm., Satzlehre* 2. 569-70), cf. on 91.5; τιμή at Eur. *Hipp.* 1402 signifies 'lack of honour'.

For *quoiei* cf. Leumann 478, Sommer 437.

4 For *uirtutei* cf. Leumann 436, Sommer 275 and *opid* 2.3 (q.v.); the *ei* spelling is non-etymological for *ī*.

5 I cannot make sense of this line (the restoration of *l[oc]eis* seems certain) unless it means *his locis mandatus* = *hic situs*; cf. *CLE* 473.3, 501.1 (these passages, though much later, seem to validate the plural, which caused reasonable surprise to Maas, *ALL* 12 (1902), 535). The omission of *h* will not be a phonetic error (common later; see on 168b.2), but due to the influence of *is* in 4. For the spelling (rather than *heis*) cf. *hic* 4, which etymologically should be *heic* (6.2 etc.).

6 In simple classical Latin this means *ne quaeratis cur honos non sit mandatus*. For the type of purpose clause (the sense might be filled out to *annos natus xx, <quod dictum est> ne quaeratis*) see my note on Juv. 15.89 *ne quaeras*; for the prolepsis of *honos* into the governing clause ('I know thee who thou art') HS 471, KS 2.579; for *minus* = *non* HS 454-5; for *quei* (the old instrumental *qui*, with non-etymological *ei* for *ī*) *OLD*, *qui* (2) 1c.

It has been suspected that *mandatus* (for which see *TLL* vi.3. 2926.47) is an error by the ordinator due to 5, but we must not impose our sense of elegance on archaic inscriptions, and the composer may have thought that he was actually being elegant.

Metre

4 and 5 are standard Saturnians; otherwise this composer uses exclusively six-element cola if we scan *minu'* in 6. In 2 *posidēt* retains its original quantity. 3a would be an orthodox seven-element colon, and the line a standard Saturnian (cf. above p. 29), if *quoiei* were a spondee, but that scansion before a consonant leads a precarious life only at *CLE* 368.2, Plaut. *Bacch.* 225; the same question arises with *quoius* in the similar line 10.3. Monosyllabic scansion is much more likely.

13

CLE 958 = *CIL* 1.15 = 6.1293 = *ILS* 6 = *ILLRP* 316.
Photo: *Imagines* 137; Coarelli fig. 16 (drawing fig. P).

The deceased (*RE, Cornelius* 347) speaks in his own person, as in the tiny fragment *CLE* 10 = *CIL* 1.14 = 6.1292 = *ILLRP* 315, which is no doubt from a Saturnian poem. He was praetor in 139 B.C. (the dates of his other offices are unknown), but died before reaching the consulship. For the sense of family tradition Botteri, *Ktema* 5 (1980), 77 compares Diodorus Sic. 34-35 fr. 33 ἀκόλουθον ἔσχε τῇ τοῦ γένους διαδοχῇ καὶ τὴν τῆς ἀρέτης κληρονομίαν (referring to Scipio Nasica Serapio cos. 111,descended from Scipio Nasica the son of Calvus, cf. on 9); the same sense can be seen in 11.5.

1 For the form *mieis* cf. *TLL* viii.913.61, Leumann 46, Sommer 351, 413, 416, SP 53, 92 (and below 59.1). It is here a monosyllable.

2 *progeniem genui* is an etymological figure, picking up *generis* and accompanied by alliterations in 1-2. He makes a point of this because at this time some noble houses were beginning to die out (the son of Africanus (on 11) had had to adopt); in 131 Metellus Macedonicus felt it necessary to deliver his famous speech *de prole augenda*. Hispanus 'emulated' the deeds of his father, who was consul in 176 but from whom no notable deeds are recorded.

3 For *sibei* see on 7.1.

4 He must imply by the tense of *laetentur* that the *maiores*, though dead, can still feel pride in their descendant. The form *honos*, as in the earlier inscriptions, has now been supplanted by *honor*.

Ennius introduced the elegiac metre as a corollary of his introduction of the hexameter, and in it wrote two epitaphs (fr. 43-4 *FLP*), apparently purely literary, on Africanus; one of these begins *hic est ille situs* (cf. 12.4), in the other Africanus speaks from his own mouth (cf. 13). Ennius' influence has now driven the Saturnian from the field.

I C : OTHER REPUBLICAN INSCRIPTIONS

14*

Fragmenta Poetarum Latinorum ed. W. Morel p.32
Discussion: O. Vessberg, *Studien zur Kunstgeschichte der röm. Republik* (1941), 37

The temple of Juno at Ardea, mentioned Verg. *Aen*. 7.419, has been identified, but without any proof, with a three-cella temple on the acropolis there, the architectural terracottas of which are now in the Villa Giulia at Rome; in fact Livy 22.1.19 suggests that the temple of Juno was in the forum. The artist is Marcus Plautius (for the order of names cf. on 10.1); we can hardly identify his patron since the only Plautii known to have a connection with Asia (which may not even be relevant) belong to the first century B.C., which is too late for this inscription, and the praenomen of the painter need not be identical with that of his patron (see on 18). Pliny 35.17 mentions other paintings in temples at Ardea which he describes as *antiquiores Urbe;* see also Serv. *Aen*. 1.44. Since this inscription uses hexameters, it will have been later than Ennius.

1 For the proverbial *digna dignis* see my note on *vers. pop.* 10 (*FLP* 476). *loco* seems to be corrupt; attempts to explain it are unsatisfactory:

(a) It might mean 'opportunely', but that seems detrimental whether it is linked with the preceding or the following. It is still worse taken as ablative depending on either *digna* (so among others Paladini, *Epigraphica* 12 (1950), 29) or *dignis;* Hermolaus Barbarus altered *digna* to *dignu'* so that *dignis* can agree with *picturis* and have *loco* depending on it, but the loss of the proverbial expression is too high a price to pay. Somewhat better is Lachmann's proposal (on Lucr. 4.53) *dignis digna loces*.

(b) It might be a proper name, Plautius' cognomen, representing Lycon (but then it will have to be changed with Bergk to *Luco*, since *Loco* cannot be justified), but the separation at such a distance from the rest of his name is not defended by the instances quoted on 11.6-7.

(c) Mazzarino, *Maia* 3 (1950), 302 suggests that it represents *loco(m)*, on the supposition that the rest of the spelling was modernised to *templum, Plautius Marcus* but that this escaped because it was not realised that it was accusative; *templum* will now be in apposition. However *loco(m)* is totally superfluous.

There is another problem in that, whereas *supremus* is common as an epithet of Jupiter, it is not elsewhere found as a noun ('the Supreme One'). The two problems can be simultaneously eliminated if we replace *loco* with *Iouis*; the accumulation of genitives is unpleasant, but even without the emendation we have that problem.

4 i.e. *nunc laudat et semper laudabit*; for a similar ellipse cf. 112.13.

15

CIL 1.2662 = *ILLRP* 342

Photo: Dow 84-5, Taylor and West 10 (see below); A. B. West, *Corinth, Results of Excavations* 8.2 (1931), 1; Gordon, *Introduction* pl. 9 fig. 14; *ANRW* ii.7.1 pl. 4 no. 5 (after p. 528); *Imagines* 151 (a copy).

Discussion: *CIL* 1.2.4 p. 936; Taylor and West, *AJA* 32 (1928), 9; Dow, *HSCP* 60 (1951), 81; Gordon in *Corinthiaca* (Studies D. A. Amyx, 1986), 50 with photo; J. Nollé, *Side im Altertum* (1993), 70 and 234

This was found at Corinth in 1926. The traces in the erasure in 3 make it certain that the erased name was as restored. This epigram refers to the campaign of Marcus Antonius, grandfather of the triumvir, against the Cilician pirates in 102 B.C. When his grandson incurred *damnatio memoriae* in 30 B.C., the identical name of his grandfather was erased both here and in the Capitoline consular Fasti for 99 and 97, though there it was subsequently restored. In 102 Antonius was praetor with proconsular imperium (hence he is referred to as either praetor or proconsul by our sources), cf. *MRR* 3.19; on the question of his office see further H. Pohl, *Die römische Politik und die Piraterie* (1993), 211 sqq. The cognomen Hirrus appears only among the Lucilii, cf. *MRR* 1.569-70, 3.129; this man was probably nephew of the poet (West, *AJP* 49 (1928), 24).

Most of the ships for this campaign were supplied by Rome's subjects and allies in Asia, particularly Rhodes and Byzantium; from this epigram we learn, to our surprise, that some came from the Western Mediterranean and were hauled over the Isthmus of Corinth. Antonius then proceeded to Athens, where he spent a few days (Cic. *De Or.*1.82). Because of seasonal bad weather (Cicero mentions *nauigandi difficultas*, cf. *anni e tempore*) Antonius, unwilling to risk his fleet, left it at Athens under Hirrus to be got ready for action and himself proceeded to Side, with a stop in Rhodes (Cic. *De Or.* 2.3) no doubt to collect the contingents of the allies. Side is a harbour in Pamphylia which at this time was clearly allied with Rome against the pirates (Nollé 71, following Ferrary, *MEFRA* 89 (1977), 642-3); Strabo 14.3.2.664, evidently referring to a later date, speaks of it as then used by the pirates as a market for their captives. For the campaign in general see D. Magie, *Roman Rule in Asia Minor* (1950), 2.1161 n.12.

7-10 seem defensive in tone and suggest that the decision to haul the ships over the Isthmus was controversial. 1-2 seem to be encomiastic exaggeration unless there is stress on *classis*, a whole fleet; for previous instances of warships transported presumably on the diolkos see Cook, *JHS* 99 (1979), 152, MacDonald ibid. 106 (1986), 191.

It is not apparent who put up this inscription; on the general view that there was no Corinth between the sack by Mummius and the refoundation by Julius Caesar, one would have to suppose that it was brought from the Isthmus. However J. Wiseman, *ANRW* ii.7.1.495 argues that Corinth was not totally obliterated. The inscription is of strictly local reference, as C. Damon points out to me, and shows no interest in the outcome of the campaign; what is stressed is that Antony did what was necessary at the Isthmus without bothering anybody too much. One might suggest that it was put up by Roman traders settled at Sicyon.

ā is spelt *aa* in the ablative (2, 8) but not elsewhere (not even *Maarci*, cf. on 8.1); *anni* is inconsistent with *uirei*. Classical rules about caesura (5) and diaeresis (6, 8) are not observed. The alliteration in 2 and 7 is noteworthy.

1 *quisquanst* For *ms* shifting to *ns*, even though here the first word must end in *-m* to allow the aphaeresis *(e)st*, cf. Leumann 212. For the concord *quod...rem* cf. HS 431-2, KS 1.63; such things are quite common in, but not confined to, authors like Varro and Lucretius. For the general frame of the line cf. 31.3.

2 *feramus* presumably means 'you the readers and I the composer'.

3 For the order *Antoni Marci* cf. on 10.1.

5 *eire profectus* Cf. Plaut. *Rud.* 847.

6 For *constituit* cf. Nepos, *Alc.* 8.1.

7 *haec* is neuter plural, since *classem perficere* is not found.

8 For *quom* cf. on 12.2.

9 Travis ap. Dow makes it likely that *quei contra est* means 'he on the other hand who is', not 'he who is of the opposite disposition' (though *OLD, contra* 10b gives some support to the latter interpretation). In that case a predicate is needed, which he achieves by supplying *in[uidus* rather than *in[uidet;* then the line may be completed by something like *damnat* (Elder ibid.). Taylor and West compare *CLE* 334 *aemule, si qui potes, nostros imitare labores. si maleuolus es, geme; si beneuolus es, gaude* (very late). Another possible supplement would be *in[probus liuet.*
10 The most pointed supplement for this seems to be *q[uam ded]ecet id u[ideant,* which appears on the copy in the Museo della Civiltà Romana illustrated by Degrassi; unfortunately Dow did not consider this, so we do not have the benefit of his careful measurements, which exclude a number of other supplements. It will then mean (with a pun on *inuideant* and *uideant* which cannot be translated) 'let them envy provided that they understand how inappropriate this is'. That involves accepting an indicative in an indirect question, which seems acceptable enough in this composition (cf. HS 538; though they are more tolerant than I am inclined to be). Another possibility which does not involve this might be *q[uos add]ecet id u[igeant,* which gives a respectable word-play and will mean 'so long as those to whom this (i.e. flourishing) is appropriate flourish'.

16

CLE 361 = *CIL* 1.1861 = 9.4463 = *ILS* 5221 = *ILLRP* 804
Photo: *CIL* 1.2.4 tab. 96.2
Discussion: Wachter 416

The antiquity of this epitaph from Amiternum is shown by the forms of the words, and the shapes of the letters P (everywhere, but not with sharp enough corners to establish a firm dating; Wachter 323 n.767) and L (twice with the second stroke upturned, though not very sharply; twice in the later style), for which see above p. 19, are consistent with this. With *soueis* scanned as a monosyllable (cf. Metre I 1) the second line is a hexameter. The first line is also presumably an attempt at one; Pisani, *Paideia* 6 (1951), 376 suggests that it shows a mason's error for *suaueist* (*suauist*) *heicei situs.* This would leave the problem only of the form *heicei,* which could be compared with *inpeirator*, *CIL* 1.614 (note however that Wachter 287 § 118f thinks that the second *i* there was a later addition). Note *heice*, *CIL* 1.1295.7 = *ILLRP* 965. If this is wrong we have to assume (1) that *situst* is a pyrrhic either because it is again an error for *situs* scanned *situ'* or because the composer felt himself justified by the *Hedyphagetica* of Ennius in introducing an iambic shortening into hexameters (at Lucil. 580 the correct reading is *hic situs Metrophanes*, not *situst*); (2) that *ei* is used to represent ī̆ in *suauei(s)* (cf. on 20.3; *sororei* on *CIL* 1.1312 = 6.33444 = *ILS* 7975 = *ILLRP* 925 looks like a genitive rather than a dative) and ĕ in the second syllable of *heicei* to provide long syllables where needed.

This epitaph must be dated soon after the introduction of the hexameter by Ennius; it is clear that its composer was struggling with the metre. At this date it is one of the earliest testimonies for mime-actors at Rome; despite his Greek name Protogenes must have been able to perform in Latin. The fact that the name, like that of Philotimus in 19, in this early inscription is Greek is significant; verse epitaphs came in through such people and hellenising nobles like the Scipiones.

It should be added that Wachter vainly tries to make both lines or at least the first choliambic, and Gentili, *Quad. Urb.* 34 (1990), 131 to make them Saturnians.

1 i.e. Protogenes the slave of Cloelius (the form Cloulius also *CIL* 1.1479 = 14.2820, cf. *TLL onom.*, *Cloelius* 502.31 sqq. and *MRR* 3.58).
2 For *que* and *nuges* cf. Leumann 421 and on 9.1. *plouruma* is a false archaism (Leumann 66, cf. 496; Sommer 458; Wachter 419); contrast *ploirume* 9.1. For *soueis* see on 2.3, 17.4.

*17***

CLE 52 = *CIL* 1.1211 = 6.15345 = *ILS* 8403 = *ILLRP* 973

This inscription is known only from humanist reports, which vary in some details; in particular some report *pellige* in 1 and *dIxi* in 8.

Three points make this an inscription of extraordinary interest. First, it encapsulates in the last line an early Roman view of wifely duty, for which see Lattimore 297, Ogilvie on Livy 1.57.9, my note on Juv. 6.289 and Treggiari 243; cf. *CLE* 1123.3, 237.2 *lanifica* (see *TLL* s.v.) ... *domiseda*, 63.4, 1988.14. Second, in 2-3 it strikingly exemplifies that fondness for etymological play which we often find in early Latin literature (cf. 13.2). For *nomen nominare* cf. H. Haffter, *Untersuchungen zur Altlat. Dichtersprache* (1934), 20-1; e.g. Ennius, *Medea* 211-2 *quae nunc nominatur nomine / Argo, quia Argiui...* (where the etymology of Argo is added to Euripides); here indeed the figure seems to be applied somewhat inappropriately, since the parents would not actually have chosen the name Claudia (this point was made to me by C. Damon). See also e.g. *Andromacha* 92 *ui uitam euitari* and Jocelyn on 6-7. Here *sepulcrum* is derived from *pulcrum* and (regardless of the difference of quantity) the prefix *sē-*, 'apart from' (as in *securus* etc.); this etymology is also found in Charisius 93 Barwick = 73 Keil *sepulcrum hodieque manet quod sit seorsum a pulcro* and in Donatus on Ter. *Andr.* 128. The word is of course derived from *sepelire*, as *fulcrum* from *fulcire*. Third, it seems to imitate a Greek literary epigram by Heraclitus (see Swinner, *Ancient Society* 1 (1970), 41 n.10 for some doubts about the authorship), *AP* 7.465 (also imitated by Antipater of Sidon ibid. 454), an epitaph for a woman who died while giving birth to twins, one of whom also died; this poem mentions a ὁδοιπόρος and addresses him as ξεῖν(ε). That situation, not spelt out in our poem, would account for the present *locat* in 6, though *secum aufert* would be plainer. How would the Roman composer have known this poem? The obvious answer would be that he read it in the Garland of Meleager, the publication date of which unfortunately cannot be fixed; Gow - Page, *Hellenistic Epigrams* xiv-xvi think perhaps the nineties, but recognise a possibility as early as 125. The earlier dating would be needed to fit this epigram, since *pulcrai* would not be so spelt after about 120 B.C.; but these hypotheses cannot be pressed, and knowledge of Heraclitus might have come from Antipater himself, who visited Rome and whose death is put c. 125 B.C. (Gow - Page 1.xv, 2.32). One may note that the first recorded funeral *laudatio* for a woman was delivered about this time or a little later (Cic. *De Or.* 2.44). The spelling is notably inconsistent (note in particular *pulcrai feminae* and *suom...souo*, for the latter of which see on 2.3; it survives as late as Sullan times, *CIL* 1.727 = *ILS* 34 = *ILLRP* 176).

1 For the address to the *hospes* cf. on 8.2; for *pellege* cf. 20.2. 'I' seems to be the speaking tomb, as probably 19.4; cf. Burzachechi, *Epigraphica* 24 (1962), 37 for Greek instances (e.g. *GVI* 1171-92).

2 *pulcrai* is another way of spelling *pulcrae*, not *pulcrāī*.

5-6 *alterum...alium* is imposed by metre; cf. *TLL* i.1742.5, Munro on Lucr. 4.688. It was assumed above that *locat* is present; instances of the perfect in -*āt* are very few (Sommer 564, who quotes *pugnat, CIL* 10.7297; Alpers, *Glotta* 49 (1971), 260 with some very dubious cases; Munro on Lucr. 1.70; note *decoraat, CLE* 56.3 = *CIL* 1.1570 = *ILLRP* 977; the transmitted *deierāt* at Lucil. 818 is not likely to be right). Despite 4.6 and 10.6, it would also be very implausible to suppose a historic present.

7 This line is rather disjointed here; somewhat similar is 20.9-11. Her gait was 'becoming' (cf. e.g. Plaut. *Most.* 254-5, *Asin.* 401, Nepos pr. 1), not like that of a harlot (Cic. *Pro Cael.* 49, Catull. 42.8).

18

CLE 53 = *CIL* 1.1210 = 6.32311 = *ILS* 1932 = *ILLRP* 808

M. Granius cannot be identical with the witty *praeco* Q. Granius known to Cicero in his youth and to Lucilius, but he no doubt was a partner in a family business of auctioneering. For *Olus* = *Aulus* cf. Salomies 24 and for the *ō* - *au* variation in general Leumann 72, SP 68. Here the less vulgar *A(u)* is retained in the formal subscription; cf. *CLE* 1785 (p. 824) = *CIL* 4.2353 (p. 219) = *ILS* 6442b *Aulus Olo suo salutem.* For the name Stabilio see Kajanto, *Cognomina* 259; the examples in *CIL* 1 belong mainly but not exclusively to slaves and freedmen. The convention that freedmen took the praenomen of their former owner was not firmly established until about Augustan times; cf. *ILS* index p. 926, *ILLRP* index p. 488b, Ruggiero, *libertus* 910-11, Fabre 108, Thylander 57.

This epitaph shows the influence of pattern-book formulae, for which see 19 and my commentary on the epitaph of Pacuvius (*FLP* 49), or at least standard formulation; it is however more elegant than the parallels, particularly with the introduction of the neat paradox *rogat...tacitus* (for which cf. *GVI* 1887.9, 1994a.1, p. 689 and *CLE* 512.1 quoted on 190.8). For the construction of 5 (= *uoluit ne hoc nescires*) see *FLP* ibid., Turpilius 65, Löfstedt, *Syntactica* 1.156 and *CLE* 90.5 *memor esse* with accusative. 3 is fairly standard praise, cf. *CLE* 1868.4, where however there is no mention of the *fides* needed by a business man (cf. on 127.8) and expected of a freedman in his dealings with his patron (Fabre 228). The long I in *OlI* suggests a dating (on 7.6). *quoius* 2 is monosyllabic.

2 *umbram* 'le simulacre du mort encore vivant au fond de son tombeau' Galletier 27 n.6, q.v.

3 '*frugi* is an epithet often applied to freedmen and slaves' Shackleton Bailey on Cic. *Ad Att.* 7.4.1.

19

CLE 848 = *CIL* 1.1209 = 6.33919a = *ILS* 7703 = *ILLRP* 821 = J. B. Frey, *Corpus Inscr. Iudaicarum* 1 p. 573 no. 72*.
Photo: *Imagines* 311; A. Rostagni, *Storia della Letteratura Latina* (1952-4), 1.200; Diehl, *Tabulae* 6d; P. Batlle Huguet, *Epigrafia Latina* (ed. 2, 1963), pl. 2.4.

The prose at the end was added subsequently and in instalments (see Degrassi); the Jewish angle (whence its inclusion by Frey) comes from the name *Manchae*.
1 *sax(s)us* is masculine *CLE* 415, 1580.6, etc.; it is an instance of the drift from the neuter into the masculine (HS 10) which we often see in Petronius and which led to the disappearance of the neuter in Romance (cf. 40.1-4, 94a.2, 179.20). *tametsi properas* is a traditional topic of epitaphs; see Nisbet - Hubbard on Hor. *Odes* 1.28.35.
2 For the spelling *scriptust* see on 172.8.
3 The need to incorporate the name leads to the abandonment of the metre (senarii), cf. p. 23. Since the metre is abandoned, it is hard to see the reason for the order *Maeci Luci* (for which cf. on 10.1) and the separation of the cognomen (for which cf. 11.6-7). For the spelling of the name P(h)ilotimus see Leumann 160.
4 For *ni* = *ne* cf. 165.6, 168b.1, HS 535, Walde - Hofmann s.v., Väänänen 88, Vine 255; it comes from *nei*. *-m* is nearly always written in republican non-Saturnian inscriptions (cf. p. 19); its absence (cf. 57.3) here is due to the line-end (for the lay-out see on no. 6). For the 'I' intended see on 17.1.

The epitaph of Pacuvius quoted by Gellius 1.24.4 runs thus:

adulescens, tametsi properas, hoc te sax<ul>um
rogat ut se aspicias, deinde quod scriptum est legas.
hic sunt poetae Pacuui Marci sita
ossa. hoc uolebam nescius ne esses. uale.

This and 19 derive from a pattern-book or other model in which the name and *ossa*, as in 18 and 19, were fitted neatly into one line, and from which 19 varies by introducing a vulgar gender *saxsolus*.

20

CLE 55 = *CIL* 1.1214 = 6.10096 = *ILS* 5213 = *ILLRP* 803.
Drawing: T. P. Wiseman, *Catullus and his World* (1985), 31 with discussion
Discussion: Anderson, *PCPS* 166-8 (1937), 8; Popova, *Eirene* 7 (1968), 60

The portions marked by square brackets are not on the stone now but were when it was first discovered.

The problem in this poem lies in the interpretation of 10-11, from which the one clear thing that emerges is that Eucharis danced. She was certainly not the first female dancer to appear on the Roman stage; for the date of the poem see on 6, and for an earlier performer see the *saltatricula* Dionysia mentioned by Gellius 1.5.3, referring to 62 B.C. (she is also known from Cic. *Rosc. com.* 23 of 76 B.C.). We then have the following alternatives:
(1) *prima* is not nominative but ablative, which seems unlikely.
(2) *prima populo apparui* means 'was judged top-class by the people', which also seems rather improbable.
(3) *prima apparui* means 'I made my first appearance' (so Anderson); but this line should mention something of which Eucharis is proud, and her first appearance does not in itself seem something to boast about.
(4) *Graeca in scaena* has some particular meaning which justifies the boast. Our only exact parallel is *CIL* 6.10095 *denunttiator ab scaena Graeca,* which tells us nothing. Our best lead seems to be that the *ludi honorarii* appended to Augustus' secular games consisted of *ludi Latini* and *Graeci,* of which the latter were divided into *astici* (i.e. performances of dramas, as in the Athenian City Dionysia) and *thymelici* (performances consisting of music and dancing). Eucharis would fit in well with the last, and her boast would presumably be that she was the first female to appear at Rome in such formally-constituted games, discounting *mimae;* Anderson denies that *prima apparui* would be how one would express 'I was the first female to appear', but verse demands less precise and more concentrated forms of expression than prose. Under the republic such games would naturally be put on through private initiative of *nobiles* (as indeed were, it seems, the *ludi honorarii*); I do not see this word as contrasted with *populo.* Cicero, *Ad Att.* 16.5.1, *Ad Fam.* 7.1.3 mentions *ludi Graeci* rather scornfully (Beaujeu, *Hommages H. Le Bonniec* (CL 201, 1988), 10 improbably takes this to mean athletic contests);

she could also have appeared on the occasion when Brutus (Plut. 21.3) fetched performers from Naples. Perhaps she danced to a libretto in Greek, after the fashion of the later pantomime; Julius Caesar (Suet. 39.1) *edidit...ludos etiam regionatim urbe tota et quidem per omnium linguarum histriones* (and likewise id. *Aug.* 43.1 *uicatim ac pluribus scaenis*). Cic. *Ad Fam.* l.c. mentions also *ludi Osci*, which means performances in the Oscan dialect (Strabo 5.3.6.233). This view of Eucharis' epitaph is taken by Mommsen (*History of Rome*, English translation 5.516, almost the last page of the work); Wiseman's view l.c. fails to account for *prima*.

The earlier terminus for the dating is fairly clear, but the question might be raised whether the inscription could belong to the first century A.D. This is discouraged by the mention of the *nobiles* and the increased difficulty of justifying *prima* as time proceeds, but see on 6. For the apices in 1 and 7 cf. p. 19 and Leumann 13-14.

1 *heus* calls the attention of the passer-by, cf. *CLE* 119.1, 120.1. For *oculo errante* cf. Cic. *Har. Resp.* 37; he is looking vaguely around the tombs and is asked to look specifically at hers. Cf. *oculo properante* in a similar context at Ovid, *Tr.* 3.3.71.

3 For *parenteis* = *-ĭs* cf. 16.1 and Leumann 64, SP 65, Wachter 250.

4 *ubei* is a pyrrhic, cf. on 7.1.

5 *heic* (*hic* 18) presumably means 'here on earth'. For the emphasis on *artes* and culture here and in 9 see Sanders in *Cultura Epigrafica dell' Appennino* (1985), 55.

6 *et* is not elsewhere found postponed before Vergil's *Bucolics*, so this poem cannot be earlier than c. 40-30 B.C. Since Eucharis was aged fourteen when she died, she can hardly have been born before 55 B.C. For another girl who started her theatrical career very young see Pliny, *NH* 7.158 (unfortunately the exact numbers in Pliny's text are subject to some doubt).

Cf. Prop. 2.10.23 *laudis conscendere* †*carmen*† (*culmen* Itali, alii alia); this might count as an imitation of Augustan poetry stronger than Popova's examples.

7 In later epitaphs *properauit aetas* becomes a set formula.

9 Cf. 180.6 *quam Pallas cunctis artibus erudiit*, *CLE* 1965 *docta nouem Musis*, 1570.2. For the spelling *erodita* (also in the prose introduction) cf. *CIL* 6.10127, Leumann 51, SP 62. The nominatives hang, to be taken up by *nostri* 12.

13 For the spelling *infistae* (if rightly read; on Wiseman's reproduction it looks like *inflstae*) cf. SP 54-5, for the song of the Parcae (not an old conception; see E. Fraenkel, *Horace* (1957) 375 n. 2 and

Wilamowitz there referred to) *TLL, carmen* 464.43, *CLE* 1141.16, 1169.3, 1533.4. *deposierunt* = *deposiuerunt*, cf. *TLL* s.v. 576.7, Leumann 601, Sommer 573.
17 For this poignant reversal of the order of nature, often bewailed on epitaphs, cf. 187.7-8.
18-19 Likewise one is said to carry one's years into the grave (*CLE* 387.5, 1069.3); cf. 177.4. *tenebris tenentur* is a striking homoearchon (cf. 124.16).
20 Cf. Tib. 2.4.49-50. This is the first allusion at Rome to the notion *STTL*, cf. on 178.4 and my note on Juv. 7.207; this notion comes from Greece (Sullivan, *TAPA* 70 (1939), 508). However it does not well match the other grecising conception of death in 13 and 19 (cf. 70.15 as contrasted with 11-12). One will note that these grecising conceptions appearing here for the first time do so in association with the Greek name Eucharis and with the milieu of the theatre which did much to introduce such ideas.

21

CLE 185 = *CIL* 1.1219 = 6.24563 = *ILS* 7976 = *ILLRP* 983.

For the form *ossua* cf. *TLL* s.v. 1094.47. This is the first Roman epitaph to convey this message, cf. Lattimore 260-2 and id. 154-6 for Fortuna in epitaphs; this is the blind Greek Tyche (cf. *deludite* 70.14), an idea which, one will note, here comes from non-Romans (Sullivan [on 20.18] 505-7). For living for the day and the hour see Cic. *Phil.* 5.25 and *TLL, dies* 1040.70. *Proprius* is a legal term meaning 'held in perpetuity' (*OLD* 1a); the idea is that of the famous line Lucr. 3.971 *uitaque mancipio nulli datur, omnibus usu*, where among other passages Bailey quotes Accius 422 *neque uita ulli propria in uita est*, cf. id. 159, Lucil. 701. See further *GVI* 1132 and Lier (1903) 598.

The metre is intended to be senarii, but the first line is too long; *Fors* for *Fortuna* would put the metre right. This suggests faulty use of a pattern book or other model. Since *Primus* is a common slave name (cf. 171), Solin, *Arctos* 7 (1972), 184 n.3 thinks that the deceased was Prima the slave or freedwoman of Pompeia. Salvius is an Oscan and Umbrian praenomen also used, like Statius, as a slave name (Kajanto, *Cognomina* 134, 177), no doubt from Italian captives.

22

CLE 961 = *CIL* 10.2971 = *ILS* 7781

This inscription was found at Naples, and the scansions *Stalliu'* and *Hauranu'* suggest republican date, since this feature became obsolete in literary verse in the 50s B.C. (of course later sub-literary inscriptions are a different matter). In that case its subject can be convincingly identified with the C. Stallius who with his brother (?) M. between 63 and 51 B.C. rebuilt the Odeon of Pericles at Athens after its destruction by Sulla (*IG* III.541 = ed. min. II-III 3.3426 = Dittenberger, *OGIS* 354), apparently as architect or contractor. This identification will fit the flourishing of Epicureanism in Campania in the late republic and early Augustan times. Stallius however seems not to have been a serious Epicurean, but one who took the creed as an excuse for a voluptuous life; the tone is very much that of *Epicuri de grege porcum*, sharpened in Cicero's attack on Piso. Note *CIL* 6.37813 to a *philosophus Epicureus*.

1 *Gaius* is normally a dactyl; as a trochee it is rare and late (L. Mueller 305, Leumann 129, SP 108, Allen *HSCP* 2 (1891), 71; add *CLE* 1225.1 for trochaic scansion and 12.1 in Saturnians for dactylic). In Greek for dactylic scansion see *GVI* 1796 = *CIL* 12.306 etc., for trochaic *GVI* 1314.3 = IG 9.2.650 (I do not know why editors print the word with a diaeresis). Here the writer did not wish to scan *Gaiu' Stallius* leaving -*ŭ* before *St-* (though Lucretius permits this at 6.195 and 943) and preferred to reverse the names, cf. 10.1.

The name Hauranus is not found elsewhere; Hagenbuch (quoted by J. C. Orelli, *Inscriptionum lat. sel. collectio* (1828) on his no. 1193) suggested *Gauranus* (cf. *CIL* 10.2229 from Puteoli), which would suit the Campanian setting, since mount Gaurus, probably identical with Monte Barbaro, is on the north shore of the Bay of Naples.

2 For *choro* cf. Cic. *De Fin.* 1.26 *tu quidem totum Epicurum paene e philosophorum choro sustulisti*, Dion. Hal. *De Comp. Verb.* 24.8 Ἐπικουρείων χορός; comparable ironical uses of χορός occur in Plato. The termination *-eius* of the first adjective is pure Greek; for the remarkable type of compound in the second Leumann 396 compares *ueliuolans, stellumicans*.

23

CIL 1.3109a
Discussion: Solin, *ZPE* 43 (1981), 357 with plate XVb; Cugusi, ibid. 61 (1985), 26 (adds nothing); Tatum, ibid. 83 (1990), 299

On a wall belonging to c. 80 - 30 B.C. at the entrance to the theatre in Terracina. Professor Vine suggests to me that *Publi(us)* should be so understood, comparing *Mummi(us)* 3.1 and other instances in republican inscriptions (see Kaimio, *Arctos* 6 (1970), 23). The pretentious diction (*letum* instead of *mortem* (cf. Enn. *Ann.* 389 *occumbunt letum*), *progenies* (with which cf. Cic. *Pro Cael.* 34 *ne progenies quidem mea Q. illa Claudia*)) suggests to Solin a somewhat ironic tone, something like that of Lucr. 3.1025 *lumina sis oculis etiam bonus Ancus reliquit*; even one with the family background of Publius Clodius had to submit to death (at the hands of Milo in 52 B.C.). Tatum on the other hand reads it as the beginning of a serious elogium and relates it to the origin, which he seeks to establish, of Clodius' henchman Sex. Cloelius from Terracina. On the wall the second line is inset as if a pentameter is intended.

II: IMPERIAL INSCRIPTIONS

A: EMPERORS, NOTABLES, MATTERS OF STATE, PUBLIC BUILDINGS

Under this heading one might include the epitaph of Verginius Rufus (*FLP* 364), and nos. 67, 74-6, 111, 134, 141, 149, 180 below. *CLE* 881 is discussed in *FLP* 481.

24

CLE 18 = *CIL* 10.3757 = *ILS* 137

This inscription was found at Acerrae in Campania, and undoubtedly refers to Augustus and his adopted sons C. and L. Caesar. Mommsen's supplement *her[oibus* in 1 imports enormous difficulties, and preferable seems *her[edibus* (L. R. Taylor, *The Divinity of the Roman Emperor* (1931), 224), though it too is not without problems. Mommsen's purpose was to avoid the need to postulate a cult of the Caesares in Italy during their lifetime, since direct cult of living members of the imperial family within Italy was avoided, by making this a cult of the Lares Augusti with which they could be associated, but *CIL* 11.3040 = *ILS* 106 is a dedication of *aedem et signa* to Augustus and the Caesares during their lifetime (the stone comes from near Viterbo). Mitford, *Annual British School Athens* 42 (1947) 222 no. 9 publishes an inscription of a priest of Augustus and the Caesares also during their lifetime from Cyprus. In Gaul the Maison Carrée at Nimes was perhaps dedicated to the Caesares during their lifetime (*CIL* 12.3156), though this is doubtful (R. Amy - P. Gros, *La Maison Carrée* (*Gallia* suppl. 38, 1979), 1.189); the sixteenth legion, which was dissolved by Vespasian, was continuously stationed at Mainz during this period (*RE, legio* 1761). Some fine distinctions might be blurred in the municipalities and provinces; in any case *templum* cannot be pressed (cf. 141.2, 154.2). Note that Ovid, *AA* 1.183 hints that C. Caesar is a *deus*.

On the stone it is plain that we have the beginning of this inscription, but *heredibus* could not stand without definition; there must have been a preceding slab which said something like 'to the greater glory of Augustus'. His adoptive sons of course did not carry the actual name Augustus; the 'name of Augustus' which they carry is Caesar. For the wish that this may remain cf. Ovid, *Ex Ponto* 1.2.98-100 *nihil maius Caesare terra ferat /utque diu sub eo, sic sit sub Caesare semper* (Housman 928 = CQ 10 (1916), 140; *terra* codd.) / *perque manus huius tradita gentis eat,* which as Housman explains means 'may it be for ever under *a* Caesar'; cf. also *Fasti* 4.859-60.

The metre is senarii, with no caesura in 1 and 7 (see Metre II B d).

3 Some word in the ablative meaning 'government' is to be supplied.

4 *deum* is accusative singular.

5 *repetes* The wide-spread idea that the soul belongs to the sky (cf. the inscription of Fabatus quoted on p. 14) is well-suited to ruler-cult; cf. Hor. *Odes* 1.2.45 *serus in caelum redeas,* where Nisbet - Hubbard quote Vell. Pat. 2.123.2 (cf. also 124.3) and Manil. 1.799 *descendit caelo caelumque replebit, / quod reget, Augustus* (which means 'will fill with his also-to-be-deified posterity'; *repleuit...regit* codd.), Germanicus 558-60. See A. Alföldi, *Die monarchische Repräsentation* (1970), 202 = *Röm. Mitt.* 50 (1935), 84.

mundum reges He will be a κοσμοκράτωρ (see LSJ s.v. for application of this word to third-century emperors). Cf. Mart. 7.7.5 *mundi rector*. Manil l.c. hints at an equation with Jupiter, cf. also 916 *in ponto* (i.e. at Actium) *quaesitus rector Olympi*. Hor. *Epist.* 1.19.43 and Ovid, *Fasti* 1.650 show that colloquially Augustus was referred to as 'Jupiter'.

6 *felicibus uoteis* All their wishes are to come true; cf. *TLL* vi.1.446.54. Cf. the letter of Augustus quoted by Gell. 15.7.3 ἀνδραγαθούντων ὑμῶν καὶ διαδεχομένων *stationem meam*.

25

CLE 990 = *CIL* 14.2298 = *ILS* 1949

Discussion: Popova, *Eirene* 7 (1968), 58 (unconvincing).

Found on the Appian Way near Alba. M. Aurelius Cotta Maximus was son of the famous M. Valerius Messala Coruinus and an Aurelia belonging to the family of the Cottae; he was later adopted by an Aurelius Cotta, and became consul in 20 A.D. He was a friend of Ovid, and receives as many as six letters in *Ex Ponto* 1-3, after probably three in the *Tristia*. He was famed for his generosity (Juv. 5.109, 7.95), which Tacitus, who takes an unfavourable view of him, interprets as prodigality (*Ann.* 6.7.1 *egens ob luxum*). On him see R. Syme, *History in Ovid* (1978), 117-131, *The Augustan Aristocracy* (1989), 229-239.

1 *legetur* on the tomb.

3 It is hard to know how literally to take this; a one-time gift of equestrian census to a freedman is mentioned Mart. 7.64.2, cf. Schol. Juv. 5.109 with *Laus Pis.* 109-11.

6 For such contributions to or of a dowry cf. Cic. *De Off.* 2.55, Pliny, *Ep.* 2.4.2, 6.32.

7-8 The son served out his time (*emeruit*) as military tribune. Some strings will have had to be pulled to secure an equestrian office for a freedman's son (Mommsen 3.452; Demougin 315, 655). The name Cottanus, not found elsewhere, was coined as a tribute to the patron, cf. Vopiscianus *CIL* 14.4242 = *ILS* 1044.

9 *quid non Cotta dedit?* is a formula of closure, cf. 199A.A86.

10 *dedit* i.e. he commissioned the verses.

26

CLE 271 = *CIL* 3.77, 12076

This inscription, now in the British Museum, was found at Talmis in Nubia, which was a *statio* on the Roman road on the west bank of the Nile, now called Kalabsha (or a similar transcription of its Arabic name). It was first seen by B. G. Niebuhr lying in the court of the huge temple of the Nubian god Mandulis, which was temporarily flooded as a result of the Asswan dam but has now been removed and re-erected. The acrostich gives the name *Iulii Faustini M-*; he is otherwise unknown, and presumably this was his grave-stone. M. Petronius Mamertinus was prefect of Egypt 133-137 and heard (7-9) the 'statue of Memnon' (on which see below nos. 75-6) near Thebes in 134 (*CIL* 3.44 = Bernand 40); *signa* 9 is poetic plural. He evidently travelled as far south as Talmis, and

Bücheler suggests that where the poem breaks off it was about to describe the bursting forth of a spring during his visit.

1 Every emperor introduces a new *saeculum*, cf. 6 and my note on Juv. 4.68. The Muses are 'victorious' because they are contemporaneous with an 'invincible' emperor.

2 *crinitus Apollo* Ennius, *trag.* 28, Verg. *Aen.* 9.635.

3 An elegant 'golden' line like 9; other lines too show a partiality for two adjectives and two nouns (1, 4, 5, 11, 12, 13). *Serenificus* is not found elsewhere.

4 For the spelling *frus* cf. *CIL* 1.583.64 (this inscription elsewhere has *fraus*), Lucr. 6.187 and occasionally as a variant in manuscripts (in the verb too); it is doubtless a back-formation from *defrudo.*

6 This must be either *Hadriăno* or *Hadrjano;* so also in 121.3 (cf. Metre I d) and quite often in Greek epigrams, e.g. those of Balbilla on Hadrian's visit to Memnon (Bernand 28-31), in one of which (28.12) she says δῆλον παῖσι δ' ἔγεντ' ὤς ϝε φίλισι θεοί. Previously the gods had fled like Astraea (Justice) after the Golden Age. Presumably the *inuictus dux* contrasted with Hadrian during whose reign poetry did not flourish is Trajan.

7 *peroccultus* is not found elsewhere, but if we read *per occultas,* as texts do, we shall be left with an unexampled and harsh construction of *rimata.*

8 *tempora prisca* The 'Golden Age' now revived.

9 Martial 13.117.1 has *Māmertinus,* which is what we should expect.

10 *superum fides* Lucan 2.17.

11 Isis = Io = the daughter of Inachus, but *Inachias* means more than just 'Egyptian'; Isis was particularly patroness of the district of Talmis (E. Bernand, *Inscriptions métriques de l'Égypte Gréco-Romaine* (1969), no. 166 (p. 577) 20-21).

sospes is said in view of the dangers of the journey. *diti pede* on Bücheler's interpretation will mean 'an enriching foot', because where it treads a spring bursts forth. *pede pressit harenam* Ovid, *Met.* 8.869.

12 *sedilia* on which the devotees sit.

13 From personal inspection I can verify that the last letter, though damaged, is T. That seems to permit only the supplement *at[ris,* but I cannot interpret this and suspect that it may have been an error for *artis,* the crowded houses of the town.

27

CLE 1861 = *IGRR* 1.1207 = *ILS* 8908 = E. Breccia, *Inscriptiones Graecae Aegypti II Inscrr. nunc Alexandriae in Museo* (1911), 49 no. 66 = F. Preisigke, *Sammelbuch gr. Urkunden* 1 (1915), 307 no. 4282

From Egyptian Thebes; Sulpicius Serenus is probably identical with the Ser. Sulpicius known from *IGRR* 1.1200 = Preisigke, *Sammelbuch* 5. 8340; cf. Bernand 20.1. Clearly he pursued a marauding band of Agriophagi. This tribe, supposed to live on the flesh of wild beasts, is mentioned by Pliny *NH* 6.195, *Peripl. Maris Eryth.* 2 and located on the southern border of Egypt near to Berenice; perhaps Sulpicius was prefect of the garrison there just before Hadrian abolished it (see on 76).

In 1 *arăm instruxit* is so scanned (see Metre I c), in 2 the metre (trimeters, not senarii) is temporarily abandoned to accommodate the proper name (cf. p. 23).

3 i.e. *periit*.

4 A few more letters have been deciphered in this line, but they are neither certain nor intelligible. Somewhere the line must have had a finite verb.

5 The camels were brought by the Agriophagi to carry off the booty.

28

CLE 1814 = *CIL* 6.34001 = *ILS* 9022

The initial letters are separated from the rest of the line, as presented above, to mark out the acrostich (cf. 48); this is the origin of the name παραστιχίς (*Philol.* 134 (1990), 4). Each hexameter is also split into two lines of which the second is inset (cf. 40, 44); this throws the initial letters into yet greater relief. The *signum* so produced is Macarius. A *signum* is an extra name separated from the rest of the name and often substituting for it; see *RE* xvi.1663, ii A 2448, Kajanto *Supernomina*. Such *signa* proliferated under the Roman empire; Kajanto 53 sees this as the first occurrence of the word in this strict sense.

This man was *procurator ad oleum* (*CIL* 14.20 = *ILS* 372; 175 A.D.), in charge of distributions of oil to the people. The joint rule of Marcus Aurelius and Commodus under which he held this post was in 176-180 A.D.

1 For the scansion *Aeliu'* see Metre I h. Here the writer surely had in mind the cadence of Enn. *Ann.* 329 *catus Aelius Sextus.*

2 Contrast the correct *in luce moranti, CLE* 1400.3. *trigintă* has been weakened from classical *trigintā*, cf. 193.3 and NW 2.290, Hallbauer 75, 77, 81-2, 84, L. Mueller 421; in Ausonius such numerals always end in -*ă*.

3 *populi* tends to encroach on *populus* (Bömer on Ovid, *Met.* 6.179, Venini on Stat. *Th.* 11.654). The alliteration of *p* is striking.

4 *Commodus* is scanned as if it were *Comodus* (cf. Metre I k), as indeed it is sometimes spelt (*TLL onom.* s.v. 547.47). *īmpĕrātor* and related verbal forms offer insuperable problems to dactylic poets, which they solve by use of this archaic form when it is unavoidable. *induperantum* ends the line in Ennius (cf. on l. 1) *Ann.* 412.

6 Cf. *CEG* 635.4 φθονερὰ τ[οῖς ἀ]γαθοῖσι Τυχ[ή].

7 For *imuenias* cf. Leumann 139, SP 196, for *dum uita maneret CLE* 2107 B2, 1829.5, *ILCV* 1096.2; *dum uita manebat* (128.15) and *cum uita maneret* are also common.

29

AE 1968, 164 = Reynolds, *PBSR* 34 = 21 (1966), 66 (photo pl. xviiib).
Discussion: Peachin, *Phoenix* 40 (1986), 446 (cf. id. in *Studien zur Gesch. der röm. Spätantike, Festgabe J. Straub* (1989), 188); Vanderspoel, *ZPE* 79 (1989), 159

This inscription comes from Southern Etruria (the find-spot is marked by '29' on my sketch-map of Italy); a few letters survive from a column to the right of this. Carpus (for the name cf. 192) and his son (at least one presumes that to be the relationship) were clearly imperial freedmen. The son was in the office *a memoria*. The father was a mint official, and if, as the wording of 4 suggests, he was actually *procurator Monetae*, he must have been of equestrian status. That raises two problems: (1) his relationship to a freedman son; (2) the fact that equites were supposed to be of free birth. In answer to (1), the son died before the father, and *iuuenem* 9 suggests at a young age (*CIL* 14.4062 = *ILS* 1673 is an *adlectus a memoria* who died at the age of seventeen), so the father could have been promoted to equestrian rank after the death of his son; to (2), imperial patronage sometimes overrode such restrictions (see P. R. C. Weaver, *Familia Caesaris* (1972), 282; G. Boulvert, *Domestique et Fonctionnaire* (1974), 250-6; Demougin 650), as Vespasian elevated the freedman father of Claudius Etruscus to equestrian status (Stat. *Silv.* 3.3.143).

The verse is of sub-literary nature; apart from the irregular pentameters and the abandonment of the metre forced by the term *a memoria* in 9 (cf. p. 23), there are instances of hiatus in 4 and 5, a lengthening at the caesura in 7, and a false quantity in 6.

1-2 i.e. *cerne nos, quos similes fecit manus* (cf. on 103a). *similis* is often applied to portraits, e.g. Juv. 2.6. Reynolds thinks that *numen* means the inspiration of the sculptor, which seems unlikely; I think that the writer has in mind the idea of passages like Verg. *Buc.* 3.60 *ab Ioue principium Musae* (Otto *Iuppiter* 1 and *Nachträge* 174, 239; Nisbet - Hubbard on Hor. *Odes* 1.12.13).

4 For *procuro* with dative cf. Ulpian, *Dig.* 43.8.2.17.

5 *mihi* is the pleonastic dative pronoun which flourished in vulgar Latin (HS 93-4), cf. 40.17, 120.1, 171.6 and specifically for *cesso mihi* E. Dahlén, *Études syntaxiques sur les pronoms réfléchis pléonastiques* (1964), 90.

10-12 He claims the hero Achilles as an ancestor, as Pallas was alleged in flattery to descend from Evander (Tac. *Ann.* 12.53.2); one can hardly suppose that an ex-slave had a human ancestor called Achilles. Achilles' portrait bust was in the middle between those of Carpus and his son. Properly speaking Bootes is a constellation and Arcturus the brightest star in it, but the two names can be interchanged (*TLL* ii.2128.60). Reynolds (who however misunderstands 11-12) suggests that *tutatus* is an etymological allusion to the second element of this name (οὖρος = guardian). After *nobiliter* there is an upper serif, which to Reynolds suggests that I or V followed; but the N of *Monetae* 4 has such a serif, which supports my supplement. Though Arcturus is patron of civil servants (Manil. 5.357 sqq.), it looks as if it is introduced merely as an ornamental comparison, and that the antecedent of *qui* is not *Bootes* but *Achillis*. In that case the hero from his distant tomb protects his alleged descendants; *maior* is rare in the singular = 'ancestor' but cf. e.g. Apul. *Flor.* 2 *maior meus Socrates*.

30

AE 1977, 762 (Barnea, *Dacia* n.s. 19 (1975), 258 with photo) = E. Dorutiu-Boila, *Inscriptiile din Scythia Minor* 5 (1980), 281 with photo.

Discussions: Solin, *Arctos* 15 (1981), 116 and 19 (1985), 198; Vassileiou, *RPh* 57 (1983), 66; Gamberale, *ZPE* 77 (1989), 43.

This stone was re-used in the surrounding wall (built around 300 A.D., whence a terminus ante quem for the inscription is derived) at Noviodunum (*RE* no. 7, col. 1191), modern Isaccea, situated just before the delta of the Danube. Noviodunum was a base of the Danube fleet, *classis Flauia Moesica*; see *RE* l.c. 1192.31 and *Moesia* 2398.39, C. Starr, *The Roman Imperial Navy* (ed. 2, 1960), 159 n.34. Nothing else is known of the prefect Postum(i)us. *alumnus* can mean 'subaltern' to an officer (Ruggiero s.v. 440b), but here looks more as if it means 'foster-son' (113, 119A etc.; B. Rawson, *The Family in Ancient Rome* (1986), 173; Nielsen, *C et M* 38 (1987), 141).

Krystallus is a rare name and would be an odd name for a Roman infant born in Spain, but certainly looks like a probable supplement. The other *alumnus* bears, as often happens, a river-name; there are many rivers called Achelous, one of them in Lydia. His origin presents a puzzle. Tyana (for the feminine form here supplemented see *RE* s.v. 1632.10) is in the south-west corner of Cappadocia, nowhere near the Black Sea (Pontus) nor the province of Pontus, nor even to the Mediterranean (understanding *ponti*), from which it is separated by about 70 English miles across Cilicia. I can only suggest that there was an otherwise unknown Tyana in the north of Cappadocia.

Poem A is in iambic dimeters, with *-s* ignored in *alumnus* 3 and the second *ae* in *primaeue* 7 weakened to ĕ (the difference of quantity marked by difference of spelling). See Metre I a and h.

A1 *fluentum Ibericum* the Ebro; cf. *flumen* with adjective (*TLL* s.v. 958.69).

A5 *longe* in effect acts as an adjective = *longinqua*, cf. Verg. *Aen.* 1.13.

A6 'On the Moesian shore', i.e. by the banks of the Danube.

A9 Stat. *Silv.* 5.3.252 *raperis, genitor, non indigus aeui.*

A10 For *florum germina* cf. *De Rosis* (OCT *App. Verg.* p. 177) 23-4, Avien. *Arat.* 738, Claudian, *In Eutr.* (20) 2.96 *laxabant germina flores.*

A11 The Thracian wind is proverbial for cold to those on whom it swoops down from the north (Hor. *Odes* 1.25.11 with Nisbet - Hubbard; *RE, Thraskias* 561.43); here as a fossilised topos it is

applied to people situated north of Thrace.
B3 For the dative *Acheloo* cf. HS 90-1, KS 1.420.
B4 For *artibus ingenuis* cf. *CLE* 1167.1, 2068.5.

*31***

CLE 279 = *CIL* 6.1163 = *ILS* 736

This poem, known from two sixteenth-century reports and a tiny fragment (*CLE* 268 = *CIL* 6.31249 = 10.1863) containing the end of 7, was on the base of the obelisk which Constantius erected on the *spina* of the Circus Maximus in 357 A.D. (*RE, Obeliskos* 1713.40) during his visit to Rome (Amm. Marc. 16.10.17); each of the four sides of the base had six verses inscribed on it. The obelisk was rediscovered in situ in 1587 and in 1588 resited in front of the basilica of St John Lateran, where it still is minus the ancient base. It is of red granite (cf. 19), and is the largest obelisk in existence, whence the insistence on the tremendous task of moving and re-erecting it. Constantine had intended to bring it from Thebes to Constantinople (so this inscription (5) says, contradicting Ammianus, whose version that Rome was the intended destination is preferred by Fowden, *JHS* 107 (1987), 54; cf. Nicholson, ibid. 109 (1989), 198). In fact he transported it as far as Alexandria, where it lay for twenty years. Ammianus' account (17.4.13-15) of the bringing of the obelisk to Rome shows verbal coincidences with this poem; compare *auulsam hanc molem sedibus suis* with 6 and 19, and he calls it *mons ipse*, cf. 12. See Nash 2.142, Richardson 273-4 with further references.

There is another obelisk inscription (that erected in the hippodrome in Constantinople in 390 A.D.) in *CLE* 286.
2 cf. *refert* ('recovers') *orbem* 35.7.
3 Cf. Sil. It. 6.152 *cui par uix uiderit aetas / ulla uirum.*
4 *condidit* cf. 24. *exaequet* shows disregard of sequence (cf. 2.6-7 and Konjetzny 337-8) if this is a purpose rather than a consecutive clause.
5 This is from the adjective *cognominis*, the city named after the emperor himself.
7 For *diuus* cf. *TLL* s.v. 1658.3, *onom.* s.v. *Constantinus* 574.20; applied to Christian emperors (*RAC* s.v. 1255, Wissowa 347) it no longer implies deification but divine favour and an aura of sanctity

which has been compared (though the matter is rather controversial) to the position of a saint (cf. 'St John the Divine'); see Bowersock in B. F. Meyer - E. P. Sanders (edd.), *Jewish and Christian Self-definition* (1983), 3.176.
9 It was as massive as the Caucasus.
10 *dominus mundi* was how Constantius wished to be known (Amm. Marc. 15.1.3). For *fretus* with infinitive see *TLL* s.v. 1319.1.
12 *haut partem exiguam montis* Verg. *Aen.* 10.128.
14 *litus in Hesperium* Verg. *Aen.* 6.6.
15 Magnentius proclaimed himself Augustus in 350, and was defeated by Constantius and committed suicide in 353. *tyrannus* under the dominate is the usual term for a usurper, cf. *CLE* 278.4 and *CIL* 6.1158 = *ILS* 731 also of Magnentius and 36.1 below; the use is frequent in SHA (cf. R. Seager, *Ammianus* (1986), 120; Wardman, *Historia* 33 (1984), 222; H. W. Bird, *Sextus Aurelius Victor* (1984), 112-3). Magnentius subjected Rome to a blood-bath after the revolt of Nepotian in July 350. Ammianus 16.10.1 says that it was largely to mark the defeat of Magnentius that Constantius visited Rome; *triumfis* in 4 and 24, if that is accepted, could be taken as poetic plural, cf. 74.5.
16-7 *locandi, spreti* sc. *doni. iacuit* is taken in two different senses by syllepsis. *crederet* would be *credebat* in classical Latin, cf. HS 575, Konjetzny 340.
18 *tantae...molis opus* Ovid, *Ex Ponto* 2.5.28; *consurgere in auras* Lucr. 6.1021.
19 *auulsa metallis* cf. Lucan 6.34; sc. *moles*.
22 *uirtute* cf. 11.
23 *uictor ouans* Verg. *Aen.* 5.331.
24 *principis* i.e. Constantine; *munus* takes up 1 and *condit* 4 by ring-composition, cf. on 35.10, 127.20, 132.6.

32

CLE 111 = *CIL* 6.1779 = *ILS* 1259 = M. J. Vermaseren, *Corpus Cultus Cybelae Attidisque* (EPRO 50) 3.246
Discussion: Polara, *Vichiana* 4 (1967), 264 (thin).
Photo: A. Momigliano (ed.), *The Conflict between Paganism and Christianity* (1963), fig. 7-8; A. Rostagni, *Storia della Letteratura Latina* 2 (1952), 712-3; Walser p. 63 no. 20 (the prose); Vermaseren pl. CXXXIII - CXXXV.

I have followed Bücheler in presenting the faces of the stone in this order; since the husband died first, it seems logical to have his epitaph before his fictitious address to his wife. For the dialogue form see on 180. The monument was clearly erected after the death of the wife, despite 41.

For Vettius Agorius Praetextatus see *PLRE* 1.722, *RE, Praetextatus* 1 and e.g. Bloch, *HThR* 38 (1945), 203-9, A. Chastagnol, *Fastes de la Préfecture de Rome* (1962), 171, J. Matthews, *Western Aristocracies* (1975), 6. Among many other high offices he was proconsul of Achaea in 362-4 and died at the end of 384 before he could enter on the consulship in 385 for which he had been designated. Since they lived together for forty years, he married his wife Paulina (*PLRE* 1.675) in 344. He was a leading champion of the pagans in their last losing battle against Christianity, and his death is deplored by Symmachus, *Relationes* 10-12 (R. H. Barrow, *Prefect and Emperor* (1973), 72-81). He exemplifies the combination of scholarship and intense religious feeling characteristic of one section of the late Roman aristocracy. Paganism is by now highly syncretistic (*numen multiplex* 15; cf. Wissowa 98-9, Latte 369, Nock 37), and the list of his religious affiliations shows three main strains under the umbrella of sun-worship (one may compare *CLE* 264, 654, 1529; he is made to expound a solar theology in Macrob. *Sat.* 1.17-23):

(1) traditional Roman priesthoods;

(2) oriental cults like Serapis, Cybele and Attis, Mithras;

(3) Greek mysteries; his proconsulship of Achaea offered a convenient occasion for initiation into these. The prose mentions the Eleusinia and distinguishes from them mysteries of Liber (the husband) and Ceres (the wife); *CIL* 6.1780 = *ILS* 1260 *sacratae apud Laernam deo Libero et Cereri et Corae* shows that this means the rites at Lerna, for which see *RE, Lerna* 2087.49 and *Lernaia; Mysterien* 1269.70; W. Burkert, *Ancient Mystery Cults* (1987), 146 n. 22. It also shows that 28 refers to the mysteries of Hecate on Aegina, for which see *RE, Hekate* 2781.20-49, *Mysterien* 1272-3, Thiersch, *Nachr. Göttingen Gesellsch.* 1928, 151; the designation of the husband as *hierophanta* and of the wife as *hierophantria* refers to this (*RE, Hekate* l.c.). As well as the Greek mysteries, the oriental cults have now developed initiation rites; this is part of the late antique longing for revelation and gnosis.

The metre is iambic trimeter, showing features of senarii in the fourth-foot anapaest in 24 and the second-foot spondee in 34 (cf.

149.8). The Bentley-Luchs law is violated in 39; it is by now generally ignored (J. Soubiran, *Essai sur la Versification Dramatique* (1988), 387), and in any case is not observed by all writers of trimeters with the same strictness as in senarii. See Metre II B e. There is a striking fondness for an anapaest in the first foot.

1 Paulina was the daughter of Aconius Catullinus, praefectus praetorio 341, praefectus urbi 342, consul 349; he too was a pagan.

2 *iam tum* is elliptical, sc. when he married me; cf. on 123.6.

4 It is odd that we cannot pin down assertions of the distinguished family of Praetextatus, and do not know his father. He is generally supposed to be the son of C. Vettius Cossinius Rufinus, praef. urb. 315-6, cos. 316.

6 Praetextatus was highly respected by pagans and Christians alike.

8-12 This suggests that Praetextatus participated in the work of correcting manuscripts of pagan classics like the members of the circle of Symmachus, of whose activity we have record in manuscript subscriptions; for Praetextatus himself we have no record, but such work by his descendant Vettius Agorius Basilius Mavortius is recorded in the manuscripts of Horace, and also in Par. lat. 8084 of Prudentius (what an irony that a descendant of Praetextatus should study a Christian poet!). Cf. Symmachus, *Ep.* 1.53.1 (to Praetextatus) *remissa tempora et ab negotiis publicis feriata libris ueterum ruminandis libenter expendis.*

9 This recalls the words put into the mouth of Scipio by Ennius in his epitaph (44 in *FLP*) *mi soli caeli maxima porta patet*. For *soforum* cf. 70.5 and *CLE* 434.5 *studiumque sophorum,* i.e. philosophers; Praetextatus is known to have translated into Latin the commentary of Themistius on Aristotle's Analytics. See also Pfligersdorffer, *WS* 65 (1950-1), 131.

11 *solutis* i.e. in prose; *OLD* s.v. 9.

13 One might better spell *mustes,* cf. *TLL* s.v. 1758.33.

14 Cf. 45 *arcana mentis.*

19-20 Symmachus, *Rel.* 12.2 says of Praetextatus *gaudia corporis ut caduca calcauit. parua* takes up 13.

21 This imitates a phrase of Symmachus in the poem in *Ep.* 1.1.5 (375 A.D.) *bis seno celsus...fasce cluis* (*FLP* 448).

23 *puram ac pudicam* is an alliterative phrase not listed by Wölfflin; cf. also 57.

26 *Dindymenes* i.e. Cybele. Firmicus Maternus, *De Errore Prof. Rel.* 18.1 speaks of an Ἄττεως μύστης; this form of the genitive is not found elsewhere. For Cybele and Attis in this connection see R.

Duthoy, *The Taurobolium* (EPRO 10, 1969), 63-6.
27 In the taurobolium the initiate stood in a pit and was spattered with the blood of a bull slaughtered on a grid above the pit; see M. J. Vermaseren, *Cybele and Attis* (1977), 101.
28 *trina* because of the common identification of Hecate with Selene and Diana-Artemis (141.2).
29 'The Greek Ceres' is Demeter.
30 *omnis* is nom. pl., cf. on 2.6.
32 *ignota* indicates the female virtue of not being spoken about (Thuc. 2.45.2; cf. *infamis*, *CLE* 1988.27, which does not mean 'infamous').
34 For the adjective *Romulus* cf. *OLD* s.v. b, and in general for the creation of adjectives from proper names without suffixation HS 427, KS 1.233.
35 Their son set up *CIL* 6.1777 = *ILS* 1258.
39 *felix* sc. *futura*, 'I would have been happy'; cf. 70.9.
41 For the three tenses cf. HS 708, Ellis on Catull. 21.2, Leo, *Ausg. kl. Schr.* 1.164-5.
42 *consortio* is nom. sing. of the third-declension noun. *Consors* and *consortium* are often applied to partners in marriage; see Treggiari 9, 251.
45 For *arcana mentis* cf. Stat. *Silv.* 2.1.57.
48 *coniugali* for the sake of the metre replaces *coniugis*, which would correspond to the other genitives.
51 *aetatis usu* means the experience brought by life, *consecrandi foedere* their shared initiations.
52 *iūgi* from the adjective *iugis*; *iugi concordia* Gell. 12.8.6 (one may note that the *Noctes Atticae* was well known to Macrobius, who introduces Praetextatus as a character in his *Saturnalia*).
56 cf. Tac. *Agr.* 6 *uixerunt...in uicem se anteponendo.*

33

CLE 2046 = *ILS* 8987
Discussion: Mommsen, *Sitzb. Berl. Akad.* 35 (1902), 836 with photo.
Drawing: B. Thomas, *Römische Villen in Pannonien* (1964), 272.

A bronze tablet found near Magyar Boly in Pannonia; since this is in the middle of nowhere, one will infer that it was the site of the villa of Valerius Dalmatius (who is otherwise unknown). Similarly in *CLE* 329 = *CIL* 13.921 = *ILS* 6117 the province of Lugdunensis Senonia presents *tabulae* to its former governor, calling him its *patronus, tantis pro meritis,* and says that it would really have preferred to present statues. Since that inscription was found in a country district in Aquitania, one must infer that that governor too had retired to his villa; for such retirements see Matthews, *Aristocracies* (on 32) 44. The *prouincia Lugdunensis tertia,* which comprised Brittany and la Touraine, is not heard of until nearly the end of the fourth century (the *Notitia Dignitatum* and *Chron. Min.* (MGH, AA 9) 1.538; see A. Alföldi, *Die Untergang der Römerherrschaft in Pannonien* 2 (1926), 61), from which we deduce a dating. For such subdivided provinces cf. 161.

1 *Ius* means 'administrative power', which in ancient and modern times need not be exercised in accordance with *iustitia;* cf. Cic. *Phil.* 9.10. For the spelling *aequm* see on 188.9.

2 *alma Fides, CLE* 1376.10 etc.

3-4 The Twelve Tables, the praetorian edicts and the imperial *constitutiones*. It is an open question whether *condita* is governed by *doctus* or by *tenet*.

5 Cf. Cic. *Pro Clu.* 46 *legum ministri magistratus, legum interpretes iudices,* and note the difference of viewpoint. Juv. 4.79 *interpres legum* (the urban prefect) is closer. Note the chiastic word-order.

6 *Prudens* is the mot juste in connection with the law, cf. *OLD* s.v. 2 and modern 'jurisprudence'.

7-8 *multis pro meritis* is an emphatic epanalepsis.

9 *publica uota, CLE* 2099.10 etc.

10 *patriae* i.e. of Dalmatius.

11 These are the *publica uota* of 9; they hope that he will eventually attain to a prefecture (one cannot conceive immediate elevation to this eminence after the governorship of such a backwater as *Lugdunensis tertia*).

13 *celebratus amore, CLE* 400.2.

15 For the spondaic hexameter see Metre II A i.

16 *Clienta* is similarly used only by Auson. *Parent.* 24.12 (to be dated c. 380 A.D.).

34

AE 1927, 48 = 1948, 54 = 1951, 251 = V. Beševliev, *Spätgriechische und spätlat. Inschr. aus Bulgarien* (1964), 74, with photo taf. 26.

Discussion: Stroux, *Hermes* 79 (1944), 192; *Sitzb. Berl. Akad.* 1949.1 (almost identical).
Photo; *Recueil M. Niedermann* (1954), frontpiece.

This was found at the village of Vojvoda in Bulgaria, and probably came from the port of Odessus, modern Varna. The harbour wall had collapsed (*hanc r[uinam* 9), and its masonry had turned into a danger to shipping (*obiecta scrupea* 8), so that some ships were wrecked in the apparent safety of the harbour; Eusebius (who cannot be identified) cleared away this hazard and repaired the mole.

The metre is so defective that analysis of its faults is pointless. The writer however has read his Horace; with 1 and 5 cf. *Odes* 1.3.10 *qui fragilem truci / commisit pelago ratem*.

1 The subject was *aliquis*, often used like τις to mean 'many a one'.

3 *classem* = 'ship', cf. *TLL* s.v. 1283.60, adding Catull. 64.53 and 212 in view of 249; *amissam classem* Verg. *Aen.* 4.375.

5-6 'Shipwreck in harbour' was proverbial (Otto, *portus* 1 with *Nachträge* 115, 202, 284). Cf. Verg. *Aen.* 10.55 sqq. *quid pestem euadere belli / iuuit....*

7 His deeds surpassed the expectations aroused by his name 'Pious'; for such puns on names see on 176. The old antithesis between λόγος and ἔργον underlies this.

9 *rettulit in melius* Verg. *Aen.* 11.426.

10 'He restored its lost good name to the harbour and the harbour to use'; for the latter cf. *ILS* 5701 and the restoration on 5888.

35

CLE 893 = *CIL* 5.7781 = *ILS* 735
Discussion: various authors, *Maia* 27 (1975), 3; F. Della Corte, *Romanobarbarica* 5 (1980), 94 = *Opuscula* 7.226 (a far-fetched claim that the author is Rutilius Namatianus)
Photo: N. Lamboglia, *Albenga* (ed. 2, 1957), 16 fig. 9; id., *Rivista Ingauna* 31-2 (1976-8), 36.

This is from Albigaunum, modern Albenga, on the coast about halfway between Genoa and Monaco. The discovery of two new fragments of Rutilius Namatianus by Ferrari, *IMU* 16 (1973), 15 has thrown much light on this epigram. The relevant portion of the second fragment reads

1]unt in propugnacula rupes
meritum machina tollat [
<3-6 the walls of Thebes and Troy>
7 conditor(?) ips]e nouae consul Constantius ur[bis
]tium consiliumque dedit.
belli]gerum trabeis thoraca secu[
Latii nominis una salus.
inuictaque pectora curis
12 rep]etit Martia palma[
19 hostilibus ille recepit.

One will note the verbal coincidence *recepit* 19 (and *conditor* 7, if that is right) with the epigram 2 (and 6). It is now plain, since the journey of Rutilius is to be dated to 417, that the reference is to the Flavius Constantius who defeated the usurper Constantine III at Arles in 411, thus recovering Gaul, was consul in 414, 417 and 420, married Galla Placidia in 417 and became co-Augustus with Honorius as Constantius III in 421, in which year he died (*PLRE* 2, Constantius 16). The hostile races referred to in 9 were the Goths, whose army was hovering menacingly in the south of Gaul, having withdrawn there after Alaric's sack of Rome; it was obvious prudence to fortify Albigaunum.

3 *recenti* = fresh-cut, cf. Caes. *BC* 3.96.1 *r. caespitibus*.

4 *parta* seems to mean 'which he set up' (*TLL* x.1.403.27).

5 Bücheler prefers to take *portus* as genitive depending on *commercia*, but the asyndetic list of nouns (cf. 1) is much more stylish, and this form of line becomes very popular in late Latin (cf. *CP* 79 (1984), 310). The exact sense of each item is not to be pressed (cf. on 53); e.g. *ciues instituit* do not fit well together. For other such lists see 50.2 and 4, 199.1.

7 Cf. Rut. Nam. 1.66 *urbem fecisti quod prius orbis erat* (not that, as Della Corte points out, this is the only occurrence of the combination; see more in *TLL* ix.2.916.15 and Bréguet, *Hommages M. Renard* (CL 101, 1969), 1.140, culminating in the papal blessing *urbi et orbi*, and add *CLE* 1254.7, 2100.1-2). *refert* = 'recovers', cf. 31.2.

8 shows that the inscription was placed above the city gates.

10 *Constanti nominis* by ring-composition takes up 1, cf. on 31.24.

36

CLE 285 = *CIL* 3.735, 12327 = B. Meyer-Plath and A. M. Schneider,

Die Landmauer von Konstantinopel 2 (1943), 124 no. 8.

This inscription, reconstructed from the nail-holes which once attached bronze letters, stood above the Golden Gate at Constantinople, the first verse written inside, the second outside. It certainly refers to Theodosius II and the suppression of the usurper Ioannes Primikerios in 425, since we have the explicit testimony of Malalas (*Corpus Scr. Hist. Byz.* 28 p. 360) that it was Theodosius II who gilded the doors of the Golden Gate (which became the triumphal gate of the emperors); so Meyer-Plath and Schneider 43, Speck in H. G. Beck (ed.), *Studien zur Frühgeschichte Konstantinopels* (1973), 141 with other references. That gives us a date for this poem, but only a terminus ante quem for the gate itself, since Malalas' wording suggests that Theodosius II gilded already existing bronze doors. The gate is a puzzle since, as can be clearly seen in the photo in Meyer-Plath and Schneider taf. 27, or D. Talbot Rice, *Constantinople* (1965), pl. 18 facing p. 58, or Salway [see on 161] 285 (the last two, like others, refer this poem to Theodosius I and the usurper Maximus), it is not integrated with the city walls.
1 *Theudosius* (also in *CLE* 287.1 etc.) circumvents the problem of *Thĕŏdŏsīus* (cf. *CLE* 286 and Bücheler on 286.3; L. Mueller 316); Greek poetry had long availed itself of this device, and the spelling is quite common in e.g. Sidonius and found also in prose inscriptions. For *tyranni* cf. 31.15.
2 Just as each emperor opens a new *saeculum* (on 26.1), so each opens a new Golden Age; see my note on Ablabius in *FLP* 424. Meyer-Plath and Schneider quote an acclamation of 457, χρυσέους αἰῶνας βασιλεύουσα εὐτυχῆς εἴη ἡμῖν ἡ βασιλεία σου.

37

CLE 898 = *CIL* 5.8120.3, 13.10032.7a, b = *ILS* 1307 = R. Delbrueck, *Die Consulardiptychen* (1929), 26-8 pp. 141-3, taf. 26-8 = W. F. Volbach, *Elfenbeinarbeiten der Spätantik* (ed. 3, 1976), 25-7 pp. 38-9, taf. 12-13.

Three specimens of this consular diptych survive. The couplet is on the inside, and the outside reads

Fl. Petr(us) Sabbat(ius) Iustinian(us) u(ir) i(nlustris) com(es) mag(ister) eqq. et p(editum) praes(entalis) et c(onsul) o(r)d(inarius).

This is the future emperor Justinian marking his consulship in 521 A.D. while his uncle Justin I was still emperor. These ivory diptychs were mementos of the inauguration presented to senatorial friends. *meis* implies a proprietorial tone in the relations between the imperial house and the senate.

II B: BATHS AND SPRINGS, PRIVATE BUILDINGS, WORKS OF ART, FURNITURE

Under this heading one might include the epigram of Tullius Laurea (*FLP* 182).

38

CLE 865 = *CIL* 14.3911 = *IIt*. 4.1 (ed. 2, 1952) 596
Photo: *Forma Italiae, regio 1 vol. 17, Tibur, pars tertia* (Z. Mari) 316 fig. 534

Found at Tibur; it stood beneath a relief, of which only the horse's hoofs remain.

1-2 *Samis* is an unexampled and extraordinary name, and I suggest this is an error for *Samnis*, which is a cognomen on *CIL* 2.3512. The medicinal spring is *Aquae Albulae*, about five miles from Tibur on the road to Rome (now called Bagni di Tivoli). The water there was considered good for wounds (Pliny, *NH* 31.10, Galen 11.393 K) and for those suffering from loss of muscle control (Cael. Aurel. *Chron.* 2.1.48 *Albae siue Albulae quae sunt appellatae solutione laborantibus a ueteribus sunt approbatae;* cf. Pliny l.c. 59 *est autem utilis...aluminata (aqua) paralyticis aut simili modo solutis*). For *medicis...aquis* cf. Claudian, *Carm. Min.* 26 (Aponus) 86.

3-4 The subject is *articulus*. This is an incoherent way of saying *turgebat et solutus erat dente apri Russellani ex Etruria;* cf. 70.11-12. Rusellae in Etruria is usually so spelt; as here *CIL* 11. 6689.78 and a well-supported variant at Livy 28.45.18. For Etruscan boars and the good hunting there see my notes on Juv. 1.22 and Hadrian (?) fr. 4.4 (*FLP* 385).

5-6 *graciles* because the swelling had gone down. *accepto* sc. *Sam<n>ite;* he had recovered enough to ride again. For the 'Sandhi' in *ian nerui* cf. *CLE* 2138.2, *ianiam CIL* 14.4167 and Leumann 213-4.

9-10 'Where the lord of Tibur looks down on your shrine as you, spring, face him'. The lord of Tibur is Hercules, who had his large temple on the hill overlooking the plain where the spring is. What sort of shrine there was at the spring we do not know, but there was evidently some syncretistic cult; *CIL* 14.3534 = *IIt* 4.1.34 is a *sacerdos m(atris) d(eum) m(agnae) I(daeae) ad aquas Albulas,* and Mancini *NS* 1926, 417 publishes an inscription = *IIt* 4.1.592 in which a statue of

Diana is presented to *Albula Isis* (or perhaps *Albula* and *Isis* with an asyndeton). See also Mari, *Forma* l.c. 40. For the scant remains of paint on exterior surfaces of Hadrian's famous villa on the foothills of Tibur see P. Gusman, *La Villa Impériale de Tibur* (1904), 215.

39

CLE 273 = *CIL* 3.6306, 8153 = Sasel, (1940-60) 20 = M. Mirkovič - S. Dusanič, *Inscriptions de la Mésie Supérieure* 1 (1976), 48 (with photo).
Discussion: Marcovich, *ZPE* 56 (1984), 231.

This was found at Singidunum (Belgrade). The acrostich produces Ael. Tertius. During her lifetime his wife ran a bath-house for the veterans of *legio IV S(eueriana) A(lexandriana)* (*CIL* 3.8173 = *ILS* 2377), which was stationed at Belgrade (*RE, legio* 1543); after her death her husband Aelius Tertius with their daughter Aelia Tertia re-established it under the name of his dead wife. This name may have been stated on a previous slab, or we may follow Marcovich in restoring *[Faus]ta* in 11, where *[cas]ta* is usually read.

By classical standards the versification is deplorable; various features are remarked in Metre I a, d; II A d, f, h, j (i), l. In 5, if *Alexandriae* is correct, it is uncertain whether we should understand *Alexandrjae* (cf. I d) or shorten the last syllable, as in the other instances listed under I a; the beginning of the word is also scanned as *Ales-* (for Ἀλέσανδρος imposed by an acrostich in *GVI* 967 see Robert, *Gnom.* 31 (1959), 25; note also *Alesan[der]* on *CIL* 7.133 = *RIB* 375); cf. on 188.10.

3 *ipsis* must mean 'the very veterans who now use it'. *haec] tamen* is usually read, but seems too large for the space even with the ligature of AE found elsewhere in this inscription; perhaps *me] tamen*, though this involves scanning *lacu(s)* (see Metre I h).

4 For *tunc* before a guttural see on 199A.A35.

5 *quondam* no doubt goes with *emeritis*, or possibly, on the assumption that the legion has now been renamed *Gordiana* (*RE, legio* 1549), with *dignae*. I would then restore *Alexand[riae*; the normal adjective from Severus Alexander is *Alexandrianus*, as given above in the expansion of *CIL* 3.8173, but we find mention in the *Notitia Dignitatum* (one hopes that the text is sound) of a *legio Iulia Alexandria* which should doubtless be connected with him (Parker, *JRS* 23 (1933), 176

dissents, but without offering an alternative; A. H. M. Jones, *The Later Roman Empire* (1965), 3.375 suggests that it came from Egypt, but this should be *Alexandrina*). Then one will understand *legionis*.
6 A 'Golden Line', reinforced by the elevated compound adjective.
7 Cf. Claudian, *De Balneis Quintianis* (carm. min. 12) *lympharum dominum...inter dura uiae balnea qui posuit*.
8 *conse[crare]* is usually read, but it is blatantly unmetrical and far too long; moreover the letters *se* cannot be read. For the verb which I supply cf. Sen. *Dial.* 11.18.2 *cetera quae per constructionem lapidum et marmoreas moles aut terrenos tumulos in magnam eductos altitudinem constant*; its subject is *opus*.
10 *exordia* is fitted in pleonastically and with indeterminate grammatical construction. Professor Vine suggests to me that it may be an error for *ex ordine* due to the frequent occurrence of *exordia* (cf. 109.9) and the like in the context of acrostichs (cf. on 42.5); at Lucr. 2.1062 the opposite corruption has taken place.

40

AE 1929, 7b = *IRT* 918 = T1 Pikhaus

Discussion: Bartoccini, *Africa Italiana* vol. 2, anno 7 (1928-9), 55-8 with photos; Lavagnini *RFIC* 56 (1928), 416; 58 (1930), 216; Kroll, *Glotta* 19 (1931), 151; Vetter, *Mitteil. des Vereins kl. Philologen in Wien* 8 (1931), 43; Rebuffat, *Karthago* 1 (1987), 93 with plate p. 98; M. A. Marwood, *The Roman Cult of Salus* (1988), 77

From the baths (see *CRAI* 1972.331 [another acrostich inscription found there] and Brouquier - Reddé fig. 105 p. 180) at Bu-Ngem, a frontier fortress on the eastern boundary of Tripolitania established in 201 A.D.; it is uniform with *IRT* 919 from the same baths, which reads *centurio leg. III Aug. faciendum curauit*, and that centurion was no doubt Q. Avidius Quintianus, who emerges from the acrostich here. The baths were finished by 203 (*IRT* 913, redated by Rebuffat and Vita-Evrard l.c. 107). The name of the legion on 913 and 919 was erased after the legion itself was disbanded for its part in the murder of the Gordians. See Y. Le Bohec, *La Troisième Légion Auguste* (1989), 441-3.

Each line of verse is split into two of writing, so the format is like that of 28 and 44.

1 *quaesii* scans as if it were *quaesiui*; conversely in *CLE* 1144.8 *siuere* is scanned as if it were *siere*. The construction is *quaesii quod uotum commune memoriae traderem proque reditu redderem*, except that the writer hesitates between masculine (see on 19.1; cf. *CIL* 8.5667, 8248) and neuter gender for *uotum*; for such hesitation cf. Pieske 57, *CIL* 8 index 317b. *castra* also in 2 follows the path generally taken in late Latin and Romance from neuter plural to feminine singular (*CLE* 1616.12, *TLL* s.v. 548.44, Kübler 172).

2 *prae* takes the accusative in the vulgar speech of Petronius and often in late Latin. *agens prae cunctos milites* must mean 'commanding all the soldiers'; cf. the *agentes in rebus*. For the prosody see Metre I e.

3 Most of the first garrison was dispersed on operations; the return took place in 205 (*IRT* 920 and an inscription in *Libya Antiqua* 9-10 (1972-3), 122, cf. Rebuffat 128). Speidel, *Ant. Afr.* 24 (1988), 99 thinks that the reference is rather to the hoped-for relief of the garrison by its successor and its return to the legionary base.

4 sc. *uotos*.

7 *quem* is used as feminine, cf. Väänänen 114, Sommer 439, Pieske 38-9, Konietzny 306; cf. on 94e for *quendam* and *qui* = *quae* in an inscription quoted on 179.1. This is clearly on the road to the Romance simplification of the declension of the relative pronoun.

8 *quandium* (scanned as a spondee by synizesis; or it might be a dactyl, like *quandiŭcunque* in *CLE* 1988.43, since this writer was hardly sensitive to split anapaests, for which see Metre II B e) = *quamdiu*; the writer has omitted *m* so often that in compunction he now adds it hyper-correctly. For *Salus* = Hygieia cf. *RE* s.v. 2058-9, Wissowa 308, Le Bohec o.c. 557 n.218; *salus* is often associated with baths (*AL* 175.1, 179.6, 350.6, 377.12), cf. *salutiferas* 43.1. The archaism *sient* stands at the end of the senarius, as this and other archaisms often do in the old scenic poets; see Leumann 523, Dziatzko - Hauler, *Phormio* (ed. 4, 1913) p. 71.

10 sqq *Veras* because they belong to *Salus* as well as *salus*; the pun is intended also in 18, cf. *CIL* 13.6621 = *ILS* 602 *Salut(i) pro salute*, *CIL* 6.20 = *ILS* 2092 *Asclepio et s(S)aluti commilitonum*. The following construes *ut corpora* (nom.) *delenirent solis flammas tantis ignibus feruidas in istis collibus nutantis austri*. *nutare* often means 'to lean from the vertical', and when one envisages, as is natural, north as 'up' and south as 'down', the verb can mean 'inclining towards the south' (cf. Manil. 2.906); so here *nutantis austri* in effect means *australibus*. *istis* = *his* (see on 116.3); *hārenacis* (with a false quantity)

= *-iis* (cf. on 190.3).
15 *aestuantis* is scanned *aestvantis*; *fucilari* = *focilari*.
16-17 i.e. *laudem reddere <ei> qui*, cf. HS 555-6, KS 1.282. For *tibi* cf. on 29.5, and Dahlén (there cited) 120 specifically for *sanus sibi*. *pigere* looks as if it is used personally, cf. HS 417.

41

CLE 1802, 1911 = *CIL* 8.20267 = *ILCV* 229

This was found in the middle of the baths at Satafis, and is dated by the subscription between 359 and 388 A.D.
1 *fabrica mole* ends *CLE* 2041.5 also (from Carthage).
4 The beginning is usually supplemented *ac uir]es*, which, so far as I can judge from published reports, is too short. I propose e.g. *corpus, [nomen op]es* (*nomen* = fame); a reference to *opes* fits very well with the responsibility of rebuilding the baths. Cf. Sen. *Ag*. 805 *cuncta pollentis*. *suae* is not likely to be used for *tuae* (HS 176; cf. on 194.1); if it is not just an error, it probably means 'appropriate to the *nomen*' (or whatever else is restored), cf. HS 175, Housman 936-7 = *CQ* 10 (1916), 148.
5 The first word must have indicated the emperor.
7 *honos iste* (involving a false quantity which would have been avoided by *honor*) clearly refers back to the *honore* of 6, and we need an antecedent for the *quem* which must be assumed for the beginning of 8. I therefore propose something on the lines of *ex surrec]turis.../ per te, que]m*; you were once appointed governor over the Moors, now respect for you will spring up again as a result of the baths which will spring up through your agency.

42*

AL 120

Since Statius and Martial the themes of baths and warm springs had developed into a sub-genre for ecphrasis and epigram. Many surviving specimens are purely literary, but others, though preserved in literary traditions, have palpably been copied from actual buildings, and in *Hermathena* l.c. 38-42 I have tried to show that this is the case with some preserved in the Latin Anthology. In this poem we have an acrostich Filocali and a telestich Melaniae, perhaps distinguished respectively as *conditor* (cf. *AL* 213.7, *Epigr. Bob.* 2.1) and (if we accept that *prima* 6 is a psychologically easy corruption of *summa*) *auctor* of the baths. This may be interpreted to mean that Filocalus put up the baths, and the suggestion that he should do so was made by Melania; however it has to be admitted that *auctor* would normally be synonymous with *conditor* (cf. 39.7 above and Sidon. Apoll. *Carm.* 22.142-4), and it may be preferable simply to admit that the telestich is not referred to in the poem (this may have been felt unnecessary if it was originally rubricated). In *CP* 82 (1987), 237 J. Evans-Grubbs and I suggested that Filocalus can be identified with a subdeacon known from the correspondence of Augustine as *Hipponensium primarius* and *uir honorabilis*, and Melania with the younger of two prominent Roman aristocratic ladies of this name. She and her husband decided to live a life of Christian asceticism, sold off their estates in Western Europe and North Africa, and settled at Thagaste c. 410-417. As a noted philanthropist she might well have suggested the erection of baths, and indeed have put up some or all of the money for their construction. Cameron, *CP* 87 (1992), 140 prefers the elder Melania and the calligrapher Filocalus, but (1) we do not know of any connection between these and Africa: (2) Cameron thinks that the part of Filocalus was to engrave or compose the poem, but we do not know that he ever composed anything himself, and *condens* 1 and *condentis* 5 then have to be taken in different senses.

1 *domini* cf. 39.7.

2 *fessos...uiae* Cf. Stat. *Th.* 3.395.

3 According to Augustine Filocalus was *de fundo uiri spectabilis Oronti*. The baths might have been erected on this estate, so that the *fundi praesul* would be Orontius himself. If he is meant, we have to leave uncertain the relative parts played in their construction by Orontius, Filocalus and Melania.

4 *Dulcifluus* is a word used by Dracontius and other late authors. The spelling *(h)ospis*, a retrograde formation, is quite often encountered in manuscripts, but not inscriptionally.

5 Cf. *CLE* 511.10 *inspicies, lector, primordia uersiculorum*; Latin has to use such phrases since it has no word for 'acrostich' (cf. 28.8, 39.10).

7 *Pontiuagus* is not found elsewhere. Cf. *AL* 121.1-4 *quisquis Cumani lustrauit litoris antra...hic lauet, insani uitans discrimina ponti; Baiarum superant balnea nostra decus*. Since 42.7 is tailor-made to fit the

acrostich and telestich, it seems to be the original and *AL* 121.1 the imitation. The latter shows that *Cumani litoris antra* means Baiae, which in many of these poems is used to mean the archetypal acme of warm baths (cf. 43.1 and Dunbabin, *PBSR* 57 (1989), 14 n.59).
8 *deliciae* cf. 43.6.

43

CLE 1754, 2039 = *CIL* 8.25362 = *ILS* 8960 = *ILCV* 787 = *Musée Bardo* 432 with pl. 432 = A78 Pikhaus

Found at Tunis; Gebamund was a cousin of the last Vandal king, killed in battle in 534 A.D. (Procop. *Bell. Vand.* 1.18, 1.25.15; *Chron. Min.* 2 (*MGH, AA* 11) pp. 198, 299). The Vandals much admired the culture of the Romans whom they had displaced as lords of North Africa; in particular they admired the baths, and built a number themselves (C. Courtois, *Les Vandales et l'Afrique du Nord* (1955), 228 n.3).
1 *Baias* cf. on 42.7.
3-4 The epigrammatic point sought in many of these poems is the harmonious co-existence of fire and water (cf. Speyer, *JAC* 20 (1977), 40 and my note on Hilarius, *FLP* 454). For Vulcan and Neptune cf. *AL* 270, for *certat* ibid. 213.8 *decertat fontibus ignis.* Hülsen thought that a female deity would suit *amore* better and suggested *Ne[rine]*, which the photograph shows to be too short.
4 For *f[ocum* cf. *AL* 212.2. There is a nice pun *necat...nocet,* rather spoiled to classical taste by the accusative after the latter, for which cf. Hadrian (?) fr. 4.11 (*FLP* 386) and HS 33. Perhaps the writer had in mind Ovid, *Tr.* 1.8.4 *dabit ignis aquas;* cf. also *AL* 214.9 *non hic flamma nocet.*
5 *operi* is ablative, as Varro, *LL* 5.141 (not likely to be right at Arnob. *Adv. Nat.* 5.40); cf. on 2.3. For *regalis origo* cf. Cassiod. *Var.* 8.2.3 *ex uobis qui nascitur origo senatoria nuncupatur,* Claudian, *Laus Serenae* 36 *quae maior origo / quam regalis erit?*
6 For *deliciis* cf. 42.8; for *utere* 54.

44

Marrou, *REL* 44 (1966), 373; id., *Bull. d'Archéologie Algérienne* 3 (1968), 343 with photo 344.

This was found near Thibilis by a spring. The last line directs us to the acrostich *Felice* (sc. *curante*). Each line of verse is split into two of writing, so the outlay resembles that of 28 and 40. 3-4 seem to have started life as hexameters, *merserat ante latex <riuos> ubi sentibus horrens, / funditus incassum <nisos> superante ruina* or the like; 'where previously the water, over-grown with briars, had submerged its streams, with the collapse (presumably of a Nymphaeum) totally overcoming their useless efforts'. However the components of these lines seem to have been shuffled to fit into the acrostich. In 5 the reversal is unmotivated and probably a mere error; of course it is not impossible, though it seems unlikely, to scan *morē priscŏ* (see Metre I g, j (i)).
1 *mecum partire laborem* Verg. *Aen.* 11.510. *Uraniă* is vocative; *AL* 664.8 and 664a.8 *Uraniă pŏl-* look suspicious, though they support each other, but ibid. 88.8 *Uraniă* of the mss. is changed by editors to *-ie*. For the retention of the Greek quantity one may compare e.g. *Argiă#* five times in Statius; see NW 1.83-5, Sommer § 180. The epithet given to the Muse associates her with Felix the restorer, especially as this, like 175, is an acrostich of the type discussed in *Philol.* 134 (1990), 10-11, in which the horizontal and vertical words to be read on the pivot of the shared first letter are cognate.
5 Verg. *Aen.* 5.217 *radit iter liquidum* (through the air).
6 *si* is scanned short.

45

CLE 280 = *CIL* 3.188 = L. Jalabert - R. Mouterde, *Inscriptions Grecques et Latines de la Syrie* 1459

From Apamea, above an aperture in a wall through which grapes were poured into the press. SHA 17.21.2 mentions Apamean grapes as a delicacy.
1 *Baccheia munera* Auson. *Mosella* 153, after Verg. *Georg.* 2.454 *Baccheia dona*; cf. *Bacchi munera* 175.3, 199A.A 51 etc.
2 *bitis* = *uitis; genuīt* is lengthened at the caesura.

46

CLE 882 = *CIL* 2.4284 = *ILS* 6039 = *RIT* 801 with photo taf. 139.1.

From Tarraco; Hübner thinks that it was placed outside a guest-bedroom in a private house.
1 The writer does not want to lengthen *uiuīs*, so he prefers the subjunctive even though it does not match the indicative in 2. *eccum* = *ecce* (*TLL* 25.7, 83); this is the origin of Italian *ecco*. For the spondaic hexameter see Metre II A i.
2 *patior hospitium* 'I tolerate entertaining you'. The first three letters of *pudet* are in an erasure.

47

CLE 2054 = *CIL* 4.7698
Photo: Della Corte, *NS* 1927, 93-4; Spinazzola 2.754 tav. 731-5
Discussion: Vogliano, *RIFC* 53 (1925), 220; Morgenstern, *Ph. W.* 50 (1930), 702; Todd, *CR* 53 (1939), 168; A. Maiuri, *La Cena di Trimalchione* (1945) 241 and tav. viii

Written on the walls of a triclinium at Pompeii. These are *leges conuiuales*, like the spoof *lex Tappula* referred to by Lucilius and partly preserved in a fragmentary inscription (see Konrad, *ZPE* 48 (1982), 219), or that which ends the *Querolus* concerning injuries inflicted during drinking-bouts (cf. *iurgia* c1); these are conveniently accessible in Bücheler's Petronius. Pliny, *NH* 14.140 after mention of drunkenness caused by the *lex (conuiualis)* adds *tunc auidi matronam oculi licentur*, cf. b here.
a1 Catull. 65.6 *adluit unda pedem*.
a2 *mappa* = coverlet (Cato, *De Agr.* 10.5, 11.5; Varro, *LL* 9.47). *caue lintea* = 'don't mark the cloth with your dirty feet' (not 'keep your thieving hands off the napkins').
b reminds us of fictive situations set up by Ovid, not to mention the behaviour of some emperors at dinner-parties.
c1 For *iurgia* cf. Juv. 5.26 with my note. *litis* or *lites* was read by a number of scholars, and Todd confirmed Morgenstern's supplement from Ovid, *Fasti* 1.73-4 *lite uacent aures insanaque protinus absint / iurgia*.

48

CLE 1916 = *ILS* 9351 = *ILCV* 779
Photo: J. F. Matthews, *Political Life and Culture* (1985), XI between pp. 172 and 174; Camps, *Ant. Afr.* 20 (1984), 186; *L'Africa Romana, Atti del III Convegno, 1985*, tav. xxiv after p. 128.

This was found in a mountainous region of Mauretania at M'lakou near the stream Wed-Sahel (Soummane). The acrostich and telestich produce *Praedium Sammacis;* on the stone the first and last letters are separated (cf. 28) by small spaces from the rest of the lines, which are so laid out that the final letters are exactly below each other (this cannot be reproduced in modern print). This Sammac is the Zammac of Amm. Marc. 29.5.2 and the Salmaces of id. 29.5.13. He was the illegitimate son of the Moorish chieftain Nubel, and a loyalist to the Roman sway; he was killed by his legitimate half-brother Firmus when the latter rose in revolt in 372-3 A.D. Ammianus describes him as *dominus fundi Petrensis, quem in modum urbis extruxerat;* at this time such private fortresses spring up in north Africa like medieval baronial castles (Leveau, *MEFRA* 89 (1977), 302). For the political background see Matthews 174-7. Another Sammac is known from *CIL* 8.21728, but despite *PLRE* he can hardly be identical with this one.
2 *tutat* shows a false quantity; the active (rather than deponent) form is fairly common in pre-classical Latin and occasional thereafter (e.g. *CLE* 929.2), cf. P. Flobert, *Les Verbes deponents latins* (1975), 290, 359. *fida* is taken up by *fidem* 7.
4 The rocky mountain gives the name Petra to the fort. A dedication *genio Petrae* (*AE* 1969-70, 727) was found in Mauretania, but thirty miles away from M'lakou, and it is probably earlier in date; there seems therefore to have been another Petra.
8 Cf. 53.2.

49

AE 1967.85 = G. Jacopi, *L'Antro di Tiberio* (1963), 42 (with photo).
Photo: G. Jacopi, *L'Antro di Tiberio* (guide 1965), fig. 39; Krarup, *ARID* 3 (1965), 74; Sichtermann, *Gymn.* 73 (1966), taf. xix after p. 384 (cf. p. 229); Buchwald, *Philol.* 110 (1966) facing p. 290; Säflund, *Opusc. Romana* 7 (1967), 10; Bordenache, *Studii Clasice*

14 (1972) facing p. 224; R. Hampe, *Sperlonga und Vergil* (1972), taf. 33; G. Säflund, *The Polyphemus and Scylla Groups at Sperlonga* (1972), fig. 9 p. 21; *Dial. di Arch.*. 7 (1973), fig. 27 (cf. Coarelli p. 116); *Enciclopedia Virgiliana* 4 (1988) s.v. Sperlonga p. 992.

Discussion: see the above references, and H. Lavagne, *Operosa Antra* (1988), 540

This was discovered in the grotto near Tarracina called Spelunca (whence its modern name Sperlonga) in which Tiberius was nearly crushed by a rock-fall in 26 A.D. (Suet. 39, Tac. *Ann.* 4.59). Large sculptures were also found, of which two show scenes from the Odyssey, the blinding of Polyphemus and Scylla attacking the ship of Odysseus; it has been securely proved now that the stern of a ship with a man clinging to it is part of the latter and not a separate scene, so that line 6 of the poem will refer to this group as a whole. *Fractam puppim* has been interpreted in two ways: (1) it refers to the stern broken off by Scylla; (2) it refers to shipwreck. The latter seems correct to me (in which case *puppis* will, as commonly, mean the whole ship by synecdoche; so *frangere pupp-* at e.g. Prop. 3.7.39, [Ovid], *Her.* 19.186) because *in gurgite* is pointless with the former, and, while in the state of mutilation of this sculpture it is possible that the stern was shown as broken, it is not so shown on similar representations; moreover it is hard to see why Faustinus should want to stress this detail. On those other representations Scylla, as in Homer, is plucking men off the ship but not wrecking the ship. Faustinus' words would suggest that the sculptors altered their model, which seems to have been a bronze statue, in this respect. I believe that they were influenced to do so by Vergil's modification of Homer's account (*Aen.* 3.424-5 *Scyllam caecis cohibet spelunca latebris...nauis in saxa trahentem*, a passage to which their attention was directed by the word *spelunca*).

These deductions might seem to favour the view taken e.g. by Stewart, *JRS* 67 (1977), 88, that these sculptures are of early imperial date, and that the whole complex was designed for Tiberius. The Scylla is signed by the three Rhodian artists who were also, according to Pliny, responsible for the famous Laocoon, with which similar questions arise; on Stewart's view Tiberius may have got to know their work while he was on retreat in Rhodes until 2 A.D. One may note that a statue-base from Capri, probably from the villa of Tiberius, has an attribution to Athanadorus, one of these sculptors; it is, however, not a personal signature but a later attribution (see Rice referred to below). Unfortunately this whole argument founders on the proof by Rice, *Ann. Brit. School Athens* 81 (1986), 233 that Athanadorus was active in 42 B.C. (though Rice's argument that he was then middle-aged is not compelling), and that another of the sculptors, Hagesandros, appears on a dedication dated by Rice to about 50 B.C. Therefore one can hardly suppose that they were still active after 2 A.D., but they could still have been active when the *Aeneid* was published soon after 19 B.C., so the Virgilian influence which I seem to detect on the sculptors could still operate on Rice's chronology. I personally believe that the Laocoon was also influenced by Vergil, though there is much controversy about this.

The poem likewise shows many Vergilian echoes, but it goes too far to call it a Vergilian cento. The scansion *uiuăs* 8 (see the note) in a poem with literary pretensions proves it to be a product of late antiquity, certainly not earlier than the end of the third century; the lettering has suggested the same to some, but by no means to all. The sculpture of course is much older than that, and so too assuredly is its placement, so one must enquire what the role of Faustinus was. It may be either that he celebrates the grotto in verse (in which case one will follow those who restore in 10 e.g. *ho[c concinit antrum,* as Degrassi, or *praedicat,* as Tandoi), or that he refurbishes it, in which case one will think of e.g. *ho[c expolit antrum* (for the present tense cf. 36.1). The former seems pointless, the latter is supported by the fact that the Tiberius episode shows that the grotto may have needed occasional attention. Continued use of it is proved by the discovery in it of the head of a tetrarch, dating from c. 300 A.D., and of pottery going down into the sixth century. For another suggestion see on 10 below.

2 *cederet antro* 'would grant superiority to the grotto'.

3 *adque* = *atque. dolos Ithaci* is a quotation from *Culex* 326, where it refers to the trickery by which Odysseus won the arms of Achilles over Ajax. By now the *Culex* was firmly accepted as Vergilian. *lumen ademtum* of course quotes the Vergilian description of Polyphemus (*Aen.* 3.658); *flammas* refers to the fire in which the stake was hardened to blind Polyphemus.

4 This combines *Aen.* 3.630 *uinoque sepultus* (Polyphemus), 6.520 *somnoque grauatum,* 2.265 *somno uinoque sepultam.*

5-6 Cf. *Aen.* 1.200-2 *uos et Scyllaeam rabiem penitusque sonantis / accestis scopulos, uos et Cyclopea saxa / experti* (editors for some reason shrink from the spelling *Cyclopea,* which has overwhelming manuscript authority). *speluncas uiuosque lacus,* a quotation from *Georg.* 2.469, fits oddly into this context; one has to assume that the composer is thinking of the actual setting of the sculpture in the grotto and is transferring this back to the cave of Polyphemus. The opportunity to bring in the word *spelunca* in allusion to the name of the grotto was irresistible. 6 perhaps recalls *Aen.* 5.209 *fractosque legunt in gurgite remos*; the recall may be motivated by the fact that in the sculpture (as, to judge by the other representations, in its model) Scylla is grasping the steering-oar. In the grotto the Scylla group was placed on a base in the middle of a pool, a *gurges* (the word of course does not mean 'whirlpool').

7 *ipse fatebatur* Verg. *Buc.* 3.24. The line might have ended with e.g. *fingi* or *dici* or (with a comma after *uiuas*) *adesse.*

8 The false quantity in *uiuăs* cannot be evaded either by reading *ui* instead of *ut* (this is certainly not what is inscribed, removes the correlative of *sic* and produces a metrical singularity not much less difficult than that which it tries to remove) nor, with V. Tandoi, *Disiecti Membra Poetae* 3 (1988), 156 and 175, by understanding *uiua's* (i.e. *uiua es*); this is a form of writing never found on inscriptions, and no suitable feminine noun which can be fitted into the line presents itself. *artificis* is genitive singular with the last syllable lengthened by the beat like *opūs* 2; for the end of the line the supplement *express[it dextera formas* (Buchwald; one might vary to *express[it dextra figuras*) seems admirable.

10 Stat. *Silv.* 2.2.107 *sis felix, tellus, dominis ambobus* (addressing a villa at Sorrento) makes me think that we here have *felix*, not *Felix*, and that it is neuter, not masculine (I am not sure if Tandoi 176 intends this); cf. also Mart. 1.101.2, the hand of a secretary which is *felix domino*. We should like to know who the *domini* (of the grotto, not of Faustinus) were when Faustinus wrote. Prof. D. Kovacs suggested to me that *felix* might be predicative, and that we might then restore *ho[c reddidit antrum*. In any case Faustinus intended the semantic play between his name and *felix.*

50

AE 1927, 121 = Paribeni, *NS* 1926, 284

Found on the Via Appia Nuova on a headless herm, perhaps a double herm of Socrates and the younger Cato, who are often associated by Seneca. Portraits of philosophers adorn a place, probably a peristyle garden, intended for literary recitations; for such a setting see my note on Juv. 1.12. My suggested *antra* in 2 will mean 'bowers', as often. With 5 cf. the *uiuidum pectus* of Camillus in Livy 6.22.7. I think that 5-6 mean the countenance of Socrates and the intelligence of Cato show signs enough that the type <is apparent>' (supplementing e.g. *[hinc pateat*) rather than 'the busts show the countenance of Socrates...well enough that...' The type of what? Presumably of those represented by the other busts, i.e. after identifying Socrates and Cato you can infer that they are all philosophers. *satīs* is lengthened at the diaeresis. For the lists in 2 and 4 see on 35.5.

51

CLE 889 = *CIL* 6.48 = *ILS* 3375

A statue-base found on the Aventine. This is our only evidence for a statue of Bacchus by Euphranor. Furtwängler put forward an identification from a copy (W. D. E. Coulson, *Euphranor* (Univ. N. Colorado, Museum of Anthropology, Occasional Publications in Archaeology 8, 1978), 31-2), which however is far from certain (W. Helbig, *Führer durch die öffentliche Sammlungen in Rom* (ed. 4, 1969), 3 p. 134 no. 2217). The spelling with *f* representing phi in a literate inscription (cf. 32.9, 41.1, 171.5; contrast Filocalus 42, Philocalus 66; *sofus* 32.9, *sophus* 70.5) would not be common before the end of the second century (Leumann 162; Biville 191-2), and *fastorum consul* evidently means *consul ordinarius*; the combination of these two factors makes Virius Gallus cos. 298 the most likely candidate.

52

AE 1956, 259
Discussion: Mazzarino, *Iura* 7 (1956), 137
Photo: R. J. A. Wilson, *Sicily under the Roman Empire* (1990), 332.

The dutiful brothers of Catania were famed because, while they were rescuing their parents during an eruption of Etna, the lava-flow parted around them. A statue-group commemorating them is mentioned by Conon (*Frag. Gr. Hist.* 26 F 1.xliii p. 206 Jacoby) and by Claudian (*Carm. Min.* 17). This had evidently been

carried off by the Vandal raiders who plagued Sicily from 440 until 475, and its recovery by Merulus (otherwise unknown) is commemorated in this inscription from the Greek theatre in Catania.
1 *flammifuga* ('who escaped the flames') is a word new to the lexica; it is formed like *larifuga, lucifuga* etc.
2 Both the false quantity in *hostĭlitas* and its collective sense are illustrated by Paulinus Pellaeus, *Eucharist.* (CSEL 16.304), 333 *et grauior multo circumfusa hostilitate / factio seruilis.*

53

CLE 1905

This was found at Timgad (Thamugadi), and was clearly the base of a statue commemorating some victory. This writer likes to fill his lines with lists (that in 4 involving two false quantities), the components of which do not always go very well together (thus in 5 *agere prouectus* is not an easy combination); cf. on 35.5.
1-2 Cf. 48.8 *Romuleis...triumfis* and Claudian 24 (*Cons. Stil.* 3), 205 *o palma uiridi gaudens et amica tropaeis / custos imperii uirgo.* For *praepes* cf. Matius fr. 3, Auson. *Epigr.* 26.2 p. 296 Prete = *Prec.* 1.2 p. 143 Green. Victory is a winged creature, both human (*homo*, which does not imply a male) and divine (*numen*); the other abstract appositions are tacked on somewhat loosely. *uirgo fecunda* is next door to an oxymoron.
1 *gloria palmae* Verg. *Georg.* 3.102.
5 *comitatus* = accompanied by Victoria; cf. Claudian l.c. 215 *hunc bellis comitare fauens. prouectus* is accusative plural of the fourth-declension noun. The triumphal word *palma* ends the last line as it had the first.

54

CLE 1926 = *CIL* 13.10018.82 = *ILS* 8609m

This is an inscription on an ampulla found at Strassburg; the word *felix* stands on its own beneath the handle. On the vessel the stroke after *libe* is vertical; I have misrepresented it above because in the rest of this book such a stroke is used to indicate line-division. This is usually taken to represent *Libe(ri)* (cf. 45.1 etc.). Oxé, *Germania* 16 (1932), 120 sqq. thinks it an error for *labe* (λαβέ), which appears on some such vessels; I think it more likely to represent *libentes*, comparing another such inscription illustrated by Oxé 122 abb. 2, *escipe quae ferimus manibus <pedibus>que libentes feliciter*. Other such inscriptions showing the form *escipe* favoured in Germany and dactylic rhythms are *CIL* 13.10018.81 *escipe et trade sodali ut<e>re* (cf. *CLE* 338 = *CIL* 13.10016.4 *accipe me sitie(n)s et trade sodali* on a vessel found at Mainz), *CIL* 13.10025.203 *escipe pocula [g]rata* on a glass vessel, 10018.61 and 78-80. There are similar inscriptions on rings; *CIL* 10024.65 *escipe si amas pignus amant(is)*, 10024.103 = *CLE* 1925 *non tituli pretium sed amantis accipe curam*. In the last case the writer has probably, through a slip of memory, substituted the formulaic *accipe* for an original *respice*, as Heraeus 186(-7) n.3 suggested; he compared the medieval *non doni cultum sed dantis respice uultum, non donum dantis, sed respice cor tribuentis (...pectus amantis)*, for which see Walther *Proverbia* 3 p. 250 nos. 17520-22. Cf. also P. Wuilleumier, *Inscriptions latines des trois Gaules* (*Gallia* suppl. 17, 1963), 570 *escipe si amas*. Such inscriptions may be compared with Martial's formulae for presenting a gift; 13.102.2 *accipe fastosum, munera cara, garum*, 14.89.1 *accipe felices, Atlantica munera, siluas* (a table of citrus wood). For *utere* cf. 43.6.

55*

AE 1941, 53 = *AL* 487d = Sasel, (1902-40) 1980A = A206 Pikhaus
Discussion: G. Sanders, *Lapides memores* (1991), 524

Possidius in his life of Augustine 22 reports that Augustine had the above distich inscribed on his table (cf. also Migne, *Patrol. Lat.* 40.1279); a late antique or medieval Yugoslavian inscription reproduces it (only the first halves of the lines survive, as indicated above). The couplet became very widely known, was much quoted, and also acquired a separate manuscript transmission (see Riese, de Rossi, *Inscr. Chr. Urb. Romae* 2 p. 279 no. 4 and add e.g. Brux. 1372 = 9581-95, mentioned in *MGH, AA* 15 p.40, and Turicensis C 58 / 275 saec. xii, mentioned by Weymann (see below)). The manuscript tradition of Possidius shows many variants, including *hac mensa...suam* (so also Bede in Migne 91.1010 etc.) which means 'let him know that his own <life> is unworthy of this table'. This reading seems to be due to a failure to appreciate the sarcasm of 'let him know that this table is unworthy of him'; for *indignus* with the dative in later Latin see *TLL* 1190.62 (e.g. Augustine, *Quaest. Test.* 1.113.3 [*CSEL* 50.300.15] *rem sibi indignam*). Some manuscripts also read *sui* (which also is a possible construction with *indignus*) or *sua* (sc. *uita*). In addition Bede and others quote with *carpere* in place of *rodere* (cf. Hor. *Serm.* 1.4.81 *absentem qui rodit amicum*), and there are other variants too (*famam* for *uitam*, *hanc mensam uetitam nouerit esse sibi* for line 2). For the medieval quotations see Walther, *Proverbia* 4 p. 405 no. 25526 and *Initia* p. 842 no. 16148 and p. 938 no. 17909. C. Weymann, *Beiträge zur Gesch. der christlich-lateinischen Poesie* (1926), 112 remarks that the phraseology *quisquis...nouerit* has the air of an official proclamation. The imitation of Theodulf (62.9-10, *MGH, PLAC* 1 p.556) runs thus:

quisquis es hic adstans, hominem ne detrahe quemquam;
absentum uitam rodier est facinus.

In 1 *dictis* means 'witticisms', as often.

56

CLE 2048 = *CIL* 4.6635
Photo: *MAL* 8 (1900), 2 (the inscription); *NS* 1900, 199 (the whole picture).

This is written in the corner of a Pompeian wall-painting showing a young woman suckling an old man; the figures are identified by the names Micon and Pero beside them. According to the story Micon was imprisoned and starved, but was kept alive by being suckled by his daughter Pero (called Xanthippe by Hygin. *Fab.* 254) on her visits; this story is recounted by Hyginus and Val. Max. 5.4 ext.1, who comments *stupent hominum oculi cum huius facti pictam imaginem uident*. Several other representations of the story in various media have been found at Pompeii (Wick, *Atene e Roma* 8 (1905), 211; Gigante 223); all must derive from some well-known original. For these and other representations see W. Deonna, *Deux Études de Symbolisme Religieux* (CL 18, 1955) = *Latom.* 13 (1954), 140 and 356; Gricourt in *Hommages M. Renard* 3 (CL 103, 1969), 272.

3 For *aeuo* cf. Lucan 9.981, Quintil. 11.1.10; this reading is due to Mau.
4 Some imperative form of *aspicio* seems highly probable, but exact certainty depends on whether the strokes after the obliteration are read as *m* or *ut*. For *micant* cf. *TLL* s.v. 929. 33. The ancients thought that wine entered the veins (*OLD* s.v. 2a; e.g. Verg. *Buc.* 6.15 *inflatum hesterno uenas...Iaccho*) and thence the lungs (see my note on Juv. 4.138).
5 The idea is that she rubs her father to restore the circulation. This is not plain on the representations, in which she holds her breast for her father with one hand while the other (presumably that envisaged as rubbing him) is draped over his shoulder.
6 The alliterative pair *pietas* and *pudor* is not listed by Wölfflin; cf. Ovid, *Met.* 7.72 *pietasque pudorque.*

II C: POEMS WITH LITERARY, EDUCATIONAL AND PHILOSOPHICAL CONNECTIONS

One might here include 85, 96, 123, 148, 152 and the poets of 75, 188.

57

CLE 42 = *CIL* 4.1877

This is a riddle, written in the basilica at Pompeii. As Schenkl, *WS* 8 (1886), 172 explains, the *mulier* is the principal of a loan, the *filius* is the interest. This riddle has a Greek origin, since the Greek for 'interest' is τόκος, which also means 'offspring', and 'to produce interest' is τόκον φέρειν. Schenkl compares Aristotle, *Pol.* 1.10.1258b5 (τόκος is so called), ὅμοια γὰρ τὰ τικτόμενα τοῖς γεννῶσιν αὐτά ἐστιν, ὁ δὲ τόκος γίγνεται νόμισμα ἐκ νομίσματος. The speaker of the second line is like a husband suspecting his son of being a bastard; cf. the argument about paternity at Menander, *Epitr.* 944 sqq. Sandbach. The word *adulterinus* is applied both to counterfeit coinage and bastard offspring.

The first line is a senarius, the second has probably been distorted from one (ending *uellem meum*) by a slip of memory; then the writer adds a comment of his own. The form is one occasionally found in riddles, the narration of the outline of a situation; *Anth. Pal.* 14.109 is quite similar. Hesychius has αἴνιγμα · ζήτημα (the Latin equivalent is *quaestiuncula*, Pompeius *GLK* 5.311); the word is also on *CIL* 4.1878 (written above the present riddle, perhaps in the same handwriting) and the prose subscription to *CLE* 447 (see also Bücheler's note here for *CIL* 4.5341). For *uoleba(m)* cf. 19.4 (with a special justification there). The verb *similo* is not elsewhere found intransitive.

58

CLE 938 = *CIL* 8.2265.480

Scratched on the rim of a *patera* from Caesarea in Mauretania. If you write a billet-doux in gold letters, Danae will immediately invite you to visit her as a lover; for *ueni* cf. Ovid, *Am.* 1.11.24 and perhaps Prop. 2.25.2, for *rescribet* Martial quoted on 86. Jupiter's visit to Danae as a golden shower was often rationalised as her seduction by a shower of money (see my note on Petron. 137.9 in 'The Poems of Petronius' (1991)); e.g. Fulgentius, *Myth.* 1.19 *Danae imbre aurato corrupta est*, and *CLE* 359, 1983 (*CIL* 4.4207 is mysterious). For writing in gold letters see T. Birt, *Kritik und Hermeneutik* (1913), 306, Bischoff 17, LSJ s.v. χρυσογραφία; we even hear of 'golden books' (Birt 257-8), whatever they were.

59

CLE 1532 = *CIL* 6.35887 = *ILS* 8168
Discussion: Peek, *Zeitschr. f. Kirchengeschichte* 61 (1942), 26.

1 The first half of a hexameter (with which cf. *CLE* 1036.1) with the second half of a senarius.
2-3 The metre is very shaky (see Metre I c, h; II A f). This imitates an epigram which the scholiast on Hom. *Il.* 22.414 says is ascribed to Epicharmus (296 Kaibel, 64 Diels - Kranz)

εἰμὶ νεκρός · νεκρὸς δὲ κόπρος, γῆ δ' ἡ κόπρος ἐστίν ·
εἰ δ' ἡ γῆ θεός ἐστ', οὐ νεκρὸς ἀλλὰ θεός.

This is also used in an epitaph from Eretria (*IG* 12.9.290 = *GVI* 1126)

εἰ θεός ἐσθ' ἡ γῆ, κἀγὼ θεός εἰμι δικαίως ·
ἐκ γῆς γὰρ βλαστῶν γενόμην νεκρός, ἐκ δὲ νεκροῦ γῆ.

Cf. also *GVI* 1941, *CLE* 974.4 = *CIL* 6.29609 *cinis sum, cinis terra est, terra dea est, ergo ego mortua non sum* and Ennius in his *Epicharmus* (fr. 37 *FLP*) *terra corpus est*. All this is put in syllogistic form.
4 Cf. 168 (and of course there are other forms of violation of tombs), Lattimore 119.

60

CLE 1936 = *CIL* 4.9131

A wall-inscription in Pompeii from the cleaning establishment of Fabius Ululitremulus, who derives his name from a proverbial expression alluded to by Varro, *Sat. Men.* 539 *eum peius formidant quam fullo ululam* (*tremo* = *formido*). The owl is the sign of two cleaner's shops at Pompeii, and there are also *CIL* 4.4118 *Cresce(n)s fullonibus et ululae suae sal.* (= *ILS* 6441e), 4112 *Cresce(n)s fullonibus* | *ululamque canont*. For all this see Moeller 88, who thinks that cleaners respect (*formidant, tremunt*) the owl as the sign of their patroness Minerva. This however hardly suits Varro's *peius*, and while the noun *formido* is used of religious veneration (*OLD* 1b), the verb is not. I suspect that there was some fable which we do not know behind the phrase. Another possibility is suggested by the Pompeian wall-painting reproduced by Moeller 23, which shows an owl perching on a drying-frame in a fulling establishment (for tame owls see Aelian, *NA* 1.29); perhaps then what the fullers feared is that such tame owls kept as mascots might soil the cleaned clothes with their droppings.

This verse may be a sardonic comment on the fact that a painting of Aeneas carrying Anchises and leading Ascanius appears on the facade of the workshop of Ululitremulus (illustrated *NS* 1913, 144; Spinazzola 1.149-50 with figs. 182-3, tav. x and xviib). On the other side of the doorway is a picture of Romulus with the *spolia opima*; below that is the shop-sign, and this inscription is below that.

61

CLE 1491 = *CIL* 4.5112

A graffito on a Pompeian wall. The end of the pseudo-Vergilian *Copa* (38) *Mors aurem uellens 'uiuite' ait, 'uenio'* is modelled on such sentiments as we read here and in *CLE* 485-6, 802-3, 1231. For *uiuo* = 'enjoy life' cf. 199.4, *OLD* s.v. 7, Brelich 50.

62a

CLE 1989 = *CIL* 13.7127

62b

AE 1941, 43

Discussion: L. Leschi, *Études d'Épigraphie* (1957), 179; Zarker, *Helikon* 8 (1968), 396 with plate, *Acta of the Fifth International Congress of Epigraphy 1967* (1971), 452 with pl. 48.

(a) is from Mainz, (b) from Lambaesis; the latter is accompanied by an inscription referring to the mother. The two both imitate the poem attributed to the juvenile Vergil

Monte sub hoc lapidum tegitur Ballista sepultus;
nocte die tutum carpe uiator iter

(see *FLP* 257). Ballista was a robber, so the point of the second line in [Vergil] is plain; not so in either of these imitations. The second is closer, but has substituted *his ipse* for *Ballista* (thus causing the lengthening *tegitūr*) and *uia* for *die*; the second substitution seems unmotivated and may be just an error of anticipation, the first is all but unintelligible (*his* seems to mean *lapidibus*). In (a) the alteration of *monte...lapidum* to *forte...lapidē* involves the indicated lengthening at the caesura (see Metre II A d).

63

CLE 97 = *CIL* 9.1164 = *ILS* 2953
Discussion: Alfonsi, *Epigraphica* 26 (1964), 59

From Aeclanum; from *CIL* 9.1111 Mommsen deduces that it was made a colony by Hadrian, and with this will have come the institution of *duouiri* as the municipal magistrates, which will give a terminus post quem. Mommsen however also works out a family tree which makes Bassulus grandfather of L. Eggius Pomponius Longinus (this is a few out of his many names), who was consul in 126 A.D. and *duouir quinquennalis* at Aeclanum before that. Chronologically the combination of the two deductions seems highly implausible, and I think that Mommsen's family tree must be erroneous, no doubt because of homonyms in different generations. Cantria Longina is also on *CIL* 9.1153.

For interest in comedy under Trajan see Pliny, *Ep.* 6.21 on the compositions of Vergilius Romanus (*scripsit comoedias Menandrum... aemulatus*). Bassulus, who as 10 shows himself composed this epitaph (since *hoc* must be accusative, not ablative), took care to give an archaic flavour to his diction.
1 is Sallustian in thought and diction; cf. *more pecorum* in *Hist.* 3.48.6

M (p. 187 Reynolds) and also *Cat.* 1.1. Though in late Latin *transfunctorius* is coined ('perfunctory'), *transfungi* is not found elsewhere and is no doubt partly due to contamination with e.g. *uitam transire,* used in contexts like this by Sallust, *Cat.* 1.1, 2.8.

3 *ipsus* is derived from comic diction. An example is sometimes quoted from Fronto, but the correct reading there is *ipsius;* the instance in Auson. *Bissula* 1.6 is probably due to a reminiscence from comedy.

4 *mandatum* sc. *est; diu* = *iamdudum,* a usage of which there are few indubitable instances (Apul. *Apol.* 66 is one). For such modesty about one's own literary production cf. Catull. 1.8-9 *quicquid hoc libelli / qualecumque quidem* (as should be read).

8 For *mortem potiri* (with the archaic accusative) cf. Gellius (an also archaising contemporary) 13.15. This no doubt implies that Bassulus committed suicide; for justification of this by *taedium* Cugusi 93 n.3 quotes Jerome *Ol.* 189.4 (Atratinus), 194.1 (Porcius Latro); see also Sen. *Ep.* 24.22, Pliny, *NH* 2.156 and 7.186, Tac. *Hist.* 5.10.1, Gell. 6.18.11 (but the implication is not inevitable; see Sen. *Ep.* 98.18).

ea] is usually supplied, but if the space permits perhaps *quae*] would be preferable; then Bassulus in his senarii, like Apuleius fr. 2 (*FLP* 393), would observe the Senecan rule for trimeters that the fifth foot must be a spondee except with quadrisyllables, as in 6 and 9 and six times in Seneca. One will also note that a final iambic word is rarely preceded by a tribrach (C. Questa, *Introduzione alla Metrica di Plauto* (1967), 192).

9 Cf. *CLE* 220.3 *leuamen hoc doloribus*.

10 He allows hiatus at the caesura, as at least Plautus seems to have done; cf. Metre II B c. The word *elogium* seems to be a portmanteau formation in which *eloquium,* λόγος and ἐλεγεῖον all played their part. It is first found in Cato, *Origines* fr. 83 Peter in reference to the Greek Leonidas, and Cicero applies it to the epitaph of Calatinus (see on 9); cf. also *CLE* 1537.7 *hoc lecto elogio.* Cicero, *Cato* 73 uses it to mean just 'elegiac poem'; Varro fr. 303 Funaioli makes the connection with *elegia*.

12 Cic. *Consolatio* fr. 9 Müller *in hos scopulos incidere uitae.*

13 The image of the harbour is common (Bonner, *HThR* 34 (1941), 49; Lier (1903) 567; Soubiran in *Mél. M. Labrousse* (1986), 483). Passages which particularly resemble this are Enn. *Thy.* 298, Cic. *Tusc.* 1.118, Verg. *Aen.* 7.598, Sen. *Ep.* 70.3, *Ag.* 591-2.

14 *perpes* is an archaic adjective (Plautus etc.) formed on the analogy of *praepes;* it reappears in Apuleius and later writers.

64

CIL 4.6819
Discussion: Lebek, *ZPE* 57 (1984), 70
Photo: *Arch. Class.* 17 (1965), tav. lxxx.1

As an example of ambiguity Quintilian 7.9.8 quotes a line *quinquaginta ubi erant centum inde occidit Achilles*, which is of course nonsensical if *quinquaginta* is taken as nominative and *centum* as accusative. This is a Latin version of πεντήκοντ' ἀνδρῶν ἑκατὸν λίπε δῖος 'Αχίλλευς (where Quintilian seems to reflect a variant κτάνε) quoted in a similar context by Aristotle, *Soph. El.* 166a.37, and the garbled version from Pompeii shows that it was established in the school curriculum.

64A

Della Corte and Ciprotti, *Studia et Docum. Hist. et Iuris* 27 (1961), 325 no. 1
Discussion: Lebek, *ZPE* 42 (1981), 59

An Ostian graffito which, as Lebek explains, incorporates a riddle. The first letter is the doleful exclamation *a*, the third is *i*, the imperative of *ire*. The second and fourth need not only to be understood as single letters for the the word spelt out by the riddle, but also as letter-names for the clue (as e.g. in Greek the letter Φ has a name Φῖ, and in English the letter h has a name 'aitch'). Here the second letter is *s*, and its name is *es*, which is the imperative (*iubet*; originally wrongly read as *lubet*) of *esse*, though not a very common form (NW 3.595), *esto* being usual. The fourth letter is *n*, and its name is *en*, which can be an exclamation of sorrow (Ti. Claudius Donatus on Vergil's *en Priamus* [*Aen.* 1.461] remarks *en non tantum demonstrantis est, verum etiam dolentis*; Lebek goes wrong here). That so far gives *asin-*, which with the addition of the vocative ending *-e* produces an insulting (*inuidiam*) reaction to a silly action (*facti*). Since the inscription apparently is to be dated c. 200 A.D. (so Solin ap. Lebek on palaeographical grounds), this shows that the letter-names such as *es* and *en* originated earlier than is sometimes thought, and confirms the credibility of the statement attributing them to Varro (fr. 241 Funaioli); see A. E. Gordon, *Letter Names of the Latin Alphabet* (1973), 14.

65a

Szilagyi, *AAntHung.* 2 (1953-4), 307 with abb. 2.
Discussion: Guarducci, *Arch. Class.* 17 (1965), 249 with tav. lxxxi.2.

65b

Della Corte and Ciprotti, *Studia et Docum. Hist. et Iuris* 27 (1961), 328 no.14
Discussion: Guarducci l.c. with tav. lxxxii.1 and drawing p. 255.

Szilagyi for (a), a tile-brick at Aquincum, and Guarducci for (b), an Ostian graffito, saw that we have here the *uersus recurrens* quoted as *illud antiquum* by Sidon. Apoll. *Ep.* 9.14.4 *Roma tibi subito motibus ibit amor,* which is the same whether spelt forwards or backwards (*FPL* p. 186 no. 92 Morel = p. 216 no. 93 Büchner); (a) also has the *rotas - sator* square written in capitals (whereas the palindrome is in cursive). In the Middle Ages another palindrome *signa te, signa; temere me tangis et angis* was prefixed to this line and the story was evolved that a pilgrim changed Satan into a beast of burden, and that as he was impatiently riding the Devil to Rome the latter said to him 'Cross yourself, cross yourself; you are rash to touch and pain me. Suddenly through my movements Rome, your heart's desire, will come to you'. See Walther, *Initia* p. 954 no. 18191, *Proverbia* 4 p. 1052 no. 29616; the line is quoted also in an anonymous poem edited *MGH, PLAC* 3.556. For *uersus recurrentes* in general see Teuffel - Kroll, *Gesch. d. röm. Lit.* (ed. 6) 1 (1916), 46 § 26.4, L. Mueller 580, *Suppl. Hell.* note on 996.11-14, Polara in *Studi di Fil. Cl. in Onore di G. Monaco* (1991?), 3.1335.

66

CIL 4.10241
Discussion: Lebek, *ZPE* 23 (1976), 21, with references to earlier literature and drawing; Hiltbrunner, *Gymn.* 88 (1981), 45; Gigante 88 with tav. x after p. 128; Semmlinger, *Ziva Ant.* 31 (1981), 191.

Primigenia was popular enough to have her address recorded on *CIL* 4.8356. This couplet is written on a tomb outside the porta Nucerina at Pompeii; a second copy with minor variations and without the heading was found in the house of M. Fabius Rufus (Solin in *Neue Forschungen in Pompeii*, ed. B. Andreae - H. Kyrieleis (1975), 253; photo pl. 241). In both these copies *pressa* was read by Solin 253 n. 42 in place of the previous decipherment *missa* (cf. Gigante, *PP* 29 (1974), 200). The new reading is taken by Hiltbrunner to be nom. fem. sing., but I still prefer it to be neut. acc. plur., cf. Ovid, *Her.* 2.94, Mart. 6.34.1. The variant mentioned in the apparatus, which contains only the beginning of the hexameter, was found *ad dextram primi ostii a uico lupanaris*; it is however not the original form since it would violate the sequence of tenses, and is perhaps due to a reminiscence of Ovid (see below) 9 *o utinam fieri subito mea munera possem.*

The interest of this distich lies in its combination of Ovidian and Vergilian motifs. For the second see *Aen.* 1.683 (Venus asking Cupid to transform himself into Ascanius) *tu faciem illius noctem non amplius unam / falle dolo* (*falle* = 'imitate deceptively'). The Pompeian composer has introduced hiatus by adjusting *noctem* to *hora,* and has preferred the ablative of duration to Vergil's accusative (the context of Seneca's *non amplius una* (*AL* 427.9) is mutilated); for this ablative cf. 27.2, 28.2, 100A.1, 109.15, 117.8, 129.3, 146.1 etc. For the first cf. *Am.* 2.15, in which Ovid, giving a ring to his beloved, wishes for transformation into that ring so that he may have physical contact with the girl (a common literary motif; see Lebek and my article in *BICS* suppl. 51 (1988), 18); one form of this contact will be receiving a kiss so that he/it will not stick to the wax in sealing (cf. l.c. 20 n.2 and my note on Juv. 1.68).

There is hiatus at both the caesura of the hexameter (see above) and the diaeresis of the pentameter, in the former case accompanied by lengthening of a short open vowel (see Metre II A a, f); the latter could have been avoided by substituting *sauia* or *basia,* but neither was on quite the right stylistic level (see my note on Pliny 1.8 in *FLP* 368).

67

CLE 1530 = *CIL* 6.537 = *ILS* 2944
Photo: A. Rostagni, *Storia della Letteratura Latina* 2 (1952), 734.

Discussion: Seagraves, *Actes du viie congrès international d'épigraphie* (1979), 468; Smolak in R. Herzog, *Die lat. Lit. von 284 bis 374 n. Chr.* (1989), 320; J. Soubiran in the Budé Avienus (1981), 13 sqq., 293 sqq.; Matthews, *Historia* 16 (1967), 484.

A still unpublished inscription, part of which is quoted by Matthews and by Cameron, *CQ* 17 (1967), 392-3, reads *Abienii. Eximiae integritatis uiro ac mir(ae) bonitatis exemplo, Postumio Rufio Festo*. That and this inscription refer to the poet known under the name Auienus, and show that the proper form of this name may be Auienius, though this is not certain (Matthews 490; a descendant, cos. 502, calls himself Rufius Magnus Faustus Auienus). It also shows that this name is a *signum* (on 28; for the genitive cf. Cameron l.c., Soubiran 18 n.2), so that he is properly referred to as Postumius Rufius Festus signo Avien(i)us. He was proconsul of Achaea at an unknown date (*IG* II-III 3.4222; that will have been when he saw Delphi, *De Orbe Terr.* 603-4, cf. *Arat.* 71), and the new inscription suggests that he was proconsul of Africa; these will be the two tenures of this office mentioned in A4. Absolute dates for his life and career are hard to fix beyond the broad dating to the fourth century. His family traced its origin to the Neronian Stoic philosopher Musonius Rufus (A1), who came from Volsinii (Suda 3 p. 416 Adler), and Matthews follows out its history, securely based on nomenclature, over more than three centuries. See also M. T. W. Arnheim, *The Senatorial Aristocracy in the Later Roman Empire* (1972), 134.

A1 *suboles prolesque* in the same position in the verse *Arat.* 370. The meaning of the line is not clear, but it probably is 'descendant of Musonius and son of Caesius Avien(i)us, from whom the *aqua Caesiana* (?) derived its name'. The *aqua Caesiana*, if that is what it was called, is unknown.

A2 Cf. *Arat.* 497 *Aones hoc latici posuerunt nomen equino / pastores*.

A3 Nortia, the Etruscan equivalent of Fortuna, has a well-known cult at Volsinii. His birth-place is contrasted with his domicile (4).

A5 adjusts the common *integer aeui* to match the preceding phrase. For the spelling *aeum* see *TLL* s.v. 1164.54 and on 188.9.

A6 We cannot identify any children other than Placidus.

A7 Avien(i)us in his *Aratea* is fond of the archaic *olle*, often placed at the end of the line.

A8 Stoicism, not unexpected in a descendant of Musonius and translator of Aratus, comes through strongly here; for *trahentur* cf. e.g. Lucan 7.46.

B1-2 The son adapts his father's *Aratea* 2 *reserat dux Iuppiter aethram*...4 *Iouis imperio mortalibus aethera pando. candidus Iuppiter* covers both 'clear sky' and 'propitious Jupiter'. I prefer this interpretation to that of *TLL* iii. 241.33, where *candidus* 'dressed in white' is referred to Avien(i)us and taken with *uenias* (but see ibid. 36 for the word's application to gods).
B3 Cf. Claudian, *De ui Cons. Honorii* praef. 16 *plaudebant numina dictis / et circumfusi sacra corona chori* and *Pan. Lat.* 6.7.2 (p. 190.26 Mynors) *receptusque est consessu caelitum, Ioue ipso dexteram porrigente* (referring to Constantine's father); likewise in Christian imagery Eusebius, *Vit. Const.* 4.73 and J. P. C. Kent, *Roman Imperial Coinage* 8 (1981), index 582 s.v. 'Hand of God'. See the illustration in Rostagni 735, Koep, *JAC* 1 (1958), 99 = A. Wlosok (ed.), *Röm. Kaiserkult* (1978), 509. Cf. also on 183.34.

68

CLE 91 = *CIL* 10.3969 = *ILS* 7763

This seems to have been brought to Naples from Capua; beneath the inscription is a relief of a teacher sitting on a chair and two pupils, a boy and a girl (illustrated in S. Bonner, *Education in Ancient Rome* (1977), p.43).
1 *animula* is a form popular in the second century (Hadrian 3.1, Sept. Ser. 16-17 and perhaps Apuleius 6.5 in *FLP* 397), but see also Servius ap. Cic. *Ad Fam.* 4.5.4 *unius mulierculae animula.* For the metaphor of *castellum* cf. Cic. *Cato* 73 *de praesidio et statione uitae, OLD* s.v. *statio* 5a, διαπεφρούρηται βιός Aesch. fr. 265 (this is inscribed on the gravestone of B. L. Gildersleeve in Charlottesville, Virginia; see W. W. Briggs - H. W. Benario (edds.), *Basil Lanneau Gildersleeve* (1986), 106, W. W. Briggs (ed.), *The Letters of B. L. Gildersleeve* (1987), 324). Most Greek occurrences of words like φρουρά in such contexts (e.g. Antiphon the sophist 87 B 50 Diels-Kranz) are ambiguous, since they probably mean 'prison' (Boyancé, *Rev. Ph.* 37 (1963), 7), like *custodiae* in Cic. *Somn. Scip.* 15.

The reversal of the two conjunctions would be an easy error by the ordinator, and the correction produces an enormous improvement. The structure now is *Auruncus erat qui parce uixit dum licitum est, cum haberet animulam clausam*; cf. *CLE* 1082.2 *uixi ego dum licuit dulciter ad superos.*

3 For *omni tempore* = *semper* see on 199A.A57.

Wölfflin does not note the alliterative combination *parce pudensque*; for the linking of adverb and adjective by *-que* see HS 172, 817.

4 The proper name sets the metre astray (see p. 23), and the repetition of *erat* is inelegant; probably a formula from a pattern-book or other model has had to be adjusted. The Aurunci had been wiped out at the end of the fourth century B.C.; their name survived only in Suessa Aurunca, and Philocalus, with a schoolmaster's pedantry, is indicating that he came from there. For the separation of the names Furius Philocalus cf. on 11.6-7.

5 *-i* for *-ii* in adjectives is rare (Sommer 339).

6 For *quom* (but *cum* 7) cf. on 12.2. Notoriously many schoolmasters could not make the claim of this line and of *pudens* 3 (see my note on Juv. 10.224).

7 Now his moonlighting profession, for which cf. *CIL* 10.4919 = *ILS* 7750; *testamentarius, CIL* 2.1734 = *ILS* 7749 and *OLD* s.v. b, E. Champlin, *Final Judgments* (1991), 70.

8 *ius*, if right, will mean 'did not deny to anyone what he was entitled to'; there are reasonable parallels in *TLL, ius* 691.63, but one will do even better to take it as the response to phrases like *ius petere, postulare* etc. (Lodge, *Lexicon Plautinum* s.v. *ius* II 3 a). For the spelling *quoiquam* see on 86.1.

9 *decurrere uitam* is a metaphor from the race of life (*TLL* v.232.52), cf. 199.2. *fidus* takes up *fide*.

10 This refers to the *centuriae* of his *collegium funeraticium*. For the internal organisation of such *collegia* see Waltzing 1.358, *TLL* (834.36) and Ruggiero (189) s.v. *centuria; RE, collegium* 418-9. *centuris* = *-iis* (see on 190.3).

69

CLE 107 = *CIL* 8.26672 = *ILS* 7772 = A103 Pikhaus

This is from Thugga, and Terentius was evidently a rhetor who had moved from Hippo. The metre is senarii; it goes astray in 1 because of the name (cf. p. 23; it could be restored by the removal of the cognomen) and in 5 (see below; it could be restored by removal of *in se de analogia*), and the split proceleusmatic in the second foot of 4 is horrible (Lindsay 94; see Metre II B e), unless *diarytos* was really intended.

1-2 Cf. Val. Max. 2.2.3, where Cicero is *litterarum...abundantissimum fontem*, Apul. *Flor.* 20 *Karthago camena togatorum*, Augustine, *Serm.* 36.7.7 *opimi pietate*. Perhaps one should remember that the Camenae were originally spring-goddesses (see my note on Juv. 3.13).

2 Like many words which in Latin express abstract concepts, *sapere* does so metaphorically and originally had a concrete sense, 'to have good taste', applied either to food or men. 'Wisdom' is not always a suitable translation, and here too 'taste' in the sense of 'discrimination' seems better.

3-4 See *TLL onom.* s.v. *Diarr(h)ytos*; Hippo is so called because the outlet of a lagoon flows through it to the sea.

5 Arithmetic, like proper names, sets the metre awry (see p. 23). *TLL, in* 744.76 puts this with other cases of *uiuere in se* in inscriptions, but in all the other cases the subject is plural, referring to two spouses, and the phrase means 'live together, with each other' (Löfstedt, *VS* 115 n.2; Funck, *ALL* 6 (1889), 258). I think that the line means 'he lived the square of the base number from the proportion of Pythagoras'. The proportion of Pythagoras is 6:8::9:12, the ratio of the chief musical intervals (Boethius, *Inst. Mus.* 1.10, Nicomachus of Gerasa p. 279 *MSG*). The base number of this is 6; 6 squared = 36. The technical term for 'to square a number' is *multiplicare (TLL* 1598.18) or *ducere (TLL* 2156.14) or *facere (OLD* 4b) *in se*, an expression which here seems to be abbreviated. In Greek this would be τὸν τῆς τοῦ Πυθαγόρου ἀναλογίας ἀριθμὸν πυθμενικὸν ἐφ' ἑαυτὸν πολλαπλασιωθέντα. My best thanks are due to Professor W. Knorr for help with this note.

70

CLE 434 (cf. p. 855) = *CIL* 11.6435 = G. Cresci Marrone - G. Mennella, *Pisaurum I Le Iscrizioni* (1984), 155 with plate.
Photo: *Pesaro nell' Antichità* (1984), p. 29.
Discussion: Mariotti, *Arch. Class.* 25-6 (1973-4), 395, with photo tav. lxxx.

From Pisaurum; the surviving stone goes as far as the end of the fifth line of verse, with the ends of the lines missing. The slave Antigenides was the son of his owner Hilarus (see Cresci Marrone - Mennella no.111 = *CIL* 11.6396 for another occurrence of this name) and a slave-woman (cf. *CIL* 5 index p. 1215 *liberti iidem filii*); his father would have given him his freedom and would have been his patron (10 = *patronus <futurus>*, cf. 32.39) as well as his father had the boy not died prematurely. Even before his manumission he carries the gentilicium of his owner, as *uernae* sometimes do (see Thylander 150 and Mariotti). For third-declension forms of patronymics in late Latin see *CP* 79 (1984), 310-1, where this case should be added.

1 With *ujator* this line can be roughly scanned (see Metre I b, d). *pede stricto* seems to mean 'a foot laced up in a shoe'.

3 The writer seeks the variation *duōs* - *duŏs* as an elegance (Hopkinson, *Glotta* 60 (1982), 162); cf. 187.12. For *soles* cf. *CLE* 1224.2; for the precision 115.4-6, 117.8, 179.2-3.

4 For *feci* see *TLL* s.v. 121.59. *at* = *ad* = *apud*, as in 11.

5 For *meauĭ* (which is used = *percurri*; see on 143.3) see Metre I j (iii) and *CLE* 1114.3, for *sophorum* cf. 32.9.

6 His literary curriculum seems to have been like that in the school run by Statius' father (*Silv.* 5.3.146 sqq.). *Pia* seems to be in enallage; it is Homer himself who is *pius*, as poets because of their devotion to Apollo etc. are (Catull. 16.5, 14.7).

7 Either *praescripta tulisset* = *praescripsisset*, governing *quid* (cf. on 18.5), or *quid* is an error for *quod* = *quot*. *Tulisset* is used as in *legem ferre*. We tend to associate the abacus with numerical calculations, but essentially it just means a flat board which could be covered with sand and used for geometrical figures too; see Marquardt 99, Blümner 323, Kissel on Persius 1.131.

8 *uernae* were allowed considerable licence (Blümner 288 n.8, Marquardt 167; for *procaces* cf. Hor. *Serm.* 2.6.66).

10 *contraria fata*, *CLE* 102.1.

11 *TLL* viii.1310.65 quotes two instances of *nunc modo*, a typical late and vulgar Latin pleonasm, from Cyprian. The archaic form *Acheruns* is still used by Fronto.

12 This line is presented according to the report of Iucundus; two other reports rewrite it in widely different ways to make it into a hexameter. One should not however dismiss the possibility that the end of the line may have been hard to read and that Iucundus too could be in error; as the line stands *-que* is incoherent (cf. on 190.6). The composer is thinking of Verg. *Aen.* 6.641 *sua sidera norunt*, which alludes to the idea that the underworld occupies the southern hemisphere (Cumont, *Recherches* ch. I 1, *LP* 191; Mynors on Verg. *Georg.* 1.243), a Pythagorean view according to Lactant. Plac. on Stat. *Th.* 4.527. The same passage of Vergil is recalled on an inscription from Mactaris (*AE* 1948, 107) *solemq(ue) super ac sidera noui*, the meaning of which is much discussed (Pindar fr. 133 Snell also implies a second sun in the underworld). These *sidera* are *taetra* like everything in the underworld. Löfstedt, *Eranos* 10 (1910), 173 wrongly interprets *sidera* to mean 'night'. *Tartarei* goes with *Acheruntis* in recollection of *Aen.* 6.295 *hinc uia Tartarei quae fert Acherontis ad undas*; for its placement cf. 38.3-4. See also 183.19-20 *non ego Tartareas penetrabo tristis ad undas, / non Acheronteis transuehar umbra uadis.*

13-14 This is a traditional sentiment, for which cf. 112.12, 172.8, *CLE* 1498.1 [see *AE* 1980, 767], 2139.1; *AP* 9.49, 134 [Palladas], 172 [also Palladas], Grenier, *MEFRA* 25 (1905), 72, Kleberg, *Eranos* 33 (1935), 156, Tudor, *Latom.* 39 (1980), 643 (also an epigram published by M. G. Schmidt, *Chiron* 20 (1990), 102). Its introduction produces a heptameter in 13. *Tumidam* implies the metaphor of the stormy seas of life and the harbour of death; cf. 63.12-13, *CLE* 1516.5 *mundi inter tumidas quietus undas.*

15 *est* was clearly added to regularise the line; as it stands cf. Metre II A f. Eternal life in the tomb does not well match the conceptions of 11-12; cf. on 20.20.

70A

AE 1939.162 = 1941.4-6

Discussion: Calza, *Die Antike* 15 (1939), 99, with abb. 1 (general view), 2 (Solon), 3 (Chilon); H. Schaal, *Ostia* (1957), 99

Photo: G. Calza - G. Becatti, *Ostia* (guide, 5th English ed., 1965), pl. 75 and *AJA* 42 (1938), 409 fig. 4 (Chilon); C. Pavolini, *La vita quotidiana a Ostia* (1991), fig. 97 (Solon and Thales); G. M. A. Richter, *Portraits of the Greeks* (1965), figs. 325, 331

These are from a wine-shop at Ostia of Trajanic - Hadrianic date which was subsequently converted into baths. In its former state it had pictures of the Seven Sages, of which three survive (Solon and Thales on one wall, Chilon on the adjacent one), portrayed sitting on latrine benches and with the above verses painted beside them in elegant rustic capitals; the verses of course debunk the gnomic pearls of wisdom traditionally attributed to the Seven Sages, and the representation as a whole parodies portrayals of the Seven Sages such as those listed by Richter 1. 81 nos. 3-4 (figs. 314-5).

(a) The same edifice has an inscription (Calza 103 and Abb. 4) *amice fugit te prouerbium / bene caca et irrima medicos*; I do not understand how Pallares, *Minerva* 7 (1993), 170 can make a septenarius out of this.
(b) For *durum cacare* cf. Catull. 23.11, Mart. 3.89.2. The verb *nitor* is used in the sense 'strain at stool' by Suet. *Vesp.* 20 and probably *CLE* 51. The writer had not room in his verse for *niterentur*, so he ignores the sequence of tenses and makes the verb active; Diomedes alleges that Cicero (*De Rep.* fr. 2) used the active imperative *nitito*.
(c) Cf. Petron. 47. The verb *uissire* 'fart' is found in 80 below and *AL* 205.12 and is implied at Cic. *Ad Fam.* 9.22.4 (whence Quintil. 8.3.46) and [Acro] on Hor. *AP* 355 (cf. on 98); it survives in Romance derivatives.

II D: INNS, TRAVEL AND TOURISM

71

CLE 930 = *CIL* 4.3948

From the wall of a *caupona* in Pompeii. For *acuam* = *aquam* cf. *TLL* ii.346.80, Väänänen 54, Leumann 133; for the reduction of *nd* (as in 2 B 1 above) Väänänen 67, Leumann 216, SP 179. Probably *uendis* (with the last syllable lengthened by the metrical beat) and *bibis* are meant; for the *-es* ending see on 79.1. There is hiatus at the diaeresis of the pentameter (see Metre II A f). Dilution of the liquor is a standing reproach to proprietors of bars (cf. Mart. 1.56.2), whence Trimalchio puts them under Aquarius (Petron. 39.12). This one does not even dilute but serves pure water while himself drinking unmixed wine; the two extremes crowd out the usual ancient practice of mixing water with wine.

72

CLE 931 = *CIL* 4.1679

From the wall of a *caupona* in Pompeii. Edone = Ἡδονή is the name of the *copa* (Solin 1238), also mentioned in a prose inscription above this (*calos Edone* = καλῶς Ἡδονή). *quattus* = 4 asses; the word is found *CIL* 4.5448, 8.25902.3.19, 11.5717 = *ILS* 6643 (cf. *CIL* 4 suppl. 2 p. 463 and Willis, *HSCP* 76 (1972), 234-5), and *septus, octus, nonus, decus* are also attested (F. Hultsch, *Metrologici Scriptores* 2 (1866), 67-8). It has to be remembered that the *as* and its subdivisions the *unciae* were units of weight (hence *dupundium* = 2 asses) before they were monetary units; this takes us back to the days before there was coined money at Rome, and metal ingots, as in Sparta, were the medium of exchange. Cf. Gell. 20.1.31 *librariis assibus in ea tempestate populus usus est;* see *Cambridge Ancient History* (ed. 2) 7.2.416, 476.

73

CLE 932 = *CIL* 4.4957

This inscription is most simply understood with the above punctuation; cf. Prop. 2.22.14 *quod quaeris 'quare?'* Those who object to *dices* = *quaeres* (but without reason; see Mart. 1.70.16) prefer to understand 'I admit that I have done wrong if you will explain why there was no chamber-pot', with an indicative in an indirect question. For the perfect *mixi* cf. *TLL* viii.604.27 and 43, 998.33; it is found in two other inscriptions (one quoted on 157), *minxi* in none (cf. Hofmann, *Glotta* 29 (1942), 44). Cf. Lucil. 1248 *permixi lectum*.

74*

CLE 270 = *CIL* 3.21 = *ILS* 1046a
Discussion: van de Walle, *Chron. d'Égypte* 38 = 75 (1963), 156; Friedlaender (Eng. tr.; not in ed. 9-10) 4.137.

This was read on one of the Pyramids while they still had their outer coating by a fourteenth-century pilgrim. It was written by the sister (whose name was presumably signed separately) of Decimus Terentius (Groag *RE* 48) Gentianus (scanned Gentjani; see Metre I d), known also from *CIL* 3.1463 = *ILS* 1046 *Te]rentio Gentiano trib. militum...consuli pontif. cens. prouinc. Mace[d.] colonia Ulpia Tra. Aug. Dac. Sarmizege(tusa) patrono* and other sources collected by Groag, whose reconstruction of his career has to depend largely on hypothesis in the paucity of verifiable dates (for one thing the Fasti Ostienses have now put his consulship in 116, not in 117). In the poem *censor* (*TLL* 800.35, missing this instance) means *censitor*, the official who estimates the value of estates for tax purposes (Ruggiero, *census* 176). This activity of Gentianus is attested also by *AE* 1924, 57 (a Macedonian boundary-stone of 120), and a rescript of Hadrian from 119 preserved by Ulpian concerning those *qui terminos finium causa positos abstulerunt*; an inscription of 194 shows the arrangements of Gentianus still in force. He was regarded as a potential successor to Hadrian (SHA 1.23.5, which seems to refer to the period c. 134-6 A.D.; either this, as is likely, or Groag's dating of this poem to 130 on the assumption that Terentia then accompanied Hadrian to Egypt is wrong). D. Terentius (*RE* 68) Scaurianus (see

Molisani, *Tituli* 4 (1982), 499; Wachter, *Klio* 72 (1990), 473), who was governor of Dacia and established the colonia Ulpia Traiana Dacica around 110, was clearly a relative, probably father. Gentianus was hardly old enough (see on 6) to participate in Trajan's Dacian wars, for which he won his second triumph in 107, so 5 either refers to Trajan's posthumous triumph for his Parthian war (E. M. Smallwood, *Documents illustrating the Principates of Nerva, Trajan and Hadrian* (1966), 54) with a grandiloquent plural (cf. on 31.15), or is merely metaphorical (but still meaning the Parthian war).

On the sister see further M.-T. Raepset-Charlier, *Prosopographie des femmes de l'ordre sénatorial* (1987), no. 573; on the brother Papazoglou, *Ziva Antika* 29 (1979), 242.

The sister introduces a number of literary references (see below).

2 *moesta* is probably the spelling of the reporter of the inscription, though it is found on *CIL* 9.1069 (very late). For *quod potui* cf. 180.17, *CLE* 576 B 1, 1253.7, Catull. 68.149 (a poem much concerned with the death of Catullus' brother, though not in the immediate context), Ovid, *Fasti* 5.472 *quod potuit, lacrimas in mea fata dedit* (Romulus weeping at the death of his brother), Rossberg, *Jahrb. kl. Phil.* 129 (1884), 647.

3 Hor. *Odes* 3.11.51 *nostri memorem sepulcro / scalpe querelam* (v.l. *sculpe;* cf. 114.4); Ovid, *Her.* 11.125 *uiue memor nostri lacrimasque in uulnera funde.*

6 He attained these offices before the age of thirty. Since he was *censitor* in Macedonia in 119, and the prose inscription quoted above indicates that this came after his consulate (the verse inverts the order for the sake of metre), this would indicate that he cannot have been born before 90 A.D. Under the empire the normal minimum age for the consulate was 32, and that only for the most privileged, but (apart from the rights conferred by the *ius trium liberorum*) imperial favour could give exemptions; see Morris, *Listy Filologicke* 87 (1964), 323 (on 332 he accuses Terentia of substituting *sex* for *septem* partly for reasons of metrical convenience, as if the scansion of the two would not be identical here; the true inference from the quite exceptional promotion of Gentianus is confirmation that he was a potential successor to Hadrian), R. Syme, *Tacitus* (1958), 2.653. Morris points out that of ten consuls aged 30 or less, seven were imperial princes, Agrippa was the eighth, and the ninth was in the tumult of civil war in 69 A.D.

lustra has a double point: (1) it links with the original sense of *censor*; (2) because year of birth was often not recorded, it is quite common to find ages approximately counted in five-year periods, as with a pet 203.2; this is not to say that the ages of Gentianus and the dog were not exactly known. The role of the official *lustrum* in this phenomenon is challenged by R. Duncan-Jones, *Structure and Scale in the Roman Economy* (1990), 81 and in *Chiron* 7 (1977), 336.

75

CLE 227 = *CIL* 3.47 = Bernand 54-5 and pl. xxxix.

By Egyptian Thebes there was a huge statue of Amenophis III, of which the upper part had been overthrown by an earthquake, probably in 27-6 B.C., so that after the cold of night the rapid expansion of the loosened stones in the sudden change of temperature caused vibration of the material and air-currents through the cracks. So there was produced a musical sound in the morning at sunrise, and this motivated the identification with Memnon, the son of Aurora. The statue became a tourist attraction, and from Augustan or Tiberian times tourists recorded their presence in graffiti on the statue, of which this is one. For fuller details and bibliography see my note on Juv. 15.4 and add Gardiner, *JEA* 47 (1961), 91. The statue fell silent in the third century, which Bowersock, *BASP* 21 (1984), 24 suggests was the result of a reconstruction by Zenobia (there is no evidence for the often-repeated statement that it was reconstructed by Septimius Severus). Cf. also 26.7-9 above.

Some distance above this on the left leg in a prose inscription T. Statilius Maximus Seueru[s] declares that he heard Memnon on 18 Feb. 136 A.D. (*CIL* 3.46 = Bernand 48). Bücheler points out that the scholia to Clem. Alex. *Protr.* 4.49 mention a Maximus who had visited the pyramids and written a Greek epigram (*IGM* 222), and suggests an identification with a Statilius (*RE* 22) Maximus who was idios logos. Note also the Statilius (*RE* 23) Maximus who was epistrategos of the Heptanomia in 156 and for some years previously (M. Vandoni, *Gli Epistrategi nell' Egitto Greco-Romano* (1971?), 29). The Bernands suggest that the writer of my 75 was the epistrategos and that the writer of their 48 was his father and the idios logos. They point out that their 48 is written in large letters high up the leg and my 75 in small letters farther down (the respective locations are indicated on their pl. lxxii as 1 and 10-11), and see in this a symbol of subordination. But there is no substance in this; the two are separated by other inscriptions and are in no visible relationship. They also argue that *quoque* 3 means 'as well as my father', which is by no means inevitable.

These epigrams are in trochaic tetrameters and iambic trimeters (not septenarii and senarii).
2 Hor. *Odes* 1.17.13 *dis pietas mea / et musa cordi est*. For *camenas* = *carmina* cf. *TLL onom.* s.v. 117.55; for the present tense *audit* cf. *CLE* 28 = *CIL* 3.62 = Bernard 85 and the inscription of Statilius Maximus Severus.
3 Val. Fl. 2.452 *uox accidit aures*, Plaut. *Stich.* 88.
4 I can only understand the syntax of this line as indicated by my punctuation, 'let everyone call out the name "the poet Maximus" ' (in which of course we will also understand *maximum*).

76

CLE 272 = *CIL* 3.55 = Bernand 14 and pl. xxiv

The offices listed in 4 upset the metre, just as proper names often do, and produce a heptameter, though if the last word is read as it is written, in abbreviated form, it yields a hexameter (see p. 23).
2 *exanimi* is genitive of *exanimus* agreeing with *Memnonis*, *inanimem* (which chooses the alternative declension of adjectives compounded from *anima*) does not, as usual, mean 'that which is deprived of *anima*', but is given a new etymology and calqued on ἔμψυχος, 'that in which there is *anima*'; *TLL* compares Pacuv. 3 *inanima cum animali sono* (a tortoiseshell used as a lyre). For the scansion *ĭn-* see Metre II A h, for *clarumque sonorem* Lucr. 4.567.
3 For *cepi* see *TLL* s.v. 321.39; *sumsi* has an analogous meaning, 'I took to myself, enjoyed'.
4 An *ala ueterana Gallica* is recorded in various places in Egypt in the second and third centuries (Daris, *ANRW* ii.10.1.752; he is over-cautious in suggesting that this inscription need not refer to that *ala*). For prefects of the garrison at Mount Beronice on the West coast of the Red Sea at the southern boundary of Egypt see *RE* iii.281.34, Ruggiero 1.285a, Rostovtzeff, *Röm. Mitt.* 12 (1897), 78, *CIL* 3.13580, Bernand 37, 56 (who suggest that the office was abolished by Hadrian in 130; that would give a terminus ante quem for this poem). For another prefect of Beronice who heard Memnon see *CIL* 3.32 = Bernand 4.

3 For *canorum* cf. 75.1.
5 I cannot find any Roman name beginning with Abararo or anything like it, and to interpret as A. Bararo brings no help.

II E: EROTIC

Nearly all of these inscriptions are scratched or painted on walls etc., not incised on stone.

(a) A General Comment on Graffiti

77

CLE 957 = *CIL* 4.2487 (photo in Calabi Limentani 417), 2461, 1904
Drawings in *Literacy in the Ancient World* (1991), 83

The above version is a blend of the three occurrences, each of which shows slight variation. There is a pun in *sustineas;* the wall cannot bear the tedium of the effusions, and it literally cannot support their weight (the same point in *Priapea* 61.13-14). 1904 is on the same wall as 79, 81, 88 below.

(b) Pompeii

One set of Pompeian erotic poems has been discussed in *FLP* 79.

78

CLE 44 = *CIL* 4.5092

The writer is travelling with a mule-train, and addresses the muleteer, who is lingering over his drink. In *Vĕnerem* 2 and *ŭbi* 5 the accent creates a long syllable; cf. Metre I i. 3 starts off as if trochaic, but passes into the beginning of a senarius (with *rogŏ*).
2 *magi* is so written in *CLE* 495.4, but the split tribrach that would be produced here is most unusual in the first foot of a senarius (Lindsay 81-2).
3 *uenustum* takes up *Venerem* 2. *punge* = 'goad the mules'. For the spelling *iamus* cf. *CLE* 1615.11 (where the initial letter is part of an acrostich), *TLL* v.2.626.53, Väänänen 37, SP 92 and on 171.3. The correction (*CIL* makes no statement whether it is in the same writing) must be intended to adjust the writer from a man to a woman.

79

CLE 45, 1864 = *CIL* 4.2360, 4008, 8229
Discussion: Housman 1179 = *Hermes* 66 (1931), 406

Housman explains that this is on the lines of the common English graffito 'whoever reads this is a fool', except that 'fool' is replaced by sexual terms; cf. 8617 *uerp(a) es qui istuc leges*, 8230 *qui lego fel(l)o, sugat qui legit*, G. Sotgiu, *Iscrizioni latine della Sardegna* 1 (1961), 183 = *NS* 1923, 293 *...d]uas berpas, [ego] tertius qui lego* (*ego* seems a better supplement than *sum*). One should not understand *uerpa(m)* (sc. *comedam*), as Bücheler and Housman do. Cf. also *CIL* 10.6616 *bene sit tibi qui legis et tibi qui praeteris*; here *qui opscultat* 'who pays attention' hardly differs from *qui leget*.
1 *scribet* and *leget* are present, cf. 93b.1, 187.19 and 22, the prose of 130, *bibes* 71.2, *futue* 94a.1; such forms, for which see SP 57, are common at Pompeii (Väänänen 21-2, Eska, *Glotta* 65 (1986), 154).
2 *osculto* is the vulgar form of *ausculto* (cf. on 18.4), and false etymology as if *ob* were involved does the rest; *obsculto* is offered by the ms. of Varro, *LL* 6.83, and *obscenus, obscuro* are occasionally spelt with *ops-*. For *paticus* = *pathicus* cf. Väänänen 56, Biville 157-9.
3 Cf. *CIL* 4.4951 *ursi me comed* (the last two letters uncertain) and 93b below (also at Herculaneum, *CIL* 4.10656, 10660); this is a stereotyped curse (alluded to by Petron. 66.6; Daviault in *Mél. d'ét. anc. M. Lebel* (1980), 243 quotes also Atta 6 *ursum se memordisse autumat*).

80

CLE 46 = *CIL* 4.1884
Discussion: Gil in *Filologia e Forme letterarie (Studi F. Della Corte,* 1988), 4.419

For the verb *uissio* 'fart' see on 70A. If one evacuates something in a fart, one will have ingested that previously; so the answer to the question is *uerpam*, whence it emerges that the subject is a *fellator*. A similar point is found with *mentulam cacare* (Housman 1177 = [l.c. on 79] 404; wrongly contested by V. Buchheit, *Studien zum Corpus Priapeorum* (1962), 144).

81

CLE 47 = *CIL* 4.1882

There is a pun on *accensum* = (1) adjutant (cf. 25), from *accenseo* (2) one set on fire, from *accendo.*

82

CLE 49 = *CIL* 4.4488

Old men are liable to taunts that they suffer from scrotal hernia; Lucil. 331-2 *senex...ramice magno,* Lucillius, *AP* 11.132.6 κηλῆται, Juv. 6.326 *Nestoris hirnea,* cf. 10.205. When such a one lies on his back, his enlarged testicles prevent anal penetration; the joke is that, while this practical reason why he is not sodomised is given with a straight face, the real reason is that such an old man is far from desirable.

83

CLE 50c = *CIL* 4.1820

Ritschl realised that these are senarii, with the last syllable of *ustulatae* scanned short (cf. Metre I a). For the name Chius cf. Solin 596; this and *ficus* mutually suggest each other, since Chian figs were famous (*RE, Feige* 2121-2). In contexts like this, *ficus* clearly means 'piles', which were taken to be a symptom of irritation caused by sexual penetration; see my note on Juv. 2.13 and Adams, *Glotta* 59 (1981), 246 (for the analogy with Chian figs in this connection see Mart. 12.96.9-10). *ustulatae sunt* sc. *cum pedicarere.*

84

CLE 230 = *CIL* 4.1830

For *pilossus* cf. Väänänen 59; *dignitosso* and *sucossi* are transmitted at Petron. 57.10, 38.6, perhaps wrongly. *eādem...eādem* (sc. *operā*) = *simul...simul* (cf. *TLL, idem* 208.50); the anaphora, for which cf. Plaut. *Bacch.* 49, is spoiled by *et*, which however is desired to avoid hiatus. *u[err]it* (Shackleton Bailey, *Phoenix* 32 (1978), 322) seems much inferior to Bücheler's supplement. A *cunnus pilosus* 'keeps in the heat' like a fur coat; see the opposite in 94c. *glaber* = depilated, cf. Apul. *Met.* 2.17 *glabellum feminal*.

85

CLE 231 = *CIL* 4.1939
Drawing: Varone 91

The first word, which was probably a vocative, is erased, *Vibii* is added above the line. The Vibii are a well-known Pompeian family; see P. Castrén, *Ordo Populusque Pompeianus* (Acta Inst. Rom. Finl. 8, 1975), 240.

This resembles *Priapea* 25.3-4 *sceptrum* (= *mentula*)...*quod quidam cupiunt tenere reges*, but the expression is confused; it means 'but they remained modestly content to hold their penis, just as you do, rather than a sceptre', which simultaneously deflates the Vibii, who are *reges* 'grandees', and insults 'you'. The expression is modelled on the proverb ἦσάν ποτ', ἦσαν ἄλκιμοι Μιλήσιοι, as Marx on Lucil. 959 remarks. For *itidem quod* = *ac* see HS 581.

The third line is a foot too long, and *manu* is a pyrrhic by iambic shortening, like *manus* in *CLE* 1799.1. For the spelling *fueere* see Oliver, *AJP* 87 (1966), 155.

86

CLE 942 = *CIL* 4.1860

Cf. Mart. 2.9 *scripsi, rescripsit nil Naevia, non dabit ergo; / sed, puto, quod scripsi legerat, ergo dabit* (compared by Wilamowitz, *CIL* 4 p. 464). This recalls the complaints of the elegists about mercenary girls. For *pretium dicere* cf. Hor. *Odes* 4.8.12. For the spelling *quoi* in imperial times see Quintil. 1.7.27; it is on 94b.2 (no doubt), *quoius* on *CIL* 4.5249 (cf. *quoiquam* 68.8).

87

CLE 944 = *CIL* 4.1649

An adynaton of the type classified by Canter, *AJP* 51 (1930), 34 thus: 'if the thing or condition mentioned is possible or true, then that thing or condition is possible or true which nature's laws make impossible or false'. Many occurrences of this figure relate to love and friendship or their opposites. For 'binding the winds' (no doubt implying an allusion to Aeolus) see Otto, *Nachträge* 224 (*uentus* 8). *quīs* is a false quantity (cf. 89.4).

88

CLE 945 = *CIL* 4.4091

The same couplet is found *CLE* 946 = *CIL* 4.1173 with an added couplet which is hard to read and of uncertain interpretation; the lines are there written on a picture of a papyrus roll (*CIL* 4 tab. xviii.1). The hexameter is also in 4.3199, and the first few words of it in 5272, 6782, 9130 (= *CLE* 2063), cf. on 5186. 1173 and 3199 read *noscit* = *no(n) scit*, 1173 has the spelling *uota<t>*, and there are some other minor variations. Cf. also 4509 *<quis>quis amare uetat, <quis>quis custodit amantes*, 9202 *Crescens* (so Solin, *Gnom.* 45 (1973), 274; see on 93b): *siquis am(a)t, ualea(t), quisquis ue[t]at, male pereat...*, and Prop. 1.6.12 *a pereat si quis lentus amare potest*. For *bis tanto* cf. *TLL* ii.2008.65, Löfstedt, *Synt.* 1.288.

Another version has been found in the house of M. Fabius Rufus (Solin [on 66] 254-6 and 266 no. 66; photo in Varone fig. 4 and B. Conticello and others, *Rediscovering Pompeii* (1990), 150, cf. 153, 14 l):

uasia quae rapui quaeris, formosa puella;
    accipe quae rapui non ego solus, ama.
quisquis amat ualeat.

The girl asks for the kisses (*basia*) snatched from her to be returned; the man agrees (which gives him an opportunity to kiss her again), and for good measure returns those snatched by others as well, exhorting her to love him in return, for lovers deserve prosperity.

89

CLE 947 = *CIL* 4.1824

Cf. *CIL* 4.4200 *quisquis amat, ueniat. Veneri lumbos uo<lo fractos>*, Plaut. *Stich.* 191 *lumbos diffractos uelim* (*def-* codd.). The metre would be set right by *potis* or *ualet* in 3 (as it stands we have an iambic shortening, cf. Metre II B a) and *cur* for *quit* (= *quid*; Väänänen 70) in 4 (cf. 87.1 and *quŏd* 169). This perhaps points to defective reproduction of a model. For *illae* = *illi* cf. *TLL* 341.1, Leumann 480, Väänänen 86.

90

CLE 948 = *CIL* 4.1898

ustus sc. *amore*. *AP* 5.82 (D. L. Page, *Further Greek Epigrams* p. 43) has a vaguely similar point, and so does *IG* 14.889 = Geffcken 348, an epigram from Sinuessa by a Iunior, very likely Seneca's friend Lucilius Iunior. The couplet is quite misunderstood by Adams (on 97) 188.

91

CLE 949 = *CIL* 4.1837

Various hands have added prose comments beneath this. It is based on literary reminiscences; Verg. *Buc.* 2.7 *mori me denique coges*, Ovid, *Am.* 2.5.29 *quo nunc mea gaudia differs* (cf. *Met.* 4.350, 6.514, *[Her.]* 18.3), *Her.* 3.140 *quam sine te cogis uiuere, coge mori*. The last of these seems to motivate the unmetrical word-order in 3; the metre would be put right by *te sine* or *sine te quem*. 4 presumably means 'at any rate to have refrained from torturing me will be the gift of a kind man', which implies that this was written by a woman. The metre would be restored in 1 by e.g. *<mutua> gaudia*, cf. Ovid, *Am.* 3.6.87. With 2 cf. Tib. 2.6.20 *spes fouet et fore cras semper ait melius*. In 5 the first *spes* means '<lack of> hope', cf. on 12.3.

92

CLE 950 = *CIL* 4.5296
Discussion: Copley, *AJP* 60 (1939), 333
Drawing: Varone 99

This is written on the doorway of the so-called doctor's house, IX ix f, and it looks like a specimen of verses of a type of which we hear particularly in the elegists, those written by a lover on the obdurately closed door of the beloved. The writer was apparently attempting to copy down from memory indistinctly recalled bits of a poem or poems. 1-6a look as if derived from hexameters, if we assume that in passing from the first line of writing (not of verse) to the second the writer omitted some such word as *rapta*, and from the second to the third e.g. *pupula* (voc.); in the third line of verse *i nunc* <*et*> was clearly intended, cf. Juv. 12.57. But it is very hard not to see 6b-7 as derived from elegiacs, e.g. *multos quos Fortuna fauens modo sustulit alte / proiectos subito praecipitesque premit* (cf. Ovid, *Tr.* 3.11.67-8); here too confusion sets in with the beginning of a line of writing. In this reconstruction *modo* means 'lately'; as it stands in the inscription it means *postmodo* (see *TLL* viii.1.1311.27; D. R. Shackleton Bailey, *Propertiana* (1956), 32). The speaker of the verse is a woman (5 *ego perdita*, 4 the comment on men), as in the Fragmentum Grenfellianum (Powell, *CA* 177), and Copley argues that the writer of the graffito was also, as presumably in 91 above; this deduction seems not altogether safe to me. If it is accepted, it is more probable that we here have a soliloquy (in which case *labellis* 2 will be ablative, as I have translated it) than an invitation to another woman to transfer her affections from males to females (in which case *labellis* will be dative, 'to your lips').

1 Plaut. *Rud.* 1203 *uxor complexa collo retinet filiam;* see further Mastandrea 142.

2-3 The diminutive *braciolum* is no doubt derived from Catull. 61.181; *pupula* is alien to polished style (though Catullus has *pupulus*), but is found *CLE* 56.4. These two diminutives are reinforced by the third *label(l)is*.

3 Cf. Verg. *Aen.* 10.652 *nec ferre uidet sua gaudia uentos;* Turnus following the phantom of Aeneas does not see that his joyful hopes of victory are evaporating into insubstantial wind. So here, with the ironical challenge ordinarily given by *i nunc (et)*, it means 'go ahead, base your hopes of happiness on nothing'.

5-6 Leo compares Eur. *Hippol.* 375 sqq. In 6a one has to understand

'I said'. For *supstulit* cf. *supstenet*, *CLE* 929.
7 A remarkable alliteration of *pr*.
8 Lucr. 5.962 *et Venus in siluis iungebat corpora amantum*. For *coiunxit* cf. SP 196; *ut subito* = 'as soon as', cf. Ovid, *Her*. 12.137.
10 is not securely read.

93a

CLE 953 = *CIL* 4.1645

93b

CLE 954 = *Gr. Pal.* 283, 286 with photos tab. xc, xcii.

The two copies of 93b vary between *futuet* and *-it* (see on 79.1). For the curse in 93b cf. 79.3. Crescens (cf. the commentary on 60 and 88) is the invented archetypal writer of graffiti, like the American 'Kilroy was here'; it is amusing to see him sometimes treated as an actual historical figure, as by Franklin in *Literacy in the Ancient World* (1991), 93 and Moeller 88, who is taken in by the whimsical L. Quintilius Crescens on *CIL* 4.4107, cf. 4104 (but what about the equally whimsical C. Cresces on 4113?). If he were a historical figure, we should have to suppose an eventful career not only at Pompeii but, as here, at Rome; he is not only *fullo* (often), but also *retiarius* (4352) and *architectus* (4716, 4755; i.e. ship-builder), and in 4752 he greets *conserui*. In 10126 he is even *Euanti l(ibertus)* (Solin, *Gnom*. 45 (1973), 270). I do not think that anyone is naive enough to suppose that 4734 *Cresces hic situs* is the actual site of his burial. In each copy of 93b *Crescens* stands on a line of its own, and is no doubt meant to be nominative (sc. *dicit*) rather than vocative (cf. *CIL* 4.9202 quoted on 88); it is like καὶ τόδε Φωκυλίδεω. For *uiolare puellam* cf. Tibull. 1.6.51, for *quisque* = *quisquis* 130.7, 167.1, HS 201-2, Väänänen 123, Konjetzny 333. For the lover in the wilds, as in 93a, cf. Prop. 1.18.

94a

CLE 955 = *CIL* 4.1516

For the masculine *lutus* (*TLL* 1900.65; also in *CLE* 982.1) cf. on 19.1 and Väänäanen 82, Tolkiehn, *Neue Jahrb.* 4 (1901), 181; in this case the influence of *limus, -um* may be at work. The word is applied to nasty vaginal secretion in the Priapeum *Quid hoc noui est?* attributed variously to Vergil and Tibullus (OCT App. Verg. p.152, H. Traenkle, *Appendix Tibulliana* (1990), p.51) 37. Despite *TLL* vii.2.106.36, 1904.44 I do not believe that the potential sense 'but essentially she was a worthless person' is even glanced at. *forma* no doubt should be *forte*, as in 94b, though the reading there is not secure. For *futue* see Väänänen 23 and on 79.1.

94b

CLE 955 n. = *CIL* 4.1517

For the spondee in the second half of the pentameter see Metre II A i. The general sense of what followed must have been *exulcerauerat ut uix aspicere possem* (assuming that *talis* is right). For the spelling *nuc* cf. *CLE* 1084.5, 1323.2, *tuc* 109.8 below and the references given on 71.

These two graffiti belong to a common type; cf. 97 below, *CIL* 4.4029 and

94c an inscription from B(a)elo, modern Belonia, in Spain, published by Martinez, *Atti del terzo congresso internaz. di epigrafia* (1959), 112 (photo *Bulletin Hispanique* 21 (1919), pl. x) = J. Bonneville and others, *Les Inscriptions Romaines de Baelo Claudia* (1988), 105 and pl. xl. For the spelling *cuiius* see NW 2.451 and on 124.4.

94d *CLE* 1810 (from the baths of Titus at Rome; not in *CIL*). This inscription was so emended from the preceding one by Gil, *Habis* 10-11 (1979-80), 186; with an eloquent aposiopesis (cf. 97) the graffitist refuses to complete the line for the prurient (cf. Mart. 11.63.5 with Kay's note; *CIL* 4.6640 *curioso reste(m)*, 4.4071 *curiosus Vitalio*) reader. 94c and d suggest that in an Ostian graffito, deciphered by Della Corte and Ciprotti, *Studia et Docum. Hist. et Iuris* 27 (1961), 335 no. 51 as *<e>go me memini fuisset* , the last word should be *futuisse* (though note that on *CIL* 4.2188 *fuit* = *futuit*). This *frigus* is the opposite of the *uapor* of 84.2.

94e H. Thylander, *Inscriptions du Port d'Ostie* (1952), p. 222 no. A 348. The last line is almost identical with *CLE* 1308.3; *aurea terra* also on an inscription in *Rev. Arch.* 5.3 (1916), 380 l. 14, not in *CLE* but referred to in the note on 2082. For *quendam* feminine cf. *CIL* 4.2247, Väänänen 114, and on 40.7 for *quem.*

95

CLE 2056 = *CIL* 4.6892
Discussion; Baldwin, *Emerita* 49 (1981), 145

aedeo (assimilated to *uideo*) = *edo.* This is extremely obscure, and is not helped either by interpreting Nigra(m) in 2 as a proper name (Baldwin 145 n.3) or by understanding, with Engström, *nigră* to be there meant, with a false quantity (which leaves *cum uideo* pointless). I think that the author dislikes dark girls (cf. 96), and that the rest is to be elucidated by Asclepiades, *AP* 5.210 = V Gow - Page, *Hellenistic Epigrams* εἰ δὲ μέλαινα, τί τοῦτο; καὶ ἄνθρακες · ἀλλ' ὅτ' ἐκείνους / θάλψωμεν, λάμπουσ' ὡς ῥόδεαι κάλυκες (quoted by Baldwin). Whoever loves a dark girl does not really feel the fires of love (since *nigri carbones* = unlit coals); whenever I see a dark girl, then I gladly eat blackberries (preferring their blackness to hers, or as an antidote or prophylactic). Observe *Priapea* 46.1 *o non candidior puella moro* (v.l. *Mauro*); Mart. 1.72.5. One is tempted to suspect an obscene amphiboly, but *edo* so used is apparently found only at Tertull. *Apol.* 9.12 (Novius 6 is uncertain).

96

CLE 354 = *CIL* 4.1520, 1523, 1526, 1528, 3040, 9847

The first line of this distich is an adaptation of Prop. 1.1.5 *donec me docuit castas odisse puellas,* the second is found as part of the couplet Ovid, *Am.* 3.11.35-6

odero si potero, si non, inuitus amabo:
nec iuga taurus amat, quae tamen odit, habet.

This couplet has long been recognised as an interpolation, and in *Hermathena* 143 (1987), 7 I argued that it is an illustrative quotation from another author which has been incorporated into the text. In that case the author of the Pompeian distich, after adapting a line from Propertius, will have quoted a line from another unknown poet. Here *Candida* with a pun (see on 176) on *candida* is probably meant.

Under 1520 is written *scripsit Venus Fisica Pompeiana*; for this deity cf. *CIL* 4.6865, 10.928 = *ILS* 3180, *RE*, *Venus* 838-9, Sogliano, *Atti Accad. Napoli* n.s. 12 (1931-2), 362, Latte 184, R. Schilling, *La Religion romaine de Vénus* (1954), 383.

97

CLE 2058 = *CIL* 4.9246

I have ventured on this restoration, though on Della Corte's drawing it looks as if there is a space between *uersu* and *scribere*, which I suppose might have been filled by *hoc*, rather than at the beginning of the line. For *cetera* cf. Ovid, *Am.* 1.5.25, Philodemus, *AP* 5.4.8, Argentarius, *AP* 5.128.3, with here an effective aposiopesis (cf. 94d, 154.6), as if *peregi* were to be followed by e.g. *mille modos Veneris* (not that this is positively required by the verb, which can be defended by SHA 19.4.7 *potes tricies cum muliere perficere?*, on which see J. Adams, *Latin Sexual Vocabulary* (1982), 144). Perhaps the same could be conveyed by *se]d uersu [relicum]*. Cf. in general 94. *turpe fuit* means 'it would have been shameful' (see on 187.3).

(c) Elsewhere

98

CLE 50a = *Gr. Pal.* 281, 287 (cf. 119), with photo tab. xc, xcii, xciii. Discussion: O. Skutsch, *Hermes* 68 (1933), 353

This is presented in this form to preserve the ambiguity pointed out by Skutsch; on the walls there is no spacing between words. There is a perfectly innocent reading *men tu lacessas? uer palumbos abstulit* (for the seasonal migration of pigeons cf. Pliny, *NH* 10.72 and 78, Athen. 9.394f), and we are invited to adopt this because it produces a regular iambic trimeter or senarius; but there is also the decipherment *mentula cessas? uerpa lumbos abstulit*. This is like

[Acro]'s criticism of a potential reading in Horace (on 70A) *quamuis sit* because it could be read in a text without word-division as *quam uissit*. Because the whole point is the ingenious contrivance of the ambiguity, we do not need to look for sense or point in the words.

99

CLE 943, 1811 = *Gr. Pal.* 289 (photo tab. xciii).

For monosyllabic *qu(i)es* and the like see *CLE* 197.2, 177.3, 516.7, 1223.13, Bücheler on 90.3, Leumann 130, Väänänen 40; this restoration is supported by Val. Fl. 7.244 *nulla quies animo, nullus sopor*. The second letter of *at[que]* looks more like *r* than *t*, but the restoration must be right (cf. *TLL* v.1.1039.4). Cf. Prop. 2.13.17 *mors claudet ocellos*.

100

CLE 1900

The name Lelius very occasionally appears on inscriptions so spelt, but no doubt means Laelius. This is a true versus quadratus of the type discussed in my note on *vers. pop.* 12 in *FLP* 478; the effect is enhanced by the triple repetition (see HS 811 and the repetitions in no. 1 above), which gives the air of an incantation. For *fecit* cf. the acrostich in 199. Falcula is of course a male name. This was found at Caldas de Malavella in Spain.

100A

Vassileiou, *Mél. E. Bernand* (1991), 369, with drawing fig. 3

From a bath establishment at Villards d'Héria in the Jura. The speaker has abandoned vaginal for anal intercourse, whether with the woman with whom he was previously engaged in the former manner or with a man. Vassileiou compares *CLE* 2062 = *CIL* 4.3932 dolete puellae.

pedi[care uolo]; cunne superbe, ua[le

(so supplemented by Housman 1129 = *CR* 41 (1927), 61 on the basis of *CLE* 1785 p. 824 = *CIL* 4.2210 *pedicare uolo*, a phrase also found in *Priapea* 38.3). *quod tua praeda fuit* = *penem*. Vassileiou compares Prop. 1.6.7-10 (Cynthia complains about the prospect of Propertius' departure) *illa mihi totis argutat noctibus ignes...illa minatur / quae solet ingrato tristis amica uiro.*

101

CLE 2065 = *CIL* 11.7263

This was found at Saturnia in Etruria. The top of the stone is broken off, and probably contained a phallus to which *hec poena* alludes (H. Herter, *Kl. Schr.* (1975), 645). Cf. *RIB* 983 (a lintel) *i]nuidio[s]is mentulam* with a phallus to the right; *ILA* 1.3709 *in* [two phalli] *uide f.i.* (also a lintel), 1.864 = *CLE* 2066 *inuide uiue uide* beneath two phalli (this too a lintel), *CLE* 1928 *hoc uide uide et uide ut p[os]sis plura uidere* with a phallus underneath (*CIL* 8.24670 is similar), *CIL* 3. 10189.16 *inuidis mentulam*, 14964 *inuidis hoc* on a phallus. The phallus (*RE* s.v. 1733 sqq., esp. 1735.59) is a powerful apotropaic device for warding off the evil eye; for *inuid-* in this specific sense see *TLL* vii.2.192.20, 200.2, 212.9 and cf. C. Johns, *Sex or Symbol* (1982) 66-7 with fig. 51 p. 68 (two personified phalli slicing an eye), fig. 123 p.150, Ganszyniec, *Eos* 27 (1924), 58, Marcillet-Jaubert, *Epigraphica* 27 (1975), 153, Stiewe, *MH* 16 (1959), 166, Merlin, *REA* 42 (1940), 486. Hercules too, in addition to being god of trade (*RE* s.v. 587), is a powerful protector (Wissowa 282; *RE* 593; cf. 6 above, 135a below), and so obviously is Tutela (*RE* s.v. 1599, Wissowa 178-9, Latte 331-2, H. L. Axtell, *Deification of Abstract Ideas* (1907), 40). The presence of Fides (cf. on 127.8) and the word *statio* (see *OLD* s.v. 8) suggest that an edifice used for commerce is here being protected. Cf. *Priapea* 13 *percidere puer, moneo, futuere puella; / barbatum furem tertia poena manet* (i.e. *irrumabitur*).

102a

CLE 2153 = A. Riese, *Die Rheinische Germanien in den Antiken Inschriften* (1914), 4427
Photo: *Bönner Jahrb.* 116 (1907), tav. iv.2 (cf. Bücheler ibid. p. 298)

102b

AE 1981, 28 = Solin, *RFIC* 109 (1981), 268 with drawing = id., *Tituli* 2, *Miscellanea* (1980), 80 no. 24

102a was found at Remagen (Remimagium) incised on the bottom of an urn before it was fired. The first line intended the hexameter given in correct form in 102b, the second slips into prose from failure to recall the pentameter exactly; it is less likely that it is intended as an iambic dimeter (the combination with the hexameter as in Hor. *Epodes* 14-15) with *ratione(m)*. 102b is a graffito in the Domus Aurea, with *ratjonem* so scanned. For the syncope *sacc(u)li* cf. E. Cross, *Syncope and Kindred Phenomena in Latin Inscriptions* (1930), 59, for the word in this connection *CLE* 924.

II F: MUNICIPAL POLITICS AND INSTITUTIONS

103

(a) *CLE* 194 = *CIL* 11.4126

(b) *CLE* 195 = *CIL* 11.575 = *ILS* 8206 = *Epigr. anf.* ii.27 and tav. xiv

(c) *CLE* 876 = *CIL* 2.2403, 5558 = *ILS* 4514b = A. Jimeno, *Epigrafia romana de la provincia de Soria* (1980), p. 197 no. 165

(d) *CLE* 1466 = *CIL* 10.6193

It is striking that none of these comes from Pompeii, the walls of which are covered with electoral graffiti; perhaps such appeals were recognised as a lost cause there, cf. H. Mouritsen, *Elections, Magistrates and Municipal Elite* (*ARID* suppl. 5, 1988), 58. For the use of *ita* and *sic* in stipulation cf. 123.3, 180.23, HS 634; these instances (cf. also *CLE* 2027) in *TLL, ita* 527.5 sqq.

(a) was found by a bridge on the via Flaminia near Narnia; very similar in prose is *CIL* 6.29942, and in verse *CLE* 196 = *CIL* 5.1490 from Aquileia. The interlaced word-order in 1, which usually indicates literary sophistication (see Fordyce on Catull. 66.18 and G. Williams, *Tradition and Originality* (1968), 714) here implies the opposite, cf. 29.2 and *AE* 1983, 324.2 *sic coeptum peragas, siste parumper, iter* (for this see also Buonocore in *Supplementa Italica* 3 (1987), 154), *CLE* 1307.5 *si de consulta, palmam, loquerere, ferebat*, 1225.4 *cum, fatiare, vides* = *fateare cum vides*. For these *scriptores* see J. L. Franklin, *Pompeii, the Electoral Programmata* (Papers and Monogr., Amer. Acad. Rome 28, 1980), 24, Mouritsen 187 n. 119; the modern equivalent would be 'bill-poster'.

(b) is from Forum Popilii (modern Formipopoli) in Etruria. The writer did not compose this, but wrote it from memory, introducing metrical flaws in 1 (where the original probably had *fiat aedilis*) and 2 (where *tuus* needs to be removed). It is not even established that Forum Popilii had an amphitheatre; for a vague possibility see Aurigemma, *NS* 1940, 16-7.

(c) is from Caldas de Vizella in NW Spain; it is preceded by a prose votive inscription. With *honorem agitas* sc. *mente*, 'you have office as your ambition'. 2 shows that candidates would send out their slaves to write up electoral propaganda.

(d) is from Formiae. The actual epitaph has perished apart from the last line; similar appeals appear on tombs. *atque* was read by Iucundus, but only *a* now survives (cf. *CLE* 1525 C 12, 1144.6). 3 means 'may you often carry home just-elected praetors in triumph'. Until Hadrian made Formiae (see Ruggiero s.v. 187) a colony its magistrates were aediles, thereafter duouiri, and municipal duouiri sometimes dignified their station by calling themselves praetors (*RE, municipium* 617.37; cf. the use of *censor* in 109.23). Therefore either this inscription is post-Hadrianic or it unthinkingly repeats a formula devised for somewhere else. For *parco* with accusative cf. *TLL* 339.84 and *CLE* 1883.2.

104

CLE 38 = *CIL* 4.1597, 1766, 4272, add. p. 206 ad 1251

The various recurrences of this preserve various parts and show minor variations. *Communem nummum* means the funds of a *collegium*, *censio* that the members have voted for a distribution. There was a special legal procedure regulating this; see *TLL, commune* 1978.26, A. Berger, *Encyclopedic Dictionary of Roman Law* (1953), 342a.

105

CLE 1506 = *CIL* 14.5884 = *ILS* 6270

At Ferentinum, inscribed on the side of the monument of L. Pacuvius Severus, who held the highest local offices. Cf. *CIL* 10.5853 = *ILS* 6271 (also from Ferentinum) *mulsum et crust.* and *TLL, crustulum* 1254.68 sqq., Ruggiero, *crustulum*, S. Mrozek, *Les Distributions d'Argent et de Nourriture* (CL 198, 1987), 39.
1 For the asyndeton bimembre see Grammatical Index s.v.
2 The usual hour of the *prandium* (Blümner 382, Marquardt 266).
3 Cf. *CIL* 6.579 *ni qua mulier uelit in piscina uirili descendere; si minus, ipsa de se queretur.*

106

CLE 39 = *CIL* 4.768 (cf. 1030 et p. 196) = *ILS* 6438d

Sabinus the *dissignator* responds to the request by voting for his homonym; W. Jongman, *Economy and Society of Pompeii* (1988), 287 absurdly identifies the two. A *dissignator* is a theatrical usher, so he uses metre and vocabulary (*plausus*) associated with the theatre.

107

CLE 40 = *CIL* 4.1943 (cf. p. 465)

On the walls of the basilica at Pompeii. There is a pun on *album*, the official list of *iudices* ('a *iudex* with an Egyptian father is not on the list'; see Mommsen 3.537-8) and *albus*, a white man (whereas the Romans saw the Egyptians as negroid; see my note on Juv. 15.49), 'a *iudex* does not issue from a white Egyptian father', i.e. if he had an Egyptian father, that father must have been black. The readers will have known who was meant. For *pătre* in senarii cf. Metre II B b.

108

CLE 417 = *CIL* 5.5049 = *Epigr. anf.* ii.23 and tav. xiii.
Discussion: Wistrand, *Eranos* 79 (1981), 105; Buonopane in *Supplementa Italica* 12 (1994), 162 with photo.

This was found near Ausugum, modern Burgo di Val Sugan, in the Italian Alps near Tridentum (Trento) and Feltria. A very mutilated prose subscription written in larger letters names a Claudia as having put up the inscription. She represents her deceased husband as telling how he was honoured with a gilt statue for his services to the community, but this honour caused jealousy and dissension among the citizens, and an attempt was made to drive him out. There seems to have been a second column continuing the story. The right hand portion of the stone is now lost.

The metrical beat lengthens *timidūs* 15; for other metrical features see Metre I f and on 8. Mommsen thought the lettering consistent with the first century A.D., but the poem looks much later to me; see also on 10.

2 Cf. *TLL, laxo* 1073.54.

5 *sanctus deus hic* is the god in whose sanctuary this inscription was set up; however Buonopane prefers to take *hic* as an adverb. Ovid, *Her.* 7.149 *transfer felicius.*

6 34.9, Verg. *Aen.* 11.426 *rettulit in melius,* 2.34 *sic fata ferebant* (and similarly Ovid, *Trist.* 1.3.101), *sic fata tulere AE* 1969-70, 658.3. *felicius* and *in melius* are pleonastic.

7 *auratam* sc. *statuam* (*TLL* ii.1520.65); for the transformation of adjectives (e.g. *merum*) into nouns see HS 154. For gilt statues conferred on *patroni* cf. Cic. *In Pis.* 25, *Phil.* 6.12; for gilt statues in general see Pekary, *Röm. Mitt.* 75 (1968), 144, Lahusen, ibid. 85 (1978), 385. *generatis = collectis.*

8 Hor. *Serm.* 1.6.26 *inuidia accreuit* (not raising the problem of prosody which the inscription presents; see Metre I g). *nomine* means the title of *patronus municipii.*

9 *expellere temptat* Ovid, *Met.* 4.651.

10-15 The gist of these lines seems to be that, as individually locusts are helpless, but collectively effective, so the united community had stood firm, but after it was disrupted by jealousy and faction, it became irresolute, and it was a case of every man for himself. *iunctis* 12 is contrasted with *disiunctus* 14, and that is taken up by *quisque sibi* 15; likewise *timid-* 11 and 15 relate to each other. The last letter in the gap at the beginning of 10 was perhaps *i,* which suggests *pleb]i;* the alliteration of *p* would then match that of *m* in 1 and *f* in 4-5.

10 *lŭcustae* is not found before the fourth century (*TLL* vii.2.1605.10; L. Mueller 438).

12 Forms like *secatus* (instead of *sectus*) are found occasionally from the first century A.D. onwards, cf. *CLE* 1335.12 *secata,* 643.8 *secarunt* (see Sommer 611, NW 3.375, 530).

13 For *hominum pecudumque* (which depends on *pabula*) cf. Verg. *Aen.* 6.728.

109

CLE 1238 = *CIL* 8.11824 = *ILS* 7457 = B74 Pikhaus

Discussion: *DAC* s.v. *Moissoneur* with plate; Pikhaus in C. Saerens

and others, *Studia Varia Bruxellensia* (1987), 81.
Photo: *CRAI* 1884, 64; E. A. Lowe *Codices Latini Antiquiores*, supplement (1971), pl. vii.b, cf. p. vii; Palaeographical Society, Facsimiles, ser. 2 vol. 1 (1884-94), pl. 49 (a fine reproduction); Picard and others, *Ant. Afr.* 4 (1970), 147; H. Degering, *Die Schrift* (ed. 4, 1964), pl. 24; Bassi, tav. lvi.156 (cf. p. 110); Ireland 228.

This inscription was found at Mactaris, with mutilated prose titles above and on the sides; only a few letters can be read in the first couplet. *AE* 1946.62, also from Mactaris, is of comparable content.

The metre shows remarkable freedom in lengthening *-ă* (6, 9, 17, 20, 26), sometimes but not always at caesura or diaeresis; in 19 *-ŭs* is also lengthened at the diaeresis (see Metre II A c, d, e). For *nēque* 4, *undecĭm et* 15, *uixĭ* 5 see Metre I c, f, j (iii). See also on 14.

This inscription is of exceptional interest to palaeographers, because it is one of a group of African inscriptions (*CIL* 8.2391 = 17910, 2400 = 17911, 2409 = 17909, 17912, *AE* 1895, 111 and 1909, 156; all of these from Timgad, about 250 kilometers from Mactaris), some of which can be dated in the first half of the third century, which use letter-forms developed from the old Roman cursive and looking forward to uncial script. To these should now be added an inscription from Mactaris, illustrated *Ant. Afr.* 4 (1970), 163 and discussed by Mallon ibid. On the development see Bischoff 68-70 (unfortunately the foot-notes are wrongly numbered on these pages), and for *litterae africanae* ibid. 76 with n. 165 (not 164). See also Perrat in C. Courtois and others, *Tablettes Albertini* (1952), 16. This inscription too is dated to mid-third century.

3 A striking alliteration of *p*.

5 He evidently had a small plot, and after he had finished its cultivation he engaged in migrant work.

6 *ruri*, having been a locative in 5, now becomes a dative. *semper* = *umquam*. Cf. *CLE* 1095.4 *labor a puero qui mihi semper erat*.

8 For the form *tuc* cf. 94b.1.

9-10 For migrating harvesters cf. Suet. *Vesp.* 1.4; for gangs of them R. MacMullen, *Roman Social Relations* (1974), 42. The *Iouis arua* cannot be securely identified, and it is unclear whether *Nomados* goes with *Cirtae* or *Iouis*. Cirta is about 250 kilometres distant from Mactaris; however A. Berthier, *La Numidie* (1981), 150 takes Cirta to mean Colonia Iulia Veneria Cirta Noua = Sicca Veneria, about 60 km. north-west of Mactaris.

12 *tergus* (*OLD* 1b; add Manil. 5.248) is not often applied to the back of a human. For *pos terg-* see *TLL* x.2.156.80. *gremia* = *manipulos (TLL* 2320.10, cf. Kübler 191 and LSJ ἀγκάλη III).

14 No doubt *opera* was intended; he was promoted from workman to foreman, cf. *duximus* 15. For *posteă* (as if the second part were neuter plural accus., not abl. fem. sing.) cf. *TLL* 186.22 (fourth century onwards), Metre I j (i). *factus eram* = *factus sum*, cf. 187.3, 188.15, KS 1.140, HS 320-1.

15 For the ablative of duration see on 66.1.

16 *Numidae* is collective singular.

17-18 Though it may be possible to construe 'life content to thrive on a little', it is much more likely that *paruo contenta* means 'content with a little' (see *TLL* iv.678.66, x.1.560.31). In that case *fecere* has two constructions, first with infinitive (cf. 136.12, *TLL* s.v. 115.37), then with direct object, and the first *et* in 18 will mean 'and' (whereas with the rejected alternative it would mean 'both'). Another possibility is that the lack of a pentameter, which might have provided a smoother construction, after 17 is an error of the ordinator and not the composer.

dominum domus, unlike his father (4).

21 For the form *scribtus* see Leumann 196, SP 180, 185, *CIL* 8 index, 309a at top. Note the idiom of following a compound verb with a simple; see Watkins, *HSCP* 71 (1967), 115, Renehan, *CP* 72 (1977), 243, Adams, *Eikasmos* 3 (1992), 295. *et ipse* is repeated in 23; in both places it emphasises his rise from obscurity.

22 *ordinis in templo* i.e. *in curia*, cf. *CIL* 8.18328 = *ILS* 5520. Technically *delectus* would be *adlectus*, meaning a decurion coopted without having served as a magistrate; cf. C. Lepelley, *Les cités de l'Afrique romaine* (1979), 1.141; F. Jacques, *Le privilège de liberté* (CEFR 76, 1984), 448-9.

23 Though we occasionally encounter censors in municipal contexts, here the word is a tractable and stylish equivalent of *duouir quinquennalis* (for such at Mactaris see *CIL* 8.686); the duouiri of every five years were responsible for revision of the citizen lists, and the post was regarded as a special honour.

24 He means *genui iuuenes, uidi nepotes. carosque nepotes* Verg. *Aen.* 6.682. As *non vidisse* misfortunes is a consolation (see my note on Juv. 10.265), so *vidisse* descendants is a boast; cf. Auson. *Epic. in Patrem* (a broadly similar poem), 50.

27 *sine crimine uitam / degere* Verg. *Aen.* 4.550.

28 *sic* = like me.

110

IIt 3.1.267 = *Epigr. anf*. iii.65 and tav. xxvii.4
Discussion; H. Solin, *Zu lukanischen Inschriften* (SSF, CHL 69, 1981), 54.

This was found at Tegianum, in the north of Lucania, where the Luxilii were a locally prominent family (see *CIL* 10 p. 1044; Bracco, *RAL* 21 (1966), 124-5); beneath it was another mutilated inscription. A frieze shows the weapons and armour alluded to in the inscription (see the drawing in Della Corte, *NS* 1926, 259). The youth of Luxilius and the word *ludendo* make it highly probable that he was a member of the local Iuuentus, the paramilitary organisation promoted for *iuuenes* by Augustus and succeeding emperors (see on this *RE* suppl. vii.315, x.159.57); one aspect of their *lusus* was the performance of the *lusus Troiae*. For their military exercises in general see 119.5-6, Balsdon 161-3, Ginestet 151. For *campus urbis* see Devijver and van Wonterghem, *ZPE* 54 (1984), 198-9; one should hardly prefer *Campus Urbis*, the Campus Martius at Rome.

arma ludendo (the supplementation must be correct) is a construction which lacks exact parallel, but has reasonable analogies in *ludere trigonem, aleam, proelia* etc. (*TLL* vii.2.1780.70 sqq.). One should not compare 119.7 *feras lusi*, which means 'made sport of wild beasts'. For a place as *testis* to what goes on in it see Nisbet - Hubbard on Hor. *Odes* 2.1.30.

G: GAMES, PUBLIC PERFORMANCES AND PERFORMERS

Under this heading one might place Eucharis (20).

*111***

CLE 251 = *CIL* 14.1 = *ILS* 3385

On a marble column at Ostia. This is the P. Catius (*PIR* ed. 2, C 571) Sabinus who as praetor urbanus dedicated no. 134 below; he also held office as *curator aedium sacrarum* and was cos. II in 216 A.D. *AE* 1956, 204 is a dedication to various gods by him from Apulum. A festival in honour of the Castores was held on 27 January on an island at the mouth of the Tiber, celebrated by an urban praetor (cf. 5 here) or consul (*CIL* 1 p. 308, *IIt* 13.2 p. 403). Cf. *AE* 1955, 166 = H. Bloch, *NS* 6, 1953, 245-6 no. 10 *Neptuno Castori Polluci L. Catius Celer pr(aetor) urb(anus)*. This a was a descendant of Catius Sabinus; the recurrence of Neptune makes it likely that this god was associated with the Castores in this festival, and that there is no reference to the Neptunalia of 23 July. For the cult of the Castores at Ostia see R. Meiggs, *Roman Ostia* (ed. 2, 1973) 343; like Neptune, they had a role (as the St. Elmo's Fire) in protecting merchant sailors. Though there are other possibilities, it would seem likely that the *certamen* (3) was a regatta; Catius has put up a picture or relief of it.

2 The general level of the piece justifies us in supposing *exibuisse* to represent the spelling of the ordinator, not of the composer; see p. 13.

3 *munere* means the privilege of putting on the show.

4 Cf. Verg. *Aen.* 8.301 *uera Iouis proles.*

5-6 For *fascibus auctum* cf. *CLE* 734.1 and probably 686.

7 For the separation of the names see on 11.6-7.

112

CLE 500 = *CIL* 2.4315 = *ILS* 5301 = *RIT* 445 with photo taf. 82.2 = Piernavieja 18 p. 87 (cf. p. 239).

From Tarraco, where another charioteer-epitaph (*CLE* 1279 = *RIT* 444 = Piernavieja 17 = *CIL* 2.4314) was also found. On the circus

there see J. H. Humphreys, *Roman Circuses* (1986), 339.
1 For funeral-altars cf. 131.9, 171.5, 177.1, 188.8, Lattimore 131, Ruggiero 1.602, *TLL* ii.388.40 and in general Altmann; Verg. *Aen.* 5.48 *sacra uimus aras* (the tomb of Anchises), *CIL* 6.1969 = *ILS* 1955 *hoc sepulcrum siue ara,* 28646 = *ILS* 8087 *ara ossuaria. Factjonis* is so scanned.
2 *certi* = faithful, reliable, *studiosi* = supporters, fans; the latter word is followed by a hiatus. Cholodniak tentatively suggested that *certi* might be an error for *circi.*
3 *m. et p. a.* is a quotation from Verg. *Aen.* 5.538, 575.
4-7 A striking pattern of recurrence of the *-isti* ending at caesura and the beginning and end of lines; the Barcelona *Alcestis* 60-63 all end in *-isse. fato obire* means to die a natural death, contrasted with *ante diem obire;* cf. Gell. 13.1, *OLD, fatum* 2b, W. Schulze, *Kl. Schr.* (ed. 2, 1966) 139, Pease on Verg. *Aen.* 4.696.
8 Cf. *CLE* 303.3 *talis, res publica, quaere,* 1239.4 *quem quaerit patriae maximus hic populus,* 1305.1 *subsiste, uiator.*
10-14 are punctuated by editors in a way which obscures the relationship between *Fortunam metuant omnes* and the dismissal of her power in *Fortuna, ualebis* (for which see on 70.13); for the imperatival future here (another instance quoted on 8.3) contrasted with the imperative there and 172.8 see HS 311.
12 *bene habet* is a traditional valediction to the dead (*TLL* vi.2.2451.48). *contegat ossa lapis, CLE* 1142.2.
13 We shed tears when he died, now <we pour> a libation in burying him; cf. *CLE* 1256.5 *possint nostris Bacchum miscere fauillis,* 1107.7 *ossibus infundam quae nuncquam uina bibisti* (tubes for carrying wine to the ashes are found at many tombs, cf. Toynbee 51 and pl. 14) and, for the ellipse, 14.4, Sen. *Ep.* 6.12 *ante senectutem curaui ut bene uiuerem, in senectute ut bene moriar* (where it has been proposed to insert *curo*), Hor. *Serm.* 1.4.56-7.

*113***

CLE 399 = *CIL* 6.10078, 33940 = *ILS* 5300

Above this stood a representation of a boy in a two-horse chariot holding a palm in his left hand and with a horse-rider preceding him. The word *bigarius* is elsewhere found only in the Notae Tironianae and in Greek transcription in John Laurentius the

Lydian; beginners started with *bigae* before becoming *quadrigarii* (see *CLE* 1279. 1-4, referred to above on 112). The first line needs another word to become a hexameter, e.g. <*quondam*> *bigarius*. It looks as if Florus died in a chariot-accident, with *dum* in its causal sense as in 160.2 (see my note on Juv. 6.176); he was probably a child entertainer (see K. R. Bradley, *Discovering the Roman Family* (1991), 115).

114

AE 1971, 44 = Panciera, *Arch. Class.* 22 (1970), 151 with photo pl. 57.2

This was found on the outskirts of Rome. Underneath there is a relief of a charioteer holding a whip-handle in his right hand and a banner (*uexillum*) in his left. It is no doubt as a charioteer that Vetulenus was *delicium populi*, but it is hard to see how he could also (*quoque*) be a *praeco* or *cursor* in the circus (if *nuntius* is so interpreted, as by Panciera 154 n.7), or what the significance of the banner is. Panciera thinks that he was the *uexillarius* of a *collegium iuuenum*, comparing *AE* 1927.45 *collegio iuuenum Racilianensium* (i.e. from the vici Raciliani minoris and maioris in regio xiv); for the banners of such collegia cf. Waltzing 1.425, 2.186-7 and representations listed by Panciera 163 n.40 and *RE* viii A 2442.22. For the first problem one might suggest that, since he was aged 44, he may have retired as a charioteer and become a *nuntius*. One is still left feeling that this does not add up to a unified picture. *Lauicano* = *Labicano*.

1 *Priapea* 27.1 *deliciae populi* (a female dancer), Plaut. *Most.* 15 (an insult to a city slave), *CIL* 6.10151a = *ILS* 5222. This nominative is in anacoluthon, since it is taken up by a dative in 3; cf. 162.1-5. *ampli* no doubt means *māxĭmī*.

2 Regio vi is Alta Semita, vii is Via Lata. *idem* = *item*, cf. *TLL* vii.1.294.29, HS 188-9.

3-6 Cf. *CLE* 572 *cui cari sodales hoc titulo fixerunt nomen aeternum*, 802 *haec, postquam posuere sepulchrum, kari scripsere sodales*, and ἑταῖροι often act similarly on Greek epitaphs. *coniuuenes* is a new word for the lexica; it no doubt indicates fan-clubs of the type meant by Callistratus, *Dig.* 48.19.28.3 *solent quidam qui uolgo se iuuenes appellant in quibusdam ciuitatibus turbulentis se adclamationibus accommodare...spectaculis eis interdicitur*. *sui* means something like 'their moral obligations'.

115

CLE 489 = *CIL* 3.10501

From a sarcophagus from Aquincum, illustrated by W. Walcker-Mayer, *The Roman Organ of Aquincum* (1972), 14 fig.3; that organ (for which see Hyde, *TAPA* 69 (1938), 392; J. Perrot, *The Organ* (Eng. tr. 1971), 109) was not identical with that of Iustus, as it was found in the headquarters of the *centonarii* and seems to have perished in a fire somewhat before the likely date of Iustus. He was probably attached to the second legion in order to play at its gladiatorial shows (see the references given on 117 and Hyde 407); quite a few legionary camps have amphitheatres attached to them, and Aquincum had an amphitheatre in the *canabae* (*RE* suppl. ix.84.64 and 127.31). As civilian support staff he earns a *salarium,* not *stipendium;* see Mommsen on *CIL* 3.10988 and (a military architect) *AE* 1936, 12, also Nagy, *Acta Arch. Hung.* 28 (1976), 81. For ancient water-organs see Wille 205 and the other references given above. A woman is shown playing one at gladiatorial games on the Zliten mosaics (*La Mosaïque Gréco-romaine* (1965), fig. 17-8 after p.155; K.Dunbabin, *Mosaics of Roman North Africa* (1978), pl. 46, 49; *Antike Welt* 13 (1982), 25; Perrot, pl. 2 after p. 117; Balsdon pl. 13a after p.176).

For metrical anomalies see Metre I g, j (i) and (ii), II A a, d, f.
1 For the ablative *lapidi* see Lucr. 1.884 and on 2.3.
3 Stat. *Silv.* 4.4.53, 5.5.31 *pollice chordas / pulso;* for other lines so ending see Mastandrea 671, Lissberger 110. For monosyllabic *ei* in dactyls see L. Mueller 321 (in senarii *CLE* 80.5 etc.).
4-6 She died aged 25 years, 3 months, 14 days; for the precision see on 70.3. Auson. *Parentalia* 4.23 *tu nouies denos uitam cum duxeris annos.*
7 For *regebat* cf. *Aetna* 297. *hydraula* is here declined like *organa;* so a variant at Nicomachus, *Ench.* 4 (*MSG* 243.11).
8 Verg. *Aen.* 1.330 *sis felix nostrumque leues quaecumque laborem.*

116

CLE 1510 = *CIL* 10.1948 = *ILS* 5265

This is from Puteoli; it must have been preceded by the name of the performer and at least one line such as *cum pallam cithara canens trahebat* (Bücheler).
1 For the *syrma*, a long trailing robe of tragic actors, see *RE* s.v. and my note on Juv. 8.228; like Nero there referred to, this man probably sang arias from tragedy accompanying himself on the lyre. For such performances see Friedlaender 2.123, 175 = 2.99, 351; A. Dihle, *Der Prolog der Bacchen* (Sitzb. Heidelberg Akad. 1981.2), 30 sqq.; B. Gentili, *Theatrical Performances* (1979), 26. Cf. Sen. *Oed.* 423 *fluidum syrma* of Bacchus.
2-4 *hic* probably = *ego* (cf. HS 180) and *istis* = *his* (cf. 40.11, 145.3 and my note on Juv. 4.67) = *meis*.
3 *plaude* as if they were watching him perform even after his death. Cf. *GVI* 681.8 (a request for applause for a dead actor).
4-6 The construction is *dignus fauore et ut uiuam*. For *dignus ut* (rather than *qui*) see *TLL* v.1.1152.24.
5 For such disturbances see Friedlaender 2.142-4 = 2.115-17.

117

CLE 1319 = *CIL* 10.4915 = *ILS* 5150

From Venafrum. It does not need to be shown in detail that the metre is very shaky; 9 looks like an attempt at a pentameter.
1 *substa* is in place of the usual *subsiste* (e.g. 112.8).
2 *concipe* = 'perceive, hear', cf. Sen. *Phoen.* 224, Apul. *De Mundo* 15.
4 This probably implies that he was a second son; see Thylander 110.
6-7 He was an 'oboe'-player (this is a better translation than the usual 'flute'; see my note on Juv. 2.90) at the gladiatorial games; for the orchestra there see Wille 202, *RE* suppl. iii. 781, and for a representation of an oboe-player there see G. Ville, *La Gladiature en Occident* (1981), 373 n.61.

ancentu is evidently written in place of *accentu* (cf. Amm. Marc. 16.12.36, 24.4.22) through confusion with *incentu;* see M. G. Mosci Sassi, *Il Linguaggio Gladiatorio* (1992), 73. The writer has in mind Verg. *Aen.* 6.165 *aere ciere uiros Martemque accendere cantu*, 9.22 *quisquis in arma uocas*, 10.241 *uocari / primus in arma iube*, as well as *Buc.* 5.14 *carmina...modulans alterna notaui*. This last is itself obscure,

and appears to mean 'as I set the poems to music I marked the alternations of voice and instrument'. Here the expression seems too confused to permit exact analysis.
7 The verb *gladiare* is not found elsewhere; it is a retrograde formation from *gladiator*.
9 For *acerba* see on 119.20.

118

CLE 523 = *CIL* 8.696, 11914 = B99 Pikhaus

From the neighbourhood of Mactaris. Some of the supplements, which are due to J. Schmidt and Bücheler, are obviously purely exempli gratia (the report in *CIL* suggests *]ire* rather than *]ere* in 3). This is the epitaph of a toreador (*taurocenta, CIL* 10.1074 = *ILS* 5053). Bull-fighting was introduced to Rome from the Greek world by Julius Caesar; see Friedlaender 2.88 = 2.71-2, Aymard, *LEC* 23 (1955), 259, L. Robert, *Les Gladiateurs dans l'orient grec* (1940), 318, Blázquez Martinez and others, *Ant. Afr.* 26 (1990), 155 (for the red cloak still used cf. Ovid, *Met.* 12.102-4, Sen. *De Ira* 3.30.1 and on representations (Blázquez Martinez fig. 19, 52 etc.)).
2 Cf. Verg. *Aen.* 9.770 *uno desectum comminus ictu* (sim. Stat. *Th.* 8.469, 658), 347 *pectore in aduerso totum cui comminus ensem / condidit*.
3 'A bull covered in foam', cf. Cic. *Prognostica* fr. 3.3 (in *De Div.* 1.13) *saxa...salis niueo spumata liquore,* Vitruv. 10.3.6 *remi maris undis spumati.*
4 He means *demisit; d. in umbras* Sil. It. 15.47, cf. *CLE* 1150.1 *Stygia<s> delatus ad umbras,* Prop. 3.18.9 *Stygias uultum demisit in undas.* Note however *Il. Lat.* 431 *Stygias dimittit* (v.l. *demittit*) *ad umbras.*
5 Verg. *Aen.* 11.25 *animas...decorate supremis / muneribus.* For *sŭppremo* so spelt cf. 187.7 and *CLE* 563.5; for the spelling itself, with the common late Latin duplication of the consonant, see Leumann 219 and cf. 130.2, 179.8, 181.5.
6 This is framed on the famous 'Epitaph of Vergil' *Mantua me genuit...tenet nunc / Parthenope,* whence the unmetrical *tenet* here; cf. on 202.1, Hoogma 221, Cugusi 201 sqq. Tigimma is known as an episcopal seat, Thigiba (v.l. Thieba) is mentioned by Ptolemy, *Geogr.* 4.3.29 and is presumably the name of the place where the stone was found. If *Tigimma* is envisaged as fitting the metre exactly, it is scanned like *Tigima,* cf. Metre I k.

119

CLE 465 = *CIL* 12.533
Discussion: Rémy, *Gallia* 42 (1984), 117 with photo; Carabia, *Mél. M. Labrousse* (1986), 105 with photos.

This comes from Aix-en-Provence. A is on the front of the tombstone, B 14-15 on the right side, B 16-21 on the left. For metrical features see Metre I j (i) and (iii).
1 *Paulo* should be *paulum*, cf. *CLE* 580.2, 1305.1.
2 *inuida fata, CLE* 647.2.
5 For the military-style exercises of the *iuuenes* see on 110. *Lusus iuuenum* is the regular term (*TLL* vii.2.2.28.81, 736.41, 1890.19); this is the only reference outside central Italy. His membership explains why he specifically addresses a *iuuenis* in 1. It looks as if he came from a freedman family; families of this rank could achieve sufficient status locally for their members to belong to the rather upper-crust *iuuenes* (Ginestet 124). For engagement of the *iuuenes* in *uenationes* in the amphitheatre cf. *CIL* 11.4580 = *ILS* 6634 = *Epigr. anf.* ii p. 53 no. 33 *editori Iuuen(alium) ob insignes uenationes ab eo edita[s]*, Ginestedt 150, Pleket, *Mnem.* 22 (1969), 283. Pleket takes *ursarii* to mean actual hunters, not performers in *uenationes*, as it pretty certainly does in *CIL* 13.5243 (from Zürich, doubtless referring to the bears of the Alps); see M. Kleijwegt, *Ancient Youth* (1991), 110 n. 215.
6 *ille* suggests that the nickname *Pulcher* (cf. 17) was generally attached to him. Perhaps 5-6 refer to actual gladiatorial combat, or at least a semblance thereof, which seems to be attested for the *iuuenes* (cf. Buonocore in *Epigr. anf.* iii p.94; in my note on Juv. 3.158 I was wrong to doubt Rostovzeff's interpretation of *pinn(irapus) iuuenum* on *ILS* 6635 = *Epigr. anf.* ii p. 58 no. 39, q. v.). Then *Pulcher* may have been his gladiatorial name (cf. *Bonner Jahrb.* 118 (1909), 335). Cf. Lucan 8.264 *nullis circumdatus armis*.
7 *is* = *iis* (cf. 166.3), i.e. *feris*; so he was a veterinarian (*TLL, medicus* 548.83; *CIL* 6.33879 *Hyla medicus factionis Venetae*) as well as a *uenator*. Nutton, *ZPE* 22 (1976), 95 thinks that he was a physician, but this ignores *is*. For *feras lusi* see on 110.1; the same notion probably underlies Ovid, *AA* 1.89-91 *curuis uenare theatris...illic inuenies...quod ludere possis*, though editors do not remark it.
8 He associated with *ursarii* (*ursaris* = *-iis*, cf. on 190.3), *uictimarii* and (why?) *coronarii*. On any grammatical analysis this must postulate an otherwise unknown form *uictimum*, but perhaps the clausula

has just been imported from Lucan 7.167 (and 1.611).
11 For *uera* cf. *CLE* 1191.2.
14 Cf. 194.1. *titulus* in 11 discourages us from postulating here the neuter *titulum* sometimes found.
16 *depleo* = 'deduct'; 20 years with some months deducted = 19 years, cf. 3.
17 *uirtute potens* Verg. *Aen.* 12.827.
19 For *fatorum ordo* cf. Verg. *Aen.* 5.707 and *CLE* 432.2; Ovid, *Tr.* 4.3.35 *tua damna dole.*
20 Presumably *ut <in arbore>* was intended, as in the parallels to this traditional sentiment of tombstones (*CLE* 1490, 1542.7-8, 1543, *AE* 1982, 409, *Altercatio Hadriani et Epicteti*, ed. L. W. Daly - W. Suchier (1939), p. 185 no. 33). Cf. Macrob. *Sat.* 3.19.4 *mala citrea, alia enim praecerpuntur, alia interim maturescunt*; Cic. *Cato* 71 *quasi poma ex arboribus, cruda si sunt, ui euelluntur, si matura et cocta, decidunt*; Marcus Aurelius 4.48. The comparison in these lines underlies the common metaphor *mors acerba*, an unripe, i.e. premature, death (117.9, 123.3, 179.19).

120

CLE 927 = *CIL* 4.1595
Discussion: Wojaczek, *WJA* 14 (1988), 248
Drawing: F. P. Maulucci Vivolo, *Pompeii, i graffiti figurati* (1993), 189

This is written in the shape of a coiled serpent, starting from a picture of a serpent's head. The name Sepumius is elsewhere unknown, and is likely to be an error for Sepunius (Schulze 277 n.1) or Septumius. He was probably a Marsian, since that race was famous for snake-charming, demonstrating his art as a side-show to a theatrical or circus performance; but 1-2 seem also to point to his pride as deviser of the technopaegnion incorporating his advertisement.
1 Ovid, *Met.* 9.538, [*Her.* 20.205] *si forte notasti*; here too second persons would have harmonised better with 3-4. For *sibi notare* cf. on 29.5 and Heraeus 123.
3 i.e. *<siue> spectator siue es studiosus*, cf. HS 670, KS 2.436-7. *studiosus equorum* is quoted from Ovid, *Am.* 3.2.1, *Met.* 14.321.
4 Cf. *Codex Iustin.* 10.73.1 *aurum...aequa lance et libramentis paribus*

suscipiatur (when being equated with *solidi* or payment in kind). 3-4 mean 'then (*sic*, taking up *si*) may you never be cheated by a shopkeeper putting false weights on the scales'.

*121***

CLE 411 = *CIL* 6.10118 = *ILS* 5201

The *parasiti Apollinis* were a guild of actors, cf. e.g. *CIL* 14.4198 = *ILS* 5200 *L. Faenius Faustus quartar(um) par(asitus) Apol(linis)*, which also illustrates the supplement in 3; for them see Jory, *Hermes* 98 (1970), 237; H. Leppin, *Histriones* (Antiquitas, Reihe 1 Band 41 (1992), 93; Balsdon 282-3. It is not clear exactly what *mimi saltantes* were, though dance is attested for mimes by Festus 326M and in the Charition mime (D. L. Page, *Literary Papyri* 346). *Fabulae salticae* in the Vacca life of Lucan doubtless means pantomimes, but they cannot be meant here, since they were essentially solo performances accompanied by a chorus, which does not suit *quartarum*. *adlectus* means 'co-opted'; for the *adlecti* see Jory 253, Leppin 184 and *CIL* 14.2408 = *ILS* 5196 *L. Acilio...nobili archimimo, commun(i) mimor(um) adlecto, diurno parasito Apoll(inis)...quem primum omnium adlect(i) patre(m) appellarunt, adlecti scaenicorum* and on this Jory, *Philol.* 109 (1965), 307. It is not clear to what body they were *adlecti*. 1 *mandata referre* (see Mastrandrea 479) probably means that he performed parasite roles (cf. the parasite in another mime in Page 358-61), in which he would execute commissions and report back. 3 *quartarum* sc. *partium*; cf. *CIL* 14.4198 *quartar. par. Apol.* and Leppin 9 n.39, *RE, Mimos* 1748.

122

CLE 925 = *CIL* 6.10115 = *ILS* 5197

Discussion: H. Bier, *De Saltatione Pantomimorum* (1920), 79; O. Weinreich, *Epigrammstudien I, Epigram und Pantomimus* (Sitzb. Heidelberg Akad. 34, 1944-8), 45

On a clay theatre-ticket, which on the other side has *Theoros uictor pantomimorum* and round the edge the names of the pantomimes Pylades, Nomius, Hylas, Pierus in the accusative with their places of origin; no doubt these are the pantomimes defeated by Theoros, with victory symbolised by the palm-fronds which decorate the inscription (Jory, *BICS* suppl. 51 (1988), 76 and in *Maistor, Studies R. Browning* (1984), 64). The first three of these are known to be Augustan (at least there was an Augustan Pylades, though later pantomimes also took this name), Pierus is known from *CIL* 4.1901 *M. Pilei Piere lux Pompeianorum s(al.?)* and 2366 (assuming this to be the same man), *NS* 14 (1936) p. 321 nos. 113, 124. One then asks who could have defeated the enormously popular Pylades, and the only answer is his rival Bathyllus; a competition between the two seems to be indicated by Dio Cass. 54.17.5, Macrob. *Sat.* 2.7.19, though the latter names Hylas instead of Bathyllus. For such competitions see Lippen (on 121) 152. It is therefore concluded that C. Theoros, the freedman of Maecenas, took the stage-name Bathyllus made famous by Anacreon, and was thereafter known by it. Theoros is mentioned on *CIL* 4.1917, Theoriani in the obscure *CLE* 926 = *CIL* 4.1891, and *CIL* 6.10128 = *ILS* 5263 is another ticket inscribed *Sophe Theorobathylliana arbitrix imboliarum*; she was evidently director of the entr'actes in the troupe of Theoros-Bathyllus when his original name had not been supplanted by Bathyllus. The suffix *-ianus* in theatrical contexts seems to refer to members of a fan-club (Franklin, *AJP* 108 (1987), 103-4), but in the case of Sophe must imply something more. Note *Bathylian[* on a broken inscription *CIL* 6.13677.

deum clearly refers to an emperor, who on the above conclusions will be Augustus; for such casual popular references, not implying cult, cf. Hor. *Serm.* 1.6.52, Prop. 3.4.1, 4.11.60, Ovid, *Fasti* 4.954 etc., Manil. 1.9.

1 This should be *Theorest*.

2 For *imitare* active (not deponent) see *TLL* s.v.432.70. Lines begin with *an dubit-* at Stat. *Theb.* 7.126, Juv. 13.153.

123

CLE 1111 = *CIL* 6.10097, cf. 33960

Found on the Via Appia. It is not clear exactly what profession its subject followed. This composer likes lines with two nouns and two adjectives.

1 For *limen* applied to the tomb cf. 199A.B 17 and often in prose inscriptions. Prop. 2.1.75 *si te forte meo ducet uia proxima busto, /*

esseda...siste.
2 Cf. *CLE* 1327.1 *qui properas, quaeso, tarda uiator iter.*
3 For *sic* cf. on 103; *sic numquam doleas, CLE* 215.3.
5 An Ovidian line; *Trist.* 4.10.3 *Sulmo mihi patria est, Met.* 3.583 *humili de plebe parentes,* and six times *media de plebe* (*TLL* viii.589.73).
6-7 would run better if *tunc* and *quondam* could be interchanged; the writer probably composed 7 before 6. However, for a 'then' only vaguely defined by the context see 32.2 and Mastronarde on Eur. *Phoen.* 142.
10 *adque = atque.*
13 For *Maeonio carmine* cf. Ovid, *Ex Ponto* 3.3.31.
14 This would naturally mean the Forum Iulium, but could no doubt apply to any of the imperial Fora, in any of which there might be schools (for one in the Forum Iulium which has left Vergilian graffiti see M. della Corte, *Bull. Comm.* 61 (1933), 124) and cultural activities. Bookstores (Mart. 1.117.10) and textual studies (recorded in the famous manuscript subscriptions such as that in one family of the mss. of Martial after 13.3 referring to the Forum Augustum) are hardly relevant, but see Ven. Fort. 7.8.26 *aut Maro Traiano lectus in urbe foro,* 3.18.7-8 *uix modo tam nitido pomposa poemata uultu / audit Traiano Roma uerenda foro,* which probably reflect the persistence of earlier conditions.
15 Cf. *CLE* 1148.7 *omnia Ditis habet praeterquam nomen eoru(m),* Ovid *Am.* 3.9.59.
16 *maest. ut. par.* 195.5, *CLE* 1055.8.
18 Ovid, *Am.* 3.9.60 *in Elysia ualle.* Elysium is a fairly vague concept, and *fusus* seems to indicate that here it means little more than the actual tomb; cf. *CLE* 1188.4, 1326.2 and, less distinctly, my 199A.A3, Galletier 56.
19 *quod = quot.* The Dolphin has 9 or 10 stars (see Le Boeuffle on Hygin. *Poet. Astr.* 3.16), Pegasus next door to it 15 or 18 or 20 (see *RE, Equus* 326.14, *Pegasus* 62.51). Since the number of stars in the two cannot be equal, the sum total must be meant, which means a minimum of 24 and a maximum of 30.

124

CLE 29 = *CIL* 6.9797, 33815a = *ILS* 5173
Discussion: Mommsen, *Ges. Schr.* 8.189; Champlin, *ZPE* 60 (1985), 159 (a fantastic and untenable interpretation)

Not exactly a public performer in the same sense as the others included above, but this seemed the best place for this poem. It is in senarii, with hiatus at a pause in 6, at the caesura in 8 and 10 (cf. Metre II B b, c), and a 'prosodic hiatus' *dĕapotheca* in 11 (for parallels see Hodgman, *HSCP* 9 (1898), 146). For lengthening of the *A* of *Agrippae* before mute and liquid cf. ibid. II B a (short is certified as the natural quantity by Manil. 1.798).

1 He was the first Roman citizen (*togatus*) to play with glass balls (which of course demand expert players so that they are not dropped). Bücheler compares Pliny, *NH* 7.159 *primus togatus saltare instituit (Stephanio)*, but Sabellicus emended that to *togatas*, no doubt rightly, since Stephanio is the *St. togatarius* of Suet. *Aug.* 45.4.

4 For the spelling *Traiiani* cf. 94c.2 and Leumann 127.

6 For *pilicrepi* cf. *CIL* 4.1147, 1905, 1926; 6.6813; Sen. *Ep.* 56.1 (where he seems to be keeping the score, cf. *CIL* 4.1936); Stat. *Silv.* 1.5.57 *tabulata crepantes / auditura pilas* (in the baths of Claudius Etruscus); see Blümner 440. Ursus associates himself with the other *pilicrepi* in 13, and calls both himself and them *senes* (12, 16), unless in 16 'we' means 'I'.

7 For violets and roses (but not here for the dead) see 177-8.

8 *marcidus* seems an odd term of praise; it must mean *uetusto*, since age improves perfumes (Pliny, *NH* 13.19). For the perfuming of statues see *RE, Salben* 1857.63. 'Foliage' seems to be meant by *folio* rather than 'nard' (see on 186.6).

10 For *nigra Falerna* see Fitton Brown, *CR* 12 (1962), 193-4.

11 *uinum dominicum* at Petron. 31.2 is wine of the quality served to the host, contrasted with that served to inferior guests. Here I think it means that Ursus' friends are to raid his cellar with his blessing (n.b. *meum* 9). Galen 14.27-8 K does not say what Mommsen and Bücheler allege. *uiuo* presumably means that this statue has been set up during the lifetime of Ursus, not as a memorial after his death, cf. 127.

14 For *uicit antecessores* cf. *CIL* 7.451.

15 *decore* takes up *decenter* 2.

16 An emphatic cumulation of the syllable *uer-* (cf. 20.19), followed with a pun on *Verus* in 18.

17-8 This is M. Annius Verus, cos. III in 126 A.D. (*PIR* ed. 2, A 695); his daughter married Antoninus Pius, and their son-in-law, nephew and adoptive son M. Aurelius was also fond of ball-playing (SHA 4.4.9) and was brought up in his grandfather's house (ibid. 1.8, 10). The family tree is this:

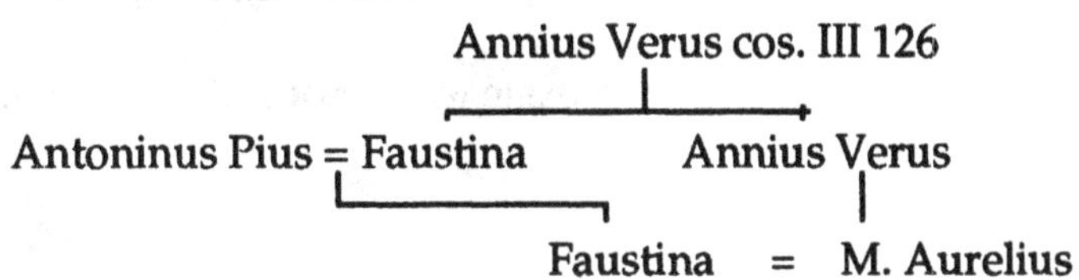

19 *exodiarius* is metaphorical; Ursus is to Verus as a light after-piece in the theatre is to the main play. Similarly *exodium* = *finis* in Varro, *Sat. Men.* 99, 174, 520.

II H: TRADES AND PROFESSIONS

One might count here the mosaic worker of 187, the schoolteacher of 68, the lawyers of 145.

125

CLE 208 = *CIL* 6.9403 = *ILS* 7713

For the Ara Marmorea see *AE* 1976.13. This profession existed because the coloured stones regularly used to represent eye-balls tended to fall out; cf. Marquardt 688, Friedlaender 3.100 = 2.317, *CIL* 6.9402 = *ILS* 7714 *faber oculariarius*. This is an instance of the remarkable degree of specialization among Roman craftsmen; see my note on Juv. 6.591, Blümner 595, Wissemann, *Münstersche Beiträge zur antiken Händelsgesch.* 3.1 (1984), 116. For the form *quaad* cf. HS 655. Prose here flows into verse; for the converse cf. 52, 140.

126*

CLE 427 = *AL* 660 = *CIL* 3.3676 = *ILS* 2558
Discussion: Speidel, *Ancient Society* 22 (1991), 277

This inscription acquired a medieval manuscript tradition, from which alone it is known. Some manuscripts name the soldier Soranus, which may be a cognomen or mean 'from Sora' (the provenance of an inscription might naturally be noted by whoever decided to record it), where, as Speidel remarks, Hadrian settled some veterans and where an *eques singularis* (see on 2) might retire. The first three verses are all leonine.

1, 9 Cf. *CLE* 426 *Ille ego qui...hic sum* and 150.15, 172.3, 180.3 below.

2 He may have belonged to a *cohors Batauorum miliaria*, which could have been the third (*RE, Cohors* 252.6); or, as Speidel thinks, to the thousand-strong *equites singulares*, popularly called *Bataui*. Presumably *fortisque* (accus. plur.) *Batauos* is epexegetic of *mille uiros; inter mille uiros* also Ovid, *Met.* 11.528, Sil. 10.173.

3 For the scansion of *Hadriano* see Metre I d. Cf. Dio Cass. 69.9.6 οὕτω γὰρ καλῶς ἤσκητο τὸ στρατιωτικὸν αὐτῷ ὥστε καὶ τὸ

ἱππικὸν τῶν καλουμένων Βαταούων τὸν Ἴστρον μετὰ τῶν ὅπλων διενήξατο. (cf. Tac. *Ann.* 2.8.3, *Hist.* 4.12.3). This is dated to 118 A.D.; see Speidel and H. Halfmann, *Itinera Principum* (1986), 195. It must not be assumed that 'Soranus' actually performed the feat under the eyes of Hadrian, as if *iudice* meant *teste*; surely the Latin can only mean 'I who, in Hadrian's judgment, could have swum across the Danube', a report of a compliment paid by Hadrian to the soldier at some time. For *profundi Danuuii* cf. Hor. *Odes* 4.15.21.
5 *abscondit in aere telum* Sil. 1.316.
6 *ex* is instrumental; for *ex sagitta TLL* v.2.1113.7 adduces a parallel from the veterinary treatise *Chironis Mulomedicina.*
7-8 Cf. 132.3. *Romanus* is explained by *miles*, *barbarus* by *Parthus* (which implies service in Trajan's Parthian war).
10 For *uiderit* cf. 199A.A21 and see H. J. Roby, *Latin Grammar* (1874), 2 p. cvi, F. Thomas, *Recherches sur le Subjonctif Latin* (1938), 184; it is future perfect indicative, not perfect subjunctive. Seven times in Ovid, as here, it appears without expressed subject in the sense '(the relative person) will have to see to it'; this goes back to an old speech-habit (HS 412, Fraenkel on Aesch. *Ag.* 71). It is a formula used for postponing judgment and putting responsibility on someone else; here its force could be conveyed by 'it is up to others to see'.

127

CLE 249 = *CIL* 14.2852 = *ILS* 3696

This comes from Praeneste, where there was a huge temple of Fortuna Primigenia with an oracle, and the consular date on the side places it in 136 A.D. Caesius Taurinus dedicates to Fortuna a statue of his grain-merchant father T. Caesius Primus, who is still alive (cf. 124). Above the inscription are depicted two sheaves of corn and two bushels filled with ears of grain.

Another verse dedication to Fortuna of Praeneste is published by Gamberale, *Dicti Studiosus* (Scritti...S. Mariotti, 1990), 117.
1 Taurinus compliments Fortuna Primigenia by pointing out that she has also a temple on the Roman Capitol (Plut. *De Fort. Rom.* 10.322f; Latte 178, J. Champeaux, *Fortuna* (CEFR 64, 1987), 15 n.57, Degrassi, *IIt* 13.2 p. 530). Cf. Stat. *Silv.* 4.2.20 *uicina Tonantis / regia.*
3 Cf. *CLE* 1293.1 *Lucius haec coniunx posui tibi dona merenti.*

5 Cf. *littera nominis, CLE* 1088.3.
7 *larga Ceres, CLE* 346.5.
8 A tradesman has to possess *fides*, cf. 18.3, 101, 128.4. *fama fidesque* is an alliterative pair (see Wölfflin 259); it ends the line again at Auson. *Parentalia* 16.3.
11 Verg. *Georg.* 4.421 *statio tutissima nautis.*
12 For *urbe sacra* cf. 128.2; according to Moore, *TAPA* 25 (1894), 53, Rome is first so called on *CIL* 6.1030 of 201 A.D., but he overlooks the dating of this inscription (quoted on p.54). See also the prose of 147.
15 For scansions like *ădicit* in compounds of *iacio* see my note on Juv. 15.16. *numero crescente* also Ovid, *Fasti* 3.125, Claudian, *Cons. Stil.* 1 (21) 304.
16-17 Iuppiter Arcanus appears again on *CIL* 14.2937, 2972, also from Praeneste. He and Apollo (a Praeneste dedication to him *CIL* 1.59 = 14.2847-8) are suitably associated with the ambiguity of the oracles of Fortuna.
19 Cf. Ovid, *Tr.* 4.10.2.
20-21 *pietate...posuit donum* resume 3 (where *dona* is poetic plural) with the technique of ring-composition, cf. on 31.24 (for such ring-composition cf. also *GVI* 1897.11 and 25). *sententia* = sentence, verdict.
23 Cf. *incolumi rumore,* Fronto p. 78.19.

*128***

CLE 437 = *CIL* 9.4796 (cf. p.686) = *ILS* 7542
Discussion: McGuire, *AJP* 67 (1946), 131

From Forum Nouum (Magliano) in the Sabine territory. In the prose prefix *se uibus* results from a mixture of *uiuus* and *se uiuo*; cf. Konjetzny 323. The name Nerusius is found elsewhere only *CIL* 6.33835 = 11.2619; for Mithres (which indicates freedman descent) see Solin 1.374 and McGuire.
1 *respice lector* ends the line also at *CLE* 1495.1.
3 A few reports show *exibui* (cf. 111.2), which is probably right, though I have not ventured to put it in the text; *exhibui* is likely to be a regularization.
2, 4 For *urbe sacra* and *fides* see on 127. 12, 8.

5 *feci* = *uixi* (*TLL, facio* 121.59, with not very exact parallels). *struxi mihi marmora* i.e. this tomb. *ueata* = *beata*.
6 He paid his taxes. *manceps* is a contractor or dealer. The substantival use of *fiscalia* is not earlier than the third century (*TLL* s.v. 821.82), which is presumably the date of this inscription.
9 *CIL* 6.32049 *coniux...communis fidelibus amicis;* also *CLE* 1304.3, 2096.5.
11 i.e. the tomb; to some extent cf. *CLE* 1190.1 *hic lapis et tutamen erit post morte(m) sepulcri,* and 199A.A 62-76 for the relationship with the heirs.
14 *re propria* i.e. in ground owned by himself; cf. *CLE* 698. 3-4 *malluit hic propriae corpus committere terrae / quam precibus quaesisse solum.* For *fama loquetur* cf. *CLE* 2090.1, Catull. 78.10.
15 Cf. 173.1, *El. Maec.* 167 *exemplum uixi te propter molle beati* (*beate* codd.). For *dum uita manebat* cf. on 28.7. There is much emphasis on *laus* in this epitaph (4, 10).
16 He solicitously looked after many and provided a resting-place for them in this tomb.

129

CLE 1521 = *CIL* 8.241, 11347 = *ILS* 7801 = B30 Pikhaus
Photo: *MEFRA* 101 (1989), 445 fig. 42 (cf. 444 no. 65)

Found at Sufetula in Numidia Byzacena. 2, 3 (with *ferĕ*; the parallel quoted by *TLL* 492.7 from 'Ausonius' is fictitious), 5, 6, 7 (with *tertjum*), 8 are ionic dimeters, 1 and 4 (with *trigintă et*) are iambic dimeters catalectic, what 9 is meant to be is hard to say. The stone is broken at the top, so something probably preceded the poem.
3 For the approximation cf. *CLE* 1341.2, 2165 etc.; since here no close relatives are mentioned, probably nobody knew his exact age. For the ablative see on 66.1.
5-9 He died three days before the gladiatorial show which he was putting on. For the construction *ante tertium muneris* see HS 64.
8 TLL iv.1156.20 quotes *monacha...in die gelata frigore, per noctem cremata igne* from Ven. Fort.; *crematus* is stronger than the usual *ustus, tostus*.

130

CLE 484 = *CIL* 8.1027, 12468 = *ILS* 1710 = A20 Pikhaus

From Carthage. Above the inscription is *D. M. S.*, to the right of this *Vitalis Aug. n(ostri) tabellarius uiuet et conuiuat* (*uiuet = uiuit*, cf. 79.1, Pieske 73-4) and to the left *et* (? *Fl.*; the inscription is hard to read in places, and transcripts differ in details) *Antigona uiuet et conuiuatur. Vitalīs* 1 is lengthened by the metrical beat; note also 1 *fecĭ* (but 6 *fecī*), 5 *perduxĭ*, for which see on 3 here and Metre I j (iii).
1-2 A pun (cf. on 176). For the spelling *sepulcrhum*, as in 7, cf. 187.5, Leumann 161-2, *CIL* 8, index 315a; for *transseo* *CIL* 8, index ibid. and on 118.5. For *meos uersus* cf. *CLE* 512.1 *ego...uersibus mea(m) uita(m) demonstro*; neither need imply that the deceased was the actual composer.
3 For *circare* (the origin of Italian cercare, French chercher) see *TLL*. *diploma* must be ablative of a first declension noun, a type of formation applied to Greek neuter nouns in - μα from the earliest days of Latin (Leumann 454; Ven. Fort. *Vit. Mart.* 4.423 still has *celeumā*); elsewhere in Latin the word remains neuter. It seems easiest to follow Wölfflin, *ALL* 11 (1900), 418 in scanning *diplōmā circauĭ tŏtam* (Wölfflin quotes *tŏtus* from Commodian), 'I traversed the whole *pedestris* region with a *diploma*'; cf. Fronto p. 11.14 *nauibusne an equis an diplomatibus*? The *diploma* is an official pass entitling the recipient to be conveyed by the horses and vehicles of the *cursus publicus*, the imperial post. Here however the presence of *pedestrem* causes a problem, which I think is best solved by following Wilmanns in taking *regio pedestris* to mean 'the sphere of activity on dry land' (*pedestris* contrasted with *marinus* as at e.g. Pliny, *NH* 3.101, Ulpian, *Dig.* 43.12.1.14). Carthage being by the sea, *tabellarii* will often have had to use ships to deliver their messages, and provision was made for this in the *cursus* (see *RE*, *Dromonarii* and s.v. *Nachrichtwesen* 1526, *Postwesen* 1009). Vitalis will be distinguishing himself as a *tabellarius* for the hinterland of Carthage from messengers whose duties took them to sea.
4 sqq. Now his diversions.
5 This scans *posteă* (cf. 109.14) *potjones*. For *perduxi* see *OLD* s.v. 11.
7 *quisque* i.e. *quisquis*, cf. 93b.1. For *uiuo* cf. the prose prescript of 128.

131

CLE 219 = *CIL* 13.8355 = *ILS* 7756 = B. and H. Galsterer, *Die röm. Steininschriften aus Köln* (1975), 334 and taf. 74.
Discussion: Rubensohn, *Archiv f. Stenographie* 55 (1903), 104
Photo: *Hermeneus* 50 (1978), 419; *Kölner Römer Illustrierte* 1 (1974), 225; Walser 240-1

Found at Cologne. 9 was clearly intended to be the beginning of an epitaph, and the lettering of 9-22 is somewhat larger than that of 1-8. What seems to have happened is that initially 9-22 were inscribed with the intention that at the head of the stone should stand a relief, but before the stone was passed from the letterer to the sculptor a second slave died, and it was decided to make the one stone serve for both and prefix an epitaph of at least 9 lines for Sidonius. The mason who inscribed the top half started off with the hope of finding room for this, but after line 4 saw that he could not hope to fit in more than 8 lines and from that point, as Rubensohn 107 n.3 points out, began to leave larger interlinear spaces. The result is that 8 breaks off in the middle of a sentence, since *acris* has nothing to agree with. Of the three instances which *TLL* quotes for this form as nom. sing. masc., one is genitive sing. and one is accus. plur., leaving only Celsus 8.4.21, where we should probably adopt the variant *acres*; to take it as nom. sing. masc. here is extremely improbable, and the writer must have intended to continue e.g. <*calamos, at alter Xantias*>.

The metre is iambic dimeter (the first syllable of the second metron always long, as is the practice of many other authors also), except that 5 and 22 are glyconics, the latter perhaps intended as a clausula, the former arbitrary.

Xanthias was a shorthand-writer, *notarius*. Ausonius has a poem *In Notarium* (p. 330 Prete, 12 Green) in the same metre as this (though allowing the second metron to start with a short), which can hardly be a coincidence; if the inscription is older than Ausonius, he may have seen it at Cologne.

7 *consonanti* indicates that he was a *symphoniacus*.

9 For the altar-tomb see on 112.1.

12-14 His pen raced to abbreviations of so many letters and words (*OLD, nomen* 5) because of his skill in taking down in shorthand what the tongue, also racing, said. Others understand *quod* as *quot*, which causes problems.

16 Cf. Manilius 4.198 (also about shorthand) *quique notis linguam superet.*
18 Cf. Auson. l.c. 1-2 *puer, notarum praepetum / sollers minister, aduola.*
19 I cannot make sense of this unless it means 'to be summoned to assume the role of *auris proxima,* closest confidant', but I cannot corroborate this interpretation; cf. however the Persian official known as 'the ear of the king' (Xen. *Cyr.* 8.2.10 etc.). *at* = *ad.*

132

CLE 483 = *CIL* 12.722 = *ILS* 7715

Found at Arles. Two (or three, if 4 be counted) of the six lines are heptameters, and in 3 *fuit* would have to be removed to make a hexameter. On either side of the inscription are depicted a plumb-line and an adze. Candidia Quintina is also on *CIL* 12.775. For *corpora* of *tignarii* at Lyons and Arles see O. Schlippschuh, *Die Händler im röm. Kaiserreich in Gallien...* (1974), 113, 119.
3 Cf. 126.7-8.
4 e.g. pumps.
5 Mart. 7.86.10 *pascis munera...non amicos, CLE* 470.1 *quat ualeas abeas pascas, multos tu habebes amicos* (i.e. *quoad ualeas habeas;* also from Arles).
6 A pun on his cognomen (cf. on 176); *simplex animoque benigno, CLE* 548.4. *studio docilis* takes up *studium doctrina* from 1 (and also 3 *doctior*), cf. on 31.24.

133

AE 1972, 74 = Virro Bugno, *RAL* 26 (1971), 691 with photo tav. iv.
Discussion: Gelsomino in *Antichità paleocristiane e altomedievali del Sorano* (edd. L. Gulia - A. Quacquarelli, 1985), 71.

This inscription, first published in 1930, was found at Aquinum, where a cheap purple dye was produced (Hor. *Epist.* 1.10.26). Zetus is Zethus; cf. Zetus and Amphio, named after the Theban twins, on *CIL* 6.29633. This is a cenotaph (Blümner 488).
1 *resiste* would be more usual and more metrically obvious. For *consiste* cf. *CLE* 980.1 and probably 1877.1.
2 Since he was an ex-slave there would be no record of his date of

birth. For the genitive cf. KS 1.284, HS 70, Konjetzny 313 and e.g. *CLE* 85.1 *decem et octo annorum natus*, 959.5, 1257.5; it is most simply explained as an amalgamation of a genitive of quality with *natus* + accus.

II J: RELIGION

Here one might include 101, 111.

134

CLE 228 = *CIL* 6.313 = *ILS* 3402

This is on a round marble altar. For other verse dedications by praetors to Hercules cf. *CLE* 22 = *CIL* 6.319 (30735), 868 = *CIL* 6.312, 869 = *CIL* 6.316; for Catius Sabinus see on 111.

These are pure tetrameters (not septenarii), except that in the proper name the licence *Euāndreo* is permitted.
2 *urbis* in prose would be *urbanus*, though note *CIL* 8.6706 *quaestor urbis*. In Varro LL 6.54 *pr<aetor> urbis* is not necessarily corrupt.
4 i.e. Potitiis (see on 190.3). Praetors had taken over this ceremony since the Potitii died out (Latte 217-8, Ogilvie on Livy 1.7.12).

135a

CLE 23 = *CIL* 6.329, 30738 = *ILS* 3469

135b

CLE 26 = *CIL* 3.5561

Cf. *CIL* 4.1454 (over the oven of a bakery) *hic habitat Felicitas* with a phallus (illustrated in G. Vorberg, *Glossarium Eroticum* 180 and in M. Grant, *Eros in Pompeii* (1975), 109); see on 101 and Herter (below) 645. For Poverty and Wealth imagined as living in the house see West on Hes. *Theog*. 593; cf. also *CIL* 4.8417 *Bonus Deus hic abitat in domo Act(ii)*. Both of these inscriptions are in senarii; (a) is on a small marble altar, (b) is from a Salzburg (Iuuauum) mosaic. (a) is closely related to a Greek inscription (*IGM* 213)

ὁ τοῦ Διὸς παῖς καλλίνικος Ἡρακλῆς
ἐνθάδε κατοικεῖ · μηδὲν εἰσίτω κακόν

found with minor variations at *CIL* 4.733 (the entrance to a tavern) and often elsewhere; see on this Weinreich 1.258 = *ARW* 18 (1915), 8, L. Robert, *Hellenika* 13 (1965), 265-6, Fraenkel on Aesch. *Ag*. 1334,

H. Herter, *Kl. Schr.* (1975), 642, Gigante 75. (a) 1 demands the pronunciation *Hercles*; the name is so spelt on *CIL* 1.563-4 (= 14.4105-6 = *ILLRP* 1198), 2486 (= *ILLRP* 143), 2659 (= *ILLRP* 129); 5.4213, 5498; 7.751, 1114 (= *RIB* 1781, 2177); 12.5733; 13.4293, and the same is implicit in the exclamation *hercle*, which comes from an Oscan form *Herclos* (Leumann 107). At Plaut. *Stich.* 223 *Hercules* is scanned as a dactyl. For *hic aduenisti* = *huc* see *TLL* 6.3.2763.34, J. Svennung, *Untersuchungen zu Palladius* (1935), 387 (this occurrence 390); even in classical Latin the notions of rest and motion are not always kept distinct (HS 276-7). There is no other attestation that Hercules is *Siluani nepos*, but the two are often associated (Wissowa 215 n.2, *RE, Hercules* 590-1, Dorcey (on 151.1) 51); for a statue showing the attributes of both see H. von Heintze, *Roman Art* (Eng. tr. 1990), 147 figs. 136-7.

136

CLE 1519= *CIL* 8.2632 = *ILS* 3374

From Lambaesis. Ionic dimeters, many of them anaclastic; 9 and 14 vary from the strict pattern with - - - x replacing - ◡ - - in the second metron, and because of the proper name 1 consists entirely of long syllables. Synapheia is observed except after 11 and 13. For the cult of Liber Pater in North Africa see A. Bruhl, *Liber Pater* (1953), 223, Ahlem, *L'Africa Romana* 9 (1992), 1049, Brouquier - Reddé 84, 269-70, 285-86; he is clearly the *interpretatio Romana* of a native god (Bruhl 230).

2 Cf. *somno monitus* in the prescript to 155 and often. For such admonitions delivered in dreams see Gramaglia, *Augustinianum* 29 (1989), 511, 517, 532.

3 For the spelling *Leiber* in the empire see p. 20. Bacchus' first mother was Semele, his second the thigh of Jupiter. The ordinator's eye has slipped from *bimat-* to *nat-us* in **4** in the copy provided to him.

9-11 *'ades filiis simul seruans matrem'* Bücheler; this is better than (with Leo, *Ausgewählte kleine Schriften* 1.76) to understand *natis* *<sospitibus>*. Pan is often associated with Dionysus (*RE* suppl. viii.1001.42).

10-12 This may mean 'bring it about that I see Rome' (cf. SHA 19.8.6) or (so Froehner, *Philol.* 71 (1912), 168) 'that Rome sees me'.

12 Cf. 149.8 *tu me meosque reduces Romam sistito.*

13 *dominis* (dative of agent) must refer to joint emperors, perhaps, as Bücheler suggests, M. Aurelius and Verus.
14 *mactum* is elsewhere applied to men only in fossilised phrases with *macte*. For similar uses of *mactare* cf. *TLL* s.v. 21.57.

137

CIL 8.10488, 11001 = *IRT* 231 (cf. *PBSR* 23 (1955), 142) = *AE* 1953, 186 = T6 Pikhaus
Photo: Aurigemma, *Africa Italiana* 7 (1940), 80 fig. 16.
Discussion: Guey, *Revue Africaine* 96 (1952), 25.

This is from Oea, and records the dedication of two elephant tusks (cf. on 138) to Liber. The metre is iambic dimeter.
5 As supplemented, this will mean 'on behalf of the city and my spouse' (cf. *OLD*, *uicis* 8a), with ἀπὸ κοινοῦ word order (cf. 120.3) = *urbis coniugisque uicem*. The exact circumstances implied cannot be clarified, except that the dedicator is apparently a woman.
6 The story is that when the Romans encountered elephants for the first time in the army of Pyrrhus in Lucania, in perplexity they called them 'Lucanian oxen' (see *TLL* ii.2142.44, *OLD* s.v. *Luca*, Clausen, *CQ* 41 (1991), 546, Arena, *RFIC* 116 (1988), 185, Sandoz, *Latomus* 48 (1989), 757). For similar expressions in Greek see Munro on Lucr. 5.1302 and *LSJ* βοῦς Ic.

138

AE 1942-3, 2 = *IRT* 295, with photo pl. viii.1 = T3 Pikhaus
Photo: Aurigemma (on 137) 79 fig. 15.

This is from Lepcis Magna, the home city of Septimius Severus (3); if *principum* is right in 8, it will date after his association of Caracalla with himself in 196. Liber Pater is one of the main gods of Lepcis (see *IRT* 275, 294-8). Here he is described as the *Lar patrius* of Severus (since *Iouigenae* in 4 is clearly dative); we may compare *CLE* 1527 A 2-3 *nostri publice Lar populi, / sancte Medaure* (i.e. Aesculapius; the stone is from his shrine in Lambaesis), *CIL* 8.10867 as read by Pflaum in *ILA* 2.487 *[L]ari Libero A[ug.] sacr[um* (from Cirta), and *AE*

1928, 106 *deo patrio Libero Patri conseruatori dominorum nostrorum Augustorum* (an inscription from Lambaesis dated 209-212 A.D.). On many coins of the Severi and *IRT* 289 (also from Lepcis) Bacchus and Hercules appear and are labelled *di patrii* (see Lipinski, *Ancient Society* 24 (1993), 41; Brouquier - Reddé 84-5, 280, 285-6). For the temple of Liber Pater in the forum of Lepcis and a sculptured pilaster in the basilica showing him see Brouquier - Reddé 81 and R. Bianchi Bandinelli and others, *The Buried City* (1966), pl. 88, 128, 135, 138.

The metre is intended to be iambic dimeter, but the flaws are so numerous that analysis of them is unprofitable. At least with elisions neglected each line has eight syllables.

1, 4 *Iouigena* is a new word for the lexica; for its point cf. 136.3-4. Cf. *Phoebigena* 143.2.

4 Severus is the sun of the writer. For this topic in ruler-cult see Housman on Manil. 1.385, 4.765, G. Chalon, *L'Edit de Tiberius Julius Alexander* (1964), 97 n.15.

6 Cf. SHA Severus 3.3 *praetor designatus a Marco est, non in candida sed in competitorum grege* (i.e. not as *candidatus Caesaris*).

11-12 The writer is blurring the distinction between Indian and African elephants in order to bring in a mythological allusion to Bacchus' conquest of India. Naturally the dedication consisted of the tusks of an African elephant; see H. H. Scullard, *The Elephant in the Greek and Roman World* (1974), 24. This must have been relatively frequent in Roman North Africa, since a ready-made line (cf. 137.6) was available to express it. For a statue of an elephant from Lepcis see Scullard pl. xix a (after p. 160), Bianchi Bandinelli etc. pl. 56, Aurigemma l.c. 67; for other references to dedicated tusks see Brouquier - Reddé 286.

139

CLE 256 = *CIL* 10.3796 = *ILS* 3261 = A. de Franciscis, *Templum Dianae Tifatinae* (1956), p. 58 no. 16

From Tifata (elsewhere neuter plural, not fem. sing.) near Capua, a district sacred to Diana, who had a temple there (*CIL* 10 pp. 366-7, 1132, 1151); the site of this is now occupied by the church of S. Angelo in Formis (Ferrua, *Rendic. Pont. Acc.* 28 (1955-6), 55; de Franciscis, op. cit.).

2 He means *Latoa* or *Latonia*. *haec miracula* = *donum hoc* 6 = a pair of antlers; for such a dedication cf. Leonidas, *AP* 6.110 = xcvi Gow - Page, Antipater of Thessalonica, ibid. 111 = xlvi G-P, Verg. *Buc.* 7.30, J. Aymard, *Essai sur les Chasses Romaines* (1961), 508, Meuli in *Gestalt und Geschichte, Festschr. K. Schefold* (1967), 159 and below 141.10.
5 For *signo* see on 28. Delmatius becomes a popular name as a sign of loyalty to the Dalmatian emperor Diocletian and his successors, not necessarily implying any local connection (contrast 33 above); see Solin in W. Eck (ed.), *Prosopographie und Sozialgeschichte* (1993), 23-4.
6 *hoc* = *tale*. *anteă* is found only in late writers, cf. *posteă* 109.14.
7 Without further context the precise meaning of the end of the line remains obscure, though the general drift is clear.

140

CLE 1520, 2148 = *CIL* 6.124, 30700 = *ILS* 3258

Two glyconics (with *dea(m)* scanned as a pyrrhic) enclosing a pherecratic; these are the metrical units used in Catullus' hymn to Diana (34). The first syllable of *Dianam* may be either short or long (cf. Catull. l.c. 1), *fĕrarum* shows an iambic base like ibid. 4 and Septimius Serenus fr. 9, where see my note (*FLP* 410). Cf. [Ovid], *Her.* 9.117 *claua domitrice ferarum*, *CIL* 8.9831 = *ILS* 3257 *Dianae deae nemorum comiti, uictrici ferarum*. *PLRE* 1.142 identifies Auxentius with the man who was governor of Cilicia before 384 A. D. and subsequently *v.c.*

141

CLE 1526 = *CIL* 2.2660 = *ILS* 3259-60 = M. del Carmen Fernandez Aller, *Epigrafia e Numismatica en el Museo Arqueologico de León* (1978), p. 28 no. 5 with photo pl. 3 - 4a = Piernavieja 4 p. 35, cf. p. 235 (partial photo fig. 1) = M. A. Rabanal Alonso, *Fuentes literaries y epigraficas de León* (1982), 1 p. 44 inscr. 4 and pl. ii-iii = F. Diego Santos, *Inscripciones Romanas de la Provincia de León* (1986), 17-18 and photo lam. xiv and xviii.
Discussion: Pena, *Mél. P. Lévêque* 4 (1990), 329 with photo.

This is from modern León in Hispania Tarraconensis; the name is derived from *legio*, since this was the base of the seventh legion (*RE, legio* 1632-3; P. le Roux, *L' Armée et l'Organisation des Provinces Ibériques* (1982), 151; Jones, *JRS* 66 (1976), 52; L. A. Curchin, *Roman Spain* (1991), 74). The date is fixed between Vespasian (who gave the legion the name *felix*) and Severus (who added *pia*); *RE* l.c. 1314.55 and 1637. The dedicator is no doubt identical with the Q. Tullius (*RE* no. 44) Maximus who in the 160's was governor of Thrace; Groag identifies him also with the eloquent African (cf. 3 *e Libya*) senator Maximus known from Aelius Aristides (see C. E. Behr, *Aelius Aristides and the Sacred Tales* (1968) 47 (-8) n. 26).
2 Hor. *Odes* 3.22.1-4 *uirgo...triformis, Pervig. Ven.* 38 *uirgo Delia;* cf. 32.28. For the 'temple' cf. on 24.1.
3 The two place names are in antithesis.
4 He could have written *posset*, so he is trying to elevate his style; cf. Clausen, *CP* 59 (1964), 95-6. *figere ceruos* Verg. *Buc.* 2.29, Sen. *Herc. fur.* 1129 etc.
5 Cf. *siluicultrix* (Catullus) and *siluicola*. For the wild horses of Spain see Varro, *RR* 2.1.5, Strabo 3.4.15.163.
6 Bücheler compares *disice* with *obice* and *subice*, which are derived from *iacio*, and concludes that this is the name of an instrument and that *ferri* is genitive of *ferrum*, so that *cursu certare* relates to *pedes* and *equo* in 7, and *disice ferri* to *arma* and *iaculator;* then *disice* will correspond to uses of *disicere* such as those quoted *TLL* 1383.8 sqq. The genitive *ferri* is presumably genitive of material (best discussed by Kenney, *CQ* 43 (1993), 458; e.g. Lucan 2.72 *uincula ferri*). If *ferri* is taken as the passive infinitive of *fero*, then *disice* is inexplicable. Cf. Plin. *Pan.* 81.2 *certare cum fugacibus feris cursu.*
8 For dedications of boars' tusks see Stat. *Theb.* 9.589 with Dewar, Symmachus, *Ep.* 5.68.1.
10 *altifrons* is unknown elsewhere and no doubt modelled on ὑψίκερων ἔλαφον Homer, *Od.* 10.158. For the dedication of antlers cf. 139.2.
12 *paramus* is an Iberian word (surviving in Spanish and Portuguese páramo = a barren plateau) found in the place name Segontia Paramica and some modern Iberian place-names; *TLL* quotes an occurrence as a noun (so here) and one as an adjective (*in campo paramo*). Cf. 1 *aequora campi* and Hubschmid in *Enciclopedia linguistica hispanica* 1 (1960), 484; A. Tranoy, *La Galice Romaine* (1981), 34-5. S. Mariner Bigorra, *Inscripciones Hispanas en verso* (1952), 71 refers this to El Páramo, a district about 30 kilom. SW of León; if this is

right we should print *Parami*.
13 For *feroci sonipede* cf. Verg. *Aen.* 4.135.
14 sqq. Trochaic tetrameters split into two cola each as in *CLE* 235-6 so that they look epodic; cf. my note on Septimius Serenus fr. 6 (*FLP* 409). The ablative *pelli*, which is apparently attested by Charisius 51.30 B = 43.14 K (v.l. *peluis*), is restored in Lucr. 6.1270.
19 Cf. 142.2.

142

CLE 1800 = *CIL* 11.5262

Found at Hispellum on an altar in a shrine of Diana, with a sculpture of a huntsman underneath; the stone has now disappeared, and Bücheler casts doubt on its authenticity.
1 *sancta uirago* ends the line at *Il. Lat.* 533 (there Athena); Diana is again *virago* on *CLE* 217.1.
2 *cornigeram* is not elsewhere found as a noun; it is an instance of 'kenning' (see my note on Juv. 8.155). *uirtute et laude* forms a hendiadys = *laude uirtutis*; for *laude potitus* cf. Stat. *Th.* 3.185.
3 The metre goes astray at the end with the false quantity *tū̆um* (cf. 138.12).

143

CLE 1528 = *CIL* 6.520 = *ILS* 3200 = *IGUR* 161 with partial photograph = *IG* 14.978.

On a herm set up, as the Greek verses show, by an Attius.
1 For Hermes as god of gain, κερδῷος, cf. e.g. *ILS* 3199, 6037; for him as god of speech see *RE*, *Hermes* 781-2, Nisbet - Hubbard on Hor. *Odes* 1.10.3, Housman 956 = *CQ* 12 (1918), 35.
2 Usually Hermes is said to have invented the lyre, not wrestling, as an infant.
3 *interpres diuum* is from Verg. *Aen.* 4.356, 378, and the composer also has in mind ibid. 6.849 *caelique meatus*. Here *caeli terraeque* are objective genitive; *meare* is transitive at *Anth. Lat.* 197.4 R and (in a

transferred sense) above 70.5.
4 The combination as in Horace l.c.
6 For Hermes as god of dreams see *RE* l.c. 789.
7 For the exceptional iambic base to the hendecasyllable see on 155.

144

CLE 866 = *CIL* 3.7266 = *ILS* 3853

From the temple of Aesculapius at Epidaurus, beneath a representation of two ears, cf. *CIL* 3.986. For the quantity *Cūtius* cf. *Cútius* on *CIL* 6.16701, 16706; for *Phoebigena* Verg. *Aen.* 7.773, Q. Serenus, *De Medicina* 181 *uis et Phoebigenae diuinam discere curam?* (proceeding to give a cure for deafness); for *ab* 'with respect to' *OLD* 25a.

145

AE 1945, 82 = M. Chelotti and others, *Le Epigrafi romane di Canosa* (1983), 3

A statue-base from Canusium. Each hexameter is written in three lines with the second and third inset, each pentameter in two with the second inset; five indecipherable lines containing another couplet followed. That the inscription is verse was realised by Crawford, *CR* 39 (1989), 354; for the spondaic endings to the pentameters cf. e.g. *CLE* 1058.2 and Metre II A i. *iurā* is due to the metrical beat and the hiatus after it to the diaeresis (Metre II A f); there is another hiatus after *dea* 1. *TLL* i.818.83 quotes two instances of *adŏrare* (as 3 here) from Dracontius. The lawyers of Canusium address the protectress of laws, as she appears notably in the *Eumenides* (cf. DS s.v. *Minerva* 916). The inscription appears to belong to the third or fourth century.
3 *isto* = *hoc*, cf. on 116.3.
4 *orare iura* (= *orare causas*) I have not found elsewhere; *iura* is evidently chosen because it can serve as the object of *dicentes* also. The lawyers both plead cases and issue judgments, the latter presumably when acting as *assessores* to magistrates.

146

AE 1931, 78 = *IIt* 4.1 (ed. 2, 1952) 213 with photo.
Discussion: Mancini, *NS* 1930. 353 with photos; C. F. Giuliani, *Forma Italiae, regio 1 vol. 3, Tibur, pars altera* (1966) p. 27; M. Eisner, *Zur Typologie der Grabbauten im Suburbium Roms* (*Röm. Mitt.* suppl. 26, 1986) 110 and photo taf. 43.4-8; G. Bordenache Battaglia, *Corredi funerari...* (1983), 124 with photos.

From Tibur, where Vesta had a cult (though the beautiful and well-known temple traditionally associated with her is not hers); for other Vestals there see *ILS* 6244-5 = *CIL* 14.3677, 3679. For other members of the Tiburtine family of the Cossinii see Cic. *Pro Balbo* 53, *CIL* 14.3755 (Mancini 363). A doll with Severan hair-style (illustrated by Bordenache Battaglia 132) used to be thought to be a relic of Cossinia's childhood (*captio* of a Vestal took place between the ages of 6 and 10), which would date the inscription about mid third century; but in fact this seems to come from a different burial, and the lettering of the Cossinia inscription suggests a mid first century date. For other long-serving Vestals see Tac. *Ann.* 2.86.1, *CIL* 6.2128 = *ILS* 4944.

147

CLE 1920 = *CIL* 6.2137 = *ILS* 4936

Found by the temple of Vesta in the forum; an inscription on the side dates it to 1 March 286 A.D. For other inscriptions of the same Vestal see *CIL* 6.2136-2140, 32420-1; cf. in particular 32420 *cuius egregiam sanctitatem...numen quoque Vestae probauit* and 2139 *sibi talem antistitem numen Vestae reseruare uoluit*. The seeming verse means 'since we are erecting a statue to you, at this moment it is important that you were so pious'; but it is fairly sure that the dactylic rhythm is accidental, cf. Cic. *Pro Marc.* 30 *nunc certe pertinet esse te talem ut...*

148

CLE 269 = *CIL* 6.31051

A cippus found near the gate of St. Paul in Rome. The supplementation of 1-2 is obviously uncertain, but the inscription seems to suit best a herm of Terminus, though it must be admitted that the first person and the humour would be very appropriate to Priapus.
1 *pede claudus utroque* coincidentally also *Epigr. Bob.* 55.1.
2 *procul hinc* is a common admonition in religious contexts (Appel 83). Cf. Ovid, *Tristia* 3.12.30 *plaustra bubulcus agit, Ex Ponto* 4.7.10.
4 *excutiare rotis* Ovid, *AA* 3.468.

149

CLE 19 = *CIL* 12.103 = *ILS* 3528

From Axima, modern Aîme, in the French Alps. T. Pomponius Victor is also on *ILS* 3823 from Martigny; he must have been procurator both of the Alpes Graiae (Aîme) and Poeninae (Martigny); see Kellner, *ACSD* 7 (1975-6), 386. The Augusti are probably M. Aurelius and Verus.
1 i.e. his statue is half-enveloped by the foliage of an ash-tree; he is sometimes represented between two trees.
2 *alti* because it is in the Alps. For Silvanus as a god of gardens see Roscher, *Siluanus* 851-2.
3 *musicas* i.e. poetical; *TLL* s.v. 1703.13.
4 The form *Alpicus* is found in Nepos, *Hann.* 3.4.
5 i.e. the wild animals living in the grove.
6 The construction of *fungor* with accusative never died out even after the ablative was standardised.
7 *prosperanti sospitas* both belong to religious vocabulary; the latter is particularly archaic, as cult words tend to be.
8 Cf. 136.12. *reducēs* spoils the otherwise pure trimeters, cf. 32.24 and 34. 8-10 constitute a *uotum pro reditu* such as we find to Silvanus on *CIL* 9.2100; for *reducem sistere* cf. Catull. 64.237.
10 For the spelling *mile* see *TLL* s.v. 973.3.

150

CLE 250 = *CIL* 9.3375 = *ILS* 3530
Discussion: Hoogma 164.

From Aufinum, modern Capestrano; an inscription on the side dates it to 156 A.D. This writer scans the ablative singular termination of the first declension short (*mellea* 3, *unda* 5, *causa* 10, *mea* 11, *ara* 15).

1 Cf. *magna dearum* Enn. *Ann.* 445. For Silvanus as herdsman see Roscher, *Siluanus* 845-6, P. Dorcey, *The Cult of Silvanus* (1992), 20; he is sometimes shown holding a shepherd's crook.

2 A grove is appropriate to Silvanus, but the adjective *Idaeum* is not; like many phrases in this poem, it is a floscule taken over without regard to suitability (*Idaeumque nemus* Verg. *Aen.* 3.112, Ovid, *Met.* 7.359). For Silvanus as a god of soldiers (*castrensis*) see Roscher 865, Dorcey 121. The form of the line is that of 'Relativ-Prädikation' which in prayers is often applied to a god's functions or his favourite abodes (Norden 168 sqq.; cf. Apul. *Met.* 6.4 quoted on 164).

3 Verg. *Buc.* 3.25 *tibi fistula cera / iuncta fuit,* Calp. Sic. 2.28 *Siluanus...dociles mihi donat auenas,* 6.10 *docili calamorum... arte.* This is a 'Golden Line'. The meaning of *quod* is opaque.

4 If *iungitur* is right, the neighbouring stream is the Aternus, which joins the Tirinus not far from Capestrano. 4-6 seem to explain that the *fistula* is made from a reed growing by the river-side. *procul* means essentially 'at a distance' (cf. *uicinus*), not necessarily 'far away'.

6 *nitidis a. u.* is a quotation from Ovid, *Met.* 3.407.

7 quotes Verg. *Georg.* 1.20 in its entirety; it resumes the address to Silvanus in 1.

8 Verg. *Georg.* 1.18 *adsis, o Tegeaee, fauens* (i.e. Pan, a god often associated with Silvanus). Cf. also *Aen.* 2.178 *numenque reducant. reportes* is a slightly colloquial equivalent for *referas;* cf. Livy 3.6.6 *tristiorem (nuntium) domum referentes* with a variant *reportantes* and HS 758.

9 *at tibi pro meritis* Ovid, *Am.* 3.6.105 (there a curse); for the end of the line cf. 177.1.

10 That the relative should go into the neuter after antecedents of different gender is regular enough, but *haec* should be *hanc.*

11 The second *que* has no function; cf. on 190.6.

13-14 Since *dicta* cannot be the antecedent of *quae,* the construction

hangs in the air with two objects for *resoluo. dicta resoluo = uota soluo.*
15 *ille ego qui*, the opening of the spurious four lines prefixed to the *Aeneid*, is found in a number of inscriptions (Hoogma 222; add *AE* 1968, 74); cf. also 126.1, 172.3.
16-17 Verg. *Aen.* 9.156-8 *nunc adeo.../...laeti bene gestis corpora rebus / procurate, uiri, et pugnam sperate parari.* Here the application is to an *epulum* to celebrate the dedication. 'Expect the future' is a meaningless phrase; it ought to be *futuro* (cf. Sil. It. 2.594 and similar uses of *despero*) or *in futurum*. Cf. however *CLE* 1991.12 *horum factorum tibi sunt speranda futura. donum dederunt* completes the syntax of the prose preface.

151

CLE 2151 = *CIL* 8.27764 = *Musée Bardo* 521 = A134 Pikhaus
Discussion; Chatelain, *MEFRA* 30 (1910), 81 with photo pl. 1; Pighi, *Epigraphica* 6-7 (1943-4), 40.

Found near Mactaris. 15 sqq. are inset to the right, a paragraphus indicates change of metre at 8 (actually it is misplaced before 9) and 15; there is no indication at 11 (where choriambs continue). 8-10 are choriambic tetrameter catalectic (a metre used by Septimius Serenus fr. 23) if the supplements are right (and that in 10 at least does seem to be); 11-14 are choriambic trimeters catalectic with resolutions and an iambic metron substituted for a choriambic in second place in 13 as in Serenus l.c. 4; 15 sqq. as far as we have them are cretic (for how they ended see on 17). The metres are recherché and the style extremely affected, with striking archaisms. All this is the fashion of Roman poetry from the second century onwards in writers such as Serenus.
1 *omnisata* (not found elsewhere) is no doubt ablative, *omnigena* nominative (*TLL* compares Paulin. Nol. *Ep.* 49.10 *omnigenum seminum*).
2 Cf. Lucr. 6.843 *tellus effeta calore*. Even in the affected style of this poem *tellus cata* is hardly credible; for *sata* (neuter) see *OLD* s.v.
3 *iubant* = *iuuant*; for *uiridare* transitive see *OLD* 2.
4 The rains of spring are the husband of the earth; cf. *Pervig. Ven.* 4, 60-1 *ut pater totum crearet uernis annum nubibus / in sinum maritus imber fluxit almae coniugis* (*uernus* Pithoeus, *ueris* Sanadon) and *TLL* viii.403.20, 404.8.

5 *cette,* the plural of *cedŏ,* is not found elsewhere after Accius; here it = *agite,* cf. e.g. *CIL* 10.878 *cedo cenemus.*
6 His grove echoes with the sound of plashing water; *bouant* (so Enn. *Ann.* 594 because of a false etymology from *bos*) = *boant.* For *frondea tecta* see *TLL* vi.1.1346.8.
7 *lucūs* is lengthened by the beat. Trees grow from the rocks surrounding the spring.
8 Lommatzsch's supplement *[em bidentem* best suits the cult of Silvanus, but makes *difficilem* hard to explain; Chatelain's *iuuencum* would be due to Ovid, *AA* 1.471 *tempore difficiles ueniunt ad aratra iuuenci.*
9 *falcitenens* is unique; cf. *thyrsitenens* etc., *falcifer. pater falcitenens* is *Saturnus pater,* a god with widespread cult in North Africa as the *interpretatio Romana* of a native god. *de uoce* may not have any precise meaning; if it does, it presumably suggests an oracle from Ammon, equated with Saturn. On *CIL* 8.24519 = *ILS* 4427 we find associated *Ioui Hammoni, barbaro Silvano.*
10 Silvanus often is represented with the crown of pine.
11-14 Now Silvanus speaks.
12 *Dryades puellae* 190.4 and other instances *TLL* onom. s.v. *Dryas* 260.53.
17 *rosea* will mean 'flushed from playing the oboe'. If these lines ended not with another cretic but with a clausula ⏑ - x like 8-14, an appropriate supplement would be [*Thalia;* in that case we would have *Apollŏ* in 18.
18 The apex emphasises that *biiuges* is to be scanned as a cretic, not an anapaest. Apollo is to hold back his chariot so that the day is longer for revelry.

152

CLE 1934 = *CIL* 4.7038

Stercorari looks like infinitive of purpose after a verb of motion (KS 1.680, HS 344-5), though only the active *stercorare* is found elsewhere; others take it to be the vocative of *stercorarius.* The message is 'go away from here to the wall to relieve yourself'; cf. 157, 168, and *Priapea* 35.2-4 *si prensus fueris* (so a few mss.; *precisus eris* the main tradition) *bis, irrumabo...ut poenam patiare.* This poem is placed here because, like the following, it relates to the *Priapea.*

153

CLE 193 = *CIL* 6.3708, 5173, 30092 = *ILS* 3585

From a first-century columbarium; Priapus guards a tomb placed in a garden or vineyard, cf. *CIL* 5.3634 *Dis Manib(us) C H C locus adsignatus monumento in quo est aedicla Priapi* and H. Herter, *De Priapo* (1932), 229 = his summary in the *RE* article *Priapos* 1929. Such a setting justifies *uitae locus*, because it is protected by the generative phallos (*RE* s.v. 1728; this passage 1732.9) of Priapus. The metre is iambic trimeter. With *destricto* the phallus is compared to a weapon (often called *telum* etc.); cf. uses of *stringo* in *OLD* s.v. 4.

154**

CLE 861 = *CIL* 5.2803 = *Appendix Tibulliana* (1990) p. 50 ed. H. Traenkle (1990)
Discussion: Dahlmann, *Hermes* 116 (1988), 434

This stone was apparently found at or near Padua (though see Reeve in L. D. Reynolds (ed.), *Texts and Transmission* (1983), 323 n.3), and was reported by many Renaissance sources; Scaliger's statement that it appeared in his Fragmentum Cuiacianum of Tibullus is probably an error (Hiller, *Hermes* 18 (1883), 348), but it made its way into at least one late fourteenth century ms. of Tibullus (Brit. Mus. Burn. 268, in which it follows immediately on the text of Tibullus), no doubt because of the role played by Priapus in Tibullus 1.4. This manuscript, my knowledge of which is due to an unpublished paper by B. L. Ullman in the possession of Francis Newton of Duke University, was used by Achilles Statius in his edition of 1567 (Hiller 345).
1 For *cultor agelli* cf. Ovid, *Fasti* 5.499 and Focas, *Vita Vergili* 6; *uilicus horti* is probably an interpolation from *Priapea* 24.1. For *uilicus aerari* (i.e. the municipal chest of Padua) cf. Mommsen's note, *RE, uilicus* 2141 and *CIL* 5.4503 *uilic. arkar(ii)* or *arkar(ius)*. Cf. Tib. 1.1.19 *uos quoque, felicis quondam, nunc pauperis agri / custodes*.
2 Scaliger took Perspectus to be a name, but no such name exists, though Traenkle defends it by cognates such as Cognitus. If a name is felt necessary it will be prudent to alter to Respectus (Reinesius) or Prospectus (Traenkle) or Perpetuus (Dahlmann); the sources

remark that the stone was badly worn. But *perspectus* (see *OLD* s.v. and Amm. Marc. 29.6.15) can comfortably mean 'tried and trusty'. *templa* (cf. *CIL* 11.6314 = *ILS* 3581, *Priapea* 2.10) means no more than a small shrine, cf. on 24.1.
3 *pro quibus officiis* Ovid, *Am.* 2.8.2, cf. *pro quis...honoribus* in [Verg.] *Priap.* 3.17, *pro quibus* in *Priapea* 27.5. Cf. also Hor. *Odes* 3.29.59 *uotis pacisci ne.*
6 *taceo* is an interpolation from [Verg.] *Priap.* 3.15. Aposiopesis is common in sexual contexts, cf. 94d, 97 and other examples in Traenkle and Dahlmann, e.g. Plaut. *Ps.* 1178; here *pene* or *fascino* is suppressed. *sed* as often means *et quidem* (see my note on Juv. 4.27); <punish him>, and that too with your erection.

*155***

CLE 1504 = *CIL* 14.3565 = *IIt* 4.1 (ed. 2, 1952) 66
Discussion: V. Buchheit, *Studien zum Corpus Priapeorum* (1962), 70

On a phallic herm from Tibur; it is disconcerting that Wissowa suspected it of being a humanistic forgery (*GGA* 161 (1899), 415), a suspicion which can hardly either be confirmed or refuted. The metre is hendecasyllabic, with three Sapphic lines (6, 10, 23) handled exactly as Horace handles this metrical unit in his Sapphic stanzas; 10 in fact incorporates a reminiscence of Horace, as does 43, though the main influence is Catullan. Indeed the Horatian structure of the Sapphic lines seems to run counter to that of the hendecasyllables, which all appear to begin - ⏑, since *saluĕ* 38 (for which I can find no parallel; perhaps it is due to the false analogy of *auĕ*) validates the same scansion at the beginning of six lines, *ergo* 38 and *ultro* 40 no doubt have -*ŏ*, and *neruus* 51 may be intended to scan *neruu'* (see Metre I h). The importance of this for the composer is shown by his use of *haud* 8, where *nec* would be natural.

All other literary post-Catullan hendecasyllables except those of Catullus' imitator Maecenas begin with a spondee (an iambus in 143.7 above, which also is exceptional in inscriptions), but this may not be such a big problem as it seems, since the consistency with which the trochee appears here must indicate an artificial basis in some metrical theory. Mancini (in *IIt*) thinks that this was intended to be read in the order 13-32, 1-12. I doubt if the order was very important to the composer.

For the mention of the *genius* of Priapus in the prose prefix cf. Petron. 21.7; there are dedications to the *genius numinis* of springs in *CIL* 6.151, 8.5884. For *genii* of divinities see Wissowa 180; *RE*, *genius* 1164.46.

For the *a cura amicorum* see *RE* iv.1773 and Boulvert 182 (who misses this man); this official was perhaps a member of the bureau which supervised right of access to the emperor (*officium admissionis*). It is perhaps because of his function that he refers to Priapus as *amice* 33, 47. A *Iulius Aug. lib.* must have been emancipated under one of the first three Caesars (for to think of Julius Philippus, emperor 244-9, would be a very long shot), so this inscription belongs to the first century. The absence of a praenomen is surprising, and the epithet *inuictus* is never elsewhere applied to Priapus, though the combination in which it occurs is applied to Hercules (*CIL* 6.328 = *ILS* 3434 *Herculi uictori pollenti potenti inuicto*). These facts, together with *saluĕ*, may count in favour of Wissowa's suspicions.

For *somno monitus* instead of *somnio* cf. *CIL* 3.1032 (= *ILS* 3019), 8044.

1 For *pater rerum* see on 34; *sancte pater salue* Prop. 4.9.71 (see on 7 above).

2 *da mihi* comes straight to the point; cf. Appel 133.

9 For the rare elision of *quae* see on Tullius Laurea in *FLP* 183.

10 Hor. *Odes* 1.4.16 *iam te premet nox fabulaeque manes.*

11 From Catullus 3.12, but because a subject *fata* has been introduced *negant* now means 'forbid' (*OLD* 5b), not 'deny'.

13 Catull. 42.1-2 *adeste, hendecasyllabi, quot estis / omnes undique, quotquot estis omnes.*

14-15 i.e. Dryads and Naiads. The match with 14 involves *colitīs* in 15.

19 Cf. *Priapea* 25.5, 43.2.

20-1 Cf. *Priapea* 40.3, 50.7 and Herter (on 153) 271.

24 Scan *silŭas*, cf. 49.

25 *incruenta* is contrasted with *cruentos* 23. One may wonder if it should be *incruenta[s*; usual Latin idiom would be *incruentis*, but cf. Val. Max. 6.9.14, Sen. *Phoen.* 89-90 and occasional accusatives after *licet* in comparable cases (at Hor. *Serm.* 1.4.39, Ovid, *Met.* 11.219 mss. vary between dat. and accus.). Otherwise it is predicative, 'dark silent places which remain free of bloodshed'.

26-30 See Herter 215. This function of Priapus is probably due to the frequent placement of his image by wells and springs and to assimilation to Pan. For the postponement of *et* in anaphora (*ille* 24 - *ille...et* 26) see *TLL* v.2.897.66.

34 sqq. For this cosmic interpretation of Priapus see Herter 236 = 1929-30; he obviously is easily associated with Pan, but an explicit identification is found elsewhere only at Cornutus, *Theologiae Graecae Compendium* 27, and the cosmological interpretation of Pan (based on the equation Πάν = πᾶν) also dates from the Neronian Cornutus (*RE* suppl. viii.1005). The sexual vigour of Priapus implies generative power; in Orphic Hymn 6.9 he is equated with Protogonos. The word *physis* is not found elsewhere in Latin except in a special mineralogical sense in Pliny *NH*. For the *siue* - formula in prayers, intended to ensure that one hits on the relevant appellation of the god, see Appel 76, Norden 144-7. 37 sqq. seem to adapt (some even speak of parody) traditional topics relating to Venus; cf. *Pervig. Ven.* 65 *perque caelum perque terras perque pontum subditum,* Ovid, *Fasti* 4.93 *iuraque dat caelo, terrae, natalibus undis,* Lucr. 1.2-20. 39-41 continue the association with eulogies of the power of Venus, though Priapus in his own right is a helper in love (Herter 222 = 1928). A point is often made that the might of love is such that it even compels Jupiter to abandon heaven to pursue his amours on earth; but Hor. *Odes* 1.3.40 *Iouem ponere fulmina,* which the writer has in mind, is not in a context like this.
42-6 The positive and negative (*te sine*) sides of a relationship with a deity form part of a traditional formula of invocation; see in connection with Venus Catull. 61.61-75, Lucr. 1.4 and 22. Priapus is often regarded as son of Venus and Bacchus and portrayed drinking; for his ties with Venus, Cupid and Bacchus see Herter 310 = 1938 and 304. He is not elsewhere linked with the Graces; the writer has in mind Hor. *Odes* 4.7.5 *Gratia cum nymphis geminisque sororibus.* See also Verg. *Aen.* 1.734 *laetitiae Bacchus dator. nec* 45 = 'not even'.
48-51 See Herter l.c. on 37 sqq. This is adapted from Catullus 2.13 *quod zonam soluit diu ligatam,* adopting the scansion *solŭas* and taking advantage of the Catullan fondness for diminutives (cf. *bello* 16, *blandula* 17). In Catullus the archetype read *negatam* with a variant *ligatam,* the latter of which is quoted by Priscian.

potens in 51 is intended to make us look back and see an implication not apparent at the time in *potens* 47.

156

Fragmenta Poetarum Latinorum, ed. W. Morel p. 40

The cult of Feronia was associated with freedmen (see *Kl. Pauly* s.v. *Feronia,* Latte 190, Evans 158); here we have a ritual process of emancipation (Fabre 60 sqq. with further references), clearly of the character of a *rite de passage* (cf. 66). Latte seeks a parallel in a law of Cos, but the purport of the mutilated inscription in the restoration of M. Segre, *Iscrizioni di Cos* (1993), ED 144 (with further bibliography; see also p. 291) is entirely different. It is equally futile for Bücheler, *Rh. Mus.* 41 (1886), 2 to adduce a Lacedaemonian inscription (*IG* 5.1155, Prott - Ziehen, *Leges Graecorum Sacrae* 2 p. 161 no. 55) which has never been firmly interpreted. The construction here is paratactic; 'let them sit here' = 'if they sit here'.

157

CLE 333 = *CIL* 4.813

This is written beside a picture of huge serpents, which as often designate the *genius loci*. The reason for the prohibition is that loiterers are liable to urinate; 168b.3 ends *discede cacator,* cf. Persius 1.112-4 (ending *discedo*)

'hic' inquis 'ueto quisquam faxit oletum.'
pinge duos anguis: 'pueri, sacer est locus, extra
meiite.' discedo.

The best illustration is *CIL* 6.29848b (from the baths of Titus) *duodecim deos et Deanam et Iouem O. M. habeat iratos quisquis hic mixerit aut cacarit* with a picture of two snakes; cf. also *CIL* 4.3832 *cacator cave malu(m)* with two snakes. There are often similar prohibitions by gravestones, cf. 168a; see *RAC, Genitalien* 21.

otjosis is so scanned.

158

CLE 879 = *CIL* 14.3535 = *IIt* 4.1 (ed. 2, 1952) 35 with photo
Discussion: H. Meyer, *Antinoos* (1991), 164, 210

From Tibur (where of course Hadrian had his villa, cf. 38), and no doubt from the base of a statue representing Hadrian's deified favourite Antinous with the attributes of the Celtic god Belenus, particularly worshipped in Gaul (Lejeune, *Études Celtiques* 12 (1968-71), 49 and 89) and Noricum, above all at Aquileia; the dedicator must have come from this area. Belenus (see *TLL* s.v.), whose name survives in a suburb of Aquileia called Beligna and a nearby locality named Bellune, closely resembled Apollo, to whom Antinous was assimilated. See Jan de Vries, *Keltische Religion* (1961), 31, Wissowa 297, A. Calderini, *Aquileia Romana* (1930), 93, C. B. Pascal, *Cults of Cisalpine Gaul* (CL 75, 1964), 123, Maraspin, *ACSD* 1 (1967-8), 147.

Cf. Ovid, Met. 9.718 *par aetas, par forma fuit*.

159

CLE 547 = *CIL* 6.32458 = *ILS* 4414 = *IG* 14.1366 = *IGUR* 3.1150 (with photo p. 8) = *GVI* 2012 = L. Vidman, *Sylloge Inscriptionum Religionis Isiacae* (1969), 433 = M. Malaise, *Inventaire préliminaire des documents Égyptiens découverts en Italie* (EPRO 21, 1971), pp. 131-2 no. 66.

On a marble sarcophagus universally taken to be from Rome, now in Florence. *Pastophori* were a low grade of priests, seldom women (H. B. Schönborn, *Die Pastophoren im Kult der ägyptischen Götter* (1976), 14). The representation of Alexandria on this stone might have been taken into account in the discussion of the nature of a παστός; it shows her carrying a little shrine of an Egyptian deity, and thus confirms the view of J. G. Griffiths on Apul. *Met.* 11.17, p. 279.15, that the παστός is such a little shrine (Schönborn 6 is indecisive). Alexandria seems to hold an independent priesthood of Bacchus (Latte 356); neither the Greek nor the Latin epigram suggests an identification with Osiris or Serapis. For another priestess of Isis cf. 190.

Since the stone was first reported (even then the last line of the Greek was missing) it has been damaged, and the end of the third line of the Greek is no longer present.

1 *dei* has to be scanned as a monosyllable or a pyrrhic.

2 *-quae* = *-que*.

3 For *cui* as an iamb see my commentary on Albinus, *FLP* 425 (add *CLE* 600.2, 1988.38); here perhaps the following mute and liquid have something to do with it. The supplementation of 3-4 remains uncertain. Since Alexandria was aged forty, one might think on the lines of *[nond]um i. / [lapsus* (scanning *nondu(m)*); then 3-4 will

indicate that her premature death was due to the ill-will of the Fates, since, though middle-aged, she still had her youthful bloom.
4 *Diti* = *ad Ditem;* this is inelegant in this context because of *inuida*. The Fates put their 'mark' on her.

160

CLE 850 = *CIL* 13.7661 = *ILS* 4569 = *IG* 14.2562
Discussion: Mertens, *Trierer Zeitschrift* 48 (1985), 19, with photo on 21

Found at Pommern on the Moselle near Coblenz on a column-capital, each side of which contains one Greek and below it one Latin verse. Mars (see *RE* s.v. 1949, Drexel, *Berichte der röm.-germ. Komission* 14 (1922), 25) Lenus was a local god of Trier; for the temple at Pommern see H. Heinen, *Trier und das Treverland in röm. Zeit* (1985), 185, H. Cüppers, *Die Römer in Rheinland-Pfalz* (1990), 526. We could assess this inscription better if we knew the profession of Tychicus.
1 *durum sufferre laborem* ends the line thrice in Lucretius.
2 *uagando* = *uagans*, cf. HS 379-80, KS 1.752. For *dum* with a causal implication cf. 113.2.

161

CLE 277 = *RIB* 103 with drawing = *ILS* 5435
Photo: J. Wacher, *Towns of Roman Britain* (1974), fig. 55 pp. 296-7

This comes from Corinium (Cirencester) in Gloucestershire; the prose is written on the face, the first line of verse on the back, the second on the left side. Britain was divided into four provinces (cf. 33.15) by Diocletian, though A. R. Birley, *The Fasti of Roman Britain* (1981), 178-80 casts doubt (not particularly well grounded) on this dating. For Britannia Prima as symbolically represented in the illustrations to the Notitia Dignitatum see P. Salway, *The Oxford Illustrated History of Roman Britain* (1993), 321.

This was part of a 'Jupiter-column'; many such columns are found in Celtic districts of the empire, and the datable ones belong

c. 150-250 A.D. See *RE* suppl. iv.689, vii.220, de Vries (on 153) 31, A. Ross, *Pagan Celtic Britain* (1967), 196, A. B. Cook, *Zeus* (1925), 2.1.57, G. Bauchhenss - P. Noelke, *Die Iupitersäulen* (1981), 505-6, Will in *Hommages L. Lerat* (1984), 2.873, *ANRW* ii.18.1.130. Miranda Green, *The Gods of the Celts* (1986), 61 (there is a photo of the second line of verse on p.64) quotes Val. Fl. 6.89-91 *Coralli...quis signa rotae...truncaeque, Iouis simulacra, columnae.* Jupiter here is the *interpretatio Romana* of the Celtic Taranis. On the question whether a Bacchic column-capital also from Cirencester came from a Jupiter-column see Phillips, *Journal of the British Archaeological Association* 129 (1976), 40-1. It may be that this inscription records the restoration under Julian the apostate of a pagan monument overthrown by Christians.

For *religione* scanned ⏑ ⏑ - ⏑ Wright compares Paulin. Pell. *Euch.* (see on 52) 462 *religiosa* = ⏑ ⏑ - ⏑; cf. also *oriundi* as a bacchiac Lucr. 2.991, *dominia* apparently as a tribrach Lucil 438 Marx. *signŭm et* is so scanned (Metre I c); the diphthong of *prouinciae* is treated as -ĕ.

162

CLE 253 = *CIL* 8.9018 = *ILS* 4428

From Auzia in Mauretania, dated to 246 A.D. In an age of syncretism many gods can be represented as embracing the attributes of the whole pantheon, and therefore take the title of Pantheos or Panthea (Wissowa 91-2, Latte 334, *RE, Pantheios* 743); consistently with this, the statue of Juno here is *biformis*, cf. *RE* l.c. 745.

1 Jupiter is horned because he is identified with Hammon. The nominative *Panthea* is taken up by *hanc* 5, so there is an anacoluthon as in 114.1-3.

4-5 There is an allusion to the phrase *latus tegere* (Hor. *Serm.* 2.5.18 etc.), to walk on the left (see Eutrop. 7.13.4, schol. Juv. 3.131) of another as a mark of respect. Presumably Jupiter is on Juno's left hand, i.e. on her right from the viewpoint of the spectator. *tegīt* is lengthened at the caesura.

3 It is odd that *his etiam terris* is contrasted with Mauretania, where Auzia is situated.

4 *utrumque* = *utriusque* = *Iouis et Ditis*. Perhaps *propter* rather than *inter* would make the expression easier.

5-8 He adorns the shrine with *puluinaria* (*puluinaribus altis* Ovid, *Met.* 14.827) and a *solium*, and also renovates the statues.
7 He has gone or is going through the *militiae equestres* as *praefectus alae, tribunus legionis, praefectus cohortis*; for *a militiis* see *TLL* viii.963.51, A. von Domaszewski, *Rangordnung des röm. Heeres* (ed. 2, 1967), 131, Mommsen 3.543. It is probably more exact to say that the metre is suspended for the official term (cf. p. 23) than that *ă* was intended. For the spelling *suplice* see *CIL* 8 index 314b; *supplice uoto* Pers. 2.35. Fentress, *Latom.* 37 (1978), 511 thinks that the dedicator is the Primianus of *CIL* 8.9045 = *ILS* 2766.

163

CLE 254 = *CIL* 8.4635, 16810 = *ILA* 1.1185 = A157 Pikhaus

This is from Naraggara in Numidia, modern Sidi Youssef. The goddess Tanit was widely worshipped in north Africa under the name of Dea Caelestis. She naturally has atmospheric functions; in Tertull. *Apol.* 23 she is *pluuiarum pollicitatrix*, Firm. Mat. *De Errore* 4 says *Assyrii et pars Afrorum aerem ducatum habere elementorum uolunt...hunc eundem nomine Iunonis uel Veneris virginis...consecrarunt* (Venus is a frequent identification of Virgo Caelestis), and Mart. Cap. 1.67 describes her as *fulmen dextra, laeua sonorum bombis terrentibus tympanum sustinens, sub quibus plurimum sudans ima subiecta roscidis uidebatur inundare fluoribus.* This however is not prominent in cult, and the writer here has drawn on literary and philosophical sources to elaborate it. The Stoics derived an etymology of Ἥρα from ἀήρ (with precedent in pre-Socratic philosophers; see Pease on Cic. *De Nat. Deor.* 2.66), and in poetry, notably in the *Aeneid*, Juno is often portrayed as sending clouds and storm (cf. 2-4). Here she also, by her physical interposition, separates the gods from the mortal terrestrial sphere (5-6): she props up the aether, the sphere of the stars, above her (7-9); she invisibly supports human respiration (10-12); she separates earth from heaven, while allowing passage to rain and the rays of the sun (13-15); while remaining constant in her essence, she embraces mutually opposing functions (15-16). Latte 347 considers identification of Caelestis and Tanit (or Astarte) with Juno purely literary; one would have liked him to comment on this poem and Firm. Mat. l.c. Brouquier - Reddé 263 presents an argument on the other side.

There are false quantities *intonăs* 4, *claudăs* 15; see Metre I j (ii).
1 This refers to Saturn yielding power to Jupiter.
2 *Aen.* 8.354 *(Iuppiter) nimbosque cieret.*
5 i.e. *admouissent*; assimilation (cf. *CIL* 8.2216 *amministrare*) is usually avoided in this word because of potential ambiguity with *amouere.*
8 *Aen.* 1.9 *regina deum.*
9 For *fulcires sidera* cf. [Ovid], *Her.* 9.18.
10 *Aen.* 1.440 *neque cernitur ulli.*
11 Pliny, *Ep.* 6.16.13 *meatus animae*, Lucan 4.327 *aeris alternos angustat pulmo meatus.*
16 *uirtus*, like ἀρετή, has a considerable range of meaning in the theological discussions of late antiquity; with this cf. Symmachus, *Rel.* 7.3 *caelestes uirtutes* = heavenly powers. See Nock 35.
17 *Aen.* 8.301 *salue, uera Iouis proles*, 12.830 *Saturnique altera proles*, *Georg.* 2.173 *salue...Saturnia tellus*, Mart. Cap. 2.192.33 *salue, uera deum facies.*

164

CLE 24 = *CIL* 7.759 = *RIB* 1791 (with drawing)
Drawing: *Arch. Aeliana* ser. 3, 17 (1920), 37
Discussion: Birley, *ANRW* ii.18.1.78; Mundle, *Historia* 10 (1961), 229; Stephens, *Arch. Aeliana* ser. 4, 12 (1984), 149.

This is from Carvoran fort in Hadrian's Wall. The dedicator, who held the rank of tribunus legionis but was acting praefectus cohortis, pretty certainly came from Africa, where the name Donatus and its derivatives were particularly common (another Caecilius Donatianus *CIL* 8.12161), since Donatus represents a native African name Muthun (sometimes latinized to Muttinus etc.) 'Given' (e.g. by Baal). The troops commanded by him, however, were probably the Syrian cohort of Hamii who were in the garrison here in the second century and made a dedication to Dea Syria (*RIB* 1792).

This is one of the most striking documents of syncretism. It starts off with the zodiacal sign Virgo, preceded in the Zodiac by Libra and followed by Leo. Virgo is represented as holding Spica in her hand, and is identified with Astraea or Dike, whence *iusti inuentrix* and (transferred to Dea Syria) *lance...pensitans* 5 (where *lance* alludes to Libra). Next comes Dea Syria, i.e. Atargatis, who has astral connections (M. Hörig, *Dea Syria* (1979), 117). She is linked with Rhea - Cybele, the *mater deorum*, by her mural crown (Lucian, *De Dea Syria* 15, 32, Hörig 173, *Lex. Icon.* iii.1.356 [= iii.2.264] nos. 8-10, 21, 28, on the last of which the goddess is surrounded by the Zodiac), which accounts for *urbium conditrix*, and by the association of both with lions (Hörig 108, 237; see also id., *ANRW* ii.17.3.154 n.23 for the identification with Rhea). The identification of Virgo with Atargatis is made by [Eratosth.] *Catast.* 9 (p. 84 Robert). Virgo is also easily identified with Ceres because of the Spica which she holds (Hygin. *Poet. Astr.* 2.25.2, Avien. *Arat.* 284); Ceres too is *legifera* (see my note on Calvus fr. 6 *FLP*), which fits 2, but Donatianus is probably mainly influenced by the popularity of this goddess in Africa as the *interpretatio Romana* of a local goddess (Wissowa 303). Finally the African Dea or Virgo Caelestis (alluded to with *caelesti* 1) is brought in; she, like Atargatis, wears a mural crown, is identified with Cybele (Halsberghe, *ANRW* ii.17.4.2207; Le Glay, *Les Syncrétismes dans les Religions de l' Antiquité*, ed. F. Dunand- P. Lévêque (EPRO 46, 1975), 139), and is depicted as riding on a lion; cf. Apul. *Met.* 6.4 *siue celsae Carthaginis, quae te uirginem uectura leonis caelo commeantem percolit, beatas sedes frequentas*. Compare the coins of the Severi connected with the grant of the *ius Italicum* to Carthage (Mattingly - Sydenham, *Roman Imperial Coinage* 4.1 pl. 7.9, 10.7; *Lex. Icon.* v.1.137-8) with the Galatian coins noted by *Lex. Icon.* iii.1.356 = iii.2.264 nos. 8-9. In such representations she literally *imminet leoni*. Gundel in *Mél. Cumont* (1936), 243 from an astrological ms. quotes *Virginis, cuius figura est mulier equitans in leone*. On an inscription from Apulum we have *deae Suriae magnae Caelesti* (*AE* 1965, 30; Bercin and Popa, *Latomus* 23 (1964), 473).

The upshot is that Donatianus recognizes the goddess worshipped by his troops (6) and adopts her cult himself (7), marrying it with his African worship of Caelestis. On a dating to the second half of the second century, the emperor of 10 may be Commodus or one of his successors up to 196, after which Donatianus would have written *principum*. Birley also asserts that Hamii were replaced at Carvoran by Dalmatians under Severus; his evidence for this is *RIB* 1795, which however is undated. Dalmatians are put at Carvoran by the *Not. Dign., Occ.* 40.43.

1 *imminet* is scanned as *iminet*, cf. 28.4 and Metre I k.

2 *urbium* is a dissyllable; cf. Metre I d.

3 Donatianus is indifferent to the Bentley - Luchs Law (Metre II B e). It is an easy deduction from the ancient system of civic religion that religion is a consequence of urbanisation; see Cic. *De Inv.* 1.2-3.

7 There is hiatus at the caesura (cf. 63.10, 124.8), here before a pause; see Metre II B c.
9 For *Donatjanus* see Metre I d.
10 For *in* = 'in the guise of' cf. E. Löfstedt, *Late Latin* (1959), 34; *TLL* s.v. 789.52.

165

CLE 987 = *CIL* 6.19747 = *ILS* 8522

The deceased was a *uerna* of Livilla (as she may conveniently be called), the wife of Tiberius' son Drusus; she was put to death in 31 A.D. It is not clear whether witchcraft is being blamed for a natural death or for a sinister disappearance. In Petron. 63 a story recounts the abstraction of a young boy's body by witches and the substitution of a straw effigy.
2 *esse* is placed ἀπὸ κοινοῦ.
3 *saga manus* may mean either 'a witch's hand' or 'a coven of witches'.
4 For the conjugation of *nocit* cf. *CIL* 1.1598, 10.4052 *nocias* and Sommer 509.
6 *ni* = *ne*; see on 19.4. For *fixsus* cf. 194.8, *CLE* 454.10, 1305.8; like a dagger in the heart.

II K: EPITAPHS

This section does not include the famous epitaph of Allia Potestas solely because there already exists a full commentary on it by Horsfall, *ZPE* 61 (1985), 251.

166

CLE 240 = *CIL* 10.3147 = *ILS* 8268

This was found at Baiae.

2 This refers to manumission by *uindicta* and by will; the former involves the rite of turning the slaves around, cf. Quintil. *Decl.* 342.6 *ut circumuerteres mancipium,* Pers. 5.75-9 *quibus una Quiritem / uertigo facit.../ uerterit hunc dominus, momento turbinis exit / Marcus Dama,* Epictet. 2.1.26, Appian, *BC* 4.17.135, Isid. 9.4.48, Sen. *Ep.* 8.7. This (cf. 156) is an obvious *rite de passage;* see S. Tondi, *Aspetti simbolici...della manumissio uindicta* (1967), 158. Dessau compares *CIL* 6.18104 *libertis libertabusque quos manumisi et quos manumisero.*

3 *TLL* x.2.215.5 is probably right in understanding *sepulcrum pateat ad postrema,* comparing Dictys 1.1 *Atreus...postrema sua ordinans.* This line paraphrases the *libertis libertabusque posterisque eorum* common on tombs. For *is* = *iis* cf. 119.7.

167

CLE 983 = *CIL* 5.3635 (cf. p. 1075)

From Verona; nothing can be made of a few preceding letters used as abbreviations. This seems to be an advertisement. The proprietor of this large grave plot is willing to allow an outsider to 'buy into' it, but only on condition that the latter does so in perpetuity (i.e. for his *posteri,* often mentioned in epitaphs in this context, as well as himself). The vendor warns the purchaser that he must secure a written contract; otherwise he may subsequently be unable to claim his rights. This paraphrase is based on my placing of a full stop after 2; if this is omitted, as by Bücheler, I cannot construe the datives in 3. The supplements in 2 and 4 are obviously uncertain in detail, but cannot be far wrong; *[meu]m* in 4 would alter the sense only slightly.

1 *hei* is no doubt an error for *heia; quisque* = *quisquis*, cf. on 93b.1. The punctuation given above seems preferable to Bücheler's; the sense will be 'Friend, since you are destined to die, receive your burial-plot by buying in'.
3 'I, the vendor (*danti*), must first give you a written document, so that you may be assured of your rights'. *cerea prata* is a high-flown periphrasis for 'wax tablets'; cf. Titin. 160 *arare campum cereum*, Auson. *In Notarium* (cf. on 131) 13 *aequor cereum*. The verb *desulcare* is elsewhere found only in Avien(i)us, but the underlying metaphor is quite commonly applied to writing (cf. *exarare*).
4 *tetulisse* in imperial times is found elsewhere only in verses produced by the *Historia Augusta*, a verse by the father of Symmachus (see *FLP* 453), *CLE* 1044A.6 and (in the form *tetoli*) 1079.2.

168a

CLE 838 = *CIL* 6.2357 = *ILS* 8204

168b

CIL 4.8899

(a) is preceded by a prose inscription. *set*, which spoils the metre, has been erroneously introduced in this reproduction of a stock formula. For the sentiment of 1 cf. 152, 157, of 2 cf. *AE* 1984, 142 *si tu bibis, et mihi da*; the dead experience hunger and thirst like the living (cf. 179.9 and Galletier 36, Cumont, *LP* 29).

(b) is not a tomb inscription but a graffito on an *insula*; it is therefore meant humorously. Because of the contradiction between the injunction in 2 and the prohibition in 3, we should probably assume that we have two separate epigrams. The first adapts the formula of (a) (note *gratus* in (a), *gratior* in (b)) in order to produce the 'contrary to expectation' joke (appreciated by Lebek, *ZPE* 22 (1976), 287) of the second line, in which the writer has been forced into the scansion *hūĭc*, parallelled only in the scenic poets (in *CLE* 1308.3 *quisque huic* is wrongly reproduced from an original with *quisquis*, or else *h* acts as a consonant, cf. Metre I e). For unaspirated forms of *hic* see Fele 1.436a; for *ni* = *ne* cf. on 19.4.

The second epigram also adapts a formula, for which see on

157. The point is a pun on the name of the hypothetical deceased (for the name Urtica see *CIL* 5.3637; it is also known as a female name); as the *cacator* squats, he is in danger of being stung by an *urtica*, a nettle. Cf. generally Petron. 71.8 *ne in monumentum meum populus cacatum currat*. The discussion by Koenen, *ZPE* 31 (1978), 85 seems off the point to me.

169

CLE 244 = *CIL* 6.18131 = *ILS* 8155a

This is a sentiment derived from an alleged epigram on the tomb of Sardanapallus, translated by Cicero, *Tusc.* 5.101 (*IGM* 232, *Suppl. Hell.* 335, with parodies in 338 and 355). It is often found on walls and tombs (*CLE* 187, 2207 etc.); likewise *IGRR* 4.923 (from Cibyra) ἃ ἔφαγον ἔχω, ἃ κατέλιπον ἀπώλεσα. It debases the sentiment of 172.10. See further Nock 885-6, Lier (1904), 59, Lattimore 261, *RE*, *Sardanapal* 2441 sqq. With *quŏd* (cf. *quīd* 89.4) this is a septenarius.

170a**

CLE 1499 = *CIL* 6.15258 = *ILS* 8157

170b

CLE 1923 = *CIL* 3.12274c

A similar sentiment is found in *AP* 10.112 (anon.)

οἶνος καὶ τὰ λοετρὰ καὶ ἡ περὶ Κύπριν ἐρωή
ὀξυτέρην πέμπει τὴν ὁδὸν εἰς Ἀίδην.

Though the classical Greeks were not insensible to the amenities of the baths, their prominent place here suggests rather the Roman world; cf. on an inscription from Aezani (P. Le Bas - W. H. Waddington, *Voyage archéologique* (1847-77) 277) λοῦσαι, πίε, φάγε, βείνησον, and also *GVI* 1146 = *IGUR* 1329.7-8. The view of these three pleasures taken in 164b stresses exclusively their debilitating effect (cf. Plut. *De San. Tuenda* 12.128c, *Quomodo Adulator* 28.69b, Livy 23.18.12; Ilberg, *Neue Jahrb.* 19 (1907), 396 n.8 collects passages from Celsus).

The deceased in (a) must have been a freedman of Claudius or Nero; the freedmen of the latter always have Ti., not Nero, as praenomen (*PIR* ed. 2, 3 p. 36, Ruggiero, *libertus* 911a). The form is that of *versus serpentini* or *echoici*, in which the end of the pentameter repeats the beginning of the hexameter. Such verses are occasionally used by Ovid (see e.e. McKeown on *Am.* 1.9.1) and Martial for particular effects, and were later written by Pentadius; a whole series of such is found in *AL* 38-80. (b) is inscribed on a spoon found at Gallipoli; the Greek refers to the story of accidental self-castration at a sacrifice recounted by Mart. 3.24.

171

CLE 1318 = *CIL* 14.914

Found at Ostia. Primus (for the name see on 21) was no doubt a well-to-do freedman, buried by fellow freedmen, but of another patron. For the system of punctuation applied in this inscription see Wingo 159.

2 *Lucrinis* sc. *ostreis;* so Mart. 6.11.5, 12.48.4. Cf. also Mart. 12.17.5 *ebria...fit...saepe Falerno.*

3 For the spelling *balnia,* not reliably attested elsewhere, cf. *mieis* 13.1, *iamus* 78.3.

5 The phoenix is an obvious symbol of rebirth (Bösing, *MH* 25 (1968), 169; R. van den Broek, *Myth of the Phoenix* (EPRO 24, 1972), pl. xiv); in that role it appears on coins of Antoninus Pius commemorating his dead wife (Mattingly - Sydenham, *Roman Imperial Coinage* 3.274). For the spelling, which suggests a date not much before the third century, see on 51. The altar is primarily that on which the phoenix immolates itself, but a phoenix was probably also portrayed on the man's grave-altar (see on 112.1).

6 Cf. 184.12 *reparatus item uiuis in Elysiis; reparare* of the phoenix again Ovid, *Met.* 15.392, Lactant. *De Aue Phoenice* 61 *ut reparet lapsum...aeuum.* For *sibi* see on 29.5.

*172***

CLE 409 = *CIL* 9.4756 = 11.4188

This apparently was found near Interamna in Umbria.
1 'On the side of my father (mother)'; cf. Apul. *De Platone* 1.1 *de utroque* [sc. *parente*] *nobilitas satis clara,* Auson. *Praef.* 1.5-6 (p. 3 Green) *gens Aedua matri / de patre.*
2 Verg. *Aen.* 7.517 *sulpurea Nar albus aqua.*
3 For *ille ego qui* cf. on 150.15. The word *circen* (another source reports *circile*) is not found elsewhere, but seems to be postulated by Italian cercine, Spanish cercen; Burman IV 274 proposed *circite,* for which *TLL* compares Cyprian Gall., *Exod.* 972 *circite perpetua uolucris...uoluitur annus.* For the singular *bis deno* see Housman 954 = *CQ* 12 (1918), 32-3, B. Löfstedt, *Eranos* 56 (1958), 196, NW 2.335.
4 Mart. 2.61.1 *cum tibi uernarent dubia lanugine malae.*
6-7 Cf. 180. 9-10 and Cugusi, *Epigraphica* 53 (1991), 103.
6 For *quia...quod* cf. e.g. Cic. *Ad. Fam.* 6.22.1 *ea res...quod tu ad me nullas (litteras) miseras, sed quia nec...nec...nec...reperiebam;* Cato, *Orat.* fr. 167 Malcovati *Rhodiensibus oberit quod non male fecerunt sed quia voluisse dicuntur facere?*
8 For this formula see on 70.13, for *excessi* see *TLL* s.v. 1207.9. The sources for this inscription report *actum est* or *hac lucst* (Bücheler p. 855); *actumst,* as in Bücheler's text, is most unlikely to be right, since in inscriptions this aphaeresis is almost invariably written as in my text (cf. 19.2, 188.16, Leumann 123, SP 215, E. Diehl, *De M finali epigraphica* (*Neue Jahrb.* suppl. 25, 1899), 117). Indeed Diehl could find not one single valid example of *-mst,* though now we must note *quisquanst* 15.1.
10 Cf. *CLE* 366.2 *si quid mortui habent, hoc meum erit, cetera liq(ui).* This adapts a philosophical topic exalting self-sufficiency; see Sen. *Ep.* 9.18, *Const. Sap.* 5.6 (Stilbon), and also Phaedr. 4.23.
meŭm hic is so scanned, cf. Metre I c.

*173***

CLE 423 = *CIL* 10.5920 = *ILS* 6261

From Anagnia. The institution of the *alimenta* by Trajan provides a terminus post quem. If Oppia was the wife of Firmus, as 4

suggests, their marriage violated the Augustan marriage laws which prohibited men of senatorial rank from marrying freedwomen (this was pointed out to me by Prof. S. Treggiari).
1 Cf. *exemplum coniugis bonae,* which Ovid has in various combinations at *Tr.* 1.6.24, 4.3.72, *Ex Ponto* 3.1.44. See also 128.15 above and *GVI* 404.2 καλῶν ὑποδεῖγμα φιλάνδρων.
3-4 'honour it (Oppia's soul), you, Arria, with the Roman group, and you, Laodamia, with the Greek'; i.e. Oppia is to be met by a Roman and a Greek group, each headed by a woman famed for devotion to her husband. For such a welcoming group in the underworld cf. *Culex* 261 sqq., Prop. 1.19.13, Stat. *Silv.* 5.1.254, *CLE* 1165.1-4, Hyperides, *Epitaph.* 35 etc.; see Holland, *ARW* 23 (1926), 209, Cumont *LP* 395. There are sarcastic variations on the theme at Aesch. *Ag.* 1555, Sen. *Apoc.* 13.
5 Ovid, *Met.* 13.371 *hunc titulum meritis pensandum reddite nostris* and cf. 177.7; *fama superstes* is found *CLE* 618.2 etc.

174**

CLE 436 = *CIL* 6.20674
Discussion: Wrede 227 no. 93; Kleiner 253 no. 113

This was on a huge double marble urn, with prose inscriptions to the mother Cornelia Tyche and the daughter Iulia Secunda; the husband of one and father of the other, Iulius Secundus, has put his name in the acrostich (cf. *Philol.* 134 (1990), 6). The inscription is now missing, but a drawing of the monument in its original form is published by C. C. Vermeule, *The Dal Pozzo-Albani Drawings* (Trans. Am. Philos. Soc. 50.5, 1960), 70 fig. 80. The attributes of Fortuna (e.g. a wheel and a rudder on a globe) appear on the sculpture, which constitutes a pun on the mother's name Tyche; see Ritti (on 176) 283 and tav. v fig. 1. For the layout of this inscription see Wingo 140.
1 *paussa* is on the analogy of *caussa* (Leumann 181, SP 159); it is the first instance of an archaising veneer in this poem. Cf. *CLE* 225.2 *pausum laboris hic est,* Fronto p. 236. 16 *mors...pausam laborum adfert.* Eventually the verb *pausare* is created.
3-6 This is geographically vague, and simply locates the shipwreck somewhere on the coast between Marseilles and the mouth of the Ebro; the Tagus is only there for learned ornament. Marseilles was

a colony of the Ionian Phocaeans; the adjective *Phocaicus* is used in this sense by Silius. *uersum* as a preposition preceding its noun is late (Leumann 221, NW 2.781); the form, generally driven out by *uersus*, is either an archaism (Leumann 222) or on the analogy of *adversum*. *ui* is left in hiatus and *Tagūs* is lengthened by the metrical beat. Cf. *Cons. Liv.* 159 *Drusi manus altera et altera fratris*. 4-6 present a remarkable instance of chiastic-style ordering, a b b a a b.

7 *primordia* sticks to the root sense of *ordior*, to lay the warp of a web; *exordium* is often so used. *duxere* (see *OLD* 23c) also relates to wool-working. The spelling *ollim*, this too analogical (cf. *ollis* 13), leads a fugitive life elsewhere, and is rejected as faulty by a grammarian (*TLL* ix.2.556.40).

10 *uitae dies* here clearly means 'birthday', but elsewhere I can only find it in the sense of 'day of death' (*TLL* v.1.1060.82; add *CLE* 141.6). *dies leti* is repeated in 12.

11 *nemen* is not found elsewhere, but Housman on Manil. 5.663 proposes to restore it to various literary passages, and in Hill's edition I tentatively suggested the same at Stat. *Theb*. 3.658. Given however this writer's fondness for analogical formations, and the guidance offered for this one by *neuere* 8, it is unsafe to propagate the word elsewhere. The thread is threefold because (a) there are three Fates (cf. *CLE* 98.5, *GVI* 1146.3 = *IGUR* 1329.2) (b) there are three members of this family.

12 *propagare*, which usually means 'prolong', here means 'postpone'; likewise *profero* is used in both senses.

13 For *lege perenni* cf. *AL* 198.76.

14 'which requires all to appear in court to answer to the bail-bond which they have given to death'; either *uadimonium* (*OLD* 2b) *sistere* (*OLD* 2b) or *ad uadimonium uenire* and the like is usual.

175

CLE 439 = *CIL* 11.6565

An acrostich of the type discussed on 44, *Vera* vertically and beginning *uer* horizontally. It comes from near Sassina on a cippus. As at Ovid, *Met.* 2.27-30 each season has one line; so in the scholastic *tetrasticha de iv temporibus anni* in *Anth. Lat.* 567-578, to which the mss. prefix the passage of Ovid (see also ibid. 116). More

generally one may compare *GVI* 1897.17-22, where there is one couplet for each of three seasons.
2 The trees around the tomb in summer sway with their foliage; the metrical beat lengthens *nutēt*.
3 Vines would be planted at the grave; see 188.9, *CLE* 468.5 and Toynbee 97-8. For such *cepotaphia* (the word is quite frequent on prose inscriptions) see *RE* s.v., Blümner 508, Marquardt 369, P. Grimal, *Les jardins romaines* (ed. 3, 1984), 59, Gregori, *Bull. Comm.* 92 (1987-8), 175, Frazer and Nicholas, *JRS* 48 (1958), 120.
4 An elaborate way of saying 'in winter STTL'; literally 'may the season of winter be consecrated to you light with respect to the earth'. For *hibernum* (sc. *tempus*) = *hiems* see *TLL* s.v. 2698.37, HS 155; the *h* prevents elision of *lĕuĕ*, cf. Metre I e.

176

CLE 441 = *CIL* 6.1975 = *ILS* 7737
Photo: Calabi Limentani p. 207; Altmann 246; Kleiner 213 and pl. 46 (with further references); G. Zimmer, *Römische Berufsdarstellungen* (1982), p. 197 no. 142 (with discussion)

A long prose inscription reveals the deceased as T. Statilius Aper, a surveyor who died at the age of 22. The pun of 1-2, as if Aper were an *aper* (indeed the Calydonian Boar) is reinforced by the portrayal of a boar lying by his side. For other such inscriptional puns on names see Gatti, *Bull. Comm.* 15 (1887), 114, H. Armini, *Conlectanea Epigraphica* (Göteborgs Högskolas Arsskrift 29, 1923), 21, Galletier 261, Brelich 46, McCartney, *AJA* 23 (1919), 59, T. Ritti, *Imagini onomastiche* (*MAL* ser. 8, 21.4, 1977; cf. id., *Arch. Class.* 25-6 (1973-4), 639 for Greek instances), Barbieri in *Quarta Miscellanea* (Studi Ist. Ital. per la Storia antica 23, 1975), 304, Cugusi, *Ann. Fac. Magistero Cagliari* n.s. 4 (1980), 257; in this collection 34.7, 130, 132.6, 174, 190, 195.7 and perhaps 96 (see also on 124.16-18).
1 The uirgin is Diana; cf. Ovid, *Met.* 12.28 *placandam uirginis iram* (also Diana). *innocuūs* is lengthened by the metrical beat.
2 *Meleāger* is scanned as if it were *Meleagros*. *(-it) uiscera ferro* is a common line-ending (Mastandrea 930).

177**

CLE 467 = *CIL* 6.9118

An accompanying prose inscription confirms that this was set up by Hermes to his wife Nice. Some features suggest a strong Greek linguistic substratum. The word *ion*, apart from technical contexts, is found in Latin only here and in 178, with the Greek pitch accent here turning into a Latin long vowel (cf. L. Mueller 443-4). If 7 is correctly reported, *sit qui parent* adapts ἔστιν οἵ (though εἰσὶν οἵ is more usual); cf. Prop. 3.9.17-18 *est quibus*.

Vowels are left in hiatus before a pause in 2 and 8.

1 For funeral-altars see on 112.1, and for the clausula 150.9.

2-3 Cf. Verg. *Aen.* 11.160 *uiuendo uici mea fata, superstes / restarem ut genitor*. With *faceres* understand *sedem aramque*. The husband reproaches himself for not praying for his wife's fate, to die first; cf. *CLE* 1208.6 *optaueram tumulum tu mihi ut faceres*, 1302.3-4 *cuius fatales pensare optauerat annos, / Ponticus huic coniux ultima dona dedit* (cf. the *dona* here 7).

4 For parallels to the expression *annis uiduata tuis* see H. Armini, *Sepulcralia Latina* (1916), 46, who quotes e.g. *CLE* 1017.2, 1279.5; cf. also 20.18 above, and perhaps 198.3.

5 *Diones rosa* Tiberianus fr. 4 (in my numeration, *FLP* 442) 10; see my note there for the connection between Venus and the rose. The violet belongs to Cybele because it sprang from the blood of Attis (Arnob. 5.7); for its association with funerals see *RE*, *Veilchen* 598.13 and Ovid, *Fasti* 2.539. The rose is also funereal (planted at a grave *CIL* 12.3667 etc.), whence the festival of the Rosalia (see *RE* s.v. and Lattimore 137) first attested under Domitian; see Toynbee 62-3. For association of roses and violets or Rosalia and the corresponding Violaria see 124.7 (not funereal), *CLE* 1184.15, *CIL* 6.10239, 10248 = *ILS* 8366, *GVI* 1409, *Culex* 399-400, *CIL* 5.6363 *utrumque florem*; *CIL* 1.980 = *ILS* 3682 = *ILLRP* 99 *uiolaries rosaries coronaries* takes this association back into the Republic (for roses and violets in garlands cf. Plut. *Quaest. Symp.* 3.1.647d). The colours red and purple link these flowers with the life-blood (Serv. *Aen.* 5.79).

7 i.e. even after my death may there be someone to perpetuate my annual tribute to you. *meritis* = because of your merits; cf. *CLE* 1042 *tibi...meritis paruola dona dedi* and 173.5 above.

8 Cf. Verg. *Aen.* 1.249 *placida compostus pace quiescit*, *CLE* 541.12 *hic ego sepultus iaceo placidusque quiesco*, 1981.4-5 *pia munera mortis, annua uota, diem sollemnesque ordine pompas*.

9 'The Attic nightingale' refers to the legend of Philomela; cf. 187.19, *IGUR* 1303 f 5, [Moschus], *Epit. Bionis* 41 sqq. The adjective *Marathonis* is used twice by Statius.

178*

CLE 1313 = *CIL* 9.3184

Found at Corfinium with a prose prefix indicating that Optatus died at the age of 2.5. Compare this generally with 177.
1 Cf. *CLE* 508 *hic iacet Vetedinus pietatis nobilis infa(n)s* (also from Corfinium).
2 For this wish cf. 188.7, Auson. *Epitaph.* 31 Prete = *Epigr.* 8 Green, Pers. 1.38-40, *GVI* 2005.34-5 = *IG* 14.607e

εἰς ἴα σου, Πώμπτιλλα, καὶ εἰς κρίνα βλαστήσειεν
ὄστεα, καὶ θάλλοις ἐν πετάλοισι ῥόδων

(this appears together with *CLE* 1551), and an inscription from Cyzicus published *JHS* 22 (1902), 203 no. 9, *CLE* 1184.12 sqq. ('May I see flowers growing from your tomb so that the traveller may remark *hoc flos est corpus Flauiae Nicopolis*'). See further Luck, *Philol.* 100 (1956), 279 (somewhat indiscriminate). The notion is still used by Shakespeare, *Hamlet* 5.1.239 'And from her fair and unpolluted flesh / may violets spring'. The underlying idea of renewal of fertility has powerful symbolical significance; see I. A. Richmond, *Archaeology and the After-Life* (1950), 25.
3 *sibi* is probably simply the usual *tibi* transposed into the third person instead of *ei*. *nunc* implies a contrast with his human mother. Cf. on 11.6-7.
4 For this pointed turn given to the conventional STTL (on 20.20) cf. *CLE* 1470-2 (the first of these reads *te, terra, optestor, leuiter super ossa quiescas / et tenerae aetati ne grauis esse uelis*), 1321, 2138, Lattimore 69-71. This turn has been made famous by Martial's epigram on the six-year old Erotion 5.34.9-10; for Greek precedents see Meleager, *AP* 7.461 = civ Gow - Page, *GVI* 1468.7-8 (from Pantikapaion, second century B.C.)

ἀλλ' ἔστω σοὶ ὁ πᾶς κῶφος λίθος, εἴ γε
πᾶσι πάρος ζώων ἦς συ προσηνότατος.

The sentiment becomes less convincing when *mediae* has to be substituted for *tenerae* (*CLE* 1192.10, 1472.2).

179

CLE 562 = *CIL* 6.19007

The metrical flaws are obvious and hardly need to be listed. For the dative form *Agathe* cf. *Ge* 196 and NW 1.100-1.
1 *Mater* was probably her *signum* (see on 28); Kajanto, *Supernomina* 21 quotes an inscription *moribus inbentum* (= *inuentum*) *fuerat mihi nomen Matris, mera Damula, qui* (= *quae*) *et Inbidiosa* (a girl aged nine; *mera Damula* = in my original form Damula, i.e. this was her real name). For the accusative of respect *nomen* see Green on Auson. *Epiced. in Patrem* 1; for *lege* cf. e.g. Val. Max. 2.9.1 *gignendi legem*. In general cf. *CLE* 2177 *nomine eram Maturus, non aetate futurus*.
3 For *uinti* see Leumann 153, 491, Hallbauer 68; for *uintĭ* cf. *CLE* 1332.5g and Metre I j (iii); for the precision see on 70.3.
5-6 The countenance not of a female, for which only my parents knew me, Agathe. For the hermaphroditic ideal of beauty favoured by the ancients in the young see my note on Juv. 15.135-7.
8 I think that the writer had not made up his mind whether he intended the first-declension forms in this line as nominative or ablative. Her hair was cropped like that of a boy, and at the back it was not tied up in a knot, but left unconfined. Clearly *remissa* is intended. For the spelling *posttrema* see on 118.5.
9 *conuiuae* at the commemorative meals held at the tomb (Toynbee 62, Lattimore 134, Cumont, *LP* 37-8, K. Hopkins, *Death and Renewal* (1983), 233, Blümner 510 (on 507 he illustrates a tomb in the form of a *triclinium*); for representations in art see Ghedini, *Riv. di Archeol.* 14 (1990), 35, Compostella, *MEFRA* 104 (1992), 659); cf. e.g. *CLE* 1977.3.
11 Faventius was her step-father. *perquam* (= *nimis*) *doleat* go together.
13-14 *et...nec* correspond to each other. For *amoenus* applied to persons, instead of (as usual) to scenery, cf. e.g. *CLE* 967.2 (there is there a pun on the name Amoena, which may in fact be meant here), 1142.7.
15 For *tristis* with genitive cf. HS 79, KS 1.443 (on 445 they quote *miser* with genitive). *parentes* = relatives; see Wilkinson, *CJ* 59 (1963-4), 358, S. G. Harrod, *Latin Terms of...Family Relationship* (1909), 56 (this passage *TLL* x.1.357.50).
16 For parallels see Lattimore 203.
17 *seu* may be just an error for *neu*.
20 For the masculine *letus* (also intended on *CLE* 2177) see on 19.1;

for the combination with *mortis TLL* can quote no better parallel than *CLE* 2180 *Lethes in morte* (*funus mortis* is also found).

For the postscript cf. *CLE* 247 = *CIL* 6.29952 *hoc est, sic est, aliut fieri non licet.*

180

CLE 995 = *CIL* 6.12652 = *IG* 14.1892 = *IGUR* 3.1250 (with a photo of the front on p. 110) = *GVI* 2008

Photo of all faces: Walser 42-7; H. Stuart Jones, *Sculptures of the Museo Capitolino* (1912), pl. 89. 12A 1-3; the front, Altmann 125 fig. 100

Scribonius Largus, *Compositiones* 162 (written under Claudius) mentions *Anthero<s> Tiberii libertus supra hereditates* (for this office, concerned with administering the many legacies left to the emperor, see O. Hirschfeld, *Die kaiserlichen Verwaltungsbeamten* (ed. 2, 1905), 112; Boulvert 136-7). This name, which would represent Ἄνθηρος, is usually and rightly emended to *Anteros* (Ἀντέρως), since otherwise it should be *Antherus* (Solin, *Arctos* 7 (1972), 201-2, who rightly restores this spelling on *CLE* 416). The husband in this epitaph had originally been the slave (*uicarius*) of the slave Anteros (whom it is reasonable to identify with the *supra hereditates*), and from him had passed into the ownership of Pamphilus, freedman of Tiberius, who had emancipated him. Scribonius 120 also mentions *Cassii medici colice bona...uera haec est, ut ab eius seruo Atimeto accepi, legato Tiberii Caesaris*, but this must be a different Atimetus. Treggiari, *Phoenix* 35 (1981), 48 n.14 thinks that Claudia was emancipated by Tiberius when he was still a Claudius.

In 1-10 Homonoea speaks, in 11-12 the wayfarer addressed in 1-2 replies. In 13-18, for which 9-10 prepare, Atimetus speaks, and in 19-26 Homonoea replies. For such dialogues between husband and wife, as in 32 and *GVI* 1873, see Krummrey, *Klio* 48 (1967), 148; B. von Hesberg-Tonn, *Carissima Coniunx* (1983), 111 and 128.

1-2 Cf. 119.1, *CLE* 960.1, 1125.2, 1196.2.

3 Cf. on 150.15. Ovid, *Met.* 4.56 *quas oriens habuit praelata puellis*.

5-6 Cf. generally *GVI* 1925.3-4; for 6 cf. *CLE* 1213.3 and on 20.9. This is the first appearance in Latin of *Paphie* or *Paphia* = Aphrodite (cf. 184.5), then *Aetna* 594, Colum. 10.193; I suggested it at Germanicus fr. 4.110 in Gain's edition.

8 Cf. Verg. *Aen.* 10.419, Ovid, *Am.* 3.9.20, Callimachus, *Epigr.* 34 Gow - Page (= 2 Pfeiffer) 6, *GVI* 1995.4; it is a legal metaphor from the procedure for claiming property (*TLL* vii.1.1613.67, viii.360.19; *RE* s.v. *manus iniectio*).
9-10 Cf. 172.6-7.
10 For *coniugis* cf. 19. This is probably correct for the time of her death, when they are both free; *contubernalis* in the prose prescript is retained from an earlier stage in which one or both were still slaves. See Boulvert, *Domestique et Fonctionnaire* (on 29 above) 284 nn. 143-4.
11-12 The sequence indicates that this means 'you deserved to live and long ago to enjoy your blessings'; the traveller who in the future reads the inscription looks back to the lifetime of Homonoea. For *dignissima uita* cf. Mastandrea 221-2.
13, 16 For *pensare* cf. *CLE* 1302.3 (quoted on 177.2-3), 1551 A 4 (see Lattimore 204 n.251), Stat. *Silv.* 3.3.192 (this last in reference to Alcestis, who is prominently in mind in such situations, as at *GVI* 2088a, p. 691); cf. 25-6. For *redimi* cf. Ovid, *Ex Ponto* 3.1.105 (also Alcestis). *Pensare, redimere, debere* are all commercial or financial metaphors.
17 For *quod potui* see on 74.2. Cf. *CLE* 542.2 *lucem iam nolo uidere* and for the general sense *CIL* 6.18817 = *ILS* 8006.
19 Cf. Stat. *Silv.* 5.1.179 *parce precor lacrimis* and the following context, Prop. 4.11.1 *desine, Paulle, meum lacrimis urgere sepulcrum.*
20 *sollicitare* usually has *manes, cineres* etc. for object (197.12, *CLE* 965.8, 1212.14, 1468.2), and despite 21 that is presumably the sense of *fata,* as at *CLE* 460.5, 965.3, 966.3. For the general topic see Lier (1904) 55.
22 Cf. *CLE* 1097.3, Nisbet - Hubbard on Hor. *Odes* 1.28.15.
23 For *ita* see on 103.
25-6 Cf. Prop. 4.11.95, Stat. *Silv.* 5.1.177 and other instances in my note on *vers. pop.* 21 (*FLP* 482; add Plaut. *Asin.* 610, and see also Schoonhoven in his edition of *Cons. Liv.* (1992), pp. 27-8 and Danesi Marioni, *Prometheus* 19 (1993), 211).

181

CLE 1038 = *CIL* 6.14404
Discussion: Solin, *Arctos* 12 (1978), 149

Painted on the stucco of a columbarium outside the Porta Esquilina, now faded and no longer visible.
1-2 A tomb laid on the earth (<*tumulum*> *superinpositum*), light so that it does not weigh down on the bones, by such skill as a poor man can afford (cf. Lattimore 229) is supported by the earth, which is even lighter than the tomb.
3 Cf. Ovid, *Ex Ponto* 4.13.1 *non dubios inter memorande sodales.*
4 *castarūm* is so scanned in hiatus at the diaeresis (cf. Metre I f), or else *h* counts as a consonant (ibid. I e). *h[oc e]s* is usually read, but the present tense seems very unsuitable and *hoc* has little point. I tentatively propose *h[ospe]s*, 'you, Junia, who were the glory of chaste women while you sojourned on earth'; for life on earth as a *hospitium* cf. Lattimore 168.
5 For the form *ess* (which here however may be just a mistake) see Leumann 220, Sommer 276, Enk on Plaut. *Truc.* 153; for *uerssa* see on 118.5. 'The tomb of a cicada' must have been something of a cliché derived from Hellenistic epigrams describing such (Anyte, *AP* 7.190, Phaennos, ibid. 197, Leonidas of Tarentum, ibid. 198); see Gow - Page, *Hellenistic Epigrams* 2 pp. 90-1, Herrlinger 11. When Pliny, *NH* 34.57 states that in her poetry Erinna (*Suppl. Hell.* 405) referred to such a tomb executed by Myron, he is confusing Erinna with Anyte and Myro (the owner of the cicada in Anyte) with Myron. I still prefer this interpretation to Solin's idea that Cicada is a proper name; who would she be?
6 A promise by the husband not to remarry, for which cf. *CLE* 634, *CIL* 11.1491; it is much more often the wife who vows to remain *uniuira* (see my note on Juv. 6.230), since there were no pressures of conventional morality on widowers not to remarry. Auson. *Epic. in Patrem* 37-8 makes his father boast of not remarrying; see also *GVI* 1392.

182

CLE 1063 = *CIL* 6.26011
Photo: G. Capecchi and others, *Collezione Fiorentine di Antichità II Palazzo Peruzzi* (1980), tav. LI.1 (cf. p. 155 no. 146).

The butterfly or moth emerging from its chrysalis is a powerful image of new birth, and the Greek for butterfly is ψυχή; see M. Davies and J. Kathirithamby, *Greek Insects* (1986), 99, 103. For Latin see *GLK* 4.10.31 *uappo, uapponis, est animal uolans quod uulgo animas uocant* (André, *Rev. Phil.* 36 (1962), 23). This forms the background for the frequent symbolic association of the butterfly with death and the soul, as often on gravestones and sarcophagi and at e.g. Phaedrus, app. 29 (31); see Lattimore 30 n.77, Sichtermann, *Röm. Mitt.* 76 (1969), 298. That leads to an actual identification of the two at *CIL* 2.2146 (quoted under *CLE* 1851), and the same is clearly intended here. *CLE* 1517.1 *ereptam uolucrem Cupido luget* might have a similar reference, with *uolucrem* (which elsewhere is applied to bees, wasps and flies) meaning 'butterfly'; but the status and significance of this epitaph generally are open to considerable doubt (see Martorelli, *RAL* 26 (1971), 729).

aranist = aranei est; arani is found also Lucr. 3.383.

183

CLE 1109 = *CIL* 6.21521
Discussion: Bömer, *AAntHung* 30 (1982-4), 275; Lissberger 97-8

Found outside the Porta Portuensis; only the first halves of 1-12 survive. This poem is full of reminiscences of classical poets, particularly Vergil and Ovid; these are assembled by Lissberger and Bömer, and I shall not record most of the instances. *CIL* 14.2696 reveals a Sex. Onussanius Sex. fil. Nepotianus from Tusculum, clearly a relative of the dedicator. The poem is organised on a compositional scheme of three groups each of 14 lines followed by a coda of 4.

There is of course a strong psychological urge to see the dead again; cf. e.g. *CLE* 542.5 *lacrime si prosunt uisis, te ostende uideri, GVI* 1545.7-10, 1923.11-12, *CIL* 6.18817 =*ILS* 8006; Lucian, *De Luctu* 16 envisages an apparition and exhortation in some ways comparable to this one. This urge would cause people to experience such dreams and visions as this poem records; Lucretius thinks it important to give a physical explanation of them, 4.26 sqq.

1 *quum* is a very late spelling, not found elsewhere in *CLE*; it argues against Bücheler's Flavian dating. In 7 only the *q* of this word is preserved.

3-4 Each line consists of two nouns, two adjectives and a verb.

6 *saxa mouere* is a proverbial phrase; see Bömer on Ovid, *Met.* 6.547, 9.303.

7 Dreams and visions coming after midnight were supposed to be reliable, unlike those coming earlier (full references in R. A. Pack's note on p. 16.13 of his Teubner Artemidorus; perhaps also *Suppl. Hell.* 922.1, 1046). See Cumont, *LP* 96 n. 1.

9-10 Nepos comes down like a shooting star; *sidereo* links with *sidera* 15. The end of 10 is modelled on Verg. *Aen.* 3.173 *nec sopor illud erat,* except that, like the imitation of Silius 3.198 *neque enim sopor ille,* this writer attracts the pronoun to the gender of the predicate (KS 1.34, HS 442). Cf. also *IGUR* 184.5-6 πᾶσι γὰρ [ ] εσσιν ἐμοῖς ἀναφανδὸν ἐπέστης / οὐκ ὄναρ ἀλλὰ μέσους ἤματος ἀμφὶ δρόμους.

11-12 Apparitions, like figures in dreams, are often described as being of superhuman size; see L. Deubner, *De Incubatione* (1900), 12, Hanson, *ANRW* ii.23.2.1410 and my note on Juv. 13.221.

13 Blazing eyes are a sign of divinity; this is how Philosophy appears to Boethius (*Cons.* 1 pr.1, where see J. Gruber's commentary p. 59 and *Rh. Mus.* 112 (1969), 172).

14 Verg. *Aen.* 2.593 (Venus) *roseoque haec insuper addidit ore,* Ovid, *Fasti* 6.426 *reddidit o. s.*

15 *adfinis* means a relative by marriage. I cannot understand how Bücheler, even after realising that we are dealing with a *Nepos* and not (as had been supposed previously) a *nepos,* can claim that the recipient of the vision was the grandfather or uncle of Nepos, or how he can infer this from *puer* 44.

17 Ovid, *Ex Ponto* 3.5.53 *caelesti sede receptum, CIL* 6.2160 = *ILS* 4947 *cuius spiritus inter deos receptus est.*

18 *numina* = *deum* 16. For such an outright assertion of divinity Lattimore 40 and 102 compares *CLE* 975.4 and 1551g (in the latter place, though the interpretation is far from clear, the deceased seems to be equated with Persephone, which one may compare with 35 sqq. here). See also 1057.15 *numen habetis,* 1046.3 *corpo]ris diui,* below 186.7 and in prose *CIL* 6.15696. For *laedere* cf. *CLE* 1467.3; on the normal view of death this would be *sollicitare manes* (on 180.20).

19 sqq. For these assertions cf. *CLE* 611.3, 1535 A 7-8 (*set non hic Manis nec templa Acherusia uisit, / ad caeli quoniam tollitur iste Pius;* there one understands *ad caeli* <*templa*>, which may be compared with 28 here). See too Verg. *Aen.* 5.733 (Anchises) *non me impia namque / Tartara habent, tristes umbrae, sed amoena piorum / concilia Elysiumque colo* and *GVI* 970.7 ναίω δ' ἡρώων ἱερὸν δόμον, οὐκ 'Αχέροντος, 861 (7-8 οὐ γ]ὰρ ὑποχθόνιος κατὰ γῆς 'Αίδης με κέκευθε/ [ἀ]λλὰ Δίος πάρεδρος ἀετὸς ἥρπασέ με, with a Latin version underneath), 1090, *IG* 12.5 no. 62.7. The words of the deified

Hercules to his mother in [Sen.] *Herc. Oet.* 1940-3, 1963-5 are quite comparable.

23-4 Cf. Sen. *Apoc.* 12.3.25 (Minos) *qui dat populo iura silenti. et...non* instead of *nec* lacks linguistic justification (HS 480).

27-8 In *GVI* 1993 the deceased appears to his mother in a dream and tells her that Zeus has rescued his spirit to heaven and made it immortal.

29 Cic. *Ad Att.* 8.6.3 *qui me horror perfudit!*, Verg. *Aen.* 7.458 *artus / perfundit...sudor.*

30 For the notion of the sweet scent of the gods (because their statues were often perfumed; cf. the statue of a human 124.8), which may reveal their presence to mortals, see the references given by Bömer and in general Deubner (on 11-12) 13; P. Meloni, Il *Profumo dell' Immortalità* (1975), 12; S. Lilja *The Treatment of Odours in the Poetry of Antiquity* (SSF, CHL 49, 1972), 27; Richardson on *Hom. Hymn Dem.* 275 sqq.. In particular see Ovid, *Fasti* 5.376 with Bömer's commentary.

31 This recalls the address to the deified Romulus in Enn. *Ann.* 106 *O Romule, Romule die,* and the idea of Romulus was also suggested in 28 (where cf. Enn. 54 *unus erit quem tu tolles in caerula caeli / templa*) and 18 (where cf. Ovid, *Fasti* 2.505-6 *prohibe lugere Quirites / nec uiolent lacrimis numina nostra suis*). Even 10 has a Romulean parallel (Ovid ibid. 503 *pulcher et humano maior*). At the same time there also appears to be a reminiscence of Enn. *Ann.* 60 *Ilia, dia nepos.*

32 i.e. you join Adonis as he sports with Venus; this presumably happens during the part of the year when, according to some versions, he is released from the underworld.

34 Cf. 67 B 3; Guarducci, *NS* 7 (1953), 123-4 compares a graffito from Alba Fucens (*AE* 1954.169d) which reads *te chorus omnis agat, Flauia, caelicolum.*

35 sqq. This recalls Ovid, *Her.* 15.23-4, *Met.* 8.31, Prop. 4.2.31-2; see also Auson. *Epigr.* 53 Green 5-7 *sed neque functorum socius miscebere uulgo / nec metues Stygios flebilis umbra lacus, / uerum aut Persephonae Cinyreius ibis Adonis...* When, as in Ausonius and *GVI* 438a (p. 679), such topics are applied to the dead, they are not to be considered identifications of the dead with the god, any more than depictions in art with attributes of a particular god. In each case we are dealing only with a means of idealising the deceased and, as in ruler cult, associating his qualities with those of a god. On the whole topic see *RAC, Grabinschrift* 539 and particularly Wrede; this poem is on p. 106, and e.g. identification with the Dioscuri 230, with Apollo 207-8. Nepos is rather unusual in that such identifications are usually

applied to women or children.
37 For *pascere crinem* see *TLL* x.1.596.70.
39 For the *manicae* cf. Verg. *Aen.* 9.616; for the paratactic form of condition with perfect subjunctive see KS 2.164 and other instances in my note on Juv. 3.78.
40 She will love Nepos as well as Attis. Cf. *CLE* 1339.20 *cum tuus in nostro pectore uibat amor.*
42 The rider of Cyllarus is usually represented to be Castor, but sometimes named as Pollux.
43 This recalls the religious formulation for covering all aspects of gods; see Appel 78 and on 155.34 above.
44 *puer* is presumably the son (see *OLD* s.v. 2) of Nepos; it is odd that nothing is said of his wife (perhaps he was divorced).
45 Perfumes were often offered at graves (see my note on Juv. 4.109), and the headstones were often garlanded (e.g. *CLE* 1592.8). *haec dona* may mean this poem, abrupt though that is; the topic of the immortality of poetry is contrasted with the evanescent nature of other gifts to the dead such as scented spices at Stat. *Silv.* 3.3.37 *nos non arsura feremus / munera, uenturosque tuus durabit in annos / me monstrante dolor.* However 127.21 suggests that it may refer to a statue of Nepos.

184

CLE 1233 = *CIL* 3.686 = M. Demitsas - A. Oikonomides, *Sylloge Inscriptionum...Macedoniae* (1980), 1042-3
Discussion: F. J. Dölger, *Antike und Christentum* 2 (1930), 107; W. Vollgraff, *Hommages Bidez - Cumont* (CL 2, 1949), 353.

This was found near Philippi, and was written in a script in which some letters were hard to distinguish from others (e.g. *i* and *t*), the writing was very crowded and sometimes the letters were linked to each other; in addition there were some obvious errors, most of them not recorded by me. The initial allusion to the relationship between Hercules and Hylas and the mention of the boy's station in 8 make it plain that, though not handsome, he was a *puer delicatus*, and that this epitaph was put up by his master.
1 *infractum* may mean 'broken down by grief' (*infringere animum* in this sense is quite common), or it may mean 'unbreakable', a sense

found first in the fourth century. *conuellere pectus* [Ovid], *Her.* 17.111.

2 *Tamen* is fairly often elliptical (some of the instances in *OLD* s.v. 4 belong here); in this case it means 'in spite of all that might discourage weeping' (further explained by 4).

3-4 *Homerus laudauit* in *Il.* 2.674. The expression is rather confused, but the meaning is plain enough; Achilles was handsome in body, whereas you had an attractive disposition. *Aeacide* = *-ae*. *corpus Achilli* is quoted from Prop. 2.9.13, and *Achilli* is a genitive form of the fifth declension; see Leumann 447, 458.

5 *sortita Paphon* = Venus, cf. 180.5.

6 Your character had *uenus*, attractiveness.

7 *sobria uirtus* represents σωφροσύνη.

8 His *uirtus* was greater (*non minor* = *maior* by litotes) than his age and greater too than his station.

12 For *reparatus* cf. 171.6. *Elysiis* sc. *campis*, cf. *GVI* 1486.5, Lucan 6.699, Mart. 9.51.5 and quite often in Latin inscriptions (Fele 1.299a). Cf. *CLE* 1189.16 *uiuis in Elysium*.

13-14 For the idea that bliss in the afterlife is a reward for piety in this life cf. *CLE* 435, 525, 1970, *GVI* 1916.

15 The word *castificus* is found on another inscription from near Milan, published *Aevum* 11 (1937), 459 no. 4, and in Sen. *Phaedr.* 169. *cursu* sc. *uitae*, cf. *CLE* 695.1 *iustis bis senos cursibus annos / egit*; for the metaphor of the race of life cf. 68.9.

16 Cf. *CLE* 1088.4 *tam simplici uita / quae superis semper tam grata fuisti*. If there is any specific reference in *iussa*, we do not know what it is.

17 Cf. the chorus of initiates in the underworld in the *Frogs* of Aristophanes; sarcophagi often show Bacchic thiasi (Cumont, *Recherches* 344, though the caveat must be entered that a firmer methodology than Cumont's is needed to interpret such scenes on sarcophagi; see Nock 616 and 639). Cf. *CLE* 607. 4-5 *(c)ui sonus auditur et uox imago Lyei, / murmurant et chitari cord(a)e cum uoce decores*. *Bromio* is presumably dative of agent, though it might be an adjective (*TLL* s.v. 2204.23) agreeing with whatever is concealed at the end of the line. *signatae* has been taken to mean 'tattooed', but Dölger points out that when Bacchantes are shown tattooed, they are so as Thracian women, not as Bacchantes (cf. Jones, *JRS* 77 (1987), 145); Vollgraff's contradiction is vain. The line therefore remains wholly obscure.

18 The flowery meadows are in Aristophanes too (see Dover's edition p. 60), and also *GVI* 1830.3-4, Hom. *Od.* 11.539, 573 and

24.13, Pindar fr. 129 Snell, [Plato] *Axiochus* 371c. A painting in the tomb of Octavia Paulina, who died at the age of six, shows children plucking flowers in the Elysian Fields (illustrated e.g. by J. Prieur, *La Mort dans l'Antiquité Romaine* (1986), 131). *floriger* is a late word, whereas *florifer* is classical. The end of the line seems to mean 'in an assemblage of the Satyrs'; *congrex*, elsewhere an adjective, is turned into a noun, and this form of the ablative is chosen to provide a correption *congregĭ in* in preference to a hiatus *congregĕ in*. Of course undue confidence would here be misplaced.

19 'The nymphs seized X' is a euphemism for 'X died' (*GVI* 952.1 and 1595.10 = 1344 *IGUR*, q.v.; *CIL* 6.29195 = *ILS* 8482 *raptus a nymphis*); cf. Nock 924. That is not relevant here, but Stat. *Silv.* 2.6.101 *forsan Auernales adludunt undique mixtae / Naides* (in an epicedion for a *puer delicatus*) is. The Naiads are κανηφόροι (*canistriferae* is not found elsewhere; *canistrariae* appear in this function); in the baskets they may be carrying flowers or (more likely) mystic objects (cf. Stat. *Th.* 4.378), like human *cistophori*.

20 A *pannychis; ducibus = praecedentibus.*

21 i.e. function in whatever capacity befits the age which you attained; *perferre* is similarly used *CLE* 1075.5, 1501.1. For *quicquid ero* in similar contexts see Lissberger 62.

185

CLE 1247 = *CIL* 6.7193a, 33241

This is a label from a columbarium on the Via Latina; another fragmentary inscription from the same or a neighbouring columbarium displayed the same epigram. Prose inscriptions reveal this one as the burial-place of a freedman Ancarenus Nothus.

1 The meaning of *quod superest homini* is not entirely plain; probably 'what we all come to in the end'. Cholodniak's idea that it is an error for *hominis* is not plausible.

3-4 *pensiones* means 'rent-payments'; these are so high, as they notoriously were at Rome (see my note on Juvenal 3.225), that the renters themselves are pawned in order to pay them. The contrast with *gratis* is obvious. The archaic accusative after *careo* re-appears quite commonly from the second century onwards. The lines are meant to be divided *arra et / gratis*; Bücheler compares *CLE* 1155.5-6 *patronae / et comprecor*, 475.9-10 and 476.9-10 *beata(m) / et semper* *honoratam*. The subject of *GVI* 1570 = *IGUR* 1168 also celebrates release from gout. The metaphorical sense of *hospitium* (188.4, q.v.; *TLL* s.v. 3042.47) fits neatly with the literal 'apartment'. *pensjonibus* is so scanned.

186

CLE 1508 = *CIL* 6.30102

1 *rara fides* Hor. *Odes* 1.35.21, with other occurrences in Nisbet-Hubbard's note.
6 Embalming was unusual at Rome; see Toynbee 41 and Stat. *Silv.* 5.1.225 sqq. *folium* was a perfume of which one of the ingredients was nard (see my note on Juv. 6.465 and Kay on Mart. 11.27.9); for the vulgar form *foleum* cf. *CIL* 10.1784, 14.1823.
7 *merentis* picks up *meritis* 4. For *ut numen colit* see on 183.18.
8 Because she might summon him to join her. *p* alliterates in this line and the next.
11 For the lamp in the tomb cf. *CLE* 1308.2, Blümner 510 n.13, Lattimore 134, Marquardt 367-8, Cumont *LP* 46 sqq., Scheid, *Archeol. e Storia antica* 6 (1984), 121. Here perfume is the fuel instead of lamp-oil; at Petron. 70.9 perfume is thrown on the lamp. Cf. *CIL* 6.10248 *lucerna lucens sibi ponatur incenso inposito.*

187

CLE 1549 = *CIL* 6.25063

1 *dua* (also on *CLE* 857.1) is a barbarism (Quintil. 1.5.15) not found in any literary text except apparently Accius 655 ap. Cic. *Or.* 156 (*TLL* s.v. 2241.81, NW 2.277). *funera mersa* looks as if it has been developed from the common *funere mersus*, with *funus* adapted to the sense 'corpse'.
2 *flebile* may be an interjection (*TLL* s.v. 891.41 quotes instances from Silius) or used adverbially.
3 *Porthmeu* i.e. Charon; see my note on Juv. 3.266 and add now the Barcelona *Alcestis* 82. *fuerat* = *fuit* or *erat* (see on 109.14). English idiom is 'it would have been enough'; for the Latin indicative cf.

97.2, KS 1.171-2, HS 327.

5 The construction of *adicio* with infinitive is a hebraism elsewhere known only from Christian authors (*TLL* i.674.30). For the wandering *h* in *Chloto* cf. on 130.1. *iteratum* = *iterum petitum*. There is hiatus at the caesura (Metre II A a).

7 For *morti occumbere* see *TLL* ix.2.380.37 (omitting this instance); for *sŭppremae* (contrast 21) see on 118.5.

8 The writer loses control of the construction; it should be *teque*. The sentiment of 7-8 is extremely common; cf. on 20.17.

10 *dunc*, which is found quite frequently (a variant at 199.4), is formed on the analogy of *tum - tunc*. Here it means 'until'; until you read the ages of the dead, do not rush to read their names, because the former contributes more to the tragedy. Then in 11-12 the ages are in fact given before the names.

11 i.e. *bis senos*, as 15 shows. If the mother died at the age of 22 and the son at the age of 12, then the son will have died some years after the mother (cf. 6); and in fact the emphasis of the poem is very much more on the recent wound of the son's death.

12 *hŭic* (a scansion introduced by Statius)...*huic* (monosyllabic as usual) is like the effect remarked on 70.3. For the genitive *Athenaidis* see KS 1.420.

16 *credebant* people in general.

17 The colour of the wool of the Parcae depends on whether they spin good or ill fortune (see my note on Juv. 12.65); here good turns into ill, cf. perhaps *CLE* 2297.15 (but note the revised reading of that line in A. Merlin, *Inscr. lat. de la Tunisie* 1166).

18-23 Apart from Echo, all these are birds or winged creatures with funereal associations. Philomela and Alcyone bewail Itys and Ceyx, the swan its own death (cf. 123.12) in its 'swan-song' (Nisbet - Hubbard on Hor. *Odes* 2.20.14; H. Donohue, *The Song of the Swan* (1993) 22 sqq.); the Sirens too are associated with death (Cumont, *Recherches* 327; Pollard, *CR* 2 (1952), 63). *GVI* 923 has nightingales, sirens and perhaps swallows.

19 For *dabet* here and *resonabet* 22 see on 79.1. For the *Attica aedo* cf. on 177.9; only here does this Greek word acquire a Latin termination (contrast *aedon* l.c.).

22 *et Echo* = 'Echo too'; for *et...et* so used see *TAPA* 114 (1984), 332.

23 The swan is called 'Spartan' simply as a literary reference to Zeus visiting Leda in that form.

188

CLE 1559 = *CIL* 6.13528
Discussion: Cumont, *Recherches* 87-90 (partly far-fetched)

1-12 were written by the poet Laberius himself as the epitaph for his wife Bassa; 13-16, whether composed by him or not, were added when he too was buried in the same tomb. 1-3 are now missing from the stone. After 5, 12 and 14 there are interlinear dashes, and presumably there was once one after 3.

1 *Labēri* here, but the correct scansion *Labĕri* (not necessarily written by the poet himself) 13. Bücheler thinks that the lengthening here is due to the accentuation *Labéri* (cf. Metre I i), but it is not clear that this genitive accentuation is anything more than a whim of Nigidius Figulus (see Leumann 425, Sommer 344, Allen 88 n.2).

coniuga is found in *CLE* 112.2 and Apuleius (thrice); cf. Kübler 172, A. Traina, *Poeti latini (e neolatini)* 3 (1989), 160. See on 200.3. For the bosom of earth-mother cf. 11.6-7.

2 *frugeae* (not found elsewhere) = *frugiferae*. For *moribus priscis* cf. Juv. 6.45 with my note.

3 These appear to be tetrameters, not septenarii, and if that is so one must scan *animu(s)* (see Metre I h). See also on 14.

4 He tells his wife to prepare a lodging for both of them; cf. 185.4, *CLE* 89.4, 242, 1293.2 *precesti hospitium dulce parare tuis* (= *praecessisti*), Lattimore 168.

5 This marriage in death, unlike that in life, is to be for ever; cf. *CLE* 1249.6, 1567.10, 1571 and more in Cumont l.c.. *haec* apparently = *hae*, the only well-documented occurrence of this form outside old scenic verse.

6 i.e. *bene odora*; this looks like a nominative lengthened before *st-*.

7 Cf. on 178.2.

8 *amens* with grief, cf. *CLE* 1523.10, but perhaps also with a glance at poetic frenzy at the end of the line. For the grave-altar see on 112.1. Cf. Suet. *Claud.* 11 *coronauit comoediam*.

9 i.e. *uuarum* (cf. Consentius, *GLK* 5.393.1); Leumann 135 quotes instances of *iuenis* (cf. 199.9, *TLL* s.v. 734.5) etc. See also 67 A 5 *aeum*, 33.1 *aequm*, and Väänänen 48-50; Wachter, index 545 s.v. *'ökonomische' Schreibung*. *racemo* is collective singular.

10 For the vine at the tomb cf. 175.3. For the weakening of the consonant in *amplesa* (which however still leaves the syllable long) cf. Leumann 221, SP 185 and on 39.5. *de* is instrumental, as often in late Latin (HS 126, 262).

11 The foliage forming a backdrop weaves a double shade, that of the tall elms and of the vine-shoots which entwine them. The vine is 'spouse' of the elm (this is not just a poetical metaphor but an actual term of Italian farmers), but no doubt we are also to think of the human wife.
13 Cf. *CLE* 591 *terrenum corpus, caelestis spiritus in me, / quo repetente suam sedem nunc uiuimus illic* (see p. 14 for this epitaph). *GVI* 1369.6, though mutilated, must have expressed the same thought as *spiritus...ortus*.
14 Varro, *Sat. Men.* 32 *in reliquo corpore ab hoc fonte* [i.e. *a corde*] *diffusast anima, hinc animus ad intellegentiam diffusus*. This also illustrates *animus* - *anima* 3, except that there the *animus* is the seat of the emotions rather than of the intelligence. For *fontem animae* cf. also Avien. *Arat.* 49-52.
15 *modo* = *nunc*, cf. *TLL* s.v. 1308.28; *fueram* = *fui*, see on 109.14. This reads almost like a riddle. Cf. *AP* 10.118.3 (anon.) οὐδὲν ἐὼν γενόμην · πάλιν ἔσσομαι ὡς πάρος ἦα, *CLE* 1341.3, 1496, *GVI* 1906.14. See too Ovid, *Tr.* 3.11.25 *non sum ego quod fueram* (i.e. dead instead of alive, as the following context makes plain).
16 Lattimore 84 n.468 compares Eur. fr. 639 N τίς δ' οἶδεν εἰ τὸ ζῆν μέν ἐστι κατθανεῖν, / τὸ κατθανεῖν δὲ ζῆν κάτω νομίζεται. see also Cumont 89 nn.1-2. For *itidest* = *eadem* cf. *TLL* s.v. 564.25; for the spelling see on 172.8.

189

CLE 1996 = B54 Pikhaus
Discussion: Kleberg, *Eranos* 27 (1929), 148

This is from Ammaedera, modern Haidra.
1 *doctrinā* is ablative, despite the scansion; for the *asyndeton bimembre* cf. HS 829, KS 2.149. Merlin suggested that *puella* is an error for *puellas*.
2 'taken away' (to the underworld, cf. *CLE* 542.1, 997.1) 'because of your father's evil destiny'.
3-6 A 'Priamel'. Cf. Sen. *De Ira* 3.35.5 *auro pretiosora* and other instances in Otto, *Nachträge* 138. For Spartan purple see my note on Juv. 8.101 and *AE* 1984, 207. *cylindro* is collective singular.
5 If the emendation correctly represents the intention of the composer, it involves a synizesis.

6 Lommatzsch interprets this as *liquebat*, comparing *esse liquebat* at Ovid, *Met.* 11.718; for the spelling see *TLL* s.v. 1477.75.
7 Despite the scansion *lanifica nulla* are nominatives; cf. 109.20.
8 He means *Pandionias*, i.e. Procne and Philomela, daughters of Pandion, turned into nightingale and swallow. For the Siren cf. the Greek epigram prefixed to 180.
9 *superasti* is required by the sense, but *superas* by the metre. Lommatzsch takes this to mean 'you excel things which are above all description', comparing Petron. 126.14, but I still prefer to understand 'you excel all the above-mentioned'.
10 Kleberg compares *CLE* 1005.11 *me memini Gallis natum Caroq(ue) [p]are[nte* (rather than *caro*); here too the metre of *sată ēs* (for the lengthening of the latter see Metre I e) shows that the pattern-book or other model had *nata*, which was varied because of *nata* 11. For the adjective *Graiugenus* cf. *CLE* 1355.9 *Graiugenam...linguam*. The easiest interpretation of the line (so Kleberg) is that her father was actually called Heros (cf. e.g. 21).
11 Sc. *annos*.
12 *rogo* means 'tomb'; this sense can confidently be accepted in Prop. 4.11.8 *herbosos...rogos*, somewhat less confidently id. 3.7.10 *cognatos inter humare rogos*.

190

CLE 1997 = *ILA* 2.809
Discussion: Grenier, *MEFRA* 25 (1905), 63

From Cirta; *ILA* 2.810 is a second inscription using 7-8.
1 *Felix* was doubtless her *signum*; for this particular pun cf. *CLE* 1862, 1869. 15, *CIL* 10.365, 6.16003, *RIT* 447.10, Sblendorio Cugusi, *Ann. Fac. Magistero Cagliari* n.s. 4 (1980), 271. *Sidoniā* is lengthened at the caesura (see Metre I d).
2 *nefăs* is a false quantity. The end of the line is a commonplace in epitaphs (e.g. 187.17) and literature. *stemina* is a blend of *stamina* and στήμονα or *subtemina*. *ante diem quam* is usually misinterpreted, but is perfectly correct Latin for 'on the day before (her marriage)', cf. Vell. Pat. 2.30.2 *Pompeius ante diem quam consulatum iniret urbem inuectus est*. This is quoted by Grenier, who for some reason rejects this sense. It is true that brides who die on their wedding day form something of a literary commonplace (Kenney

on Apuleius, *Cupid and Psyche* 4.33.4; Lattimore 194), but literature is not totally divorced from life; Armini, *Eranos* 34 (1936), 123 compares the bride who died three days before her wedding in *ILS* 8529a, and similar actual occurrences are indicated in *CLE* 441.6, *GVI* 1238, 1522 and apparently 228. Chastagnol, *Bull. Soc. Nat. Antiquaires de France* 1988, 280 discusses an inscription about a bridegroom who died on his wedding day; a fiancée of the emperor Claudius died on the day appointed for the wedding (Suet. 26.1).
3 The adjective *hymen(a)eus* is found also at Mart. Cap. 9.888.2. *nuptiis* is a spondee and could have been written *nuptis*, cf. *CLE* 383.2 quoted on 5 and my 40.11, 68.10, 119.7 and 8, 134.4, 166.3; also *gratis* 185.4 = *gratiis*. *contigit* is a surprising word (we should have expected e.g. *incendit*), and its tense and mood also surprise (we should have expected *contingeret*, like *iniret* in Vell. Pat. quoted on 2).
4 For *Dryades puellae* cf. 151.12.
5 Lucina is an old Roman goddess of birth usually identified with Juno, but in poetry sometimes with Diana. She appears here for two reasons: (1) she laments that the child to be expected from the marriage will never be born (2) she provides the point that the goddess who, as her name indicates, brings the child into the light of day now exstinguishes her own *lumen*, i. e. her torch. This implies the very common *locus*, apparently introduced by Erinna (*AP* 7.712.5-6 = Gow - Page, *Garland of Philip* 1793-4), which contrasts the torches of the marriage and burial rituals (Blümner 492 n.3, Shackleton Bailey, *Propertiana* (1956), 315-6; add Ovid, *Her.* 2.120); in inscriptions see *GVI* 950.3, 1005.3-4, 1234.5-6, 1522, 1823.1-4, 1989.7-8 and 19-20, *CLE* 634.4-5 (even with uncertain supplements), 383.1-2 (likewise)

> ereptam e gremio qum ia[m sibi posceret Hymen
> finissetque] diem nuptis, faxs altera morti[s...

and an inscription from Puteoli published by D'Arms, *AJA* 77 (1973), 165 no. 16 (= *AE* 1974, 260). Cupid is represented as carrying *sine luce faces* at the funeral of Tibullus in Ovid, *Am.* 3.9.8, but that is in allusion to Tib. 2.6.16, now ironically fulfilled, and to depictions showing Cupid carrying reversed torches at funerals (see *Lex. Icon.* iii.1.931), and is not to be supposed to represent anything in actual funeral ritual. Likewise here the point of *demerso lumine* is wholly verbal; I do not think that it means anything more than *extincto*.
6 *que* is functional only for the metre; cf. 70.12, 150.11, perhaps 198.2, *CLE* 5, 2199.5, 2203.3 and Ahlberg, *Eranos* 8 (1908), 41 (in Swedish),

Löfstedt, *VS* 56, *Spätlat. Stud.* (1908), 27. Awareness of the proper use of this tricky conjunction, which has to be added at the end of a word, declined in late Latin.
7 'The goddess of Memphis' is of course Isis. Grenier thought that *sistratae* (with the last syllable scanned as -ĕ) was an error for *sistrata*, comparing Mart. 12.29.19 *sistrataque turba*.

I have punctuated so that *haec* takes up the nominatives of line 1, but it may be that those nominatives simply hang. Cf. on 114.1-3.
8 For *silet* (with the last syllable lengthened at the caesura) cf. *CLE* 512.1 *hic ego qui taceo, uersibus mea(m) uita(m) demonstro* (the neat paradox, with which cf. 18.1, shows that this is not to be altered to *iaceo*) and *silentes* = the dead (*OLD*, *silens* 2). 20.15 is to some extent comparable. *aeterno* is a slight hypallage for *aeterni*.

191

Sasel (1902-40) 2940

From Solentia, modern Solta; *CIL* 3.3111 is the tombstone of a M. Octavius Pullus from the same locality.
2 i.e. *periit*; the word is written twice on the inscription.
4 Quintilian 9.3.16 quoting Catull. 62.45 *sic uirgo dum intacta manet, dum cara suis est* (*tum cara* the mss. of Catullus) remarks *prius dum significat quoad, insequens usque eo*. Cf. also Catull. 56 *sic uirgo dum intacta manet, dum* (so V: *tum* T) *inculta senescit*. Here too we have this idiom, 'while...during this interval'. Lommatzsch improbably understood *CLE* 1944.3 in the same way, and Lambinus without warrant introduced it again at Plaut. *Truc*. 232 *dum habeat, tum amet*.
8 i.e. close my eyes; for the act see Blümner 483 n.3, for *premere lumina CLE* 1030.3 etc. For *vultus* = *oculi* cf. Sen. *Phoen*. 43, 178, *Tro*. 966.

192**

CLE 462 = *CIL* 9.6281 = *ILS* 7671

From Beneventum.

1 The end of this line appears to be the second half of a pentameter.
2 The omission of *cupit* would make this into a proper hexameter. He was presumably fixing e.g. mosaic *tessellae* in a ceiling, cf. Stat. *Silv.* 1.5.42 *uario fastigia uitro / in species animamque nitent* in a bath; here the building is a cultural centre.
3 *H* acts as a consonant to lengthen *ĕt*, cf. Metre I e.
4 The metre goes badly astray.

193

CLE 1007 = *CIL* 13.7070 = *ILS* 8511 = Walser 154-5 with photo = U. Schillinger-Häfele, *Lat. Inschr.* (1982), no. 11 p. 44 with photo.
Discussion: Wolters, *Bönner Jahrb.* 74 (1882), 24 with taf. 1 after p. 225; W. Boppert, *Zivile Grabsteine aus Mainz* (Corpus Signorum Imperi Romani II 6, 1992) no. 52 with taf. 34.

From Mainz; beneath is a relief of a shepherd with a dog, sheep and a ram. The freedman is given a servile form of designation instead of the normal M. Terentius M. l. Iucundus, cf. e.g. *CIL* 1.1390 = 6.26947 *Anthus Sulpicianus Postumi l.* and Fabre 104. For other slaves who murdered their owners see *GVI* 1120, Pliny, *Ep.* 3.14, 8.14, Tac. *Ann.* 14.42-5, Sidon. Apoll. *Ep.* 8.11.1 and the comment in Sen. *Ep.* 4.8.
1 *CLE* 2024 *consiste uiator* .
2 For *uidĕ* see L. Mueller 418; for *indigne* in such contexts Cugusi, *Epigraphica* 53 (1991), 103.
3 For *trigintă* cf. 28.2. The form of expression seems to be unique; usual would be *plus xxx annos* or *plus quam xxx per annos* or *plures quam xxx annos*.
4-5 are each a foot short; one could suggest e.g. *uitam <prauos>* and *sese <demens>*. *sesse* seems to have no real existence as a form. For *erupuit* (contrast 6) see Leumann 87-8, SP 90, Housman on Manil. 3.352 with addenda.
6 i.e. *uitam*; Moenus is the river Main. For the elision *domin(o)* see Metre II A (i).

194

CLE 1037 = *CIL* 6.5302 = *ILS* 8513
Discussion: Cervelli, *Ann. Fac. Lett. e Filos. dell' Univ. di Napoli* 14 = n.s. 2 (1971-2), 41.

This is from a columbarium on the Via Appia. The metre is obviously very defective; in 1 probably <*tu*> *quicumque* is intended (cf. 119.14; this would still produce a defective heptameter), in 2 <*teneros*> *uincire*, in 6 <*sic*> *neque* (the assumption of *nēque*, as in 109.4, will still not cure the metre).
1 The generalising tone justifies *sua* instead of *tua*, cf. HS 176.
2 Cf. Tib. 1.9.69, Ovid, *Her.* 9.59.
3 *artus* i.e. *bracchia*.
4 For *praemia d. f.* cf. Verg. *Aen.* 1.605, Ovid, *AA* 2.702.
5 *uestitu nimio indulges* Ter. *Ad.* 63; *uestitu* is dative. *indulge* and *supprime* are antithetical.
6 If she is without finery she will not be attacked by robbers nor will she attract adulterers (cf. Tib. l.c. on 2); but the logic of *nam* 7 is loose.
7 This seems to mean *ab domina*, an extraordinary piece of Latin. Apparently a serpent bracelet (such are very common) scratched (or 'bit'; cf. Stat. *Th.* 10.171 *consumptaque bracchia ferro* of a devotee of Cybele) the woman's arm, the wound became infected and in the absence of antibiotics she died from massive septicaemia.
8 *infixum uolnus* Verg. *Aen.* 4.689; cf. on 165.6.

195

CLE 1059 = *CIL* 14.1808

This was found at Ostia. In the prose prescript *Sp. f.* is the regular way of indicating a bastard (Salomies 54; B. Rawson, *Antichthon* 23 (1989), 29; Kubitschek *WS* 47 (1929), 130). Since bastards took their name from their mother, she must have been called Volusia. One will therefore infer that while Q. Volusius *pater* was still a slave he had this son by a freedwoman who had been his fellow-slave. The tomb will have been constructed for the boy trampled by oxen; the subscription and the other burials will have been subsequent, and the wife Silia Felicula will not be the mother of this boy. The Q. Volusius Q. f. Anthus mentioned in the subscription will be a younger son given the same name as his dead half-brother. The identity of the other people mentioned in the subscription remains obscure. A similar death is recorded in *CLE* 457.

This writer likes to spell double consonants singly.

1 The common parent is earth (Colum. 1 pr.2, *TLL* x.1.364.8; cf. also Livy 1.56.12). Here and in 3 *forte*, as often, like τυγχάνω expresses temporal coincidence; for the doubling cf. Verg. *Aen.* 6.186-190 *sic forte* (so MP; *uoce* in R is an interpolation) *precatur...uix ea fatus erat, geminae cum forte columbae...uenere.*

3 For *boues nouelli* cf. Varro, *RR* 1.20.2, 2.5.6, also Ovid, *Ex Ponto* 3.7.16.

5 *maestus u. p.* cf. 123.16.

7 *Anthus* and *deflorentibus* pun together; cf. *GVI* 1038 = *IG* 14.1386 (from the Alban hills), 1244 and on 176 above.

8 I think that this combines *pietate pari* (cf. *CLE* 1188.3) and *pro pietate.*

196

CLE 1159 = *CIL* 6.29436 = *ILS* 8524

CLE 502 refers to a similar death, there during the festivals of 1st January; here the occasion was probably, though not necessarily, the *agon Capitolinus* (Herodian 1.9.2 mentions the crowds attending this festival). For the dative *Ge* in the subscription cf. *Agathe* 179.

2 *tulit* = *abstulit* (*TLL* vi.1.559.12-41). Cf. *CLE* 405.1 *abstulit una dies; NS* 1926, 246-7 no. 4 *aetatem, flores, processus abstulit una dies* (from Saepinum).

4 i.e. *una petiere.*

*197***

CLE 1198 = *CIL* 13.2219

This was found in a Christian cemetery at Lyons. For Murra as a male name see *CIL* 10.45, 6325. For the accidental death cf. Antiphon, *Tetral.* 2. A similar incident in *GVI* 1155 does not seem to have been wholly accidental. The Twelve Tables (8.24a Riccobono; see Höbenreich, *ZRG* 107 (1990), 256) had a provision covering such situations; cf. the discussion in Plut. *Pericles* 36 with Stadter's commentary p. 328.

1 Stat. *Th.* 8.642 *moribunda...uox generi.* The *moribundae uoces* seem to be 11-16. *perlege* = 'read to the end', contrasted with *legis;* so *CLE* 639.1, 986.1-2, 1191.1-4, 2068.1-2.

4 *amborum* sc. *parentum.*

6 Boys as well as girls needed to watch their reputation; cf. *CLE* 213.5, 1196.8.

9 *clauus* here seems to mean *claua* (*TLL* iii.1297.12), a dummy weapon for exercise.

12 For *sollicitare* cf. 180.20.

13-14 The disparity of age, and the fact that these are the dying words of Murra, suggest that Verecundus died first, hence my supplement in 11. 13 addresses the parents, who (with my e.g. supplement) have hardly recovered from their grief for Verecundus. Then 14 rather awkwardly addresses Verecundus himself, with *sepulte* attracted from the nominative (HS 25-6, KS 1.255-6); cf. *miserande iaces, CLE* 1075.4 and in an epitaph published *AAntHung* 1 (1951-2), 193.

198

CLE 1534B = *CIL* 3.2197

From Salonae. An associated inscription reveals the dedicator as M. Attius M. l. Faustus, who buried his freedwoman in the same tomb as his sons.

1 *uenēficae* is scanned like *beněficae;* Faustus probably pronounced them identically.

2 Unless *-que* is just superfluous (see on 190.6), the understood object *Attiam* has two qualifications, *florente aetate* and *abreptam. aegrotauerit* should be *aegrotauisset.*

3 The plain ablative after *abripio* is far from well attested (Hygin. *Fab.* 125.14), and this combined with the repetition of *aetate* from 1 has caused suspicion, which cannot be either corroborated or refuted, that the ordinator has committed an error; hence *abrepta maesta* (ablative, with the punctuation after 3 removed) Gil, *Cuad. Fil. Cl.* 13 (1977), 283. However for *abreptam aetate* we may compare *annis iam uiduata tuis* 177.4, q.v.

199

AE 1947, 31
Photo: *Folia Archaeol.* 14 (1962), taf. xii; *Archaeologiai Értesitö* (ser. 3) 4 (1943), tav. xxi.
Discussion: Schmid, *Rh. Mus.* 100 (1957), 315

This is from a sarcophagus at Aquincum; a fragment from another sarcophagus with the first halves of the lines of the same poem was found nearby (*AE* 1965, 165). In the first copy *dum* in 4 was written twice; the second varies with *dunc* 4 (see on 187.10), *colens* (for *tenent*) 5, *iuuenis* 9 (see on 188.9). There is an acrostich *Lupus fecit* (= ἐποίησε as ποιήτης), which one may compare with that in the *Epicharmus* of Ennius *Q. Ennius fecit*, or the *Italicus scripsit* which begins and ends the *Ilias Latina*; cf. also *Licinius fecit* 100. Who Lupus was we cannot tell. Egger, *JÖAI* 39 (1952), 146 points out that the cohort mentioned was apparently raised by Alexander Severus, which will give a terminus post quem of 222 A.D. (see *RE, cohors* 334.45).

For metrical features see Metre I j (i) and (ii), II A d, e; in 9 *uĭr* is lengthened by the metrical beat.

1 For *lubrica* cf. Sen. *Ep.* 99.9, Stat. *Silv.* 2.1.221. *leuis* means 'fleeting'. For *bona uel mala* cf. *CLE* 1497.1 *uita bonum est et uita malum*. Generally one may compare *GVI* 789.5-6 ἄστατος ὄντως / θνητῶν ἐστι βίος καὶ βραχὺς οὐδ' ἄπονος. For a line consisting of a list cf. on 35.5.

2-3 The lines were punctuated and understood as indicated above by Schmid; *non certo limite* is ablative of description. The *creta* denotes, in a metaphor from the circus, the chalk line which marks the finish of the race of life; cf. Hor. *Epist.* 1.16.79 *mors ultima linea rerum est*, Eur. El. 955-6 πρὶν ἂν πέλας / γραμμῆς ἵκηται καὶ τέλος κάμψῃ βίου. Schmid 326-7 quotes parallels like τὸ δυσπαράγραφον (τοῦ βίου), ἡ τοῦ βίου παραγραφή or κορωνίς. See *TLL, creta* 1186.34. *per uarios casus* is a quotation from Verg. *Aen.* 1.204. For *pendens* cf. Ovid, *Ex Ponto* 4.3.35 *omnia sunt hominum tenui pendentia filo*; see also 183.2 *Parcarum putria fila*.

4 *uiuito* 'enjoy life' cf. 61 and *CLE* 190.7 *uiue dum uiuis*, 486.3 *uiuite, morta[les, moneo: mors] omnibus instat* (supplemented from 485.5). For the end cf. Verg. *Aen.* 9.107 *tempora Parcae / debita complerant*.

5 recalls Hor. *Odes* 1.7.19-21.

6-7 The message is *es, bibe, lude* (*CLE* 935.19, 1500 and 169 above). For *pinguia* cf. 28.3; i.e. olive oil, whereas the gift of Ceres is bread

(127.7) and that of Bacchus, said to have been raised on Mount Nysa, wine.

8 The logic of this line is disputed. One view links it with what follows and understands in an ironical sense, 'live an honorable life and you will still die' (cf. Ovid, *Am.* 3.9.37). The second half of the line, however, looks much more like a positive injunction, and to understand it so brings the advantage that the imperative does not have to be interpreted differently from those in 6-7 (this is why I have punctuated with a semicolon after 7). Schmid sees a reference to the Epicurean idea that the clear conscience brought by a just life contributes to ἀταραξία. Like *serenus, candida(m)* is probably a metaphor from clear sky; cf. *candida semper gaudia* Stat. *Silv.* 2.2.149 in an Epicurean ambit.

9-10 The punctuation linking 9 with 10 and not with 8 is due to Seelbach, *Rh. Mus.* 106 (1963), 350; he compares Ovid, *Met.* 10.523-4 *iam iuuenis, iam uir, iam se formosior ipso est, iam placet*. The sense is 'quickly becoming boy and youth, quickly a man and and an old man, in the tomb you will be dead'. *Talis eris* is found in a similar context *Epigr. Bob.* 43.4 (taken from a tomb on the Via Latina); i.e. *qualis ego*. For the end of 10 cf. Ovid, *Met.* 7.543 *ueterumque oblitus honorum; CLE* 1202.7 *hic nulla est diuitis ambitio*. In relation to the dead *superi* means 'men on earth', whereas in relation to men on earth it means 'the gods'.

199A

CLE 1552 = CIL 8.212-3 = B25 Pikhaus

Discussion: *L'Afrique dans l'occident romain* (CEFR 134, 1990) 49; *Les Flavii de Cillium* (CEFR 169, 1993) with photographs. The latter, to which my notes are much indebted, is referred to as *Fl.*

This poem is written in a very high-flown and elaborate style which often makes it difficult to tie down the exact sense with precision. Because of this style it is extremely difficult to write a commentary on the poem; most of the notes would consist of statements either that the sense is elusive or that no good parallels can be found for phrases or verbal usages. In the latter case I usually leave this unsaid; in the former, unless alternative possibilities need to be considered, I usually let my view of the meaning emerge from the translation. Accordingly the notes are intentionally lean.

The poet brings himself personally forward in a way that is

highly exceptional in epitaphs, and talks with the heir, praising his filial piety in erecting such a monument, and emphasizing how monument and poem unite in perpetuation of the dead. The second poem shows an engaging sense of humour, especially in B 15-16. This is a writer of pronounced individuality.

An accompanying prose inscription (*CIL* 8.211; photo in *Fl* fig. 33 after p. 80) reads in part as follows:
T. Flauius Secundus filius fecit T. Flauio Secundo patri pio. mil(itauit) an. xxxiii, uix(it) an. cx; h(ic) s(itus) e(st)... T. Flauius T. filius Pap(iria tribu) Secundus ipse flamen perp(etuus) uix(it) an. liii; h(ic) s(itus) e(st)...

These inscriptions come from a large mausoleum at Colonia Flavia Cillium, modern Kasserine, in Tunisia; this was made into a *municipium* by Trajan, in whose tribe, the Papiria, its citizens were enrolled. Based on a podium of four steps (A 43-4) are three storeys. The poem is inscribed round the doorway of the lowest, but is ill laid out in three columns, the first of which includes A 1-60, the second above the doorway A 61 - B 14 (44 lines), the third B 15-20. The first column is just broad enough for the lines; ligatures are found at their ends, and 16 has to be squashed at the end. The next storey, slightly smaller in circumference, has four pilasters on each side (A 48). The top storey, it too smaller than that below, has an open arch and once held a statue of the father (A 49). The tomb was crowned with what seems to have been a weather-cock (A 46, B 11-16), the only one known from antiquity, though the 'Tower of the Winds' at Athens had a weather-vane consisting of a Triton (Vitruv. 1.6.4); I am sceptical about the attempt in *Fl* 155, 235 to see this as a funerary symbol of astral immortality. For a later mausoleum at Cillium with two storeys, pilasters and inscriptions (one in verse; *CLE* 450) see *CIL* 8.217-8 and *Fl* 149-151 with fig. 30 no. 1 (after p. 48). *GVI* 1983 is from a Syrian grave-tower with three poems round the door and a dove-cote (11-12) on top.

The elder Flavius was clearly the first Roman citizen of his family, a discharged soldier who had been settled in Cillium (*patrias arces* A 60). If one computes the dates of the Flavian emperors and the age and length of service of the deceased, it becomes apparent that the poem dates from mid second century or a little later.

This is the longest existing Latin verse epitaph; Bücheler remarks that the number of lines in A and B combined equals the age of the deceased. That is hardly accidental, and corroborates the impression that it is merely a literary posture that the second poem is presented as an afterthought due to an oversight. The versification is highly polished; the only elision proper (for two before *est*, A 5 and 69, do not count) is A 77 *cura operis*, and all the pentameters end in a dissyllable. The pentameters are inset by one letter. Paragraphs are indicated by a mark {——} placed at interlinear level; since these marks are clearly intended to articulate the poem, at these points I have left a blank line in my presentation, with two exceptions. These are first, that there is a mark after 22, not where it was clearly intended to stand, after 20; this misplacement is due to the palaeographical cause of homoeoarchon, and therefore shows that the marks were present in the copy provided to the mason. Second, there is a mark after 77, not 76. Though there is no mark after 37, this clearly opens a new compositional unit, which I have indicated by insetting the line. Naturally there is a mark between A and B. *Fl* 104 sqq. suggests that the composer by these marks intended to direct the mason (who, as remarked above, had them present in his copy) to leave spaces at these points, as I have presented the text, and points out that it would then have been possible, but for negligence of the mason, to distribute the poem more equably in three columns (A 1-37, A 38-76, A 77-B 20; see the diagram on p. 107).

A

1-3 All these lines have a leonine pattern of rhyme at caesura and line-end. For *parua hora* cf. *CLE* 1069.4, 1082 *longior hora*; *fugientia* = *fugacia*; *campis* would have been more usual than *terris*.
4 I think that *penso* is ablative and that with *male conscia* (for which cf. Ovid, *Her.* 7.191) one understands *sibi* ('guilty'), but *TLL* iv.373.28 compares Lucr. 3.1018 *mens sibi conscia factis* (*facti* Avantius) and takes *penso* as dative; cf. also Fronto p. 179.2 *cui rei mihimet ipse conscius sim*.
5 *blandae rationis* is probably genitive of description ('a seductively-devised substitute'), not depending directly on *imago*.
6 This is contrasted with *tempora fugientia* 1. Cf. *CLE* 1604.9 *iacuit per tempora plura*; at 1967.7 *tempora* means specifically 'years' (cf. LSJ χρόνος I 2 c). One may compare *paucas tempestates* in Plaut. *Most.* 18, which cannot be tied down to a precise sense.
7 *memoratio* is a very rare and otherwise late word, in poetry only at Maximianus 1.291.
10 Elsewhere I know *numerus* with genitive singular = 'quantity' only with nouns like *frumenti, uini, harenae,* except for *corporis numerum* Lucr. 1.436.

11 There is much emphasis on the novelty of the monument (42, 46, B 4).
12 Cf. Verg. *Aen.* 6.780 *pater ipse suo superum iam signat honore*; this suggests that we should link *alto more* (though that would be an extraordinary combination) and *patrio honore*, but in view of 78 *sublimis honor* we should over-ride this suggestion and take the echo of Vergil to be purely verbal. *more patrio agens* = acting in his father's style.
14 *mirantur opus* Stat. *Silv.* 3.1.19.
17 *melius* i.e. than the usual; to leave the comparison implicit is in harmony with the compressed style which reigned from Seneca to Juvenal.
20 *figitur* is illuminated by 68.
21 For *uiderit* see on 126.10.
24 *peregrinus* is always an insulting word for commodities at Rome, e.g. Verg. *Aen.* 11.772, Hor. *Epist.* 2.1.204, Juv. 14.187.
26 i.e. *Erythraeo* (the Persian Gulf); cf. Lygdamus 3.17, Stat. *Silv.* 4.6.18 and often in Martial. Here probably not pearls but tortoise-shell (for which see my note on Juv. 11.94) is meant.
27 *uario certamine* Verg. *Aen.* 3.128, [Ovid] *Her.* 16.361.
28 *cum* is instrumental (HS 259-60; this instance *TLL* iv.1370.13). For Spanish olive oil see Frank 3.177, 199 and *JRS* 71 (1981), 141; Bücheler adds Mart. 7.28.3, Lucian, *Navig.* 23. In this and the following lines chiasmus alternates with a b a b order.
29 *terra Libyae* Mart. 5.74.2; *orientis* i.e. *tellus*. Libya was a regular source of wild beasts for the *uenationes* of the arena.
30 This no doubt refers to impudent Alexandrian slaves, whose impudence was liked by some; see Stat. *Silv.* 2.1.73-5 with Van Dam's note, Mart. 11.13.3, Sen. *De Prov.* 1.1.6 (perhaps meant also by Ovid, *Tr.* 1.2.80), Friedlaender 1.38 = 1.36-7.

artibus actis is a strange phrase which Bücheler discontentedly compares with *CIL* 8.134 *monumentum agendum curauit*; it may incorporate *artes* = 'work(s) of art' (*TLL* ii.673. 9) and refer to such wares as Gallic metal-work (Frank 3.587; *RE, Gallia* 649). Reid, *CR* 11 (1897), 355 sugggests that there is an error and that *actibus artis* is really meant, but he interprets this in an impossible way, and in any case it hardly helps.
32 *munus amoris* Ovid, *Fasti* 4.720 (Jupiter's tribute of love to Io).
35 *breuitate* takes up *breue* 32. In manuscript traditions *tunc* rather than *tum* before a guttural is liable to arouse suspicion; see Housman, *Juvenal* xxi-xxii. Outside Christian epitaphs, which belong to a time when the form *tum* was becoming obsolete, in *CLE* it is found

elsewhere only at 39.4 above.
36 *nisi* = *quam*; see HS 596. For *uiribus aeui* cf. Lucr. 5.314.
37 'With respect for the gods' or 'with the respect of the gods'?
38 The Greek ending of *Acherontos* is remarkable, since, unlike the accusative *Acheronta*, it brings no metrical advantage over the elsewhere invariable Latin *Acherontis*. *Pallados* 28 is less surprising.
39 *si* 'A sad *if*', say Tyrrell and Purser on Servius Sulpicius in Cic. *Ad Fam.* 4.5.6 *quod si etiam inferis sensus est*. Cf. Lucan 8.749 *siquid sensus post fata relictumst* and further *Fl* 158-9, Lattimore 59, Lissberger 60-1, Lier (1904) 54, Brelich 78.
42 *sui* means the same as *sua*; see KS 1.598-9, Konjetzny 333. The monument is now covered with an ochre patina, but the original colour of the stone (not marble) was bright white (hence *nitentes*, cf. *lucentes* 48).
43 *consensus lapidum* = *lapides consentientes* (cf. B 8); see HS 152. For *consensus* cf. Vitruv. 1.2.4 *symmetria est ex ipsius operis membris conueniens consensus*; for *leuatos* see *TLL* 7.2.1236.27.
44-5 The point of *et* is not plain. *mollitae stamine cerae* seems to mean something like 'the stuff of malleable wax', with *stamen* a metaphor from weaving.
46 This must refer to the weather-cock; the casualness of this indistinct allusion is consistent with the claim in B 11 that he has failed to describe it in this poem.
47 For the reading *decores* see *Fl* fig. 44 and cf. 77 below.
49-50 *militiae titulos* in the prose inscription; *ipsum parentem* i.e. his statue, not now there. For *dederis* see on B 17. Despite the Christian overtones, one might render *numinibus* by 'the sainted dead' (see on 183.18); the idea links with that of *templa* B 4. *Fl* has confirmed that *uidentem* is the correct reading.
51-3 This picture of the activity of the father recalls *AP* 7.321 = Page, *Further Greek Epigrams* p.353. 53 refers to irrigation.
57 Just as *longo tempore* replaces *diu* and becomes French 'longtemps', so here *toto tempore* (which, sometimes in the reverse order, is quite common in Commodian) = *semper*; cf. 68.3. Within the history of French the old 'sempre' was replaced by 'toujours'. This is part of a general trend that short words are replaced by longer synonyms (HS 758); cf. *magno tempore* Petron. 125.1 with Heraeus 117, and Löfstedt, *Syntactica* 2.41.

de/seruisse/ domum/ is a type of caesura not found elsewhere in this poem.
59 *haec monumenta sequi* rather than remain in the underworld.
59 *nominibus* cf. B 17.

63 Cf. Prop. 3.11.5 *uenturam melius praesagit nauita mortem*. The sense there is defective, but this inscription confirms both *uenturam* and *mortem*, of which either or (as in Goold's Loeb edition) both are often altered, and it also, though not so positively, supports *melius*. Therefore since nothing within the line is vulnerable, I think that the defect is due to the loss of a couplet following it, e.g. *<naufragio expertus iam uiolenta freta. / aspera saepe trucem passus per proelia Martem> / uulneribus didicit miles habere metum*; homoeoteleuton could have caused the loss of such a couplet
64 For *dum uiuit* cf. 130 and the prose prescript of 128.
67-8 Either *rigore uitae* go together or *uitae = dum quis uiuit*.
71 Cf. *CLE* 1141.15-6 *Parcas quae uitam pensant* and *penso* in 4 above, referring to the amount of wool weighed out to servant-maids to be spun during the day (*OLD pensum* 1).
72 The *securitas* of 66 depends on building one's own tomb personally and not laying on an heir (cf. 128 and *CLE* 1255) the onerous obligation to do so; (75-6) now the legacy of the younger Secundus, whatever it be (i.e. even though it is smaller than it might be because the tomb has been paid for), will be totally at the disposition of the heir. The implication of all this is that the younger Secundus consciously intended the tomb for himself as well as for his father.
73 Verg. *Aen.* 1.460 *plena laboris*, the older construction.
74 This shows the only irregular conformation of the line-end in the poem.
75 But for *hoc*, *ut* would be *ne* (Livy 28.22.12 seems to venture on this even without a pronoun).
79 This probably means that because of its proximity it can more closely observe the sun's progress, rather than that its shadow tells the time.
82-5 The colossal statue of Nero originally stood in the vestibule of his Golden House; after Nero's death his head was replaced with one of the Sun, and Hadrian moved the statue to stand beside the Flavian amphitheatre, to which in the Middle Ages it gave its name. It stood 100-120 Roman feet high (Richardson 93; H. Jordan, *Topographie der Stadt Rom* 2 (1871), 37, 188; I. (=G.) Lugli, *Fontes ad Topographiam* 3 (1955), 324; Lega, *Bull. Comm.* 93 (1989-90), 347). Two obelisks stood in circuses. First, that of Augustus in the Circus Maximus, now in the Piazza del Popolo (Richardson 273, Lugli 8.2 (1962), 420-1); with the base this is 36.5 metres high. Second, that which stood in the Circus Gai et Neronis, now in St Peter's Square in the Vatican (Richardson 275-6; G. Alföldy, *Das Obelisk auf dem Petersplatz*, Sitzb. Akad. Heidelberg 1990.2); it is about 1.5 metres

higher than the other. The height of the lighthouse at Pharos is reckoned by *RE Pharos* 1868 at about 135 metres; as far as height is concerned, it is a particularly outrageous comparison, though architecturally it resembled the mausoleum, which is about 12 metres in height.

For *Romuleas...arces* cf. Stat. *Silv.* 4.4.4.

85 *flama* is so spelt also *CLE* 934.3, and *GLK* 8 p. 298.12 implicitly warns against this spelling

86 *quid non docta facit pietas* is a formula of closure, cf. 25.9. One of the apertures is illustrated *Fl* fig. 36 (see ibid. 84).

88 *cerineus* seems to be a novel blend of *cereus* and *cerinus*. For bees around tombs cf. *CLE* 468 (= *ILA* 2.2083), 1262.8.

89 *thymbraeus* is from *thymbra*, savory or Cretan thyme, a herb favoured by bee-keepers (Verg. *Georg.* 4.31, Colum. 9.4.2, 14.10). For *domus* cf. 67.

90 *florisapus* is a neologism; the late Middle Ages created *dulcisapus*.

B

1 *Fl* compares Stat. *Silv.* 3.3.1-6 *Pietas,...huc...ades. iterum* picks up A 9 and 86, where *pietas* previously appeared. Cf. Lucan 8.76 *erige mentem*; the plural *mentes* here seems to be synonymous with *mentem* (a few other examples in *TLL* s.v. 737.53; no doubt on the analogy of *animi*), used to avoid elision before *erige*.

3 *ecce iterum Crispinus* Juv. 4.1.

4 Cf. *CLE* 1255.5-8 *heres...hanc aedem posuit struxidque nouissima templa / manibus et cineri posteriisque meis*, 1551 E 1-2 *templa uiri pietas fecit.../ Pomptillae; meruit femina casta coli* (the tomb on which this is inscribed is cut out of rock in the form of a shrine: Zucca in *Rupes Loquentes*, ed. L. Gasperini (1992), 503); see further *Fl* 158. The underlying idea of divinisation links with *numinibus* A 50. For *noua* cf. A 11.

5 *quo* is most easily understood to mean 'to what purpose?' At Stat. *Th.* 1.16 *limes* means the starting-point of the poem, and it might mean the same here; alternatively it simply means the path along which the poem proceeds.

6 i.e. the subject-matter of A.

8 *iunctis locis* i.e. the stones are well set together.

12 *ebria Musa* also Symphos. *Aenigm.* 17, cf. Mart. 10.20.13; the opposite is *sobria Musa*, Auson. *Epigr.* 1.8 p. 65 Green. He presumably refers to the 'frivolities' in the concluding (hence *cadis*, implying a descent from the previous level) description of the mausoleum, A 77-85.

13-14 The cock was represented as if flying. The monument itself reaches to the clouds (A 78), the cock flies higher.
17 *iam*, like the tense of *dederis* A 50, because the inscriptions were not added until the building was complete. The *nomina* (cf. A 59) are those in the prose inscription.
18 Cf. A 8. This is sometimes taken to mean 'a life trusted because of its record of achievements', but this passive sense of *credulus* is wrongly read into Tac. *Hist.* 1.34.2, and is not found elsewhere. The meaning is more probably 'a biography which places its trust in its record of achievement'.
19 Cf. Ovid, *Her.* 7.161 *feliciter impleat annos.*
20 *fecisti* alludes to *T. Flauius Secundus filius fecit* in the prose inscription. For *monumenta legas* cf. Mart. 10.63.1-2, Cic. *Cato* 21.

II L: EPITAPHS OF ANIMALS

On this topic see generally Herrlinger. The epitaph of Hadrian's horse is included in *FLP* 384; there are new epitaphs for dogs in *Suppl. Hell.* 977, 986, and *ZPE* 100 (1994), 413.

200

CLE 218 = *CIL* 6.10082 = Herrlinger 53

As in many of these animal epitaphs, part of the point is to humanise the animal. *D.M.* works in this direction, and so does *prosata,* a grand word (Kübler 199); in the next line, however, *equinum* (a substantivalized adjective = *equitium,* 'stud') is matched by the less grand (and not found elsewhere in such a sense) *consita* 'bred'.
3 *compara* is a form not found elsewhere; cf. *coniuga* 188. For similar first declension forms intended to clarify gender see Leumann 284. Scansions like *cursandŏ* are found from Seneca onwards (see my note on Juv. 3.232). For the general sense cf. 201.3-4, and for the swiftness of African horses Aelian, *NA* 3.2.1, Strabo 17.3.7.828.
4 *uirgo* as an adjective (Tertull. *Adv. Val.* 5 *senectam uirginem;* Pallad. 1.35.16 *uirgo equa)* acquires an ablative in *-i;* see NW 2.79.
5 Statius combines *Lethen* with *subire* and *intrare.*

201

CLE 1177 = *CIL* 5.4512 = Herrlinger 52 = *IIt* 10.5.308 with photo.

From Brescia, with a relief of the horse underneath.
1 The Copori were a tribe in NW Spain; the famed *asturcones* came from nearby.
2 For Sicilian horses see *RE, Pferd* 1440.15 and Frank 352 (add Grattius 524, Oppian *Cyn.* 1.272); for Etruscan Oppian 1.170 (with Sicilian), 196, 300.
3 i.e. Cauri, cf. Sen. *Phaedr.* 736 *fugit...ocior...Coro;* for the aspirate cf. *TLL* iii.658.17. In general cf. Hom. *Il.* 10.437 θείεν δ' ἀνέμοισιν ὁμοῖοι, Verg. *Aen.* 12.84 *(equi) qui...anteirent cursibus auras.* Cf. also ὄρνις

ὄπως Mnasalces, *AP* 7.212.4 = Gow - Page, *Hell. Epigr.* 2646 in a horse-epitaph, and also *Iliad* 2.764 ὄρνιθας ὥς.
4 *stabulas* would be e.g. *quiescis* for a human.

202

CLE 1175 = *CIL* 6.29896 = Herrlinger 47

1 The beginning recalls *Mantua me genuit*, cf. on 118.6; this is part of the humanising strategy (on 200). For Gallic dogs see Fordyce on Catull. 42.9, Bömer on Ovid, *Met.* 1.533. Her name was Margarita (cf. Petron. 64.9), which is written to the left of the inscription; she was both a hunting dog and a pet, cf. Mart. 11.69.2 *uenatrix, siluis aspera, blanda domi.*
3 *incertas* i.e. dangerous; *TLL* vii.1.882.59.
4 *hirsutas...feras* in the same position Prop. 1.1.12. For *atque* in third place *TLL* s.v. 1050.6 quotes only Hor. *Odes* 1.25.17 (where Nisbet - Hubbard take it to mean 'than') and Val. Fl. 5.395, a passage which *TLL* misunderstands.
5-6 suggest an *ancilla* rather than a dog, again part of the humanising. Cf. Tib. 1.6.37-8 *non saeua recuso / uerbera, detrecto non ego uincla pedum, CLE* 1276.5 *nec uerbera sensit*, Lygdamus 4.66 *uerbera saeua* (v.l. *posse*) *pati*. For *niueo corpore* cf. Ovid, *Am.* 3.2.42.
7-8 For *sinu* cf. 204.2, Mart. 1.109.8 (though one suspects that 'Pearl' was rather larger than Issa or 'Midge'). For a luxurious dog-bed see Eubulus fr. 90 Hunter.
9 Cf. Mart. 1.109.6 *hanc tu, si queritur, loqui putabis. muto* means 'not speaking human language' (*TLL* s.v. 1733.29), as in 'dumb animals', but also suggests the paradox of the literally dumb speaking. It is hard to tell whether *canis* is intended as genitive or nominative.
11 *subi* is meant. This line again suggests humanisation, cf. *CLE* 1834.1 *causa meae mortis partus fatu[mque malignum].*

203**

CLE 1176 = *CIL* 10.659 = Herrlinger 49 = *IIt* 1.1.228 with photo (only the right half of the stone now survives).

This comes from near Salerno.
1 *Portaui* sc. *ad tumulum.*
2 i.e. as I carried you when you were born fifteen years ago; see on 74.6 (again a humanizing touch).
3 For the regretful *ergo* see Nisbet - Hubbard on Hor. *Odes* 1.24.5.
5 *merentem* is clearly humanising, and a marble tomb, when it is not specified as small as in 202.12, suggests the same.
4 The writer has been influenced by Mart. 1.109.8 *collo nixa cubat,* which however means that the dog sleeps curled up so that it seems to be lying on its own neck.
6 *semper* i.e. *in aeternum,* cf. *CIL* 8.79.11.
8 Cf. Verg. *Aen.* 11.57 *ei mihi, ...quantum tu perdis, Iule.*
10 *gremio* i.e. while lying in the lap.

204

CLE 1512 = *CIL* 13.488 = Herrlinger 48
Discussion: Walters, *CW* 69 (1975-6), 353 (far-fetched)

This was found in Aquitania near Augusta Ausciorum, modern Auch. It is modelled on Catullus 3, and is very carefully constructed symmetrically round a central core like Catullus 17 (see *BICS* 32 (1985), 94): 1-3, refrain, 5-6, refrain, 8-10.
1 Cf. *CLE* 2155.1 *quam dulcis fuerat primus natalis meis*. For *benigna* applied to an animal cf. εὔνους *IG* 12.2.459.4 = *GVI* 691, εὔνοια *IG* 14.1647.2 = *GVI* 587 = *IGUR* 1230.
2 Cf. 202.7, *quem in sinu tenebat* Catull. 2.2.
3 *conscia* i.e. companion, cf. Prop. 3.15.5.
4 From this Goold, *Phoenix* 11 (1969), 200 proposes to restore *o factum male, quod, miselle passer, tua...* in Catull. 3.16; cf. also Cic. *Ad Att.* 15.1.1 *o factum male de Alexione.*
5-6 *riualis* i.e. another dog; *dominae* is dative depending on *adcubaret* (in the *cubile* of 3). The rival is 'presumptuous', which emphasises Midge's proprietary attitude.
8 *altum* has much the same point as *marmorea* 203.5.
10 *renides* i.e. showing the teeth while pretending to bite.

INDEX OF PLACES

A: municipalities

Discovery-sites not mentioned in the text are in italics; modern names are in capitals

B: provinces, tribes, rivers etc.

NAMES

A: EMPERORS AND THE IMPERIAL FAMILY, USURPERS

B: NOMINA

B: COGNOMINA

C: GREEK AND BARBARIAN NAMES

D: SIGNA (some doubtful); cf. 28

E: OTHER

F: NAMES OF ANIMALS

G: MYTHOLOGY, ASTRONOMY and HISTORICAL GREEK CHARACTERS

SOLDIERS, OFFICIALS AND ADMINISTRATION

A: MILITARY

B: CIVILIAN

DATED INSCRIPTIONS

The dates given are mainly those of events referred to in the poems; the actual inscriptions may have been executed some time later. All inscriptions from Pompeii and Herculaneum (*CIL* 4) pre-date the eruption of 79 A.D.

date BC	poem no.
190	5b
189	5a
145	3
129	4
102	15
52	23
17BC - 2AD	24
date AD	
after 118	126
130?	74
130-138	158
134-8	26
136	127
156	150
196-211?	138
203?	40
286	147
298	51
357	31
before 372	48
after 384	32
411-421	35
425	36
521	37
before 534	43

RELIGION

A: DEITIES etc.

B: CULT, SUPERSTITIONS etc.

DEATH, BURIAL, AFTERLIFE

GRAMMAR AND STYLE

* = All occurrences of the phenomenon in this selection listed ad loc.

LATIN WORDS AND PHRASES

LITERARY MATTERS

(References to authors are selective)

GENERAL INDEX

INDEX OF BEGINNINGS

CONCORDANCES

CLE	Courtney
1	1
2	2
3	3
4	6
6	9
7	10
8	11
9	12
11	8
18	24
19	149
23	135a
24	164
26	135b
29	124
38	104
39	106
40	107
42	57
44	78
45	79
46	80
47	81
49	82
50a	98
50c	83
52	17
53	18
55	20
91	68
97	63
107	69
111	32
185	21
193	153
194	103a
195	103b
208	125
218	200
219	131
227	75
228	134
230	84
231	85
240	166
244	169
248	7
249	127
250	150
251	111
253	162
254	163
256	139
269	148
270	74
271	26
272	76
273	39
277	161
27	31
280	45
285	36
333	157
354	96
361	16
399	113
409	172
411	121
417	108
423	173
427	126
434	70

436	174
437	128
439	175
441	176
462	192
465	119
467	177
483	132
484	130
489	115
500	112
523	118
547	159
562	179
838	168a
848	19
850	160
861	154
865	38
866	144
876	103c
879	158
882	46
889	51
893	35
898	37
925	122
927	120
930	71
931	72
932	73
938	58
942	86
943	99
944	87
945	88
947	89
948	90
949	91
950	92
953	93a
954	93b
955	94a
955n	94b
957	77
958	13
961	22
983	167
987	165
990	25
995	180
1007	193
1037	194
1038	181
1059	195
1063	182
1109	183
1111	123
1159	196
1175	202
1176	203
1177	201
1198	197
1233	184
1238	109
1247	185
1313	178
1318	171
1319	117
1466	103d
1491	61
1499	170a
1504	155
1506	105
1508	186
1510	116
1512	204
1519	136
1520	140
1521	129
1526	141
1528	143
1530	67
1532	59

1534b	198
1549	187
1552	199A
1559	188
1754	43
1800	142
1802	41
1810	94d
1811	99
1814	28
1859	4
1861	27
1864	79
1900	100
1905	53
1911	41
1916	48
1920	147
1923	170b
1926	54
1934	152
1936	60
1989	62
1996	189
1997	190
2039	43
2046	33
2048	56
2054	47
2056	95
2058	97
2065	101
2148	140
2151	151
2153	102a

CIL

1.2	1
1.6-7	10
1.8-9	9
1.10	11
1.11	12
1.15	13
1.364	2
1.626	3
1.632	7
1.652	4
1.1202	8
1.1209	19
1.1210	18
1.1211	17
1.1214	20
1.1219	21
1.1531	6
1.1861	16
1.2662	15
1.3109a	23
2.2403	103c
2.2660	141
2.4284	46
2.4315	112
2.5558	103c
3.21	74
3.47	75
3.55	76
3.77	26
3.188	45
3.686	184
3.735	36
3.2197	198
3.3676	126
3.5561	135b
3.6306	39
3.7266	144
3.8153	39
3.10501	115
3.12076	26
3.12274c	170b
3.12327	36
4.768	106
4.813	157
(4.1030)	106
4.1516	94a

6.10118	121	8.11001	137
6.12652	180	8.11347	129
6.13528	188	8.11824	109
6.13696	8	8.11914	118
6.14404	181	8.12468	130
6.15258	170a	8.16810	163
6.15345	17	8.20267	41
6.18131	169	8.25362	43
6.19007	179	8.26672	69
6.19747	165	8.27764	151
6.20674	174	9.1164	63
6.21521	183	9.3184	178
6.24563	21	9.3375	150
6.25063	187	9.4463	16
6.26011	182	9.4672	7
6.29436	196	9.4746	172
6.29896	202	9.4796	128
6.30092	153	9.62	117
6.30102	186	10.5290	173
6.30700	140	10.5708	6
6.30738	135a	10.615	103b
6.31051	148	11.3078	2
6.31587-8	10	11.4126	103a
6.32311	18	11.4188	172
6.32458	159	11.5262	142
6.33815a	124	11.6435	70
6.33919a	19	11.6565	175
6.33940	113	11.7263	101
6.33960	123	11.7483	2
6.34001	28	12.103	149
6.34072	8	12.533	119
6.35887	59	12.722	132
7.759	164	13.488	204
8.212-3	199A	13.2219	197
8.241	129	13.7070	193
8.696	118	13.7127	62a
8.1027	130	13.7661	160
8.2265.480	58	13.8355	131
8.2632	136	13.10018.82	54
8.4635	163	13.10032.7	37
8.9018	162	14.1	111
8.10488	137	14.914	171

8204	168a
8206	103b
8268	166
8403	17
8511	193
8513	194
8522	165
8524	196
8609m	54
8885	4
8908	27
8960	43
8987	33
9022	28

ILLRP

4	1
122	3
136	6
149	7
192	2
309	10
310	9
311	11
312	12
316	13
335	4
342	15
803	20
804	16
808	18
821	19
970	8
973	7
983	21

IIt

1.1.228	203
3.1.267	110
4.1.35	158
4.1.66	155
4.1.213	146
4.1.596	38
10.4.317	4
10.5.308	201
13.3.90	4

AE

1927.48	34
1927.121	50
1929.7b	40
1931.78	146
1939.162	70A
1941.4-6	70A
1941.43	62b
1941.53	55
1942-3.2	138
1945.82	145
1947.31	199
1948.54	34
1951.251	34
1953.186	137
1956.259	52
1967.85	49
1968.164	29
1971.44	114
1972.74	133
1977.762	30
1981.28	102b

IRT

231	137

Frag. Poet. Lat. (Morel)

p. 32	14
p. 40	156
p. 186 fr. 92	65

Other inscriptions incidentally discussed

CLE 1055-6 p. 15
1517 - 82
1925 - 24
2062 - 100A
CIL 4.9202 - 88, 93
10.7296 = ILS 7680 p.11
Stud. et Docum. 1961, 335 no. 51 - 94d
Iscr. della Sardegna (Sotgiu) 183 - 79
Neue Forsch. in Pompeii (Solin) no. 66 - 88

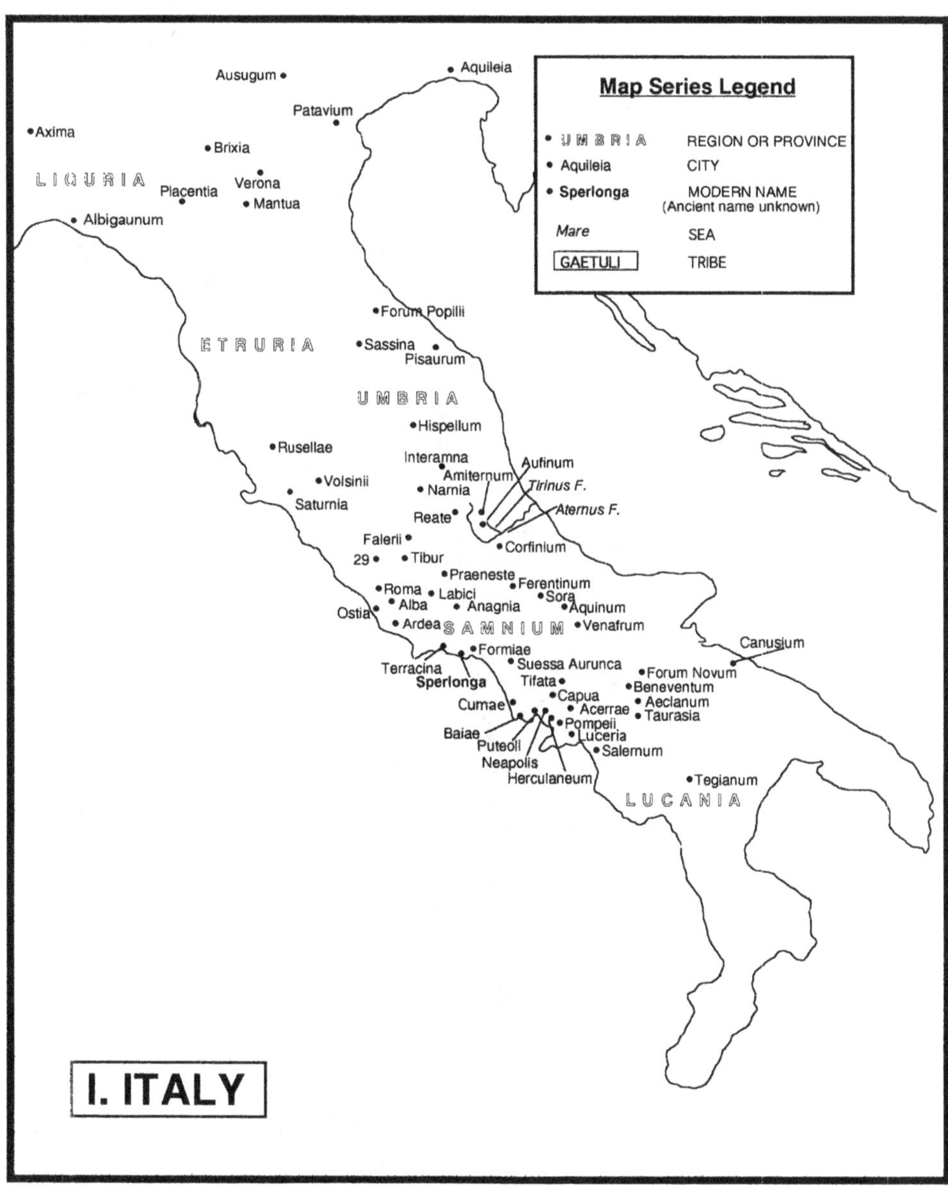

Map Series Legend
UMBRIA
REGION OR PROVINCE
Aquileia
CITY
Sperlonga
MODERN NAME
(Ancient name unknown)
Mare
SEA
GAETULI
TRIBE
Aquileia
Ausugum
Patavium
Axima
Brixia
LIGURIA
Verona
Placentia
Mantua
Albigaunum
Forum Popilii
ETRURIA
Sassina
Pisaurum
UMBRIA
Hispellum
Rusellae
Interamna
Aufinum
Amiternum
Tirinus F.
Volsinii
Narnia
Saturnia
Aternus F.
Reate
Falerii
Corfinium
29
Tibur
Praeneste
Ferentinum
Roma
Labici
Sora
Alba
Anagnia
Aquinum
Ostia
Ardea
SAMNIUM
Venafrum
Canusium
Formiae
Terracina
Suessa Aurunca
Forum Novum
Sperlonga
Tifata
Beneventum
Capua
Cumae
Aeclanum
Acerrae
Taurasia
Pompeii
Baiae
Luceria
Puteoli
Salernum
Neapolis
Herculaneum
Tegianum
LUCANIA
I. ITALY

II. European Provinces
Carvoran
Corinium
BATAVI
Rhenus F.
Colonia Agrippina
Remimagium
Moenus F.
Pommern
Moguntiacum
Argentoratum
GALLIA
LUGDUNENSIS
Danuuius F.
Iuuauum
Aquincum
Noviodunum
PANNONIA
Villards d' Heria
Magyar Boly
TAURISCI
Lugudunum
Axima
Aquileia
Singidunum
Augusta Ausciorum
COPORI
Arelate
Aquae Sextiae
Salonae
MOESIA
Vodvoda
Odessus
Leon
El Paramo
Iberus F.
Massilia
Solentia
Constantinopolis
Caldas de Malavella
Caldas De Vizella
Aleria
Philippi
CORSICA
Gallipoli
Tagus F.
Tarraco
Athenae
B(a)elo
Catina
ACHAIA
Corinthus
Epidaurus

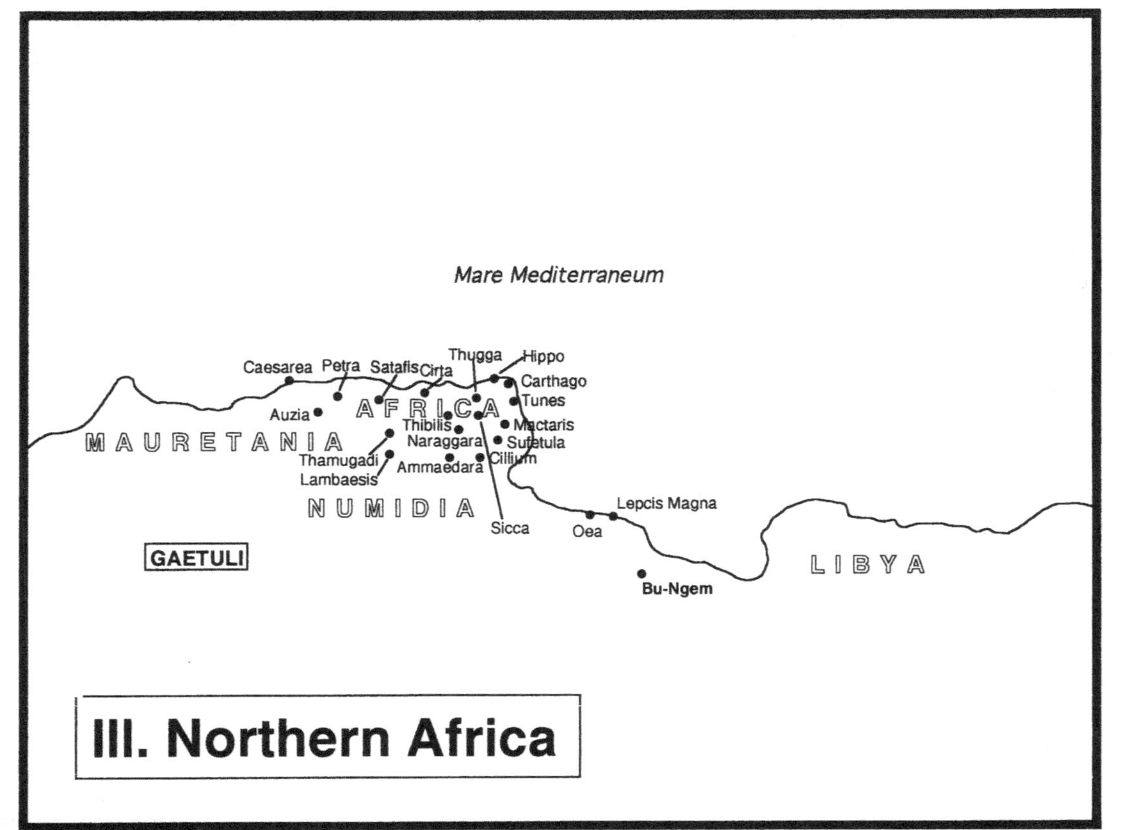
Mare Mediterraneum
Caesarea
Petra
Satafis
Cirta
Thugga
Hippo
Carthago
Tunes
Auzia
AFRICA
Thibilis
Mactaris
MAURETANIA
Naraggara
Sufetula
Thamugadi
Ammaedara
Cillium
Lambaesis
NUMIDIA
Sicca
Oea
Lepcis Magna
GAETULI
LIBYA
Bu-Ngem

III. Northern Africa

IV. Eastern Mediterranean
Pontus Euxinus
PONTUS & BITHYNIA
CAPPADOCIA
Tyana
Side
Apamea
Pharus
Nilus F.
Thebae
Beronice
Talmis

CPSIA information can be obtained
at www.ICGtesting.com
Printed in the USA
LVHW030102080821
694192LV00001B/2

9 780788 501425